Financial Markets
Tick by Tick

Other Titles in the Wiley Trading Advantage Series

New Market Timing Techniques: Innovative Studies in Market Rhythm
and Price Exhaustion
Thomas Denmark

Gaming the Market: Applying Game Theory to Create Winning Trading
Strategies
Ron Shelton

Trading on Expectations: Strategies to Pinpoint Trading Ranges, Trends,
and Reversals
Brendan Moynihan

Fundamental Analysis
Jack D. Schwager

Technical Analysis
Jack D. Schwager

Managed Trading, Myths and Truths
Jack D. Schwager

McMillan on Options
Lawrence G. McMillan

The Option Advisor, Wealth-Building Techniques Using Equity and Index
Options
Bernie G. Schaeffer

Pricing Convertible Bonds
Kevin B. Connolly

Financial Markets Tick by Tick

Insights in Financial Markets Microstructure

Edited by Pierre Lequeux

JOHN WILEY & SONS

Chichester • New York • Weinheim • Brisbane • Singapore • Toronto

Copyright © 1999 by John Wiley & Sons Ltd,
Baffins Lane, Chichester,
West Sussex PO19 1UD, England
Copyright © Chapter 3 1997 Elsevier Science

National   01243 779777
International (+44) 1243 779777
e-mail (for orders and customer service enquiries): cs-books@wiley.co.uk
Visit our Home Page on http://www.wiley.co.uk
or http://www.wiley.com

Other Wiley Editorial Offices

John Wiley & Sons, Inc., 605 Third Avenue,
New York, NY 10158-0012, USA

WILEY-VCH Verlag GmbH, Pappelallee 3,
D-69469 Weinheim, Germany

Jacaranda Wiley Ltd, 33 Park Road, Milton,
Queensland 4064, Australia

John Wiley & Sons (Asia) Pte Ltd, 2 Clementi Loop #02-01,
Jin Xing Distripark, Singapore 129809

John Wiley & Sons (Canada) Ltd, 22 Worcester Road,
Rexdale, Ontario M9W 1L1, Canada

Library of Congress Cataloging-in-Publication Data
Financial markets tick by tick/edited by Pierre Lequeux.
    p.   cm.
    Includes index.
    ISBN 0-471-98160-5 (cloth : alk. paper)
    1. Money market—Mathematics.   2. Capital market—Mathematics.
    I. Lequeux, Pierre.
    HG226.F56 1999
    332—dc21   98–35143
                                                                                CIP

British Library Cataloguing in Publication Data

A catalogue record for this book is available from the British Library

ISBN 0-471-98160-5

Typeset in 10/12pt Palatino by Laser Words, Madras, India
Printed and bound in Great Britain by Bookcraft Ltd, Midsomer Norton, Somerset
This book is printed on acid-free paper responsibly manufactured from sustainable forestry, for which at least two trees are planted for each one used for paper production.

To Finalé and Camélia

Contents

Foreword

The working of markets forms the centrepiece of economics. Economists are professionally fascinated by them. Directly or indirectly, markets help to determine our opportunities, incomes and lives. Yet we know far less about their nature and characteristics than ideally we should.

Amongst the most important markets are those for financial assets, foreign exchange, equities, bonds, short-dated financial assets (such as bills, commodities) and for derivatives of these underlying spot markets, e.g. forwards, futures and options. In these markets too there are many anomalies, whereby for example, asset prices exhibit more large jumps, and vary more than can be easily explained on the basis of publicly-known 'news' about economic fundamentals.

Some of these markets are continuous (apart from week-ends and holidays), for example the foreign exchange market. Others open and close each day at pre-determined times, e.g. most main equity markets, but are continuous whilst open. For some purposes occasional snap-shots of prices, e.g. at the close of each day, of trading volumes, say in a particular week once every two years, may suffice. But if one really wants to get inside the skin of these markets, to get a feel for their actual working, one needs continuous tick-by-tick data of price quotes and trades (number and volume), all time-stamped, to provide adequate analysis.

It is only recently, with the dramatic development of electronic information technology, that it has become possible to collect, store, manipulate and analyse the millions of events, of bytes, that capture the continuous operation of key markets. In the second paper of this book 'Modelling Intra-Day Equity Prices and Volatility using Information Arrivals', by Lin, Knight and Satchell, the short recent history of applied research in high frequency data is dated as starting with the First International Conference on High Frequency Data in Finance, sponsored by Olsen & Associates, March 29-31, 1995. I find that attribution personally pleasing because I played a role in helping to organise that Conference, (at which several of the papers in this book appeared in their initial form).

As an external member of the Monetary Policy Committee, I have been made actively aware of the perception of parts of the general public that economic academics live in a theoretical ivory tower far removed from ordinary life. That separation was once true of the financial arena also, where matters such as trading, portfolio management and risk control were viewed as best handled by the experienced practitioner, better unsullied by academic theory. Again what greatly pleases me, is how closely practitioners and academics are now working together, throughout much of the discipline of financial economics, aware of the contributions each can make to help the other advance. The editor, Pierre Lequeux, in himself gives evidence of the benefits of linking theory and applied practice, academic and practical work; and the roll call of authors shows how this subject unites academic disciplines (e.g. economics, maths, finance and physics) and practical experience in the pursuit of understanding. This book gives witness to such combined efforts.

But you cannot study markets unless there is an underlying database to study. The move towards the use of electronic systems in the conduct of trading has made the study of the high-frequency operation of trading feasible. For example, the paper by ap Gwilym, Buckle and Thomas makes use of detailed LIFFE data, where the driving force behind their provision (as MacGregor describes in his paper on "The Sources, Preparation and Use of High Frequency Data in the Derivatives Industry") came from "a particularly technically advanced section of the trading community,. . ., made up of hedge funds, unit trusts and pension funds; an 'alternative investments industry'". Fortunately, the combination of increased use of electronic systems in trading together with pressure from the practitioner and academic communities to have access (subject to appropriate confidentiality conditions) to the resulting data series has led to a huge step-forward in the availability of high frequency data sets. That process of expanding data availability is—I am happy to report—ongoing.

The resulting data series have a number of particular features, millions of consecutive data points where the events are irregularly spaced in time, a combination of deterministic intra-day seasonal effects together with marked stochastic volatility, effects of differing periodicity, large kurtosis and price jumps, etc, etc. All this leads to the development and use of a weird and wonderful collection of new statistical and mathematical methods and techniques, such as truncated Lévy flights, discrete wavelet transforms etc, etc. Whether or not you are young, and keen enough to pick up on these new techniques, there is much fascinating new information on the working of these key markets here for all of us.

Progress in understanding the working of financial markets is now being made, and quite rapidly. This book provides another milestone in this advance.

Charles Goodhart
Norman Sosnow Professor of Banking & Finance
London School of Economics.

Acknowledgments

High frequency modelling in the financial markets is a vast subject that encompass numerous techniques. It would not have been feasible to give the reader a thorough review of the topic without calling upon the knowledge of leading authorities in the field. For making this book possible by contributing their time and expertise I wish first and foremost to address my warmest thanks to each of the authors, namely: Emmanuel Acar, Mike Buckle, Dr Michel Dacorogna, Haijo Dijkstra, Michael Gavridis, Owain ap Gwilym, Allison Holland, Pr. John Knight, Shinn-Juh Lin, Dr Mark Lundin, Paul MacGregor, Raphael Markellos, Philippe Michelotti, Pr. Terence Mills, Ulrich Müller, Dr. Stephen Satchell, Dr. Thomas Schneeweis, Alison Sinclair, Dr. Richard Spurgin, Pr. Stephen Taylor, Pr. Steve Thomas, Dr Tjark Tjin, Robert Toffel, Dr. Darren Toulson, Sabine Toulson, Marcel Vernooy and Xinzhong (Gary) Xu. I also want to thank Pr. Charles Goodhart for accepting to write the preface to "Financial Markets Tick by Tick" at such short notice despite his busy agenda. Thanks goes also to Robert Amzallag, whom whilst General Manager of BNP London, shared with me his keen interest for financial modelling and gave me the opportunity to develop my career along this path. Finally, many thanks to the LIFFE who gave me support and allowed this book to become reality by sponsoring it.

Pierre Lequeux

Contributing Authors

Emmanuel Acar is a proprietary trader at Dresdner Kleinwort Benson. His current duties include elaborating and managing futures and foreign exchange portfolios for the bank account. He has experience in quantitative strategies, as an actuary and having done his PhD on the stochastic properties of trading rules. He has been trading and researching financial markets for the past eight years at BZW and Banque Nationale de Paris in London.

Mike Buckle is a Lecturer in Finance at the European Business Management School at the University of Wales, Swansea, UK. His PhD involved the development of financial forecasting models. His main research interests lie in the area of market microstructure with reference to derivative markets. He has published several papers on aspects of derivative markets and is co-author of "The UK Financial System", (MUP, 1995) and "The Official Training Manual for the Investment Management Certificate" (Institute of Investment Management and Research, 1997).

Dr. Michel M. Dacorogna after completing his undergraduate and graduate studies in Physics at the University of Geneva, accepted a postdoctoral position at the University of California at Berkeley. At both universities, he concentrated on solid-state physics, assumed extensive teaching duties and assisted in the evaluation of various computer systems. His main research interest is the application of computer science and numerical analysis to dynamic systems in various fields in order to gain insight into the behaviour of such systems. In 1986, Dr. Dacorogna joined Olsen & Associates (O&A), then a fledgling research institute, to become one of its founding members. In April 1997, he became head of the Research and Development department at O&A. He has devoted the past few years to an extensive research and development project involving a real-time, value-added information system in the field of applied economics. In addition to his research duties at O&A, Dr. Dacorogna has assumed a leadership role in organizing the first international conference on high frequency data in finance. Throughout his career, Dr. Dacorogna has gained considerable experience working with sophisticated computer environments, ranging from Crays to SUN workstations. Dr. Dacorogna has remained close to his academic background, continuing to offer internal and external seminars and publishing the results of his research in a wide range of scientific journals and internal documents. Dr. Dacorogna's mother tongue is French; he is fluent in English and also speaks German. Married with two daughters, Dr. Dacorogna favours spending his leisure time with his family.

Haijo Dijkstra, with 14 years of banking experience, has worked in Corporate and Investment Banking, and was active as a money-market and currency options trader for five years. For the last three years Haijo Dijkstra was Head of Funding and Structures, a successful team at Rabobank International involved in funding activities on behalf of the Rabobank organisation, investment-activities and tax-driven capital market transactions. Recently, Haijo Dijkstra was involved in a currency overlay project at Rabobank International.

Michael Gavridis joined BNP's Global Markets Research Team from Chase Manhattan Bank in 1996 as a Senior Quantitative Analyst. He is responsible for the evaluation and application of new modelling techniques to the forecasting of financial time series ranging from traditional fundamental economic models to more advanced time series econometric modelling. He holds a Ph.D. in Financial Economics from Brunel University and an M.Sc. in Project Analysis, Finance & Investment from the University of York.

Owain ap Gwilym is a Lecturer in Finance at the Department of Management at the University of Southampton, UK. Prior to taking this position he was a Research Assistant at the University of Wales at Swansea working on a research project on intra-day empirical regularities in LIFFE futures and options. He has a PhD in Finance from Swansea which studied the index options market at LIFFE, and has published several papers in international journals including the Journal of Futures Markets, Journal of Derivatives and Journal of Fixed Income.

Allison Holland works as policy advisor on secondary market issues at the newly formed UK Debt Management Office. Prior to this she spent a number of years at the Bank of England, which she joined in 1993. Her first two years at the Bank were spent on macro-economic analysis and forecasting of the UK and the other G7 economies. This was followed by a period of empirical research into market microstructure issues with the Bank's Market and Trading Systems Division. She holds a MSc in Econometrics from the London School of Economics and a BA (Joint Hons) in Economics and Mathematics from University College Cork. She has published papers in the CEPR's Discussion Paper series, the Bank's

Working Paper series and in the Economic Journal. She also has a number of articles in the Bank's Quarterly Bulletin and Financial Stability Review.

John Knight is a Professor in the Department of Economics at the University of Western Ontario. His recent research interests are in financial econometrics. He has an ongoing interest in theoretical econometrics, an area in which he has published extensively.

Pierre Lequeux is Assistant Vice President at Banque Nationale de Paris London which he joined in 1987. Pierre is a graduate in international trade and holds a diploma of the Forex Association. He joined the BNP Quantitative Research and Trading desk in 1991 as a dealer after gaining experience on the treasury and corporate desk. He is primarily active in the research and development of trading models and portfolio management techniques. His approach is principally based on statistical models developed by him. Pierre is a member of the Forex association and the Alternative Investment Management Association. He is a frequent contributor to academic investment conferences and publications and is a member of the editorial board of "Derivatives Uses Trading & Regulation" as well as the editor of the AIMA newsletter's currency section. He is chairman of the AIMA benchmark committee which has recently produced an acclaimed "Review of Methodology and Utilisation of Alternative Investment Benchmarks" and also a member of the AIMA Currency Advisory Group. After heading the Quantitative Research and Trading desk of BNP London where he developed a new active management currency benchmark (FXDX), he is now focusing his attention on developing Foreign Exchange Business for BNP.

Shinn-Juh Lin completed a Ph.D. in Economics at the University of Western Ontario. He now teaches at the University of Technology, Sydney. The main theme in his dissertation is modelling and examining time-series properties of information flow in financial asset markets. He is also interested in doing research on financial market structures and the impact of information dissemination on the distribution of financial asset returns.

Mark Lundin completed a doctoral degree in High Energy Particle Physics with Université Louis Pasteur, Strasbourg, France, in 1995. He also holds a Bachelor of Science degree in mathematics and computer science from the University of Illinois. His thesis research was performed both at Fermi National Accelerator Laboratory in the US and the European Centre for Particle Physics Research (CERN) in Switzerland. Soon after finishing his doctoral degree, he joined Olsen and Associates in Zurich as a Research Scientist. The emphasis of his work in the field of finance has been in the areas of dynamic currency hedging, portfolio management and the fundamental processes inherent to multivariate analysis of financial time series. Dr. Lundin has acted as an invited speaker for the Association for Investment Management and Research (AIMR), participating in their continuing education series on managing currency risk as well as participating in Olsen and Associates research workshops on high frequency data and model building. He has recently joined the Research and Strategy Group of Fimagen Asset Management in Belgium, a member of the Generale Bank Group.

Paul MacGregor joined LIFFE Market Data Services in 1994 as Statistical Manager, and extended his responsibilities to Marketing Manager for all aspects of LIFFE Market Data in 1997. He has been instrumental in the launch of LIFFE Tick Data (1995), all aspects of market data on the LIFFEnet website (1995), and more recently the launch of LIFFE's new historical data product range "LIFFEdata" in 1998. During his time at LIFFE he has worked closely with the alternative investments industry worldwide to develop and continuously improve LIFFE's market data products. Paul is a graduate in Economics, and holds a diploma in Marketing from the London School of Economics. He has previously worked at British Petroleum and the British Plastics Federation.

Raphael N. Markellos is reading towards his Ph.D. at the Department of Economics, Loughborough University, UK where he holds a Junior Fellowship from the Royal Economic Society. For the past three years he has consulted in industry on quantitative financial analysis and econometrics. His research interests and publications are mostly concerned with non-linear models and trading systems.

Philippe Michelotti moved to the UK after graduating in business studies in 1989. He then focused his interest on the energy market, primarily the electricity futures pricing. In 1994 he joined Phibro of Salomon Brothers, as an energy trader to contribute to the expansion of the electricity and natural gas trading desk. In 1996, Philippe Michelotti decided to join Creditanstalt Global Futures Investment Management Ltd. (now Bank-Austria/Creditanstalt Futures Investment Ltd.) to expand his horizon in the financial markets and derivatives funds management. As part of a small team his responsibilities have ranged from risk management analysis to structured products research. He has been instrumental in promoting and increasing the reputation of the BA/CA Futures Investment in Europe, the Middle East and Asia. Today, Philippe Michelotti, as Head of the Business Development, concentrates his efforts in advising his customers on portfolio diversification. He promotes BA/CA Futures Investment's expertise by offering the bank's futures funds or by proposing tailor made products at the client's request.

Terence C. Mills is Professor of Economics at Loughborough University, having previously held professorial appointments at the University of Hull and City University Business School and has worked for the Monetary Policy Group at the Bank of England. He is author of "Time Series Techniques for Economists" and "The Econometric Modelling of Financial Time Series", both published by Cambridge University Press, and over 100 articles in journals and books. His research interests are in the area of time series econometrics, with particular interests in finance, macroeconomics and forecasting.

Ulrich Müller studied physics and graduated at the Swiss Federal Institute of Technology, Zurich. His prize-winning Ph.D. thesis led to a patented thermoacoustic heat-pump. After his studies, he worked at an engineering company and afterwards as a self-employed consultant. His work encompassed several fields such as semiconductor optics, fluid dynamics and industrial risk analysis. In August 1985, he was one of the founding members of Olsen and Associates, Research Institute for Applied Economics, in Zurich. His pioneer work helped to create the unique Olsen and Associates high-frequency database and the O&A financial information system for banks and other financial institutions. With his colleagues, he conducted some extensive fundamental research of financial data from the foreign exchange market and other financial markets. He is (co-)author of most of O&A's scientific publications. An important piece of research is the stochastic process HARCH which reproduces the behaviour of empirical market prices by explaining their volatility as generated by traders with different time horizons. Ulrich Müller also developed forecasting and trading models. Ulrich Müller is supported by the younger researchers of O&A's research group but likes to be personally involved in the design and programming of research and development projects. He has given invited talks at several conferences and seminars in academic institutions. Ulrich Müller likes books and music of different kinds, traditional Chinese painting, bicycling and developing some sorts of computer graphics. He sings in a choir and spends a large part of his free time with his two children.

Stephen Satchell is a lecturer in Economics at the University of Cambridge, and a fellow of Trinity College. He has a keen empirical and theoretical interest in most areas of finance and is particularly intrigued by all issues of asset management, risk management and measurement. He advises a number of city companies and has published extensively in both academic and practitioners' outlets.

Dr. Thomas Schneeweis is Professor of Finance at the School of Management at the University of Massachusetts in Amherst, Massachusetts and Director of the Centre for International Security and Derivative Markets (CISDM) at the School of Management. He obtained his Ph.D. in 1977 from the University of Iowa. He is co-author of "Financial Futures: Fundamentals, Strategies, and Applications" (Richard Irwin) and the author of "Benefits of Managed Futures," published by the Alternative Investment Management Association (AIMA). He is on the Board of Directors of the Managed Funds Association and editor of the Journal of Alternative Investments. He has published over 50 articles in academic finance and management journals, such as the Journal of Futures Markets, Journal of Finance and Quantitative Analysis, Journal of Portfolio Management, Journal of Finance, Journal of Futures Markets, Journal of Derivatives, Derivatives Quarterly, and Financial Analysts Journal. He has also published widely in financial practitioner magazines such as the AIMA and Barclay Newsletters. He has been a Fulbright Research Fellow in France, taught at ESSEC in France, and is Visiting Professor of Corporate Finance at Institute of Economic Research, Lund University, Sweden.

Alison Sinclair is a consultant at Intelligent Financial Systems Limited, specializing in database management and forecasting. With a B.Sc. and M.Phil. in Economics, she previously worked as a researcher and lecturer in the UK and Germany.

Dr. Richard Spurgin is Assistant Professor of Finance at the Graduate School of Management at Clark University and Associate Director of the Centre for International Security and Derivative Markets (CISDM) at the University of Massachusetts. He holds a Bachelor's degree in mathematics from Dartmouth College and received a Ph.D. in Finance from the University of Massachusetts in 1995. He has published research in academic journals such as the Journal of Derivatives and the Journal of Futures Markets as well as in practitioner journals such as the Derivatives Quarterly. He has contributed to a number of edited books in the areas of high frequency data and alternative investment strategies and is a member of the editorial board of the Journal of Alternative Investments. Before joining the faculty at Clark University, Dr. Spurgin was Director of Fixed Income Research for Thomson Financial in Boston.

Stephen Taylor is a Professor of Finance at Lancaster University, England. From 1995 to 1998, he was head of the Department of Accounting and Finance, a department rated in the most prestigious category in the 1996 UK research ratings exercise. His numerous publications over 20 years of research include "Modelling Financial Time Series" (Wiley), in which he presented the first description of stochastic volatility models and a pioneering analysis of GARCH models. He continues to actively research a wide-range of volatility issues. He has taught his own advanced financial econometrics course in England, Austria, Belgium, Hong Kong and Australia. Professor Taylor obtained his M.A. and Ph.D. degrees from Lancaster University, following his B.A. degree in Mathematics at Cambridge University.

Steve Thomas is Professor of Financial Markets at the Department of Management at the University of Southampton, UK, and a Visiting Professor at the ISMA Centre, University of Reading, UK. He has published extensively in international journals, including the Journal of International Money and Finance, Journal of Banking and Finance, Journal of Futures Markets, Journal of Derivatives, Journal of Fixed Income and the Economic Journal, and is co-author of the "Investment Management Certificate Official Training Manual" for the IIMR. He is also consultant editor of FT Credit Ratings International and a quantitative finance consultant with Charterhouse Tilney Securities.

Dr. Tjark Tjin is recognized as a successful researcher with a Ph.D. in Theoretical Particle Physics. He has seven years of professional working experience at several first rate institutions such as the University of Munchen and Shell Research. Tjark Tjin has been involved in a currency overlay project from September 1996—September 1997 at Rabobank International. He now works at the Trading Company, one of the largest stock-option brokers in Amsterdam as Director of Research.

Robert Toffel has just completed his Undergraduate Degree in Mathematics at Imperial College, London where he obtained a First Class. He has previously been a trader at Titan Capital Management implementing proprietary trading models in the FX markets. His current focus is one of system development of numerous trading strategies and money management techniques for application across a wide range of markets.

Dr. Darren Toulson is a director of Intelligent Financial Systems Limited, a company developing financial forecasting and trading systems. He holds a B.Sc. in Mathematics and Physics and a Ph.D. in Neural Networks and Time Series Analysis from King's College London. He is the author of a number of papers on neural networks applied to time series analysis, image processing and financial forecasting.

Sabine Toulson is a director of Intelligent Financial Systems Limited. She read Economics and Mathematics at University College London and holds an M.Sc. with Distinction in Neural Networks from King's College

London. She has published several papers on exchange rate analysis using neural nets and portfolio management.

Marcel Vernooy is an experienced project manager who spent a large part of his professional career, five and a half years, with the Robeco Group. He started as a quantitative researcher at IRIS, the quantitative research institute of Robeco, and was primarily responsible for the development of forecasting models for equity markets, bond markets and asset-mix portfolios. At the same time, he acted as a consultant on these matters towards the investment departments and the foreign offices of the Robeco Group. Marcel Vernooy has been involved in a currency overlay project at Rabobank International.

Gary Xu is employed by the Bank of England. Until 1998, he was Senior Lecturer in Accounting and Finance at the University of Manchester, England, where he taught investment analysis and capital market theory. His research interests are in volatility modelling and forecasting, the efficiency of financial futures and options markets, and empirical tests of asset pricing models. Three innovative papers were published from his Ph.D. thesis on exchange rate volatility, including important contributions about the term structure and smile properties of implied volatilities. He obtained his B.Sc. from Peking University, his M.B.A from Aston University and his Ph.D. from Lancaster University.

Introduction

Financial markets are being swept by important changes affecting the way market participants inter-act and operate. As a recent example, both over the counter and exchange based market practitioners have considered and applied in some sort of way computerized trading as an alternative to open out-cry. These developments have contributed toward a more efficient market and potentially a better service to the end user of financial products. The phenomenal progress in information technology made over the last decade has been a catalyst to these changes. Maybe a less apparent but not the least important contributor to these changes is the wider use of high frequency time price series in the decision-making process. The advent of second generation microprocessors has made it possible to process large amount of data within a realistic time frame to make practical use of it. Undoubtedly the analysis of high frequency data brings us a wealth of information about the behavior of financial prices and new perspectives in the field of risk management and forecasting which were previously inconceivable. It permits market practitioners to test hypotheses and new trading strategies. It provides new resources to model and generate correlation and volatility estimates to input into pricing and risk models. Acknowledging the demand, statistical departments of financial exchanges and other data suppliers have started to release "clean" high frequency price data in convenient format. This has translated into a steady flow of research papers on high frequency modelling produced by both academics and market practitioners.

This book intends to give the reader a broad view on the uses and avenues of research presently investigated. It regroups researches from leading academics and market practitioners in the field of high frequency data. It is structured around three sections addressing practical issues that are paramount to the financial community. The first section of the book is dedicated to price volatility and risk estimators, the second section concentrates on statistical features and forecasting issues. Finally, the last section illustrates how "tick data" affect the way that market practitioners operate in the financial markets by giving practical examples of applications.

PART I HIGH FREQUENCY FINANCIAL SERIES, VOLATILITY AND RISK

Estimating risk is probably one of the most arduous and discussed issues in finance. It affects a wide area of financial activities from pricing options to managing portfolios of assets or evaluating the day to day risk of a dealing room. The interest for new measures of risk has been epitomized by the recent arrival of risk management techniques involving co-variance matrices of financial instruments, the efficiency of these models being a function of the robustness of the estimates used. Keeping this in mind, the first part of "Financial Markets Tick by Tick" gives a review of how high frequency data contributes to a better understanding and modelling of risk.

In **"Efficient estimation of intra-day volatility: a method-of-moments approach incorporating the trading range"** Richard Spurgin and Thomas Schneeweis address the difficult task of measuring intra-day volatility by introducing new historic volatility estimators relying on the trading range. These estimators are shown to provide a more accurate forecast than the traditional closing price and Parkinson estimators.

Shin-Juh Lin, Professor John Knight and Dr. Stephen Satchell investigate the choice of proxies to measure the flow of information to equity markets and their impact on price volatility distributions. In **"Modelling intra-day equity prices and volatility using information arrivals—A comparative study of different choices of informational proxies"**, they conclude that both the number of trades and the number of price changes are much better explanatory variables than trading volume itself. They find that their model reduces the persistence in volatility and consequently leads toward a better modelling and understanding of intra-day volatility.

Stephen Taylor and Xinzhong Xu use ARCH models in **"The incremental volatility information in one million foreign exchange quotations"** to compare the volatility information found in exchange rate quotations and in implied volatility. They find exchange rate quotation information to be more informative than options information. Their conclusion is supported by an out of sample comparison of forecast of hourly realized volatility.

"Correlation of high frequency financial time series" by Mark Lundin, Michel Dacorogna and Ulrich Müller, discusses the problems associated with measuring correlation at high frequency. They use a co-volatility adjusted measure which accounts for missing or non existent data. The stability of correlation over time and the exponential memory of financial time series return correlations is investigated. They find an inverse relationship between the rate of correlation attenuation and the level of activity in the instruments involved and also that returns short term are likely to be uncorrelated even if highly correlated over the long term. They do not find a "best" time interval for measuring correlation since this is dependent on the pertinence of time horizon for specific applications.

Emmanuel Acar and Robert Toffel in **"Highs and lows: times of the day in the currency CME market"** expose new stylized facts of extreme clustering for the CME currency contract. They show that contrarily to hetereoscedacity, skew and kurtosis, the impact of drift has little effect on the timing of intra-day extremes. These evidences of clustering could be of great help to a liquidity or directional trader.

PART II STATISTICAL FEATURES OF HIGH FREQUENCY FINANCIAL SERIES AND FORECASTING

Non-linear methods have provided financial market practitioners with new forecasting tools. High frequency data and faster computers have undoubtedly been the main factors contributing towards the development and use of these methodologies. The second section of "Financial Markets Tick by Tick" acknowledges this by providing the reader with insights on the statistical features of high frequency financial time price series.

Owain ap Gwilym, Mike Buckle and Stephen Thomas investigate the properties of time series and interaction of market variables in **"The intra-day behaviour of key market variables for LIFFE derivatives"**. They use a large high frequency data-set to examine the intra-day behaviour of return, volatility, trading volume, bid-ask spread and price reversal across a range of financial contracts traded on the LIFFE. They compare their findings with previous researches on other markets and find that market structure plays a vital role in determining the behaviour of these variables and this particularly at the open and close of a market.

In **"Price discovery and market integration in European bond markets"** Allison Holland examines the relationship between four major European government bonds and their associated future contracts. She finds that price discovery occurs in the future markets with the spot market following with a lag. Whereas arbitrage activity appears to be limited by the presence of market friction, the importance of spread trading is highlighted in the case of dually traded futures contracts. These are highly integrated reflecting very active arbitrage between the markets.

"A practical approach to information spillover at high frequency: empirical study of the gilt and FTSE LIFFE contracts" looks at the high frequency relationship between the LIFFE Gilt and FTSE contracts. Pierre Lequeux uses 10 years of 15-minute data for both Gilts and FTSE to investigate how the intra-day relationship between the two instruments evolved over time.

In **"High-frequency random walks?"** Michael Gavridis, Raphael Markellos and Terence Mills discuss the departures of high frequency prices from the simple random walk model and the implications for short term risk management and trading. Their arguments are supported by the analysis of 30-minute prices for 13 currency pairs. Their results suggest that although fat tails characterize the distributions of returns, variances are finite, This implies that short term investors face finite but non-Gaussian risks. They also find intra-day seasonalities in systematic risks and long-run dynamics.

Emmanuel Acar and Pierre Lequeux in **"Trading rules profits and the underlying time series properties"** provide a better understanding of forecasting strategies by using stochastic modelling. They derive tests of random walk and market efficiency from the stochastic properties of trading rules returns. Their propositions are then applied to a data-set of foreign exchange rates.

PART III HIGH FREQUENCY FINANCIAL SERIES AND MARKET PRACTITIONERS APPLICATIONS

Building on the previous sections, examples of practical applications and arguments for the use of high frequency data are presented in the four last chapters of this book.

Paul MacGregor in **"The sources, preparation and use of high frequency data in the derivatives markets"** gives us a concise description of how historical prices are generated both over the counter (OTC) and financial exchanges. Collection of data for both open outcry and computerized trading are detailed. The innovative approach of the LIFFE in supplying clean historical data whilst meeting end users' requirements is demonstrated in a "guided tour" of their LIFFE *style* product.

"The design of a quantitative currency overlay program" by Haijo Dijkstra, Marcel Vernooy and Tjark Tjin raises practical issues in designing a currency overlay program. They first provide the reader with the essential analytics to design a currency overlay program. Then they illustrate their methodology with an example using high frequency data models as a core indicator for the decision making in the currency overlay.

In **"Constructing a managed portfolio of high frequency LIFFE futures positions"** Darren Toulson, Sabine Toulson and Alison Sinclair demonstrate how discrete wavelet transform, neural networks and high frequency data can be used to design a risk-managed portfolio of LIFFE futures contracts. After detailing all the practical issues they assess the performance of the portfolio by testing their strategy out of sample.

Pierre Lequeux and Philippe Michelotti, in **"Is short term better? An insight through managed futures performances"**, quantify the economic value of short term traders and consequently the use of high frequency data. They analyse the performance of a universe of trading managers operating over three distinct time horizons: Long term, medium term and short term. They find that, generally, short term traders are less volatile and offer a better risk adjusted return than traders operating on longer time frames. They also find that the minimization of risk is better obtained through a portfolio of short term traders than long term traders.

The topic of high frequency data in the financial markets is very broad and the implications for market practitioners are numerous. We hope that the 14 chapters of this book will contribute toward a finer knowledge of this very specialized field as well as giving some orientation in terms of future research.

Pierre Lequeux

Part I

High Frequency Financial Series, Volatility and Risk

Chapter **1**

Efficient Estimation of Intra-day Volatility: A Method-of-Moments Approach Incorporating the Trading Range

Richard B. Spurgin and Thomas Schneeweis

Assistant Professor of Finance, Clark University, Professor of Finance, University of Massachusetts

INTRODUCTION

This chapter introduces new methods of estimating the historic volatility of a security from its trading range.[1] Parkinson (1980) showed that the range of a security contains considerably more information[2] about the return-generating process than does the period-to-period return. A number of papers have been published on this topic, all of which have two things in common. First, the authors assume security prices follow geometric brownian motion (GBM). Secondly, each of the several existing range-based variance estimators is based on squared trading ranges. Estimators derived from the second sample moment of observed ranges are highly efficient. However, they are shown in this chapter to be more sensitive to misspecification of the underlying process than estimators derived from lower sample moments. A new class of variance estimators is proposed in this chapter. Some members of this class are shown to provide more accurate variance estimates than existing range estimators and the close-to-close estimator as well.

There are a number of potential applications of this research. First, by correcting the biases known to exist in range-based variance estimators[3] and improving their efficiency, it may be possible to accurately estimate historic volatility over short time frames. Improved estimation would have a direct application to option and other derivative pricing. More accurate variance estimation would also allow for more efficient estimation of a security's beta, more accuracy in event studies, lead to more accurate models of the time-varying properties of return volatility, and generally improve any statistic that relies on an estimate of the variance or covariance of a security.

Review of Previous Research Trading Range Studies

The distribution of the trading range of a security that follows geometric Brownian motion has been extensively studied. Parkinson (1980) first considered this problem. Using a distribution first derived by Feller (1951), Parkinson found a variance estimator for a security whose log follows a zero-mean diffusion. His estimator is about five times as efficient[4] as the conventional close-to-close estimator. Garman and Klass (1980) extend Parkinson's approach, incorporating the open and close prices and the trading hours of the security. Ball and Torous (1984) find the minimum-variance range-based estimator by solving for the MLE of the joint distribution of high, low, and closing prices. Kunitomo (1992) and Rogers and Satchell (1991) develop estimators that allow for a drift term in the Parkinson and Garman and Klass estimators, respectively.

Despite theoretical results suggesting range-based estimators are several times more efficient than classical ones, empirical tests fail to demonstrate their superiority. Garman and Klass (1980) use simulation to show that range-based estimators are sensitive to discreteness in price changes, producing downward biased estimates. Beckers (1983) reaches a similar conclusion with actual data, and shows the efficiency of range-based estimates is only slightly better than the classical approach. Wiggins (1991, 1992) studies the properties of several estimators for a wide range of securities and finds the performance of range-based estimators is not significantly better and often worse than traditional estimators. Rogers, Satchell and Yoon (1994) find that the Rogers and Satchell (1991) estimator is accurate when tested with simulated data, but is considerably biased when actual stock data are used.

The problems may be due in part to microstructure issues. Because prices are reported in discrete increments, the true high and low of a security that follows GBM are unobservable. The rounded values distort both the trading range and the last price, but the influence on the range will be more pronounced. Marsh and Rosenfeld (1986) employ a model that shows a discretely observed range will be smaller than the true range, and thus estimators based on the observed range will give downward biased estimates of the true variance. Rogers and Satchell (1991) derive a model in a continuous-time framework that corrects this bias when the time interval between price changes is known. Ball (1988) describes the bias when estimating variance with discrete end-of-period prices, and shows that variance estimates using observed returns will be downward biased. Cho and Frees (1988) reach the same conclusion using a first-passage time approach.

Another possible explanation for the poor performance of range-based estimators is misspecification of the underlying return-generating process. Range-based variance estimators are more sensitive to misspecification of the underlying process than classical estimators (Heynen and Kat, 1993). If the assumptions of geometric Brownian motion are violated, estimators derived from the trading range will be adversely affected to a larger degree than close-to-close estimators.

ESTIMATING HISTORIC VOLATILITY USING THE TRADING RANGE

Methods of estimating historic volatility using the trading range of a security are described in this section. The approach makes use of the distribution of the range of a binomial random walk (Weiss and Rubin, 1983), the range of a diffusion process (Feller, 1951), and the distribution of the number of distinct sites visited by a binomial random walk. Prior research has focused on quadratic estimation techniques. However, estimators can easily be derived from other sample moments. This section also identifies the reasons why previous tests of range-based variance estimators have been biased.

Distribution of the Range of a Binomial Random Walk

The distribution of the range of a binomial random walk was derived by Weiss and Rubin (1983). Although this function has been known in the scientific literature for some time, it has not been explored in finance literature. The probability W that the range is exactly l is:

$$W_n(l) = -\sum_{a=0}^{S} \Delta_a \Delta_b Q_n(0| - a, b)|_{b=S-a}.$$ 1

Δ is the difference operator, $\Delta_a f(a) = f(a+1) - f(a)$. Q_n is the probability that the walk is contained within an interval $(-a, b)$ given that the starting point is 0 and there are n steps in the walk,

$$Q_n(0| - a, b) = \sum_{r=-a+1}^{b-1} U_n(r; -a, b|0).$$ 2

U_n is the probability that the walk is at price r at step n, given it is restricted to $(-a, b)$, and began at 0,

$$U_n(r; -a, b|0) = \sum_{l=-\infty}^{\infty} (P_n(r + 2l(a + b)) - P_n(r + 2a + 2l(a + b))). \qquad 3$$

P_n is the unrestricted probability that the walk is at location r at step n. If the process follows a zero-mean binomial expansion[5], this probability is a transformed Binomial distribution,

$$P_n(r) = P(y = Y), \text{ where } y \sim B\left(n, \frac{1}{2}\right) \text{ and } y = \frac{x + n}{2}. \qquad 4$$

The transformation maps the range of the random walk $[-n, n]$ to the binomial range $[0, n]$. There are other methods of deriving the range distribution of a binomial variable. A function that generates range probabilities for an n-step walk given the $n - 1$ step probabilities is described in the Appendix.

Distribution of the Range of a Continuous Random Walk

The distribution of the range of a security following a zero-mean diffusion process was first solved by Feller (1951). This function and the moment generating function are:

$$F(l, \sigma^2 t) = \sum_{n=1}^{\infty} (-1)^{n+1} n(erfc((n + 1)l/\sqrt{2\sigma^2 t})$$

$$- 2erfc(nl/\sqrt{2\sigma^2 t} + erfc((n - 1)l/\sqrt{2\sigma^2 t})) \qquad 5$$

$$E[l^p] = \frac{4}{\sqrt{\pi}}\Gamma\left(\frac{p+1}{2}\right)\left(1 - \frac{4}{2^p}\right)\zeta(p - 1)(2\sigma^2 t)^{p/2}, \qquad 6$$

where the l's are observed ranges, N is the sample size, $erfc(z)$ is one minus the integral of the Gaussian distribution, and $\zeta(x)$ is the Riemann zeta function: The distribution has one unobservable parameter, the diffusion constant σ^2.

Distribution of the Number of Sites Visited by a Binomial Random Walk

The range of a continuous process has been studied by a number of authors, but these results translate poorly to discrete processes for a simple reason: Feller defined the range differently than Parkinson. Feller defines the range as the number of sites visited by a random walk, while in finance the range is the difference between the high and low trades. Thus the continuous range density 5 is the limiting distribution of the number of sites visited by a random walk, not the limiting distribution of the range of a random walk. Although these two quantities are equivalent in the limit, in discrete time the number of sites visited (in finance, the number of distinct prices traded during the period) is generally one trade-size larger than the range.[6] This is the principal source of discreteness bias in Parkinson's estimator.

The distribution of the number of sites visited by a binomial random walk (V), is created with a transformation of the P distribution employed by Parkinson. Assuming that the number of sites visited is always one greater[7] than the range in this model, then the probability that $D(l + 1) = V(l) = P(l)$.

Comparing the Moments of the Range Distributions

Figure 1 graphs the moments of the three functions: The density employed by Parkinson (P), the discrete range density from Weiss and Rubin (D) and the PDF of the number of sites visited by a discrete random walk

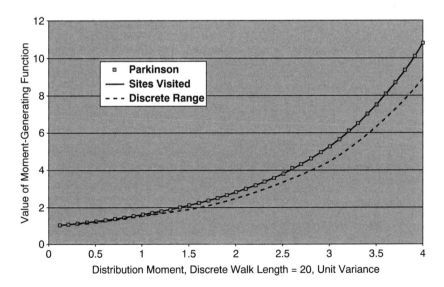

Figure 1   Comparison of Moment Functions: Parkinson, Discrete Range, and Sites Visited.

(V). Variance is normalized, and the discrete walks further assume a walk-length of 20. According to the uniqueness theorem,[8] if the V function and the P function have a common moment-generating function, then the distributions are the same. While there is no closed solution to the moment-generating function of V, Figure 1 shows that the moments of V and P are nearly identical over the first 4 moments (including fractional moments) and that the moments of D are significantly different.[9]

While Figure 1 demonstrates the similarity between V and P, they are not the same function. Since P is an approximation of V, for any given moment, V converges to a slightly different number than that predicted by P. This difference is small and easily corrected in any case. A numerical correction of this difference, termed the difference constant (C_m), is described in Appendix 2.

Parameter Estimation

The variance of a diffusion process is given by $\sigma^2 t$. It is generally assumed that time is observable, and hence the unknown parameter is σ^2. Assuming a unit time interval, Parkinson (1980) derived an estimator of the Feller distribution from the second moment of 6,

$$\hat{\sigma}^2 = \frac{\left(\sum l_i^2 / N\right)}{4 \ln(2)}.$$

7

Another estimator proposed by Parkinson is based on the first moment of the distribution[10]:

$$\hat{\sigma}^2 = \frac{\left(\sum l_i / N\right)^2}{(8/\pi)}.$$

8

The variance of a zero-mean binomial random walk is $S^2 n$, where n is number of steps taken and S is the step-size or minimum trade. The step-size is assumed to be observable and the true source of uncertainty is assumed to be the number of price changes per period. Other researchers studying this question have made the opposite assumption—that the number of steps per period is known and the variance per step is unknown (Garman and Klass (1980), Torney (1986), Wiggins (1991), Rogers and Satchell (1991)). Assuming an unknown step-size is reasonable if prices are assumed to follow a continuous process. However, assuming the walk-length is unknown seems more consistent with observed market behavior. During periods of increased volatility, it is generally the transaction rate that increases, not the size of each price change.[11]

The **V** function and the moment correction discussed in the previous section lead to a natural estimator of the variance. For example, the first moment of the **V** function can be expressed as an adjusted function of the first moment of the **P** distribution (which is calculated from Equation 6) and the difference constant (Appendix 2):

$$E[r_v] = \left(\frac{8}{\pi}(S^2 n) + .499S \right)^{1/2}.$$

9

This relationship is rearranged to form a variance estimator based on the average of observed ranges. This estimator requires transforming observed ranges into number of sites visited, averaging observed ranges, and reducing the total by about .499 times the tick-size of the security:

$$\hat{n} = \frac{\left[\sum (v_i/N) \right]^2 - .499S}{8/\pi}, \quad \text{where } v_i = l_i + S$$

10

An estimator of this type can be created from any of the moments of V and P. In general, if $v_i = l_i + S$ and C_m is the difference constant, then

$$\hat{\sigma}^2 = S^2 \hat{n} = S^2 \frac{\left[\sum (v_i^m/N) \right]^{2/m} - C_m}{E[l_P]}.$$

11

DATA

The estimators are tested with daily and intra-day data on two financial futures contracts, the CME SP500 contract and the CBT Treasury Bond contract. The tick-by-tick data, which were supplied by Tick Data, Inc., cover the period October, 1989 through June, 1994. Each trading day is broken into four segments. The day session of T-Bond trading is 400 minutes long, so each intra-day period is 100 minutes. Night trading for CBT Bonds was excluded from the analysis, as was T-Bond futures trading on foreign exchanges (Tokyo and LIFFE). The S&P500 trading session is 405 minutes long. In this analysis, the first three periods are 100 minutes, and the final period is 105 minutes (from 2:30–4:15 Eastern Time). In each intraday period the range is calculated as the difference between the high and low recorded trades. Returns are based on the nearby contract, rolling to the next contract on the first day of the delivery month.

The daily range is calculated as the natural logarithm of the high trade less the log of the low trade. The return is the log of the closing quote less

Table 1 Descriptive statistics for S&P500 and Treasury Bond Futures data.

Panel A. S&P500 futures: 100 minute periods and daily data from October 1, 1989 to June 29, 1994.

	Return (log of open/close)						Range (log of high/low)					
	1st	*2nd*	*3rd*	*4th*	*All*	*Day*	*1st*	*2nd*	*3rd*	*4th*	*All*	*Day*
Observations	1196	1196	1196	1196	4784	1196	1196	1196	1196	1196	4784	1196
Mean	−0.013%	0.004%	−0.008%	0.036%	0.005%	0.023%	0.602%	0.443%	0.440%	0.595%	0.520%	1.086%
Variance X 100	0.175%	0.097%	0.078%	0.243%	0.149%	0.661%	0.139%	0.079%	0.072%	0.157%	0.118%	0.403%
Skewness	−0.53	0.12	−0.55	−4.54	−2.53	−0.68	3.48	2.84	3.36	6.24	4.51	2.99
Kurtosis	11.40	6.90	7.09	75.41	54.65	15.98	23.41	17.57	33.90	97.07	58.82	22.89
Extreme Value	−3.44%	1.93%	−2.18%	−8.40%	−8.40%	−8.45%	4.16%	3.01%	4.10%	7.79%	7.79%	8.19%

Panel B. S&P500 data excluding "mini-crash": Friday, October 13 and Monday, October 16, 1989.

	Return (log of open/close)						Range (log of high/low)					
	1st	*2nd*	*3rd*	*4th*	*All*	*Day*	*1st*	*2nd*	*3rd*	*4th*	*All*	*Day*
Observations	1194	1194	1194	1194	4776	1194	1194	1194	1194	1194	4776	1194
Mean	−0.015%	0.003%	−0.009%	0.043%	0.005%	0.025%	0.599%	0.441%	0.440%	0.588%	0.517%	1.075%
Variance X 100	0.168%	0.095%	0.078%	0.183%	0.131%	0.572%	0.128%	0.076%	0.072%	0.113%	0.103%	0.338%
Skewness	−0.83	0.08	−0.56	−0.57	−0.55	−0.08	3.12	2.78	3.38	2.03	2.76	1.77
Kurtosis	10.31	6.84	7.11	5.73	8.50	4.92	19.35	17.42	34.13	10.53	18.19	7.97
Extreme value	−3.44%	1.93%	−2.18%	−2.01%	−3.44%	−3.78%	3.55%	3.01%	4.10%	3.25%	4.10%	4.73%

Panel C. Treasury Bond Futures: 100 minute periods and daily data from October 1, 1989 to June 29, 1994.

	Return (log of open/close)						Range (log of high/low)					
	1st	*2nd*	*3rd*	*4th*	*All*	*Day*	*1st*	*2nd*	*3rd*	*4th*	*All*	*Day*
Observations	1195	1195	1195	1195	4780	1195	1195	1195	1195	1195	4780	1195
Mean	0.002%	−0.009%	0.000%	0.013%	0.002%	0.007%	0.431%	0.320%	0.290%	0.356%	0.349%	0.727%
Variance X 100	0.088%	0.044%	0.036%	0.065%	0.058%	0.262%	0.063%	0.050%	0.043%	0.043%	0.045%	0.126%
Skewness	−0.27	−0.34	−0.77	−0.30	−0.35	−0.21	1.93	1.89	2.45	1.90	2.16	1.18
Kurtosis	7.08	6.62	11.47	7.91	8.52	3.77	8.19	8.63	16.87	11.72	11.19	4.88
Extreme value	−1.60%	1.22%	−1.81%	−1.92%	−1.92%	−1.98%	1.93%	1.43%	1.88%	2.11%	2.11%	2.53%

the log of the open. No attempt is made to account for overnight activity, as data on the overnight range are not reliable. As a result, variance estimates will underestimate the true variance per 24-hour day.

Table 1 reports descriptive statistics of the data. The first panel is S&P500 data. Results are reported cross-sectionally by time period as well as in total. There is considerable difference in variance between the time periods. The first and last periods account for 70 percent of the daytime variance and the middle two periods only 30 percent. Returns are negatively skewed, extremely so in the fourth period, where skewness is −4.54. Returns are also fat-tailed. The coefficients of kurtosis range from a low of 7.09 in the third period to 75.41 in the fourth.

The extreme readings in the fourth period are entirely due to the events of one day—the "mini-crash" on October 13, 1989. On that day the stock market fell nearly 9 percent in the final hour of trading. The second panel of Table 1B repeats the analysis in Table 1A excluding October 13 and 16, 1989. After excluding those two days, return volatility in the fourth period declines by 25 percent to .183 and overall intra-day volatility declines by 15 percent to .131. Skewness and kurtosis measures also decline sharply. Declines of similar magnitude are recorded in the volatility of the intraday trading ranges. However, the mean intra-day range declines by only .003, or about $\frac{1}{2}$ percent. Thus, estimators based on the average trading range will be only marginally influenced by the outlier, while estimators based on higher moments will be highly influenced.

Table 1C reports descriptive statistics of Treasury Bond futures data. As with the stock data, the mean return is negligible. Returns are slightly negatively skewed and fat-tailed, though not as severely as the stock data. Consistent with prior research on the empirical distribution of returns, the higher moments of the daily return and range distribution are considerably smaller than for intra-day data[12]. Skew and kurtosis for daily bond returns, for example, are −.21 and 3.77, not far from normality.

EFFICIENCY OF VARIANCE FORECASTS

In this section, the reliability of variance forecasts produced by each model is tested. Variance estimates are studied two ways. First, simulated data are used to understand the properties of the estimators, in particular the bias and efficiency of each estimator. The second test involves historical security data. Data are first segmented into non-overlapping blocks. A variance estimate is derived from the observations in each block. This estimate is used as a forecast of the next period's variance. If an estimator is a reliable forecasting tool, then the difference between the current period's estimate and the next period's estimate will be small. Forecast errors are squared and summed over the entire sample. The best forecasts will minimize mean-square error. In order to be useful, an estimator must be more accurate than simply assuming that variance is constant. Using the close-to-close estimator, Figlewski (1994) demonstrates that forecasts become more accurate as the amount of historical data used in the estimation is increased. This implies that estimating volatility over short time intervals is not productive. This notion is tested by comparing the mean square error (MSE) of consecutive forecasts with the variance of all forecasts.

Description of Variance Estimators

Tests are conducted on eight variations of the Binomial model: Method of moments estimators are calculated using Equation 11 starting with the $\frac{1}{4}$ sample range moment and continuing to the second moment in $\frac{1}{4}$ increments.[13] The formulas for each of the eight binomial estimators are given in Appendix 3. Equation 11 requires knowledge of the tick-size, S. For Treasury Bond data, the assumed tick-size is $\frac{1}{32}$ of a percent. For S&P500 the tick-size used is .05 percent. The closing price estimator,[14]

$$\hat{\sigma}^2 = \left(\sum x_i^2 / N \right),$$ 12

and the Parkinson estimator 7 are calculated for comparison.

Simulation Results

Table 2 reports the simulation results. 50-step binomial walks were simulated. The high, low and closing values of each walk were recorded. Twenty such walks were simulated and the data used to calculate each of the estimators. This process was repeated 1,000 times in order to generate information about the sampling distribution of each estimator. Results indicate that binomial estimators derived from the different sample moments are approximately unbiased,[15] while the Parkinson estimator has a downward bias of 16 percent. The CLOSE estimator is also unbiased, but its variance, at 259, is more than five times as large as the variance of the range-based estimators. There is little difference among the different binomial estimators. Estimators based on low moments outperformed the higher moment estimators by about 10 percent in terms of efficiency. The Mean Square Error of each estimator is about twice the estimator variance,

Table 2 Performance of variance estimators using simulated random walks.

50-step random walks, unit step-size, 20 random walks used to calculate variance estimate
Variance of sampling population: 50
Repetitions: 1,000

	CLOSE	Parkinson	Sample moment used to generate variance estimate							
			$\frac{1}{4}$	$\frac{1}{2}$	$\frac{3}{4}$	1	$1\frac{1}{4}$	$1\frac{1}{2}$	$1\frac{3}{4}$	2
Mean	50.51	41.93	50.19	50.15	50.10	50.06	50.02	49.98	49.94	49.89
Variance	259	45	45	46	46	47	48	49	50	52
Maximum	104.80	73.20	77.49	78.32	79.14	79.97	80.78	81.59	82.39	83.19
Median	48.80	41.42	49.73	49.65	49.59	49.40	49.61	49.54	49.44	49.43
Minimum	14.00	25.84	33.37	33.23	33.08	32.94	32.79	32.64	32.50	32.35
Estimator error	1.02%	−16.13%	0.37%	0.29%	0.21%	0.13%	0.04%	−0.04%	−0.13%	−0.22%
Normalized variance	0.102	0.025	0.018	0.018	0.018	0.019	0.019	0.020	0.020	0.021
Normalized forecast MSE	0.213	0.054	0.039	0.039	0.040	0.040	0.041	0.042	0.043	0.044
Variance efficiency ratio	1.00	4.01	5.65	5.59	5.52	5.43	5.32	5.19	5.05	4.89
Forecast MSE efficiency ratio	1.00	3.98	5.45	5.41	5.35	5.28	5.19	5.09	4.97	4.84
Variance/forecast MSE ratio	0.48	0.47	0.46	0.46	0.46	0.46	0.47	0.47	0.47	0.47

Estimator Error is the percentage difference between the mean estimate and the population value. Normalized Variance is the estimator variance divided by the square of the mean estimate. Normalized MSE is the sum of squared differences between consecutive estimates divided by the square of the mean estimate. Variance Efficiency Ratio is the ratio of the CLOSE variance to the estimator variance. Forecast MSE Efficiency Ratio is the ratio of the CLOSE Forecast MSE to the estimator variance. Forecast MSE Efficiency Ratio is the ratio of the CLOSE Forecast MSE to the estimator MSE.

an unsurprising result. MSE is the variance of the difference between consecutive estimates. If consecutive estimates are independent, the MSE will be twice the variance of a single estimate.

Performance of Variance Estimators Using Historical Data

This section reports the performance of the same 10 estimators used in the previous section, this time using contiguous blocks of observed data to calculate the estimators. Using actual data severely limits the number of estimators that can be calculated, as overlapping observations are known to introduce bias.[16] Twenty days of data are used in each estimate, so the sample size for daily results is 20. With four periods per day, each intra-day sample contains 80 observations. The 1,196 days of observations result in 59 realizations of each estimator (the final 16 days are ignored). Estimators are evaluated using the same methodology as the simulated random walks. The only difference is that the true variance of the simulated random walks is known. With S&P500 and Treasury bond data this parameter is estimated from the full sample, and hence is itself subject to estimation error. All results are divided by the square of the step-size. Thus the quantity estimated is not the variance, *per se*, but the rate at which price changes occur.

Discussion of S&P500 Results

Both the intra-day S&P500 results (Table 3A) and the daily results (Table 3B) show the range-based estimators to be negatively biased relative to the full sample estimate and the CLOSE estimator to be unbiased. For example, the Binomial(1) estimator is downward biased by 8.32 percent using intra-day data and 16.46 percent using daily data. This bias is entirely due to the influence of the "mini-crash".[17] The median estimates for CLOSE and the low-moment binomial estimators are approximately equal for both daily and intraday data.[18]

The variance of estimates is much larger with actual data than with the iid binomial simulation. The variance increase is relatively more pronounced for binomial estimators than for the CLOSE estimator. The normalized variance of CLOSE increases from .102 to 1.18, a factor of 11.6, while the Binomial(1) estimator increases from .019 to .357, a factor of 19.3. The efficiency of Binomial(1) declines to 3.98 from 5.53. There are a number of possible explanations for the reduced efficiency. First, if volatility is time-varying, a given sample is likely to have a greater concentration of high or low volatility periods than the population as a whole, resulting in greater

Table 3 Performance of historic volatility estimators using S&P500 index futures data.

Panel A: 100 minute periods, October, 1989 to June, 1994. Total of 4784 Periods, sample size 80
Population variance estimate using full sample: 56.52.

	CLOSE	Parkinson	Sample moment used to generate variance estimate							
			$\frac{1}{4}$	$\frac{1}{2}$	$\frac{3}{4}$	1	$1\frac{1}{4}$	$1\frac{1}{2}$	$1\frac{3}{4}$	2
Mean	56.90	52.62	47.66	48.91	50.28	51.82	53.35	55.53	57.80	60.38
Variance	3,815	1,585	790	834	888	959	1,057	1,198	1,412	1,739
Maximum	450.70	222.76	146.12	149.73	153.55	157.59	161.82	166.23	188.00	233.68
Median	41.06	40.10	40.18	40.86	41.58	42.05	42.70	44.19	45.73	47.34
Minimum	11.96	10.34	13.42	13.56	13.70	13.85	14.02	14.20	14.40	14.62
Estimator error	0.68%	-6.90%	-15.67%	-13.46%	-11.03%	-8.32%	-5.25%	-1.75%	2.27%	6.84%
Normalized variance	1.178	0.572	0.348	0.348	0.351	0.357	0.368	0.389	0.423	0.477
Normalized forecast MSE	1.148	0.410	0.135	0.139	0.145	0.157	0.176	0.207	0.257	0.332
Variance efficiency ratio	1.00	2.06	3.39	3.38	3.35	3.30	3.20	3.03	2.79	2.47
Forecast MSE efficiency ratio	1.00	2.80	8.49	8.26	7.89	7.33	6.54	5.55	4.47	3.45
Variance/forecast MSE ratio	1.03	1.40	2.57	2.51	2.41	2.28	2.10	1.88	1.65	1.44

(continued overleaf)

Table 3   *(continued)*

Panel B: Daily data, October, 1989 to June, 1994. Total of 1196 Days, sample size 20
Population variance estimate using full sample: 251.34.

	CLOSE	Parkinson	Sample moment used to generate variance estimate							
			$\frac{1}{4}$	$\frac{1}{2}$	$\frac{3}{4}$	1	$1\frac{1}{4}$	$1\frac{1}{2}$	$1\frac{3}{4}$	2
Mean	252.12	216.69	197.87	201.54	205.56	209.99	214.83	220.11	225.77	231.76
Variance	92,284	28,434	16,370	17,036	17,902	19,075	20,695	22,921	25,903	29,749
Maximum	2,164.4	999.31	691.47	703.77	715.43	726.35	736.40	756.45	883.69	1,022.3
Median	164.79	156.90	155.52	159.68	164.55	167.68	168.09	168.39	168.55	170.59
Minimum	34.73	44.19	53.67	53.49	53.31	53.13	52.95	52.77	52.59	52.41
Estimator error	0.31%	−13.79%	−21.28%	−19.81%	−18.22%	−16.46%	−14.53%	−12.43%	−10.17%	−7.79%
Normalized variance	1.452	0.606	0.418	0.419	0.424	0.433	0.448	0.473	0.508	0.554
Normalized forecast MSE	1.511	0.462	0.157	0.169	0.186	0.210	0.243	0.288	0.346	0.417
Variance efficiency ratio	1.00	2.40	3.47	3.46	3.43	3.36	3.24	3.07	2.86	2.62
Forecast MSE efficiency ratio	1.00	3.27	9.63	8.94	8.12	7.19	6.21	5.24	4.37	3.62
Variance/forecast MSE ratio	0.96	1.31	2.66	2.48	2.28	2.06	1.84	1.64	1.47	1.33

Estimator Error is the percentage difference between the mean estimate and the population value. Normalized Variance is the estimator variance divided by the square of the mean estimate. Normalized MSE is the sum of squared differences between consecutive estimates divided by the square of the mean estimate. Variance Efficiency Ratio is the ratio of the CLOSE variance to the estimator variance. Forecast MSE Efficiency Ratio is the ratio of the CLOSE Forecast MSE to the estimator MSE.

dispersion of estimates. Secondly, the distribution of intraday returns is know to have longer tails than the normal distribution (for example see Guillaume *et al.*, 1994, and Granger and Ding, 1994). The efficiency of all the variance estimates decreases as the tail thickness increases, and the decrease in efficiency is more pronounced for range-based estimators than for the closing price estimator.

Forecast efficiency for Binomial estimators is considerably better than for the CLOSE estimator. For example, the intraday Binomial(1) estimator has normalized variance of .357, but the (normalized) forecast MSE is .157. Thus for this estimator, knowledge of the previous estimate is a better predictor of the next period's estimate than the mean of all forecasts.[19] The Variance/FMSE ratio of the CLOSE estimator is 1.03, suggesting the most recent CLOSE forecast is no more informative than the average of all forecasts.[20] The efficiency of low moment binomial forecasts is much higher than any of the quadratic estimators. For example, Binomial ($\frac{1}{2}$) has Forecast MSE efficiency of 8.26, a considerable improvement over Binomial(2) at 3.45 and Parkinson at 2.80.

A comparison of daily and intra-day results shows that intra-day estimation with range estimators provides a reasonable proxy for daily results (for example, the daily mean estimate for Binomial(1) of 209.99 is almost exactly four times the 51.82 mean intra-day estimate). This is not true of the CLOSE estimator, however, which measures about 10 percent more intra-day volatility than daily volatility. The normalized variance and Forecast MSE of all the estimators is lower for intra-day results than daily results, generally 10–25 percent lower. This suggests intra-day data contains useful information about the return-generating process that daily data do not contain.

Discussion of Treasury Bond Futures Results

Results using Treasury Bond data are largely similar to the S&P500 data. Using daily data (Table 4B), all the range estimators are biased lower. With intra-day data the bias is mixed—low moment estimators are downward biased (Binomial($\frac{1}{4}$,−11.8 percent), those in the middle are about unbiased (Binomial(1),−1.6 percent), and larger moment estimators are positively biased (Binomial(2), 14.4 percent). The efficiency of binomial estimators is lower than with stock data or in simulation (for example, the intra-day efficiency of Binomial(1) is 1.73). The range is capturing more information than the returns, but the difference is considerably less than implied by theory.

Binomial range estimators have a higher forecast efficiency than either the Parkinson estimator or the CLOSE estimator. The Variance/Forecast

Table 4   Performance of historic volatility estimators using CBT Treasury Bond futures data.

Panel A: 100 minute periods, October, 1989 to June, 1994. Total of 4780 periods, sample size 80
Population variance estimate using full sample: 59.58

	CLOSE	parkinson	Sample moment used to generate variance estimate							
			$\frac{1}{4}$	$\frac{1}{2}$	$\frac{3}{4}$	1	$1\frac{1}{4}$	$1\frac{1}{2}$	$1\frac{3}{4}$	2
Mean	59.29	59.68	52.54	54.55	56.55	58.61	60.77	63.07	65.51	68.12
Variance	769	550	348	374	403	434	470	511	559	616
Maximum	168.46	147.14	114.48	119.19	125.50	131.41	137.76	144.61	151.94	159.73
Median	52.71	55.60	51.09	52.69	54.11	55.60	57.46	59.93	62.54	64.15
Minimum	23.45	23.04	18.77	19.83	20.97	22.22	23.58	25.06	26.67	28.40
Estimator error	−0.48%	0.17%	−11.81%	−8.44%	−5.08%	−1.62%	2.01%	5.85%	9.96%	14.35%
Normalized variance	0.219	0.154	0.126	0.126	0.126	0.126	0.127	0.129	0.130	0.133
Normalized forecast MSE	0.219	0.109	0.083	0.081	0.081	0.082	0.083	0.085	0.089	0.093
Variance efficiency ratio	1.00	1.42	1.74	1.74	1.74	1.73	1.72	1.70	1.68	1.65
Forecast MSE Efficiency Ratio	1.00	2.00	2.63	2.68	2.69	2.68	2.63	2.56	2.46	2.34
Variance / forecast MSE ratio	1.00	1.42	1.52	1.54	1.55	1.55	1.53	1.51	1.47	1.42

Panel B: Daily data, October, 1989 to June, 1994. Total of 1195 days, sample size 20
Population variance estimate using full sample: 268.21

	CLOSE	Parkinson	Sample moment used to generate variance estimate							
			$\frac{1}{4}$	$\frac{1}{2}$	$\frac{3}{4}$	1	$1\frac{1}{4}$	$1\frac{1}{2}$	$1\frac{3}{4}$	2
Mean	265.26	238.24	220.17	225.07	230.02	235.01	239.99	244.94	249.83	254.61
Variance	13,336	9,337	7,401	7,708	8,035	8,378	8,736	9,107	9,489	9,882
Maximum	716.96	574.64	532.91	544.26	555.17	565.56	575.27	584.25	592.41	599.71
Median	249.01	226.64	203.52	213.78	219.52	225.25	230.91	233.52	236.74	243.35
Minimum	90.18	104.85	81.79	84.86	88.40	92.47	97.17	102.55	108.65	115.50
Estimator error	−1.10%	−11.17%	−17.91%	−16.08%	−14.24%	−12.38%	−10.52%	−8.67%	−6.85%	−5.07%
Normalized variance	0.190	0.165	0.153	0.152	0.152	0.152	0.152	0.152	0.152	0.152
Normalized forecast MSE	0.210	0.125	0.108	0.108	0.108	0.109	0.110	0.112	0.114	0.116
Variance efficiency ratio	1.00	1.15	1.24	1.25	1.25	1.25	1.25	1.25	1.25	1.24
Forecast MSE efficiency ratio	1.00	1.68	1.94	1.94	1.94	1.93	1.91	1.88	1.85	1.81
Variance/forecast MSE ratio	0.90	1.31	1.41	1.41	1.40	1.39	1.38	1.36	1.34	1.31

Estimator Error is the percentage difference between the mean estimate and the population value. Normalized Variance is the estimator variance divided by the square of the mean estimate. Normalized MSE is the sum of squared differences between consecutive estimates divided by the square of the mean estimate. Variance Efficiency Ratio is the ratio of the CLOSE variance to the estimator variance. Forecast MSE Efficiency Ratio is the ratio of the CLOSE Forecast MSE to the estimator MSE.

MSE ratio for the binomial estimators is about 1.5, indicating the most recent estimate is a better forecast of the next period's variance than the average forecast. As with the S&P500 data, the CLOSE estimator has a Variance/Forecast MSE ratio of 1.0, suggesting the most recent estimate is no more informative than the long-run average.

The intra-day binomial estimators outperform their daily counterparts on the order of 20 percent. For example, the Binomial(1) estimator has normalized variance of .126 using intra-day data and .152 with daily data. Forecast MSE using intra-day results is .081 compared to the daily result of .109. However, the intra-day variance and Forecast MSE of the CLOSE estimator are actually higher using intra-day data than with daily data, suggesting that for this estimator, the noise introduced by utilizing intra-day data outweighs the benefits of more frequent observations.

As with the stock data, binomial estimators appear to scale better than the CLOSE estimator. The average Binomial(1) estimate of 235.0 transactions per day is almost exactly four times the average estimate of 58.61 transactions per 100-minute period. The CLOSE estimator scales poorly, with the daily estimate of 265.26 about 12 percent higher than four times the intra-day estimate of 59.29. The bias is about the same magnitude as with stock data, but the sign is reversed. With stock data, intra-day estimates overestimated the daily figure.

CONCLUSION

The variance estimators proposed in this paper outperform the CLOSE and Parkinson benchmarks. Binomial estimators have lower variance than either estimator and produce more accurate forecasts. Among binomial estimators, those based on the lower moments of the range distribution have properties that are well suited to estimating the volatility of intra-day financial time series. These estimators place less emphasis on extreme values than quadratic estimators, so they are less sensitive to the long tails generally observed in intraday return series. They also appear to scale quite accurately. On average, the sum of intra-day variances was quite close to the daily estimate. This was not true of the CLOSE estimator. While binomial estimators are clearly preferable to the CLOSE or Parkinson estimators, the estimators proposed here did not perform as well with real data as with simulated data. More importantly, they did not perform well enough to allow for accurate short-term volatility forecasts. Despite theoretical results that suggest highly accurate variance estimates should be possible with small sample sizes, none of the estimators tested here performed close to the theoretical benchmarks.

More research in this area is needed. The binomial model seems to provide more accurate variance estimates than the diffusion model, but is itself very limited. Range-based estimators derived from return models that allow time-varying volatility should prove more robust than the estimators described here. The use of low sample moments to estimate volatility should be studied further. Tests using different securities, time horizons, and different sample sizes are needed to see if the encouraging results reported here are generally applicable to financial time series or specific to the data analyzed.

APPENDIX 1: ALTERNATIVE DERIVATION OF RANGE OF A BINOMIAL RANDOM WALK

This appendix describes a generating function that provides exact range probabilities using a recursive approach. It can also be used to rapidly generate a complete set of range probabilities for any walk-length. The approach is essentially a brute-force method, as each of the 2^n possible outcomes is accounted for. In this model two attributes are sufficient to describe each of the 2^n outcomes—the range of the outcome and distance from the location of the walk to the lowest location traveled in the walk. All outcomes that share these attributes form an equivalence class. Thus there are at most n^2 different classes for each walk-length, which is a much more manageable calculation than 2^n for large n. To calculate the range density of an n-step walk, fill a three-dimensional array according to the following rules

$$a(n, j, 0) = a(n - 1, j - 1, 0) + a(n - 1, j, 1)$$

$$a(n, j, i) = a(n - 1, j, i - 1) + a(n - 1, j, i + 1), i, 1 \text{ to } j - 1$$

$$a(n, j, j) = a(n - 1, j - 1, j - 1) + a(n - 1, j, j - 1)$$

$$\text{and}, a(0, 0, 0) = 1$$

The first column is the length of the walk, the second is the trading range, and the third is the location relative to the minimum. Range probabilities are calculated by summing across the third column and dividing by the total number of outcomes, 2^n.

APPENDIX 2: COMPUTATION OF THE DIFFERENCE CONSTANT

Although the moment-generating functions of the Feller (P) and the distribution of the number of sites visited by a binomial random walk (V) are nearly identical, there is a small discrepancy which can be corrected numerically. The ratio of the expected values of any moment multiplied by the walk length will differ from the walk length by a small margin. This margin is essentially independent of the walk length, so the ratio of the expected values converges to 1 as the walk length tends to infinity. For shorter lengths it may make sense to correct for this difference. For example, the relative second moments at three selected walk-lengths are:

$$\text{For } n = 10, \; \frac{E[r_v^2]}{E[r_p^2]}n \approx 10.384, \; \text{error} = .0384$$

$$\text{For } n = 50, \; \frac{E[r_v^2]}{E[r_p^2]}n \approx 50.396, \; \text{error} = .0079$$

$$\text{For } n = 100, \; \frac{E[r_v^2]}{E[r_p^2]}n \approx 100.391, \; \text{error} = .0039$$

The 2nd moment of the V function exceeds the 2nd moment of the P function by a small constant (approximately 0.39). Estimation error induced by this difference is about 4 percent when n is 10 but only 0.4 percent when n is 100. While this difference is dominated in practice by the variance of the estimator, the discrepancy is easily corrected by adding the difference constant to the sample moment. Table A1 shows the difference constant calculated at $\frac{1}{5}$ moment increments for the first five moments of the distribution. Figures not listed can be interpolated.

Exhibit A1:   Difference constant calculated for various sample moments.

Sample moment	Diff constant	Sample moment	Diff constant	Sample moment	Diff constant	Sample moment	Diff constant	Sample moment	Diff constant
0.2	0.5624	1.2	0.4790	2.2	0.3688	3.2	0.2401	4.2	0.0989
0.4	0.5424	1.4	0.4590	2.4	0.3446	3.4	0.2133	4.4	0.0693
0.6	0.5268	1.6	0.4374	2.6	0.3195	3.6	0.1854	4.6	0.0394
0.8	0.5081	1.8	0.4153	2.8	0.2808	3.8	0.1570	4.8	0.0009
1.0	0.4986	2.0	0.3925	3.0	0.2675	4.0	0.1283	5.0	−0.0211

APPENDIX 3: BINOMIAL ESTIMATORS

The estimators used in empirical tests are derived from sample moments of observed ranges. The l_i are observed ranges, S is the step-size, and the variance subscript denotes the sample moment used to generate the estimate. Other estimators of this type can be computed with equation 11 and Table 1A. The results reported in Tables 3 and 4 are divided by the square of the tick-size.

$$\hat{\sigma}_{1/4}{}^2 = 0.41812 \left(\sum_i l_i^{1/4}/N \right)^8 - 0.5574S$$

$$\hat{\sigma}_{1/2}{}^2 = 0.40956 \left(\sum_i l_i^{1/2}/N \right)^4 - 0.5364S$$

$$\hat{\sigma}_{3/4}{}^2 = 0.41812 \left(\sum_i l_i^{3/4}/N \right)^{8/3} - 0.5128S$$

$$\hat{\sigma}_1^2 = 0.39270 \left(\sum_i l_i/N \right)^2 - 0.4986S$$

$$\hat{\sigma}_{5/4}{}^2 = 0.38448 \left(\sum_i l_i^{5/4}/N \right)^{8/5} - 0.4740S$$

$$\hat{\sigma}_{3/2}{}^2 = 0.37640 \left(\sum_i l_i^{3/2}/N \right)^{4/3} - 0.4482S$$

$$\hat{\sigma}_{75/4}{}^2 = 0.36846 \left(\sum_i l_i^{7/4}/N \right)^{8/7} - 0.4208S$$

$$\hat{\sigma}_2{}^2 = 0.36067 \left(\sum_i l_i^2/N \right) - 0.3925S$$

NOTES

1. The trading range is the difference between the recorded high and low price for a security over some time interval.
2. Informative in the statistical sense. Estimators derived from the trading range will have lower variance than estimators derived from returns.
3. For example, see Garman and Klass (1980), Beckers (1983), Wiggins (1991, 1992), and Rogers, Satchell, and Yoon (1984).
4. Parkinson and subsequent authors define the efficiency of a range estimator as the ratio of the variance of the closing price estimator to the variance of the range-based estimator being studied.

5. Assuming a zero-mean process is not a requirement of the model. However, Figlewski (1994) has shown that assuming a mean of zero yields the most efficient forecasts.
6. For example, consider a common stock that trades in $\frac{1}{8}$ point increments. If the high trade is at $7\frac{1}{2}$ and the low at 7, then the range is $\frac{1}{2}$ (or 4 times the trade size) but the number of prices traded is 5.
7. Similar results are obtained by Rogers and Satchell (1991) in continuous time. They calculate the amount by which the actual high (low) of a diffusion process exceeds the discretely observed high (low). They find the expected discrepancy to be about 0.90 (as opposed to 1.0 in the discrete case) and the expected squared difference to be 0.28 (as opposed to 0.25).
8. A proof of this theorem can be found in Freund (1992).
9. The particular example plotted is for a walk-length of 20. At smaller walk lengths, the difference between V and P will be more pronounced. As the walk-length tends to infinity, the moment-generating functions of V and P approach convergence, but this does not take place until n is very large (several thousand). For example, the first moment (mean) of a 100-step random walk evaluated with the P function is nearly 10 percent less than the V function. The reason for the discrepancy is that most realizations of a 100-step random walk will have a range of less than 10. Since the V function adds 1 to observed ranges, small-range random walks are incremented by a large percentage. The mean range of a 100-step random walk is slightly greater than 10, so adding 1 step to each range results in a difference between the two means of nearly 10 percent.
10. This estimator is not in wide circulation because it is slightly biased (Garman and Klass, 1980).
11. The size of price changes will certainly increase in periods of extreme volatility. However, for Treasury bond futures, in excess of 99 percent of all recorded price changes are in $\frac{1}{32}$ increments. Assuming a fixed walk-length and a variable trade-size would seem an unlikely approach to modeling this security.
12. See, for example, Guillaume *et al.* (1994), Baille and Bollerslev (1990).
13. Moments higher than two were excluded because preliminary tests showed estimators based on these moments are highly susceptible to misspecification of the tails and hence unlikely to provide useful forecasts.
14. The CLOSE version employed is the MLE, or population version of the estimator. This estimator is more efficient than the standard variance estimator, though it is slightly biased. Both versions were tested. The MLE version was found to be less biased as well as more efficient in the MSE sense, though the difference was very slight.
15. There is a slight bias in binomial estimators. For an analytical solution to this bias, and a correction formula, see Spurgin (1994).
16. See Figlewski (1994) for a discussion of overlapping intervals.
17. The 20-day period containing the mini-crash produces the highest estimate for both the CLOSE and the Binomial estimators. For CLOSE, this figure is 450.7 (see the Maximum column on Table 3A). This single period accounts for 7.6 percent of the mean of 56.90. However, the maximum Binomial(1) estimate of 157.59 accounts for only 2.7 percent of the mean estimate of 51.82. This difference accounts for the estimator bias.
18. This is a potentially useful result for practitioners. Estimates of historic volatility often skyrocket after an "outlier" day and then plummet again 20 or 50 days later when the data point ages out of the sample. Since low moment range estimators place less emphasis on outliers, this problem is largely eliminated.
19. The mean forecast is only known *ex post*. In a forecasting model, the mean would be replaced by an estimate from a very long sample.

20. This does not mean the most recent CLOSE estimate contains no information. If consecutive estimates were independent, then the expected value of a Variance/FMSE ratio would be 2.00. There is some information in CLOSE, simply not enough to make it a better forecast than the mean.

BIBLIOGRAPHY

Baille, R.T. and Bollerslev, T. (1990), "Intra-day and Intermarket Volatility in Foreign Exchange Rates", Review of Financial Studies, 58, 565–585.

Ball, C. (1988), "Estimation Bias Induced by Discrete Security Prices", *Journal of Finance*, 43, 841–866.

Ball, C. and Torous, W. (1984), "The Maximum Likelihood Estimation of Security Price Volatility: Theory, Evidence, and Application to Option Pricing", *Journal of Business*, 97–112.

Beckers, C.E. (1983), "Variances of Security Price Returns Based on High, Low, and Closing Prices", *Journal of Business*, 56, 97–112.

Cho, D. Chinhyung and Frees, E. (1988), "Estimating the Volatility of Discrete Stock Prices", *Journal of Finance*, 43, 451–466.

Feller, W. (1951), "The Asymptotic Distribution of the Range of Sums of Independent Random Variables", *Annals of Mathematical Statistics*, 22, 427–432.

Figlewski, S. (1994), "Forecasting Volatility Using Historical Data", *Working Paper*, Stern School of Business.

Freund, J. (1992), *Mathematical Statistics*, Prentice Hall.

Garman, M. and Klass, M. (1980), "On the Estimation of Security Price Volatilities From Historical Data", *Journal of Business*, 53, 67–78.

Granger, C.W.J. and Zhuanxin, D. (1994), Stylized Facts on the Temporal Distributional Properties of Daily Data from Speculative Markets, *Working Paper*.

Guillaume, D., Dacorogna, M., Dave, R., Müller, U., Olsen. R and Pictet, O. (1994), "From the Bird's Eye to the Microscope: A Survey of New Stylized Facts of the Intra-daily Foreign Exchange Markets", *Working Paper*, O&A Research Group.

Heynen, R. and Kat, H. Volatility, in *Advanced Applications in Finance*, T. Schneeweis and D. Ho, (eds), Kluwer Academic Publishing, 1993.

Kunitomo, N. (1992), "Improving the Parkinson Method of Estimating Security Price Volatilities", *Journal of Business*, 65, 295–302.

Marsh, T. and Rosenfeld, E. (1986), "Non-trading, Market Making, and Estimates of Stock Price Volatility", *Journal of Financial Economics*, 15, 395–472.

Parkinson, M. (1980), "The Extreme Value Method for Estimating the Variance of the Rate of Return", *Journal of Business*, 53, 61–66.

Rogers, L.C.G. and Satchell, S.E. (1991), "Estimating Variance from High, Low, and Closing Prices", *The Annals of Applied Probability*, 1, 504–512.

Rogers, L.C.G. and Satchell,S. E. and Yoon, Y. (1994), "Estimating the Volatility of Stock Prices: A Comparison of Methods that Use High and Low Prices", *Applied Financial Economics*, 4, 241–47.

Spurgin, R. (1994) "Proposal for a derivative security based on the range of another security", Working Paper, University of Massachussetts.

Torney, D. (1986) "Variance of the Range of a Random Walk", *Journal of Statistical Physics*, 44, 49–66.

Weiss, G.H. and Rubin, R.J. (1983), "Random Walks: Theory and Selected Applications", *Advances in Chemical Physics*, 33, 363–505.

Wiggins, J.B. (1991), "Empirical Tests of the Bias and Efficiency of the Extreme-Value Variance Estimator for Common Stocks", *Journal of Business*, 64(3).

Wiggins, J.B. (1992), "Estimating the Volatility of S&P500 Futures Prices Using the Extreme-Value Method", *The Journal of Futures Markets*, 12(3), 265–273.

Chapter **2**

Modelling Intra-day Equity Prices and Volatility Using Information Arrivals—A Comparative Study of Different Choices of Informational Proxies

Shinn-Juh Lin, John Knight and Stephen Satchell

Department of Finance, University of Technology, Sydney, Department of Economics, University of Western Ontario, Department of Economics, University of Cambridge

INTRODUCTION

The purpose of this chapter is to present a model for intra-day prices and volatility generation for equity. In particular, we consider alternative choices of conditioning variables, i.e. exogenous variables, to help us in modelling. Although our methodology is general, we restrict ourselves to two US stocks, IBM and INTEL. We use tick by tick data for January 1994 for these stocks, which were chosen on the basis of their high liquidity. It might be argued that this is insufficient information to carry out our analysis; our response is that our use of data here is illustrative and that a full analysis involving many stocks and longer time periods could be carried out by researchers following the methodology presented here. Our data comes from the New York Stock Exchange (NYSE) Trade and Quote (TAQ) database. This database contains virtually every trade and quote of every stock traded on major American stock exchanges.

Relevant literature on choosing suitable conditioning variables is reviewed on p 28. We present our initial models, investigate their statistical properties, and identify certain problems on p 30. We present details of the data, estimation techniques and estimation results on p 32.

We find that our information variables do not satisfy the requirement, assumed in the model on p 30, of being independently and identically distributed. On p 45, we address the problems discussed at p 44 by presenting extended models based on doubly stochastic processes. Surprisingly, these models are straightforward to estimate

Financial Markets Tick by Tick
Edited by Pierre Lequeux. © 1999 John Wiley & Sons Ltd

for all information variables except volume. We find that volume does not appear to be a suitable variable for measuring information flow, whilst the number of trades or the number of price changes seem to work very well. Finally, and importantly in our opinion, we find no evidence of volatility persistence in our model, although GARCH models measured on the same data show strong evidence of persistence. This indicates, to us at least, that the claimed persistence of volatility may be an artifact of the choice of model and does not reflect a market opportunity or a forecastable feature of the data.

LITERATURE REVIEW ON THE CHOICE OF CONDITIONING INFORMATION VARIABLES

Applied research in high frequency data, as claimed by Gourieroux, Jasiak and LeFol (1996), has a rather short history, it may be dated from the First International Conference on High Frequency Data in Finance, sponsored by Olsen and Associates, March 29–31, 1995. Due to the recent availability of data sets, researchers are now able to uncover more interesting features of asset dynamics at intra-day frequency. Goodhart and O'Hara (1997) have reviewed a host of literature which contains the availability of databases, statistical properties, problems and difficulties involved with high frequency data. There is also a long history of using trading information as the conditioning variable to explain returns/volatility dynamics at lower frequency. This literature dates back to Osborne (1959) and the pioneering work of Clark (1973) on stochastic subordination. However, little empirical evidence is available on high frequency intra-day data, except the work by Bollerslev and Domowitz (1993), and Locke and Sayers (1993). In this section, we will review some of the information variables that have been employed to explain the return/volatility processes.

Since information arrival is not observable practically, difficulties arise in determining what would be a good proxy for it. In addition to trading volume, number of trades, and number of price changes, other variables have been used. For example, average trading volume (trading volume divided by the number of trades), number of quote changes, and executed order imbalance have appeared in the empirical analysis of stock returns. We will briefly discuss each of them in the following.

Trading volume is, by far, the most often used informational proxy in the empirical study of stock returns. Ever since Clark (1973), trading volume has been used to test the mixture of distributions hypothesis, see Harris (1987); to test the price-volume relationship, see Gallant, Rossi and

Tauchen (1992);[1] and to examine stock returns volatility, see Andersen (1996) and Lamoureux and Lastrapes (1994).

However, in a recent paper, Jones, Kaul, and Lipson (1994) show that trading volume has no informational content beyond that contained in the number of trades. The use of number of trades as the informational proxy dates back to Osborne (1959), who modified Bachelier's (1900) random walk model by incorporating a diffusion process into the evolution of stock prices, with an instantaneous variance dependent on the number of trades sampled from a uniform distribution. The uniform distribution assumption on the number of trades is however dubious, because transaction time intervals are certainly not uniformly distributed, see Oldfield, Rogalski, and Jarrow (1977). Recently, several researchers have revitalized the use of the number of trades and have given empirical support for using them as alternative informational proxies.[2] Marsh and Rock (1986) find that the net number of trades (number of seller-initiated minus buyer-initiated transactions) explain as much as does the net volume. Geman and Ané (1996) demonstrate that the moments of the time change needed to induce returns normality match the moments of the number of trades for the S&P500 one minute returns. Madan and Chang (1997) propose a variance gamma stock price process and confirm that normality is attained in the trade-based measure of time. All of this new evidence indicates that the number of trades could be a better instrument for the non-quantifiable information than trading volume.

In addition to trading volume and number of trades, average trading volume is also used in the empirical analysis of stock returns. Jones, Kaul and Lipson (1994) actually use average trading volume, instead of total trading volume, in their comparison of the explanatory power of different information proxies. Their justification comes from the observation that both the number of trades and the average trading volume are highly correlated with the total trading volume; however, there is little correlation between the number of trades and average trading volume. In other words, the number of trades and the average trading volume seem to contain different information.

Quote changes are the number of times the valid market quoted prices changed throughout the day for a certain security. Although Bollerslev and Domowitz (1993) find that market activity, as measured by the number of quote arrivals, has no statistically significant effect on returns volatility, Smaby (1995) and Takezawa (1995) suggest that the number of quotes is positively and significantly related to the intra-day volatility of foreign exchange rates, in their recent studies.

The equivalent measure to the number of quote changes is the number of price changes for the trade data set. Again, this variable has not often been used as a proxy for information arrival, possibly due to its unavailability. Both the number of quote changes and the number of price changes seem to be intuitively good instruments for the discrete price-jumps often observed in equity markets. In addition to the aforementioned information variables, Locke and Sayers (1993) have also examined the impact of executed order imbalance in reducing volatility persistence.

All of these variables are observable and have empirical implication of a random rate of flow of information. In this chapter, we only examine the performance of two most often used information variables, trading volume and the number of trades, and the number of price changes.

A HOMOGENEOUS COMPOUND POISSON MODEL

In what follows, we assume that there is some variable, $N(t)$, that measures the arrival of information. Such a variable could be volume, number of trades, or number of price changes, etc, see p 29.

We shall show that log-returns are conditionally normal with mean and variance being linear functions of $\Delta N(t)$, which is the model of Harris (1987). This can be derived from the standard diffusion and Poisson stochastic differential equation describing the evolution of asset prices, a model motivated by the finding of occasional jumps in the empirical time series. The rationale of using a mixed jump-diffusion process is that it reveals systematic discontinuities. We define our price generating equation next:

$$P(t) = P(0)\exp\left[\left(\alpha - \frac{1}{2}\sigma^2\right)t + \sigma(z(t) - z(0)) + \sum_{i=1}^{N(t)} Q_i\right] \qquad 1$$

where $P(t)$ denotes the price of an asset at time t, α and σ are parameters, $z(t)$ is a standard Brownian motion, $N(t)$ is a (homogeneous) Poisson process with parameter λ, Q is a normal variate with mean μ_Q and variance σ_Q^2 in the interval $(t, t + \Delta t]$. It is straightforward to derive the probability density function (pdf) of logarithmic returns, $X(t) = \ln(P(t)/P(t-1))$, since

$$X(t) = \left(\alpha - \frac{1}{2}\sigma^2\right) + \sigma(z(t) - z(t-1)) + \sum_{i=1}^{\Delta N(t)} Q_i \qquad 2$$

We see that $X(t)$ is independent and identically distributed (i.i.d.) and

$$\text{pdf}(X(t)) = e^{-\lambda}\sum_{j=0}^{\infty} \frac{\lambda^j}{j!}\phi(\mu + \mu_Q \cdot j, \sigma^2 + \sigma_Q^2 \cdot j) \qquad 3$$

where $\mu = \alpha - \sigma^2/2$, and $\phi(a, b)$ is the normal density with mean a, and variance b.

We next compute $\text{pdf}(X(t)|\Delta N(t))$. Simple manipulations with Equation 2 show that

$$\text{pdf}(X(t)|\Delta N(t)) = \phi(\mu + \mu_Q \cdot \Delta N(t), \sigma^2 + \sigma_Q^2 \cdot \Delta N(t)) \qquad 4$$

It follows, in regression notation, that

$$X(t) = \mu + \mu_Q \cdot \Delta N(t) + \sqrt{\sigma^2 + \sigma_Q^2 \cdot \Delta N(t)}\varepsilon(t) \qquad 5$$

where $\varepsilon(t)$ is distributed $N(0, 1)$ and is independent of $\Delta N(t)$. Equation 5 may also be interpreted as a linear regression model with linear heteroskedasticity in $\Delta N(t)$, as such it is an example of the heteroskedasticity models popular in econometrics, see Judge *et al.* (1985, 419) for a survey. As long as μ_Q and σ_Q^2 are found to be significant, our assumption that $\Delta N(t)$ influences the conditional mean and variance of returns is not rejected.

To test if $\Delta N(t)$ influences the rate of returns, an appropriate test would be the joint hypothesis, that is, $\mu_Q = 0$ and $\sigma_Q^2 = 0$. We now devote some arguments to testing our various hypotheses. We shall consider the different hypotheses in turn. Let the three tests be

$$H_{10} : \mu_Q = 0 \qquad\qquad vs.\, H_{1A} : \mu_Q \neq 0$$

$$H_{20} : \sigma_Q^2 = 0 \qquad\qquad vs.\, H_{2A} : \sigma_Q^2 \neq 0 \qquad 6$$

$$H_{30} : \mu_Q = 0 \text{ and } \sigma_Q^2 = 0 \quad vs.\, H_{3A} : \mu_Q \neq 0 \text{ or } \sigma_Q^2 \neq 0$$

A test that $\mu_Q = 0$ implies that the number of trades does not influence the expected rate of returns, whilst it increases the volatility of the asset, an assertion investigated by Lamoureux and Lastrapes (1990). A test that $\sigma_Q^2 = 0$ implies that jump magnitudes are of constant size, albeit unknown to the econometricians. In this case, each arrival of new information has the same kind of effect on stock prices, i.e. each transaction generates the same amount of trading volume and, consequently, the same impact on prices. Similarly, the joint hypothesis implies that the $\Delta N(t)$ is completely independent of price changes. Since all these hypotheses are interesting, it is worthwhile estimating and testing our model. We note two of the tests above have the difficulty that the point $\sigma_Q^2 = 0$ lies on the boundary of the parameter space, so that the asymptotic distribution of the one-sided test will be non-standard, i.e. not $\chi^2(1)$. For this reason the Lagrange Multiplier (LM) test would be preferred to Wald or Likelihood Ratio (LR) tests, since it is well-known that the LM test retains its $\chi^2(1)$ distribution under H_0

even for boundary points. Here, computational ease is required at the cost of potential loss of power. It is straightforward to derive the LM test, see Breusch and Pagan (1980). The derivation of the score statistics for the three hypotheses is shown in Appendix 1. We present the results as a theorem.

Theorem 1. The LM tests for our hypotheses given in Equation 6 are:

$$LM_1 = \left(\sum \frac{(x_t - \widehat{\mu})\Delta N_t}{\widehat{h}_t}\right)^2 \left(\sum \frac{\Delta N_t^2}{\widehat{h}_t} - \left(\sum \frac{\Delta N_t}{\widehat{h}_t}\right)^2 \left(\sum \frac{1}{\widehat{h}_t}\right)^{-1}\right)^{-1}$$

$$\text{where } \widehat{h}_t = \widehat{\sigma}^2 + \widehat{\sigma}_Q^2 \Delta N_t \qquad\qquad\qquad 7$$

$$LM_2 = LM_2(\widehat{e}_t) = \frac{\left(\sum (\widehat{e}_t^2 - \widehat{\sigma}^2)\Delta N_t\right)^2}{2\widehat{\sigma}^4 \sum (\Delta N_t - \Delta \overline{N})^2} \quad \text{where } \widehat{e}_t = x_t - \widehat{\mu} - \widehat{\mu}_Q \Delta N_t$$

$$LM_3 = LM_2(\widetilde{e}_t) + \frac{\left(\sum \widetilde{e}_t \Delta N_t\right)^2}{\widehat{\sigma}^2 \sum (\Delta N_t - \Delta \overline{N})^2} \quad \text{where } \widetilde{e}_t = x_t - \widehat{\mu}$$

where LM_i is the test appropriate for H_{0i}.

It should be noted that our test procedures are asymptotically $\chi^2(1)$ for test statistics LM_1, LM_2 and $\chi^2(2)$ for test statistics LM_3. This is true despite the fact that the alternative hypothesis involves σ_Q^2 being positive, so that one may wish to use this information explicitly. This has been done in general by Rogers (1986) in which he proposes a test procedure based on the Kuhn-Tucker test of Gourieroux, Holly and Monfort (1982). This should lead to a more powerful test but involves substantially more computation; we shall not investigate this point any further.

DATA AND RESULTS

Data used in this chapter are extracted from the January 1994 Trade and Quote (TAQ) database, which is produced monthly by New York Stock Exchange (NYSE). This database contains virtually every trade and every quote of every stock traded on major American stock exchanges, such as NYSE, AMEX, NASDAQ, etc. Among the many stocks, we only choose two frequently traded stocks, namely IBM and INTEL. IBM has been employed in several intra-day trading analyses, for example Engle and

Russell (1994) and Engle (1996), and INTEL had the highest total trading volume among all the stocks available in that particular month.

In January 1994, there were 21 trading days, which are treated separately in the following study. From these 21 days, we use only the "trade" information. Variables recorded for each observation include: a time stamp, a traded price and the associated trading volume (share). Only those transactions that occurred between 9:30 a.m. to 4:00 p.m. are extracted, because both NYSE and NASDAQ, where IBM and INTEL were mostly traded respectively, were open during that period. Although there are some transactions that happened before 9:30 a.m. and some that happened after 4:00 p.m., the percentage of these exceptions is quite small. Therefore, we decided to delete these observations. We ended up with 13,095 observations of IBM stock traded on NYSE, and 72,831 observations of INTEL traded on NSADAQ. To facilitate our analysis in fixed time intervals, we then sample these tick-by-tick data every minute. The sampling procedure, adopted by Locke and Sayers (1993, 17) is described as the following:

1. Select the first recorded trade as the observation for each minute.
2. Retain the previous trade information for those following minutes with no trades.

This yields roughly 390 observations per day. While sampling the 1-minute data, not only have we extracted the price series, we have also calculated total trading volume (TVol), total number of trades (N), and total number of price changes (NPC) in each one-minute interval.

We first examine the returns processes. The stock return concept used in this paper is the one-minute log-return, defined as the difference of the logarithm prices of two consecutive minutes. By examining Table 1a and 1b, we notice that most return processes are highly kurtotic and non-normally distributed. We compute the Bera-Jarque normality test statistics, which is asymptotically distributed as $\chi^2(2)$. This test is rejected in most cases for INTEL and is rejected in every case for IBM. Also, most returns processes are not independent and identically distributed (i.i.d.), judging from the BDS test statistics proposed by Brock, Dechert and Scheinkman (1986). Another salient feature of the returns series is that most of them have significantly large negative first-order autocorrelation, as reported in Table 2. Most literature on the intra-daily analysis of exchanges rates and stock indices has indicated signs of significant negative but small first-order autocorrelation, see Andersen and Bollerslev (1997), Goodhart and Figliuoli (1991), and Goodhart and O'Hara (1997). Only Zhou (1996) observes significant large negative first-order autocorrelation for DM/US$ and JPY/US$ exchange rates. *He ascribes the high autocorrelation to the noisy*

Table 1a   Descriptive Statistics of Log-Returns (INTEL).

Date	NOBS	Mean	Variance	Skewness	Kurtosis	BJ	BDS
Jan/03/94	389	−4.1632e − 005	8.6799e − 006	−0.074	0.261	1.5	8.468
Jan/04/94	389	1.0284e − 004	7.9931e − 006	0.118	1.326	29.4	7.546
Jan/05/94	389	4.0012e − 005	7.6488e − 006	0.121	0.997	17.1	8.993
Jan/06/94	389	−4.0012e − 005	8.5810e − 006	0.096	0.656	7.6	7.886
Jan/07/94	389	9.9267e − 005	8.6340e − 006	0.030	1.665	45.0	6.582
Jan/10/94	389	2.9048e − 005	8.6570e − 006	−0.267	2.862	137.4	7.809
Jan/11/94	389	−4.8095e − 006	8.5162e − 006	0.116	0.442	4.0	6.837
Jan/12/94	389	0.0000e + 000	9.9269e − 006	−0.180	4.449	322.9	7.961
Jan/13/94	389	0.0000e + 000	6.0198e − 006	−0.000	−0.435	3.1	7.623
Jan/14/94	389	−9.3650e − 006	9.1142e − 006	0.018	0.890	12.9	6.877
Jan/17/94	389	−8.6177e − 005	9.8798e − 006	0.196	4.878	388.2	8.440
Jan/18/94	389	3.3667e − 005	1.4521e − 005	0.281	8.987	1314.1	8.817
Jan/19/94	389	−1.0221e − 005	2.0207e − 005	−0.354	17.402	4916.5	8.748
Jan/20/94	389	4.0644e − 005	1.1315e − 005	0.023	2.334	88.3	6.910
Jan/21/94	389	2.9834e − 005	7.1557e − 006	−0.033	1.116	20.3	10.691
Jan/24/94	389	1.9775e − 005	1.3870e − 005	0.018	27.735	12467.9	7.934
Jan/25/94	389	−9.8683e − 006	1.1452e − 005	0.036	36.546	21647.6	8.044
Jan/26/94	389	−5.0554e − 006	9.2477e − 006	−0.027	0.599	5.9	8.903
Jan/27/94	389	1.0061e − 005	8.1759e − 006	−0.078	0.243	1.4	7.744
Jan/28/94	389	3.9857e − 005	8.5613e − 006	0.041	−0.001	0.1	9.430
Jan/31/94	389	0.0000e + 000	7.1059e − 006	0.023	−0.373	2.3	8.876

*NOBS = Number of Observations, BJ = Bera-Jarque Normality Test Statistics $\sim \chi^2(2)$ with 5% critical value = 5.99. BDS = Brock-Dechert-Scheinkman $\sim N(0, 1)_{asy}$, Embedding Dimension = 3, Epsilon = Standard Deviation/Spread

Table 1b   Descriptive Statistics of Log-Returns (IBM).

Date	NOBS	Mean	Variance	Skewness	Kurtosis	BJ	BDS
Jan/03/94	388	3.3764e − 005	1.3221e − 006	0.229	2.210	82.4	9.6480
Jan/04/94	387	2.7636e − 005	8.6563e − 007	−0.123	3.260	172.3	6.0146
Jan/05/94	387	2.7229e − 005	7.3054e − 007	0.331	4.317	307.6	3.6733
Jan/06/94	385	−5.4684e − 005	1.0495e − 006	−0.206	1.859	58.2	4.0637
Jan/07/94	388	2.1935e − 005	8.2120e − 007	0.061	2.590	108.7	3.9882
Jan/10/94	388	2.1796e − 005	8.8587e − 007	0.048	2.146	74.6	1.2024
Jan/11/94	389	−2.1832e − 005	8.6346e − 007	−0.053	2.299	85.9	3.6332
Jan/12/94	387	−2.2085e − 005	9.0234e − 007	−0.048	2.133	73.5	3.3904
Jan/13/94	389	2.1972e − 005	7.9455e − 007	−0.143	3.809	236.5	4.5641
Jan/14/94	389	−1.0962e − 005	7.1724e − 007	0.197	4.554	338.6	5.8922
Jan/17/94	388	−5.0047e − 005	1.2484e − 006	−0.600	3.788	255.3	4.2779
Jan/18/94	389	−1.6857e − 005	1.1145e − 006	−0.164	2.000	66.6	7.2851
Jan/19/94	388	−4.0048e − 005	9.7589e − 007	−0.084	2.075	70.0	2.3455
Jan/20/94	389	−2.8917e − 005	1.1908e − 006	−0.169	1.856	57.7	4.2923
Jan/21/94	386	5.8679e − 006	9.1534e − 007	0.016	2.644	112.4	2.9040
Jan/24/94	387	1.2993e − 004	2.7850e − 005	−0.146	25.620	10585.2	9.9298
Jan/25/94	388	−2.1982e − 005	4.3778e − 006	−2.478	20.380	7112.0	2.9699
Jan/26/94	382	−1.0802e − 004	1.6862e − 006	−0.352	2.498	107.2	3.0933
Jan/27/94	389	1.6968e − 005	1.1024e − 006	−0.119	3.206	167.5	3.4422
Jan/28/94	388	−2.2266e − 005	9.9185e − 007	−0.039	1.768	50.6	5.7514
Jan/31/94	389	−5.0462e − 005	1.0457e − 006	−0.077	1.606	42.2	2.3132

*NOBS = Number of Observations, BJ = Bera-Jarque Normality Test Statistics $\sim \chi^2(2)$ with 5% critical value = 5.99. BDS = Brock-Dechert-Scheinkman $\sim N(0, 1)_{asy}$, Embedding Dimension = 3, Epsilon = Standard Deviation/Spread

Table 2 First Three Lags Autocorrelations of the Log-Returns.

	IBM (NYSE)			INTEL (NASDAQ)		
Date	Lag1	Lag2	Lag3	Lag1	Lag2	Lag3
Jan/03/94	−0.399	0.008	0.055	−0.485	0.047	−0.014
Jan/04/94	−0.302	−0.070	0.027	−0.464	0.081	−0.091
Jan/05/94	−0.255	0.032	0.029	−0.538	0.114	−0.029
Jan/06/94	−0.283	0.077	−0.125	−0.452	−0.081	0.124
Jan/07/94	−0.272	−0.042	0.083	−0.476	0.091	−0.103
Jan/10/94	−0.237	0.012	−0.027	−0.491	−0.018	0.080
Jan/11/94	−0.271	−0.136	0.053	−0.462	0.055	−0.075
Jan/12/94	−0.316	−0.041	0.026	−0.467	−0.057	0.067
Jan/13/94	−0.236	−0.074	0.058	−0.467	−0.027	−0.063
Jan/14/94	−0.292	0.129	−0.113	−0.527	0.081	−0.063
Jan/17/94	−0.227	0.008	−0.060	−0.477	−0.011	0.014
Jan/18/94	−0.248	0.022	−0.012	−0.577	0.169	−0.018
Jan/19/94	−0.287	−0.041	−0.028	−0.497	−0.045	0.137
Jan/20/94	−0.309	0.109	0.010	−0.514	0.060	−0.070
Jan/21/94	−0.275	0.028	−0.072	−0.465	−0.010	0.019
Jan/24/94	−0.554	0.154	0.001	−0.309	−0.216	0.074
Jan/25/94	0.030	0.102	−0.028	−0.524	0.032	0.047
Jan/26/94	−0.105	0.187	0.008	−0.474	0.009	−0.019
Jan/27/94	−0.203	0.023	0.011	−0.481	−0.019	0.092
Jan/28/94	−0.330	0.024	−0.073	−0.536	0.088	0.013
Jan/31/94	−0.274	−0.028	−0.048	−0.488	−0.011	0.069

*Assuming Gaussian white noise, the 95% confidence interval of the sample ACF could be calculated as $\pm 2/\sqrt{T}$, where T is the sample size. For our data set, this number is about ± 0.1014.

structure of the markets. Other possible explanations for the negative first-order autocorrelation include: bid-ask bounce, nonsynchronous trading, and brokers' inventory considerations. We will not model autocorrelation in our data set. However, in later work, we will try to account for this feature.

We provide summary statistics of the three trading variables in Tables 3 to 5 below. We observe that all three trading variables are positively skewed, highly kurtotic, and non-normal. Similar to return processes, we reject that these trading variables are i.i.d. in most cases. Comparing IBM and INTEL, two noticeable differences arise:

1. When all 21 trading dates are pooled together, as shown in Table 6 below, IBM has a lower average number of trades and price changes in each one-minute interval. On average, INTEL has 8.69 trades and 4.54 price changes in each 1-minute interval, while IBM only has 1.60 trades and 0.33 price changes. Accordingly, there is a less severe discreteness problem with INTEL than with IBM.

36 *Shinn-Juh Lin et al.*

Table 3a Descriptive statistics of trading volume (INTEL).

Date	NOBS	Mean	Variance	Skewness	Kurtosis	BJ	BDS
Jan/03/94	390	7257	1.223e + 008	3.644	21.873	8637.6	7.126
Jan/04/94	390	9778	2.395e + 008	3.648	16.515	5297.2	5.192
Jan/05/94	390	11397	3.374e + 008	3.812	18.175	6312.7	3.325
Jan/06/94	390	7621	1.069e + 008	2.665	9.259	1854.9	6.787
Jan/07/94	390	15337	5.906e + 008	3.342	13.695	3774.0	9.360
Jan/10/94	390	10946	2.030e + 008	2.912	11.483	2693.7	4.903
Jan/11/94	390	7537	1.382e + 008	3.436	14.815	4334.1	5.152
Jan/12/94	390	15224	5.142e + 008	2.838	9.350	1944.0	10.873
Jan/13/94	390	8333	1.412e + 008	2.433	6.476	1066.4	7.549
Jan/14/94	390	9849	1.944e + 008	3.253	14.595	4149.4	7.880
Jan/17/94	390	12826	3.947e + 008	4.077	25.435	11593.6	4.045
Jan/18/94	390	18317	9.682e + 008	6.341	58.890	58968.3	3.598
Jan/19/94	390	62260	3.883e + 009	1.855	4.394	537.4	11.867
Jan/20/94	390	20868	1.624e + 009	10.006	146.424	354906.8	8.643
Jan/21/94	390	22353	1.183e + 009	3.627	19.061	6759.0	3.134
Jan/24/94	390	14056	5.656e + 008	3.912	20.940	8120.2	5.407
Jan/25/94	390	10155	3.237e + 008	4.593	28.431	14506.7	3.246
Jan/26/94	390	18585	9.252e + 008	3.815	20.081	7499.1	7.063
Jan/27/94	390	14278	3.513e + 008	2.237	5.746	861.6	5.617
Jan/28/94	390	9490	2.760e + 008	3.104	11.694	2848.2	8.858
Jan/31/94	390	8823	3.594e + 008	9.540	134.074	298024.3	5.950

*NOBS = Number of Observations, BJ = Bera-Jarque Normality Test Statistics $\sim \chi^2(2)$ with 5% critical value = 5.99. BDS = Brock-Dechert-Scheinkman $\sim N(0, 1)_{asy}$, Embedding Dimension = 3, Epsilon = Standard Deviation/Spread

Table 3b Descriptive statistics of trading volume (IBM).

Date	NOBS	Mean	Variance	Skewness	Kurtosis	BJ	BDS
Jan/03/94	389	2781.0	38576492.9	6.289	54.822	51278.1	1.4729
Jan/04/94	388	3450.3	63085762.2	7.724	93.777	146029.0	3.6474
Jan/05/94	388	5356.4	152626185.8	6.238	52.767	47530.5	5.5166
Jan/06/94	386	4816.8	268190079.3	13.836	230.536	867097.6	3.2387
Jan/07/94	389	3085.9	54454619.2	7.091	69.460	81459.2	2.6029
Jan/10/94	389	3654.2	54680838.9	3.889	18.455	6500.7	0.51352
Jan/11/94	390	3145.6	98414312.6	7.440	64.934	72113.6	1.5224
Jan/12/94	388	3162.6	53332475.8	4.968	31.639	17778.7	2.6565
Jan/13/94	390	3854.6	67155595.6	4.136	24.657	10991.3	6.2859
Jan/14/94	390	3101.8	51283929.9	6.687	66.937	75715.5	2.2052
Jan/17/94	389	2930.3	40883407.4	3.894	19.024	6848.8	4.0623
Jan/18/94	390	4350.8	73731863.2	3.593	16.041	5020.3	4.4550
Jan/19/94	389	3928.5	78357611.5	4.496	24.729	11222.5	1.3763
Jan/20/94	390	4535.1	76137246.1	3.632	19.634	7121.5	0.51898
Jan/21/94	387	5741.1	240149318.0	9.786	134.918	299699.6	1.4453
Jan/24/94	388	8797.4	241820200.1	6.477	71.144	84540.7	3.8537
Jan/25/94	389	22047.8	1171816934.6	5.040	43.368	32130.5	4.8469
Jan/26/94	383	8929.5	504852033.0	12.836	209.362	710007.0	0.72295
Jan/27/94	390	4600.8	94950462.1	6.040	59.584	60062.0	4.2846
Jan/28/94	389	2800.3	53443427.8	7.468	82.443	113782.7	1.3955
Jan/31/94	390	3863.3	54664127.7	4.067	23.864	10328.7	1.0396

*NOBS = Number of Observations, BJ = Bera-Jarque Normality Test Statistics $\sim \chi^2(2)$ with 5% critical value = 5.99. BDS = Brock-Dechert-Scheinkman $\sim N(0, 1)_{asy}$, Embedding Dimension = 3, Epsilon = Standard Deviation/Spread

Table 4a Descriptive statistics of number of trades (INTEL).

Date	NOBS	Mean	Variance	Skewness	Kurtosis	BJ	BDS
Jan/03/94	390	5.6	31.1	3.427	18.411	6271.7	13.588
Jan/04/94	390	6.1	34.6	3.565	19.955	7296.8	13.303
Jan/05/94	390	7.2	62.6	5.135	38.847	26237.0	11.534
Jan/06/94	390	5.9	31.1	2.963	16.141	4804.5	13.435
Jan/07/94	390	9.8	174.6	6.211	61.325	63620.0	15.036
Jan/10/94	390	8.5	59.2	4.565	31.809	17796.9	7.959
Jan/11/94	390	6.1	30.9	3.255	16.362	5039.2	9.268
Jan/12/94	390	9.8	131.9	3.911	18.829	6755.5	15.674
Jan/13/94	390	5.4	19.9	2.148	6.437	973.3	12.973
Jan/14/94	390	7.4	60.1	4.589	32.046	18056.4	12.364
Jan/17/94	390	6.8	36.6	2.553	9.529	1898.9	13.493
Jan/18/94	390	9.2	50.5	2.199	8.540	1499.5	14.661
Jan/19/94	390	33.9	571.6	1.976	5.341	717.3	23.569
Jan/20/94	390	13.1	157.0	3.828	21.546	8496.3	18.091
Jan/21/94	390	9.5	69.6	4.554	34.008	20142.5	13.215
Jan/24/94	390	7.4	43.0	3.058	15.990	4762.7	13.266
Jan/25/94	390	5.6	25.3	2.868	11.437	2660.3	10.706
Jan/26/94	390	7.4	40.1	2.244	6.740	1065.4	12.842
Jan/27/94	390	6.6	31.0	2.177	7.164	1142.0	14.248
Jan/28/94	390	5.5	36.3	4.436	27.983	14003.7	13.969
Jan/31/94	390	5.8	55.8	8.253	97.587	159180.7	9.917

*NOBS = Number of Observations, BJ = Bera-Jarque Normality Test Statistics $\sim \chi^2(2)$ with 5% critical value = 5.99. BDS = Brock-Dechert-Scheinkman $\sim N(0, 1)_{asy}$, Embedding Dimension = 3, Epsilon = Standard Deviation/Spread

Table 4b Descriptive statistics of number of trades (IBM).

Date	NOBS	Mean	Variance	Skewness	Kurtosis	BJ	BDS
Jan/03/94	389	1.4	1.8	1.115	1.320	108.8	8.2054
Jan/04/94	388	1.4	2.1	1.315	1.953	173.5	5.1818
Jan/05/94	388	1.6	2.3	1.835	8.170	1296.7	4.0105
Jan/06/94	386	1.6	2.3	1.040	0.815	80.2	6.6650
Jan/07/94	389	1.3	1.5	0.918	0.419	57.5	2.2061
Jan/10/94	389	1.5	2.0	1.020	0.979	82.9	2.3133
Jan/11/94	390	1.2	1.6	1.159	1.553	126.5	2.3101
Jan/12/94	388	1.3	1.7	1.267	2.049	171.7	5.0166
Jan/13/94	390	1.3	1.8	1.381	2.008	189.4	6.8374
Jan/14/94	390	1.2	1.7	1.243	1.542	139.1	5.4762
Jan/17/94	389	1.3	2.0	1.290	1.367	138.2	4.1208
Jan/18/94	390	1.6	2.2	1.060	1.144	94.2	4.8445
Jan/19/94	389	1.4	1.9	1.386	2.781	250.0	1.3596
Jan/20/94	390	1.5	1.9	1.360	2.535	224.6	4.5076
Jan/21/94	387	1.5	2.2	1.292	2.246	189.1	5.0264
Jan/24/94	388	2.6	4.9	1.329	2.465	212.4	7.4080
Jan/25/94	389	3.7	6.8	0.774	0.306	40.4	6.9422
Jan/26/94	383	2.1	3.4	1.131	1.407	113.2	5.1466
Jan/27/94	390	1.4	1.9	1.166	1.184	111.1	3.1581
Jan/28/94	389	1.3	1.9	1.407	2.504	230.0	5.4202
Jan/31/94	390	1.5	1.6	1.035	1.605	111.5	0.40399

*NOBS = Number of Observations, BJ = Bera-Jarque Normality Test Statistics $\sim \chi^2(2)$ with 5% critical value = 5.99. BDS = Brock-Dechert-Scheinkman $\sim N(0, 1)_{asy}$, Embedding Dimension = 3, Epsilon = Standard Deviation/Spread

Table 5a   Descriptive statistics of number of price changes (INTEL).

Date	NOBS	Mean	Variance	Skewness	Kurtosis	BJ	BDS
Jan/03/94	390	3.0103	7.2081	1.8741	6.1987	852.7	10.415
Jan/04/94	390	3.1231	6.8691	1.7950	4.3085	511.1	4.761
Jan/05/94	390	3.6564	10.7762	2.1332	6.8053	1048.4	9.888
Jan/06/94	390	3.2026	8.6504	1.8694	5.1254	654.0	9.497
Jan/07/94	390	4.6513	18.9835	1.8770	5.0057	636.2	1.617
Jan/10/94	390	4.4718	10.1110	1.5547	3.7506	385.7	6.312
Jan/11/94	390	3.2103	9.3696	2.7147	11.4268	2600.8	8.374
Jan/12/94	390	5.3821	38.4012	3.4377	14.5498	4208.2	16.204
Jan/13/94	390	3.0923	7.5647	2.1491	7.0446	1106.6	10.286
Jan/14/94	390	4.0282	12.1560	2.4341	10.0782	2035.6	8.647
Jan/17/94	390	3.5103	10.7441	2.4117	9.8556	1956.5	8.796
Jan/18/94	390	4.8179	12.9668	1.8517	5.6909	749.1	10.623
Jan/19/94	390	17.4667	144.3575	1.9079	5.2997	693.0	21.771
Jan/20/94	390	6.7846	60.7915	5.4213	44.4658	34040.0	19.549
Jan/21/94	390	4.9538	19.9824	3.6961	22.7886	9326.9	9.765
Jan/24/94	390	4.1231	11.3833	1.9455	6.7445	985.2	9.573
Jan/25/94	390	2.9077	6.3771	1.9183	5.5525	740.2	5.993
Jan/26/94	390	3.9333	12.4480	2.1248	6.5732	995.6	9.121
Jan/27/94	390	3.3846	7.7334	1.4063	2.7355	250.1	7.200
Jan/28/94	390	2.7769	6.1481	2.0716	7.7779	1262.0	10.788
Jan/31/94	390	2.9000	7.5298	3.5401	23.4108	9720.7	4.137

*NOBS = Number of Observations, BJ = Bera-Jarque Normality Test Statistics $\sim \chi^2(2)$ with 5% critical value = 5.99. BDS = Brock-Dechert-Scheinkman $\sim N(0, 1)_{\text{asy}}$, Embedding Dimension = 3, Epsilon = Standard Deviation/Spread

Table 5b   Descriptive statistics of number of price changes (IBM).

Date	NOBS	Mean	Variance	Skewness	Kurtosis	BJ	BDS
Jan/03/94	389	0.3907	0.5531	2.0608	3.9658	530.3	9.0637
Jan/04/94	388	0.2526	0.3391	2.8183	9.4730	1964.4	4.9650
Jan/05/94	388	0.2088	0.2896	3.1204	11.6976	2841.8	3.7918
Jan/06/94	386	0.3264	0.3867	2.1803	5.5918	808.7	3.8511
Jan/07/94	389	0.2468	0.3101	2.4469	6.0589	983.2	4.6989
Jan/10/94	389	0.3033	0.3614	2.0460	3.8552	512.3	3.9948
Jan/11/94	390	0.2795	0.3613	2.5780	7.8688	1438.2	3.8849
Jan/12/94	388	0.2526	0.2926	2.1648	4.2024	588.6	2.7193
Jan/13/94	390	0.2000	0.2272	2.5245	6.5558	1112.7	4.1656
Jan/14/94	390	0.1897	0.2364	2.8549	8.8073	1790.3	5.3012
Jan/17/94	389	0.3188	0.3878	2.0971	4.3028	585.2	4.0809
Jan/18/94	390	0.3487	0.4950	2.4629	6.9755	1185.0	6.4851
Jan/19/94	389	0.2725	0.3585	2.4906	6.9718	1190.0	0.42557
Jan/20/94	390	0.3308	0.3710	1.9398	3.7109	468.4	5.3026
Jan/21/94	387	0.2248	0.2887	2.8445	9.9777	2127.2	2.3997
Jan/24/94	388	0.6005	0.9589	2.2807	6.8562	1096.3	4.2912
Jan/25/94	389	0.8483	1.1445	1.5243	2.3735	242.0	8.0694
Jan/26/94	383	0.4099	0.4938	1.7337	2.4843	290.4	4.1158
Jan/27/94	390	0.2410	0.2862	2.6665	9.2613	1856.0	2.5195
Jan/28/94	389	0.2853	0.3282	2.0529	3.8841	517.8	5.7743
Jan/31/94	390	0.3154	0.4016	2.0610	3.7419	503.6	2.3853

*NOBS = Number of Observations, BJ = Bera-Jarque Normality Test Statistics $\sim \chi^2(2)$ with 5% critical value = 5.99. BDS = Brock-Dechert-Scheinkman $\sim N(0, 1)_{\text{asy}}$, Embedding Dimension = 3, Epsilon = Standard Deviation/Spread

Table 6 Summary statistics of Tvol, N, and NPC when all trading dates are pooled together.

	IBM			INTEL		
	TVol	*N*	*NPC*	*TVol*	*N*	*NPC*
Minimum	0	0.000	0.0000	0	0.000	0.000
1st Quartile	0	0.000	0.0000	1800	3.000	2.000
Median	1000	1.000	0.0000	5700	6.000	3.000
Mean	5184	1.596	0.3259	15010	8.689	4.542
3rd Quartile	5000	2.000	0.0000	16180	10.000	6.000
Maximum	400000	14.000	6.0000	643000	170.000	92.000

2. The IBM stock has a higher percentage of no trade ($N = 0$) in the one-minute intervals, as shown in Table 7 below. Overall, there is about 30 percent of no-trades for IBM, while only about 2 percent for INTEL. In other words, the nonsynchronous trading problem is much more pronounced for IBM.

Therefore, we expect that INTEL would be more suitable for the intra-daily study conducted in this chapter.

Table 7 Frequency of No trade.

	IBM (NYSE)			INTEL (NASDAQ)		
Date	$N = 0$	*TOT*	%	$N = 0$	*TOT*	%
Jan/03/94	125	389	0.321	12	390	0.031
Jan/04/94	127	388	0.327	8	390	0.021
Jan/05/94	106	388	0.273	9	390	0.023
Jan/06/94	109	386	0.282	15	390	0.038
Jan/07/94	114	389	0.293	9	390	0.023
Jan/10/94	109	389	0.280	0	390	0.000
Jan/11/94	132	390	0.338	15 ·	390	0.038
Jan/12/94	131	388	0.338	2	390	0.005
Jan/13/94	137	390	0.351	10	390	0.026
Jan/14/94	140	390	0.359	4	390	0.010
Jan/17/94	141	389	0.362	11	390	0.028
Jan/18/94	101	390	0.259	3	390	0.008
Jan/19/94	122	389	0.314	0	390	0.000
Jan/20/94	99	390	0.254	0	390	0.000
Jan/21/94	119	387	0.307	2	390	0.005
Jan/24/94	62	388	0.160	5	390	0.013
Jan/25/94	32	389	0.082	13	390	0.033
Jan/26/94	79	383	0.206	3	390	0.008
Jan/27/94	111	390	0.285	12	390	0.031
Jan/28/94	135	389	0.347	17	390	0.044
Jan/31/94	81	390	0.208	12	390	0.031
Overall	2312	8161	0.283	162	8190	0.0198

We now turn to the estimation of Equation 5, which can be estimated by the following iterative feasible generalized least squares procedure:

1. First, we regress $X(t)$ on $\Delta N(t)$ by ordinary least squares (OLS), and calculate the residuals, say $\hat{\varepsilon}$'s, from the resulting OLS estimates $\hat{\mu}$, $\hat{\mu}_Q$. In other words, $\hat{\varepsilon} = \hat{\varepsilon}(t) = X(t) - \hat{\mu} - \Delta N(t)\hat{\mu}_Q$.

2. Regress $\hat{\varepsilon}^2$ on $\Delta N(t)$ by nonlinear least squares (NLS) to obtain $\hat{\sigma}^2$, and $\hat{\sigma}_Q^2$.[3]

3. Apply generalised least squares on Equation 5 after dividing both sides of the equation by $\sqrt{\hat{\sigma}^2 + \Delta N(t) \cdot \hat{\sigma}_Q^2}$. This will produce another set of estimates, $\hat{\mu}$ and $\hat{\mu}_Q$. Based on these estimates, calculate the new squared residual $\hat{\varepsilon}^2 = \left[X(t) - \hat{\mu} - \Delta N(t) \cdot \hat{\mu}_Q \right]^2$ and iterate on step 2 and step 3.

Estimates derived from the above procedure will converge to maximum likelihood estimates by a familiar linearized maximum likelihood argument. Usually, only the first three iterations are required to produce convergent estimates.

Initially, we use all three trading variables, Tvol, N, and NPC, as informational proxies. However, we find that whenever Tvol is employed, the above iterative procedure has trouble converging. This indicates that Tvol is not a suitable informational proxy in our model. It is also consistent with recent empirical finding on the informational role of trading volume, as described on p 29. Therefore, we exclude Tvol as one of the informational proxies in the following analysis.

The estimation results are reported in Tables 8 and 9 below. Judging from the t-statistics, neither the number of trades nor the number of price changes significantly influence the mean and the variance of returns of INTEL. In contrast, both number of trades and number of price changes have significant impact on the variance of returns of IBM. This may be related to the data in Table 6 (on p. 39 above) where the higher numbers of trades and price changes for INTEL relative to IBM mean that their impact is less important. Technically, it is as if the Poisson process may be converging to Brownian motion again.

To further investigate the effect of the number of trades and the number of prices changes, we conduct the LM test procedures detailed in Theorem 1. The results are reported in Table 10 on p. 43 below. In general, we cannot reject the null hypothesis that $\hat{\mu}_Q = 0$ for neither INTEL nor IBM. The null hypothesis that $\hat{\sigma}_Q^2 = 0$ cannot be rejected for most INTEL cases, while it is rejected for all IBM cases. These findings based on LM_1 and LM_2 are consistent with the findings based on the previously reported

Table 8a Estimation results of equation 5 (INTEL) using number of trades as the conditioning variable.

	$\widehat{\mu}$	$\widehat{\mu}_Q$	$\widehat{\sigma}^2$	$\widehat{\sigma}^2_Q$
Jan/03/94	1.99623e − 004	−4.32879e − 005	8.83767e − 006[‡]	1.31247e − 015
Jan/04/94	1.52690e − 004	−8.23055e − 006	8.42912e − 006[‡]	3.86243e − 014
Jan/05/94	−1.84342e − 004	3.11915e − 005[†]	7.84127e − 006[‡]	5.28197e − 017
Jan/06/94	1.29885e − 005	−8.96784e − 006	9.26315e − 006[‡]	4.19801e − 014
Jan/07/94	−8.05041e − 005	1.83980e − 005	9.46621e − 006[‡]	1.24699e − 014
Jan/10/94	−3.71835e − 005	7.85007e − 006	9.05212e − 006[‡]	5.31904e − 014
Jan/11/94	−3.31412e − 005	4.73006e − 006	8.63678e − 006[‡]	9.96011e − 014
Jan/12/94	1.14074e − 004	−1.17300e − 005	1.13677e − 005[‡]	1.40633e − 014
Jan/13/94	1.16775e − 005	−2.19872e − 006	4.49239e − 006[‡]	2.84593e − 007[‡]
Jan/14/94	−3.38677e − 006	−8.20296e − 007	9.38246e − 006[‡]	4.41067e − 016
Jan/17/94	−4.19065e − 005	−6.56040e − 006	8.99713e − 006[‡]	1.26637e − 007
Jan/18/94	2.18259e − 004	−2.00913e − 005	9.17177e − 006[‡]	5.78238e − 007[†]
Jan/19/94	4.65174e − 005	−1.67423e − 006	1.09268e − 005	2.72177e − 007
Jan/20/94	−3.57308e − 004	3.07089e − 005	5.67778e − 006[‡]	4.36347e − 007[‡]
Jan/21/94	−1.07105e − 004	1.45346e − 005	7.75926e − 006[‡]	6.49908e − 014
Jan/24/94	−5.80505e − 005	1.05155e − 005	1.73548e − 005[‡]	1.29492e − 018
Jan/25/94	7.78902e − 005	−1.58708e − 005	1.06255e − 005[†]	1.43156e − 007
Jan/26/94	4.80304e − 005	−7.18525e − 006	1.04176e − 005[‡]	1.68758e − 015
Jan/27/94	−4.31422e − 005	8.07815e − 006	8.16688e − 006[‡]	3.52169e − 017
Jan/28/94	−1.59122e − 004	3.63564e − 005	8.95511e − 006[‡]	4.18263e − 015
Jan/31/94	−7.14433e − 005	1.23353e − 005	7.52336e − 006[‡]	5.03337e − 020

*Superscripts [†] and [‡] indicate significant estimates at 95% and 99%, respectively

Table 8b Estimation results of equation 5 (IBM) using number of trades as the conditioning variable.

	$\widehat{\mu}$	$\widehat{\mu}_Q$	$\widehat{\sigma}^2$	$\widehat{\sigma}^2_Q$
Jan/03/94	8.47565e − 005	−3.76855e − 005	5.06112e − 007[‡]	6.01113e − 007[‡]
Jan/04/94	3.54840e − 005	−5.71942e − 006	4.60576e − 007[‡]	2.94003e − 007[‡]
Jan/05/94	1.72855e − 005	6.37091e − 006	4.39923e − 007[‡]	1.84871e − 007[‡]
Jan/06/94	−2.50751e − 005	−1.88733e − 005	6.22927e − 007[‡]	2.70108e − 007[‡]
Jan/07/94	−3.13990e − 005	4.06552e − 005	3.46749e − 007[‡]	3.59012e − 007[‡]
Jan/10/94	2.20453e − 005	−1.62833e − 007	4.95472e − 007[‡]	2.53087e − 007[‡]
Jan/11/94	−1.92161e − 005	−2.09804e − 006	4.51786e − 007[‡]	3.28378e − 007[‡]
Jan/12/94	3.58428e − 005	−4.62232e − 005	5.31211e − 007[‡]	2.93435e − 007[‡]
Jan/13/94	−5.14234e − 005	5.83860e − 005	4.26358e − 007[‡]	2.80516e − 007[‡]
Jan/14/94	1.31612e − 005	−1.96320e − 005	3.78540e − 007[‡]	2.74229e − 007[‡]
Jan/17/94	3.24073e − 005	−6.37293e − 005	6.45929e − 007[‡]	4.56689e − 007[‡]
Jan/18/94	−1.05613e − 005	−3.88737e − 006	5.49921e − 007[‡]	3.46613e − 007[‡]
Jan/19/94	−1.17997e − 004[†]	5.77178e − 005	6.74295e − 007[‡]	2.17576e − 007[‡]
Jan/20/94	3.80987e − 005	−4.57353e − 005	7.20096e − 007[‡]	3.17926e − 007[‡]
Jan/21/94	3.71696e − 005	−2.09765e − 005	5.73443e − 007[‡]	2.27453e − 007[‡]
Jan/24/94	−6.19560e − 005	7.47843e − 005	7.40194e − 006	7.93658e − 006[‡]
Jan/25/94	1.10154e − 004	−3.54554e − 005	1.90160e − 006	6.62572e − 007[†]
Jan/26/94	−4.42420e − 006	−4.93458e − 005	3.84824e − 007	6.16205e − 007[‡]
Jan/27/94	−6.88986e − 005	6.11763e − 005	6.88203e − 007[‡]	2.82413e − 007[‡]
Jan/28/94	−5.00181e − 005	2.18855e − 005	6.06988e − 007[‡]	2.99088e − 007[‡]
Jan/31/94	−1.13336e − 004	4.08308e − 005	6.94322e − 007[‡]	2.23505e − 007[‡]

*Superscripts [†] and [‡] indicate significant estimates at 95% and 99%, respectively

Table 9a   Estimation results of equation 5 (INTEL) using number of price changes as the conditioning variable.

Date	$\hat{\mu}$	$\hat{\mu}_Q$	$\hat{\sigma}^2$	$\hat{\sigma}^2_Q$
Jan/03/94	2.79663e − 004	−1.07282e − 004†	8.90754e − 006‡	1.19623e − 014
Jan/04/94	1.29022e − 004	−8.41686e − 006	7.85017e − 006‡	3.91817e − 008
Jan/05/94	−6.15312e − 005	2.77974e − 005	7.20774e − 006‡	1.12640e − 007
Jan/06/94	−1.28360e − 005	−8.49783e − 006	8.23181e − 006‡	1.02132e − 007
Jan/07/94	−2.41464e − 004	7.32694e − 005†	9.62282e − 006‡	2.47580e − 014
Jan/10/94	−1.61753e − 004	4.27296e − 005	7.12497e − 006‡	3.35560e − 007
Jan/11/94	−2.86262e − 005	7.48359e − 006	7.87763e − 006‡	1.93200e − 007
Jan/12/94	1.66276e − 005	−3.11267e − 006	1.08291e − 005‡	4.44068e − 014
Jan/13/94	6.76371e − 005	−2.20174e − 005	4.87449e − 006‡	3.65487e − 007‡
Jan/14/94	1.38520e − 004	−3.68765e − 005	8.52530e − 006‡	1.37965e − 007
Jan/17/94	−1.54735e − 004	1.95953e − 005	7.30761e − 006‡	7.28027e − 007†
Jan/18/94	1.83196e − 004	−3.10886e − 005	9.06530e − 006†	1.12965e − 006†
Jan/19/94	7.12381e − 005	−4.66889e − 006	1.09712e − 005	5.25986e − 007
Jan/20/94	−8.54747e − 005	1.86825e − 005	5.81773e − 006‡	8.16752e − 007‡
Jan/21/94	−1.68194e − 004	4.00588e − 005	6.81423e − 006‡	6.00429e − 008
Jan/24/94	−9.62666e − 005	2.82125e − 005	1.77812e − 005‡	1.68407e − 021†
Jan/25/94	2.47163e − 004	−8.90341e − 005	8.93494e − 006†	8.32762e − 007
Jan/26/94	5.77888e − 005	−1.60304e − 005	9.59514e − 006‡	2.08160e − 016
Jan/27/94	−4.74702e − 006	4.37727e − 006	6.80104e − 006‡	4.00279e − 007†
Jan/28/94	−8.70525e − 005	4.58381e − 005	7.87873e − 006‡	2.30541e − 007
Jan/31/94	−1.22786e − 004	4.24943e − 005	7.32542e − 006‡	5.38475e − 014

*Superscripts † and ‡ indicate significant estimates at 95% and 99%, respectively

Table 9b   Estimation results of equation 5 (IBM) using number of price changes as the conditioning variable.

	$\hat{\mu}$	$\hat{\mu}_Q$	$\hat{\sigma}^2$	$\hat{\sigma}^2_Q$
Jan/03/94	6.02553e − 005	−6.76212e − 005	6.17154e − 007‡	1.76942e − 006‡
Jan/04/94	7.58812e − 005‡	−1.90518e − 004	3.69360e − 007‡	1.90581e − 006‡
Jan/05/94	1.57119e − 005	5.50246e − 005	3.68642e − 007‡	1.72722e − 006‡
Jan/06/94	−5.64767e − 005	5.47722e − 006	4.85193e − 007‡	1.71530e − 006‡
Jan/07/94	−5.25477e − 006	1.09891e − 004	3.22471e − 007‡	2.00768e − 006‡
Jan/10/94	3.78886e − 005	−5.29159e − 005	4.15901e − 007‡	1.52934e − 006‡
Jan/11/94	−4.20013e − 005	7.19807e − 005	3.31776e − 007‡	1.88459e − 006‡
Jan/12/94	4.23226e − 005	−2.54346e − 004†	3.93444e − 007‡	1.91947e − 006‡
Jan/13/94	−1.27031e − 005	1.72930e − 004	2.66369e − 007‡	2.60886e − 006‡
Jan/14/94	3.21602e − 005	−2.26685e − 004	3.07903e − 007‡	2.08081e − 006‡
Jan/17/94	−3.23145e − 005	−5.54844e − 005	5.33500e − 007‡	2.22843e − 006‡
Jan/18/94	−6.46973e − 005†	1.36837e − 004	4.75595e − 007‡	1.83636e − 006‡
Jan/19/94	−6.73258e − 005†	9.98472e − 005	5.11553e − 007‡	1.66638e − 006‡
Jan/20/94	−4.76575e − 005	5.65120e − 005	5.80608e − 007‡	1.82703e − 006‡
Jan/21/94	2.32398e − 005	−7.70753e − 005	4.42601e − 007‡	2.07353e − 006‡
Jan/24/94	3.60744e − 005	1.55893e − 004	7.16779e − 016	5.06004e − 005‡
Jan/25/94	4.23419e − 005	−7.56287e − 005	1.93266e − 006	2.86363e − 006‡
Jan/26/94	−2.17494e − 005	−2.09918e − 004	7.66423e − 007‡	2.21501e − 006‡
Jan/27/94	−1.46022e − 005	1.30648e − 004	4.41051e − 007‡	2.68871e − 006‡
Jan/28/94	−2.89158e − 005	2.32429e − 005	3.72453e − 007‡	2.15573e − 006‡
Jan/31/94	−1.95561e − 005	−9.77442e − 005	4.68804e − 007‡	1.82722e − 006‡

*Superscripts † and ‡ indicate significant estimates at 95% and 99%, respectively

Table 10a　LM test statistics for equation 7 (INTEL).

Date	N LM1	LM2	LM3	NPC LM1	LM2	LM3
Jan/03/94	2.532	0.1	295879.2	3.650	0.2	418504.9
Jan/04/94	0.108	0.6	14125.0	0.023	0.0	3160.5
Jan/05/94	3.067	0.3	402552.7	0.373	0.4	73346.8
Jan/06/94	0.104	1.2	13133.5	0.027	0.2	2903.5
Jan/07/94	2.418	4.0	309104.0	4.164	2.9	533145.9
Jan/10/94	0.156	0.4	18768.8	0.713	2.9	86954.4
Jan/11/94	0.030	0.0	3365.8	0.018	0.8	14412.3
Jan/12/94	0.603	5.7	67172.3	0.013	2.2	1424.7
Jan/13/94	0.005	7.6	10195.2	0.176	5.0	101769.2
Jan/14/94	0.002	0.2	177.7	0.620	0.5	64249.0
Jan/17/94	0.051	1.1	12681.1	0.117	11.1	6623.7
Jan/18/94	0.387	15.1	20391.7	0.234	13.8	579.5
Jan/19/94	0.022	20.1	6482.2	0.044	19.0	10397.1
Jan/20/94	2.083	27.2	107935.9	0.286	37.7	11080.5
Jan/21/94	0.720	1.2	110417.5	1.524	0.2	214287.9
Jan/24/94	0.105	9.6	9392.3	0.196	10.6	18242.3
Jan/25/94	0.180	0.7	16355.5	1.161	5.8	333147.9
Jan/26/94	0.077	2.3	9226.3	0.130	0.3	14433.2
Jan/27/94	0.096	0.0	11746.1	0.006	3.5	288.3
Jan/28/94	2.073	0.7	251009.2	0.399	0.7	142218.1
Jan/31/94	0.437	1.3	65353.1	0.720	0.2	103814.5

Table 10b　LM test statistics for equation 7 (IBM).

Date	N LM1	LM2	LM3	NPC LM1	LM2	LM3
Jan/03/94	0.607	69.5	390700.6	0.289	187.0	3123695.1
Jan/04/94	0.022	41.4	420148.4	1.539	323.4	8061427.7
Jan/05/94	0.038	26.6	236021.4	0.119	303.4	33255.6
Jan/06/94	0.243	24.8	215394.7	0.002	193.6	311366.5
Jan/07/94	1.007	55.1	2286418.3	0.502	353.8	918565.3
Jan/10/94	0.000	32.0	196540.3	0.168	207.2	1960846.2
Jan/11/94	0.003	44.4	49963.4	0.256	334.2	1095101.6
Jan/12/94	1.188	34.1	1571143.4	2.618	268.4	13537747.4
Jan/13/94	2.092	41.9	14511511.5	0.813	473.6	3264487.8
Jan/14/94	0.273	48.5	295116.3	1.548	398.6	11441683.4
Jan/17/94	1.863	51.5	3808498.9	0.138	236.6	75114.1
Jan/18/94	0.010	40.9	427964.1	1.139	231.7	396386.6
Jan/19/94	1.975	18.4	3463029.2	0.482	203.6	3656040.4
Jan/20/94	1.016	25.4	1136782.0	0.168	169.5	495987.9
Jan/21/94	0.330	27.5	330127.5	0.206	288.4	1846759.1
Jan/24/94	0.328	77.9	24908.4	0.111	612.7	23515.9
Jan/25/94	0.675	29.4	96354.9	0.375	93.6	70446.8
Jan/26/94	1.734	84.3	2195317.4	2.314	155.2	2172753.1
Jan/27/94	1.785	21.8	7945025.7	0.496	330.1	3873798.5
Jan/28/94	0.247	29.9	2203044.0	0.024	297.7	77788.5
Jan/31/94	0.840	14.1	2574018.3	0.519	226.6	75852.5

t-statistics. However, the LM$_3$ test is significant in all cases. This provides an evidence that return processes are indeed influenced by the trading processes. The insignificant results are possibly due to modelling mis-specification. One way of examining the modelling mis-specification is to examine the independence of the fitted residuals from the model. Since ε_t in Equation 5 is assumed to be i.i.d., we test this assumption by running the BDS test on the standardized estimated residuals, namely

$$\widehat{\varepsilon}(t) = \frac{X(t) - \widehat{\mu} - \widehat{\mu}_Q \cdot \Delta N(t)}{\sqrt{\widehat{\sigma}^2 + \widehat{\sigma}_Q^2 \cdot \Delta N(t)}} \qquad\qquad 8$$

From those results reported in Table 11 below, the i.i.d. assumption on ε_t is clearly rejected for most cases. This leads us to the doubly stochastic modelling in the next section.

Table 11   BDS tests on the estimated standardized residuals.

Date	INTEL N	INTEL NPC	IBM N	IBM NPC
Jan/03/94	8.617	8.838	9.1082	7.3948
Jan/04/94	7.546	7.546	5.9476	3.3806
Jan/05/94	9.205	8.993	3.6334	3.5866
Jan/06/94	7.886	7.886	4.0592	2.9863
Jan/07/94	6.410	6.387	3.9121	3.5160
Jan/10/94	7.809	7.928	1.1909	0.99458
Jan/11/94	6.837	6.897	3.5701	3.8187
Jan/12/94	7.725	7.961	3.3836	2.0141
Jan/13/94	7.647	7.698	4.5410	3.0972
Jan/14/94	6.877	6.930	5.8569	4.3545
Jan/17/94	8.231	8.258	4.0395	2.5102
Jan/18/94	7.615	7.146	7.2038	5.3387
Jan/19/94	6.974	8.734	2.3438	2.5470
Jan/20/94	6.255	6.997	4.2690	3.9588
Jan/21/94	10.590	10.271	2.8906	2.8051
Jan/24/94	7.959	7.658	9.7016	−0.41132
Jan/25/94	7.923	6.734	0.57503	0.045457
Jan/26/94	8.903	8.903	2.4349	−0.58903
Jan/27/94	7.744	7.822	3.3970	1.2443
Jan/28/94	10.022	9.524	5.7085	5.0051
Jan/31/94	8.953	8.878	2.3108	1.9430

Standardized Residual: $\frac{X(t) - \widehat{\mu} - \widehat{\mu}_Q \cdot \Delta N(t)}{\sqrt{\widehat{\sigma}^2 + \widehat{\sigma}_Q^2 \cdot \Delta N(t)}}$

BDS = Brock-Dechert-Scheinkman $\sim N(0, 1)_{asy}$,
Embedding Dimension = 3,
Epsilon = Standard Deviation/Spread

DOUBLE-STOCHASTIC POISSON PROCESS

We have shown that the information variables are not consistent with the (homogeneous) Poisson process with a fixed parameter. In order to accommodate the non-homogeneous nature of the information data, we now introduce a more complex (non-homogeneous) Poisson process which allows $\lambda(t)$ to vary. By an appropriate choice of $\lambda(t)$, we can model the marginal distribution of $\ln(P(t)/P(t-1))$. There are many candidates for the process of $\lambda(t)$. Here, $\lambda(t)$ is defined in the form of a GARCH-type model as:

$$\lambda(t) = \alpha v^2(t-1) + \beta \operatorname{Var}(X(t-1)|I(t-2)) \qquad 9$$

where $v(t)$ is $N(0, 1)$ unconditional in $N(t)$, in fact, it is $\Delta z(t) = z(t) - z(t-1)$ and $I(t)$ contains information up to the end of the minute.[4] Heuristically, the expected number of jumps depends upon the previous volatility and the deviation from fundamental $\Delta z^2(t)$, see Equation 2.

It follows from Equation 5 that

$$E[X(t)|I(t-1)] = \mu + \mu_Q \cdot \lambda(t)$$
$$\operatorname{Var}(X(t)|I(t-1)) = \sigma^2 + (\mu_Q^2 + \sigma_Q^2) \cdot \lambda(t) \qquad 10$$

since $\lambda(t)$ is known given $I(t-1)$. To simplify our model we shall assume that $X(t)$ and $\Delta N(t)$ are (weakly) stationary. Under the assumption of weak stationarity Equation 9 becomes

$$\lambda(t) = \alpha v^2(t-1) + \beta \sigma^2 + \theta \lambda(t-1) = \frac{\beta \sigma^2}{1-\theta} + \alpha \sum_{j=0}^{\infty} \theta^j v^2(t-j-1) \qquad 11$$

where $\theta = \beta(\mu_Q^2 + \sigma_Q^2)$, $0 < \theta < 1$. We can calculate the mean and the variance of $\lambda(t)$, detailed in Appendix 2, as follows:

$$E[\lambda(t)] = \frac{\beta \sigma^2 + \alpha}{1-\theta}$$
$$\operatorname{Var}(\lambda(t)) = \frac{2\alpha^2}{1-\theta^2} \qquad 12$$

using the fact that $v^2(t)$ has a $\chi^2(1)$ - distribution.

Given our model, the information variable is not purely exogenous any more: its intensity is dependent upon the past history of prices. This framework is attractive because it allows a feedback effect through the variables. It can explain certain phenomena in financial time series such as volatility clustering where large price changes tend to bunch together. This non-homogeneous Poisson process also resolves the restrictive aspect of the homogeneous Poisson distribution which implies that mean and variance are equal. From the moment generating function of $\Delta N(t)$ derived in Appendix 2,[5]

$$m_{\Delta N}(s) = \exp\left(\frac{\beta\sigma^2}{1-\theta}(\exp(s)-1)\right) \cdot \prod_{t=1}^{\infty}\left(1 - 2\alpha\theta^j(\exp(s)-1)\right)^{-1/2} \quad 13$$

we can derive the mean and the variance of $\Delta N(t)$,

$$E[\Delta N(t)] = \frac{\beta\sigma^2 + \alpha}{1-\theta}$$

$$Var(\Delta N(t)) = \frac{\beta\sigma^2 + \alpha}{1-\theta} + \frac{2\alpha^2}{1-\theta} \quad 14$$

Note that the mean and the variance are not equal in the presence of stochastic $\lambda(t)$. Moreover, the serial correlation of $\Delta N(t)$ can be shown to be

$$\begin{aligned} Corr(\Delta N(t), \Delta N(t-s)) &= \frac{Cov(\theta^s\lambda(t-s), \Delta N(t-s))}{Var(\Delta N(t))} \\ &= \frac{\theta^s Var(\lambda(t-s))}{Var(\Delta N(t))} \\ &= \begin{cases} \dfrac{2\alpha^2\theta^s}{2\alpha^2 + (\beta\sigma^2 + \alpha)(1+\theta)}, & \text{if } s = 1, 2, \ldots \\ 1, & \text{if } s = 0 \end{cases} \end{aligned} \quad 15$$

Then from Equation 5, the moment conditions of $X(t)$, detailed in Appendix 3, are obtained as follows:

$$E[X(t)] = \mu + \frac{\mu_Q(\beta\sigma^2 + \alpha)}{1-\theta}$$

$$Var[X(t)] = \sigma^2 + \frac{(\mu_Q^2 + \sigma_Q^2)(\beta\sigma^2 + \alpha)}{1-\theta} + \frac{2\alpha^2\mu_Q^2}{1-\theta^2} \quad 16$$

$$Corr(X(t), X(t-s)) =$$
$$\begin{cases} \dfrac{2\alpha^2\mu_Q^2\theta^s}{\sigma^2(1-\theta^2) + (\mu_Q^2 + \sigma_Q^2)(1+\theta)(\beta\sigma^2 + \alpha) + 2\alpha^2\mu_Q^2}, & \text{if } s = 1, 2, \ldots \\ 1, & \text{if } s = 0 \end{cases}$$

Given that $\Delta N(t)$ is observable, the joint likelihood function of $X(t)$ and $\Delta N(t)$ can be written as

$$L = \prod_{t=1}^{T} \text{pdf}(X(t), \Delta N(t)|I(t-1))$$

$$= \prod_{t=1}^{T} \text{pdf}(X(t)|\Delta N(t), I(t-1)) \cdot \text{pdf}(\Delta N(t)|I(t-1)) \qquad 17$$

$$= \prod_{t=1}^{T} \phi(\mu + \mu_Q \Delta N(t), \sigma^2 + \sigma_Q^2 \Delta N(t)) \frac{\exp(-\lambda(t))(\lambda(t))^{\Delta N(t)}}{\Delta N(t)!}$$

Thus, the log-likelihood function becomes

$$\ln L = \text{const.} - \sum \ln(\sigma^2 + \sigma_Q^2 \Delta N(t)) - \frac{1}{2} \sum \frac{(X(t) - \mu - \mu_Q \Delta N(t))^2}{\sigma^2 + \sigma_Q^2 \Delta N(t)}$$

$$- \sum \lambda(t) + \sum \Delta N(t) \ln(\lambda(t))$$

$$\text{where } \lambda(t) = \beta \sigma^2 + \alpha \left(\frac{X(t-1) - \mu - \mu_Q \Delta N(t-1)}{\sqrt{\sigma^2 + \sigma_Q^2 \Delta N(t-1)}} \right)^2$$

$$+ \beta(\mu_Q^2 + \sigma_Q^2)\lambda(t-1) \qquad 18$$

Although the joint density is tractable, the marginal density of $X(t)$ and $\Delta N(t)$ cannot be derived explicitly. This is one of the characteristics of a mixture of distributions which contain several random variables.

We estimate Equation 17 and report the results in Table 12 and 13 below. In terms of the significance of coefficients, $\widehat{\mu}_Q$ and $\widehat{\sigma}_Q^2$, in the variance equation, we obtain similar results as those obtained from estimating the homogenous compound Poisson model in Equation 5. Namely, $\widehat{\sigma}_Q^2$ is highly significant for all IBM cases, while $\widehat{\mu}_Q$ is insignificant in most cases. In addition, $\widehat{\beta}$ is highly significant for all cases. From Equation 9, we know that $\widehat{\beta}$ measures the sensitivity of information arrival intensity $\lambda(t)$ to the previous period's realized volatility. This is a strong evidence for the existence of a stochastic arrival intensity process.

Another way of examining the performance of the doubly stochastic Poisson model is to compare the sample moments (mean and variance) of

Table 12a MLE estimation results on equation 17 (INTEL) when number of trades is used as the conditioning variable.

Date	$\hat{\mu}$	$\hat{\mu}_Q$	$\hat{\sigma}^2$	$\hat{\sigma}_Q^2$	$\hat{\alpha}$	$\hat{\beta}$
Jan/03/94	5.639e − 004‡	−1.381e − 004‡	9.672e − 006‡	8.246e − 014	0.15443‡	583747.6‡
Jan/04/94	−3.261e − 004	1.186e − 004‡	9.303e − 006‡	1.615e − 015	0.35850‡	649453.2‡
Jan/05/94	−2.32e − 004	3.242e − 005	7.452e − 006‡	1.788e − 008	−0.10693‡	958372.0‡
Jan/06/94	1.515e − 005	−9.444e − 006	8.585e − 006‡	2.655e − 018	0.00754	685889.6‡
Jan/07/94	4.953e − 005	9.960e − 006	8.585e − 006‡	1.393e − 016	−0.20602‡	1159475.0‡
Jan/10/94	−3.559e − 005	9.632e − 006	8.585e − 006‡	3.453e − 015	0.03946	971904.0‡
Jan/11/94	−8.066e − 005	5.879e − 006	8.526e − 006‡	3.199e − 019	0.23815‡	676035.8‡
Jan/12/94	8.054e − 005	−7.583e − 006	9.923e − 006‡	7.542e − 020	−0.19654‡	990418.9‡
Jan/13/94	7.769e − 004‡	−2.033e − 004‡	7.563e − 006‡	1.474e − 014	0.60826‡	637173.7‡
Jan/14/94	−6.017e − 006	5.009e − 006	9.000e − 006‡	9.452e − 009	−0.15981‡	815408.8‡
Jan/17/94	−5.459e − 005	−6.314e − 006	8.294e − 006‡	2.323e − 007†	−0.03512	687441.0‡
Jan/18/94	3.435e − 004	−4.281e − 005	1.204e − 005‡	2.429e − 007‡	0.19921‡	628407.1‡
Jan/19/94	−0.00351‡	−0.00131‡	4.130e − 011	6.320e − 005‡	26.02478‡	1465.0‡
Jan/20/94	−0.00347‡	6.858e − 004‡	2.098e − 005‡	2.560e − 006‡	3.12385‡	162953.5‡
Jan/21/94	−8.052e − 005	1.264e − 005	7.129e − 006‡	3.873e − 017	−0.08964	1326695.8‡
Jan/24/94	−6.506e − 005	1.107e − 005	1.384e − 005‡	2.895e − 017	−0.06754‡	537886.3‡
Jan/25/94	1.042e − 004	−2.293e − 005	1.142e − 005‡	5.4067e − 016	0.04298	477441.7‡
Jan/26/94	1.485e − 004	−2.355e − 005	8.940e − 006‡	3.214e − 008	−0.25679‡	829013.0‡
Jan/27/94	−1.203e − 004	2.973e − 005	8.179e − 006‡	3.985e − 017	0.25621‡	767316.4‡
Jan/28/94	−0.00115‡	3.371e − 004‡	1.204e − 005‡	6.746e − 014	1.12451‡	342264.0‡
Jan/31/94	−4.452e − 005	6.287e − 006	6.917e − 006‡	3.359e − 008	−0.41607‡	864783.5‡

*Superscripts † and ‡ indicate significant estimates at 95% and 99%, respectively

Table 12b MLE estimation results on equation 17 (IBM) when number of trades is used as the conditioning variable.

Date	$\hat{\mu}$	$\hat{\mu}_Q$	$\hat{\sigma}^2$	$\hat{\sigma}^2_Q$	$\hat{\alpha}$	$\hat{\beta}$
Jan/03/94	9.26139e − 005	−6.55090e − 005	3.71179e − 007‡	6.79924e − 007‡	0.06342‡	990163.8‡
Jan/04/94	5.39859e − 005	−2.76607e − 005	2.46681e − 007‡	4.45500e − 007‡	0.03976‡	1541929.5‡
Jan/05/94	3.00105e − 005	−1.35420e − 006	2.66819e − 007‡	3.08293e − 007‡	0.05504‡	2009604.5‡
Jan/06/94	−7.37708e − 006	−2.65190e − 005	3.27992e − 007‡	5.14542e − 007‡	0.06366‡	1325643.6‡
Jan/07/94	−3.43392e − 005	3.55769e − 005	1.06379e − 007‡	5.67357e − 007‡	−0.00755	1547819.1‡
Jan/10/94	2.12734e − 006	8.55687e − 006	2.28401e − 007‡	4.49718e − 007‡	0.03301†	1627898.0‡
Jan/11/94	−2.17333e − 005	1.65852e − 006	2.68531e − 007‡	5.29668e − 007‡	−0.02770‡	1371322.4‡
Jan/12/94	4.99580e − 005	−6.16387e − 005	2.40893e − 007‡	6.08497e − 007‡	0.03025‡	1213032.7‡
Jan/13/94	−3.87670e − 005	4.45740e − 005	2.75734e − 007‡	3.99232e − 007‡	0.01092	1586912.5‡
Jan/14/94	2.10130e − 005	−4.29745e − 005	2.11063e − 007‡	4.44022e − 007‡	0.04458‡	1559872.5‡
Jan/17/94	2.19451e − 005	−3.17046e − 005	4.25728e − 007‡	6.55747e − 007‡	0.03664‡	979630.5‡
Jan/18/94	−3.07887e − 005	1.02675e − 005	3.70254e − 007‡	4.98981e − 007‡	0.08873‡	1303135.6‡
Jan/19/94	−1.15599e − 004†	5.74840e − 005	5.04593e − 007‡	3.65331e − 007‡	−0.03188†	1376932.6‡
Jan/20/94	4.05827e − 005	−5.16874e − 005	4.20665e − 007‡	5.52583e − 007‡	0.03901†	1153405.3‡
Jan/21/94	3.56237e − 005	−2.24752e − 005	3.32605e − 007‡	4.28327e − 007‡	0.02057	1514227.2‡
Jan/24/94	−3.71290e − 006	5.23776e − 005	1.85761e − 005‡	3.16840e − 006‡	−0.00731	96231.3‡
Jan/25/94	1.33555e − 004	−4.69500e − 005	2.01640e − 006‡	6.16539e − 007‡	0.11846‡	833442.6‡
Jan/26/94	−4.00929e − 005	4.43977e − 006	5.30658e − 007‡	4.90919e − 007‡	0.20965‡	1215795.7‡
Jan/27/94	−4.88733e − 005	4.30131e − 005	4.52305e − 007‡	4.94893e − 007‡	0.03495†	1191080.5‡
Jan/28/94	−3.14280e − 005	1.67196e − 005	3.08099e − 007‡	5.79243e − 007‡	0.02229	1188794.4‡
Jan/31/94	−8.90972e − 005	2.34641e − 005	4.22253e − 007‡	4.40130e − 007‡	0.03690	1367253.9‡

*Superscripts †and ‡indicate significant estimates at 95% and 99%, respectively

Table 13a MLE estimation results on equation 17 (INTEL) when number of price changes is used as the conditioning variable.

Date	$\hat{\mu}$	$\hat{\mu}_Q$	$\hat{\sigma}^2$	$\hat{\sigma}^2_Q$	$\hat{\alpha}$	$\hat{\beta}$
Jan/03/94	4.38725e − 005	2.27688e − 005	9.12040e − 006‡	3.63871e − 014	0.26621‡	321238.7‡
Jan/04/94	1.19481e − 004	−5.32750e − 006	7.29000e − 006‡	2.26911e − 007	−0.02024	389596.3‡
Jan/05/94	−5.53380e − 005	2.61865e − 005	6.96960e − 006‡	1.91447e − 007	−0.00228	477996.9‡
Jan/06/94	8.36662e − 004‡	−3.98143e − 004‡	1.18336e − 005‡	2.96174e − 014	0.52591‡	231624.9‡
Jan/07/94	−9.62358e − 004‡	4.28048e − 004‡	1.26025e − 005‡	6.84708e − 015	0.75175‡	306435.8‡
Jan/10/94	−2.42177e − 004	6.93395e − 005	6.25000e − 006‡	5.40296e − 007‡	0.08595‡	505050.8‡
Jan/11/94	2.86678e − 005	2.21844e − 005	1.02400e − 005‡	5.08644e − 013	0.18531‡	374330.3‡
Jan/12/94	2.69586e − 005	−5.20307e − 006	9.92250e − 006‡	1.19362e − 018	−0.07391‡	540704.2‡
Jan/13/94	5.89247e − 004‡	−2.37391e − 004‡	7.07560e − 006‡	4.09658e − 018	0.38394‡	392595.7‡
Jan/14/94	1.29551e − 004	−3.69568e − 005	9.06010e − 006‡	1.17070e − 018	0.05039	433865.4‡
Jan/17/94	−1.80626e − 004	2.37146e − 005	6.50250e − 006‡	9.22685e − 007‡	−0.00727	359775.4‡
Jan/18/94	1.49204e − 004	−2.42288e − 005	1.14244e − 005‡	5.80243e − 007‡	0.05319	334170.4‡
Jan/19/94	−0.00366‡	−0.00174‡	1.27921e − 012	5.97529e − 005‡	12.52358‡	1339.5‡
Jan/20/94	0.00229‡	−8.21278e − 004‡	2.21841e − 005‡	1.84960e − 006‡	2.01060‡	120470.0‡
Jan/21/94	−1.67324e − 004	4.00871e − 005	6.86440e − 006‡	5.18682e − 008	0.00189	689308.2‡
Jan/24/94	−9.69851e − 005	2.78728e − 005	1.38384e − 005‡	1.29245e − 021	−0.03255‡	299702.7‡
Jan/25/94	1.87517e − 004	−7.04943e − 005	7.50760e − 006‡	1.34560e − 006‡	0.01863	251587.7‡
Jan/26/94	0.00104‡	−3.91810e − 004‡	1.19025e − 005‡	6.05096e − 014	0.46213‡	297088.3‡
Jan/27/94	8.12764e − 006	2.84223e − 006	6.86440e − 006‡	3.87651e − 007†	0.04969	407225.8‡
Jan/28/94	−5.68349e − 004†	2.36913e − 004‡	9.18090e − 006‡	7.87465e − 018	0.19006‡	299799.2‡
Jan/31/94	−1.44192e − 004	3.01406e − 005	6.91690e − 006‡	6.08535e − 008	−0.24102‡	436765.6‡

*Superscripts † and ‡ indicate significant estimates at 95% and 99%, respectively

Table 13b MLE estimation results on equation 17 (IBM) when number of price changes is used as the conditioning variable.

Date	$\hat{\mu}$	$\hat{\mu}_Q$	$\hat{\sigma}^2$	$\hat{\sigma}^2_Q$	$\hat{\alpha}$	$\hat{\beta}$
Jan/03/94	5.88619e − 005	−1.28630e − 004	3.63515e − 007‡	2.59728e − 006‡	0.03745‡	255342.5‡
Jan/04/94	7.76359e − 005†	−2.05966e − 004	2.47742e − 007‡	2.58035e − 006‡	0.03348‡	243157.4‡
Jan/05/94	1.57780e − 005	4.90352e − 005	2.83830e − 007‡	2.13562e − 006‡	0.00433	276309.3‡
Jan/06/94	−5.52392e − 005	2.05302e − 005	3.31985e − 007‡	2.36839e − 006‡	0.01939†	279091.8‡
Jan/07/94	−8.86237e − 006	1.06266e − 004	2.19982e − 007‡	2.55966e − 006‡	0.01732‡	268972.1‡
Jan/10/94	3.79020e − 005	−4.75277e − 005	2.93455e − 007‡	2.07899e − 006‡	0.01375†	312964.2‡
Jan/11/94	−4.31422e − 005	8.49964e − 005	2.34089e − 007‡	2.56000e − 006‡	0.01902‡	276424.8‡
Jan/12/94	4.09030e − 005	−2.47238e − 004	2.99769e − 007‡	2.45509e − 006‡	0.00797	261973.8‡
Jan/13/94	−1.53318e − 005	1.85197e − 004	1.95246e − 007‡	3.34890e − 006‡	0.01680‡	212449.0‡
Jan/14/94	2.67118e − 005	−2.39734e − 004	2.01976e − 007‡	3.07323e − 006‡	0.02635‡	209445.1‡
Jan/17/94	−3.02108e − 005	−1.76489e − 005	4.57235e − 007‡	2.50335e − 006‡	0.01558	240100.6‡
Jan/18/94	−7.61729e − 005†	1.49748e − 004	3.93037e − 007‡	2.07024e − 006‡	0.04545‡	270105.9‡
Jan/19/94	−6.48689e − 005†	7.65805e − 005	3.91403e − 007‡	2.43360e − 006‡	0.01424†	245865.8‡
Jan/20/94	−4.86975e − 005	6.29103e − 005	3.97417e − 007‡	2.58009e − 006‡	0.00909	257071.0‡
Jan/21/94	2.22230e − 005	−6.17122e − 005	3.09026e − 007‡	2.89508e − 006‡	0.00652	227475.9‡
Jan/24/94	4.54262e − 005	1.37931e − 004	7.67290e − 006‡	2.50000e − 005‡	7.56498e − 004	26339.1‡
Jan/25/94	7.69976e − 005	−1.32728e − 004	1.19784e − 006‡	4.15025e − 006‡	0.07287‡	164220.5‡
Jan/26/94	−5.69273e − 006	−2.40458e − 004†	6.45644e − 007‡	2.47482e − 006‡	0.06925‡	203008.8‡
Jan/27/94	−1.35794e − 005	1.33951e − 004	2.55802e − 007‡	3.45960e − 006‡	0.01755‡	203408.1‡
Jan/28/94	−2.39920e − 005	7.15266e − 005	2.90272e − 007‡	2.35052e − 006‡	0.03194‡	261737.9‡
Jan/31/94	−1.84068e − 005	−1.05984e − 004	3.26149e − 007‡	2.49640e − 006‡	0.00788	274554.5‡

*Superscripts † and ‡ indicate significant estimates at 95% and 99%, respectively

trading variables with those implied by the model in Equations 9 to 12. The results are reported in Tables 14 and 15 below. An interesting result shown in these tables is that the implied expected values, $\widehat{E}(\Delta N_t)$, of the trading variables match their sample counterparts, $E(\Delta N_t)$, quite well. To give a quick measure of how close they are, we calculate a χ^2 test statistics *TCF* as

$$TCF = \sum_{t=1}^{21} CF_t = \sum_{t=1}^{21} \frac{\left[E(\Delta N_t) - \widehat{E}(\Delta N_t) \right]^2}{\widehat{E}(\Delta N_t)} \sim \chi^2(20) \qquad\qquad 19$$

All of the *TCF*'s are well inside the critical region under conventional significance levels. By comparing the magnitudes of *TCF*s, we also find that, for both INTEL and IBM, the number of trades seem to be a slightly better proxy of information arrival. In addition, for IBM, implied

Table 14a Moments and persistence level of information arrival (N of INTEL).

Date	E(N)	V(N)	$\widehat{V}$ (N)	$\widehat{E}(N) = \widehat{E}(\lambda)$	$\widehat{V}(\lambda)$	$\widehat{\theta}$	CF
Jan/03/94	5.600	31.058	5.914	5.866	4.7703e − 002	1.1138e − 002	1.2062e − 002
Jan/04/94	6.079	34.567	6.716	6.459	2.5707e − 001	9.1279e − 003	2.2356e − 002
Jan/05/94	7.223	62.621	7.189	7.166	2.2876e − 002	1.8145e − 002	4.5339e − 004
Jan/06/94	5.928	31.090	5.896	5.896	1.1370e − 004	6.1175e − 005	1.7368e − 004
Jan/07/94	9.779	174.604	9.834	9.749	8.4888e − 002	1.1503e − 004	9.2317e − 005
Jan/10/94	8.467	59.211	8.387	8.384	3.1142e − 003	9.0166e − 005	8.2168e − 004
Jan/11/94	6.051	30.861	6.116	6.002	1.1343e − 001	2.3370e − 005	4.0003e − 004
Jan/12/94	9.831	131.946	9.709	9.631	7.7256e − 002	5.6944e − 005	4.1533e − 003
Jan/13/94	5.362	19.908	6.314	5.574	7.4047e − 001	2.6326e − 002	8.0632e − 003
Jan/14/94	7.359	60.112	7.286	7.235	5.1082e − 002	7.7275e − 003	2.1252e − 003
Jan/17/94	6.787	36.626	6.746	6.744	2.5314e − 003	1.5969e − 001	2.7417e − 004
Jan/18/94	9.213	50.461	9.258	9.177	8.1291e − 002	1.5376e − 001	1.4122e − 004
Jan/19/94	33.931	571.561	1395.703	28.760	1.3669e + 003	9.5107e − 002	9.2974e − 001
Jan/20/94	13.064	156.955	38.734	12.924	2.5810e + 001	4.9379e − 001	1.5166e − 003
Jan/21/94	9.456	69.565	9.386	9.370	1.6071e − 002	2.1208e − 004	7.8933e − 004
Jan/24/94	7.438	42.987	7.386	7.376	9.1233e − 003	6.5947e − 005	5.2115e − 004
Jan/25/94	5.579	25.283	5.503	5.499	3.6946e − 003	2.5099e − 004	1.1638e − 003
Jan/26/94	7.423	40.132	7.486	7.354	1.3198e − 001	2.7106e − 002	6.4740e − 004
Jan/27/94	6.597	30.951	6.668	6.537	1.3129e − 001	6.7783e − 004	5.5071e − 004
Jan/28/94	5.500	36.256	7.991	5.458	2.5329e + 000	3.8894e − 002	3.2320e − 004
Jan/31/94	5.808	55.806	6.079	5.732	3.4652e − 001	2.9079e − 002	1.0077e − 003
						TCF	9.8737e−001

E = Mean, V = Variance, $\widehat{E}$ = Estimated Mean, $\widehat{V}$ = Estimated Variance, $\widehat{\theta} = \beta(\widehat{\mu}_Q^2 + \widehat{\sigma}_Q^2)$, CF = Criterion Function = $\dfrac{[E(N) - \widehat{E}(N)]^2}{\widehat{E}(N)}$, $TCF = \sum_{t=1}^{21} CF_t$

Table 14b Moments and persistence level of information arrival (N of IBM).

Date	E(N)	V(N)	$\widehat{V}$ (N)	$\widehat{E}(N) = \widehat{E}(\lambda)$	$\widehat{V}(\lambda)$	$\widehat{\theta}$	CF
Jan/03/94	1.352	1.780	1.351	1.336	1.4869e − 002	0.6775	1.9162e − 004
Jan/04/94	1.371	2.053	1.353	1.347	6.0051e − 003	0.6881	4.2762e − 004
Jan/05/94	1.562	2.324	1.564	1.554	9.8332e − 003	0.6195	4.1184e − 005
Jan/06/94	1.568	2.256	1.588	1.573	1.5193e − 002	0.6830	1.5893e − 005
Jan/07/94	1.316	1.505	1.311	1.311	5.0583e − 004	0.8801	1.9069e − 005
Jan/10/94	1.537	2.048	1.516	1.512	4.6982e − 003	0.7322	4.1336e − 004
Jan/11/94	1.246	1.579	1.248	1.244	3.2484e − 003	0.7263	3.2154e − 006
Jan/12/94	1.257	1.655	1.258	1.253	4.0820e − 003	0.7427	1.2769e − 005
Jan/13/94	1.256	1.847	1.235	1.234	4.0109e − 004	0.6367	3.9222e − 004
Jan/14/94	1.228	1.724	1.235	1.228	7.6988e − 003	0.6955	0.0000e + 000
Jan/17/94	1.296	2.013	1.277	1.272	4.5813e − 003	0.6434	4.5283e − 004
Jan/18/94	1.618	2.216	1.661	1.634	2.7289e − 002	0.6504	1.5667e − 004
Jan/19/94	1.352	1.863	1.349	1.346	2.7381e − 003	0.5076	2.6746e − 005
Jan/20/94	1.467	1.869	1.463	1.458	5.1599e − 003	0.6404	5.5556e − 005
Jan/21/94	1.504	2.271	1.496	1.495	1.4632e − 003	0.6493	5.4181e − 005
Jan/24/94	2.568	4.885	2.562	2.562	1.1785e − 004	0.3052	1.4052e − 005
Jan/25/94	3.728	6.750	3.753	3.715	3.8233e − 002	0.5157	4.5491e − 006
Jan/26/94	2.129	3.539	2.257	2.121	1.3656e − 001	0.5969	3.0174e − 005
Jan/27/94	1.403	1.871	1.409	1.405	3.7588e − 003	0.5917	2.8470e − 006
Jan/28/94	1.270	1.852	1.251	1.249	1.8914e − 003	0.6889	3.5308e − 004
Jan/31/94	1.538	1.596	1.550	1.545	4.2753e − 003	0.6025	3.1715e − 005

| | | | | | | TCF | 2.7403e − 003 |

E = Mean, V = Variance, $\widehat{E}$ = Estimated Mean, $\widehat{V}$ = Estimated Variance, $\widehat{\theta} = \beta(\widehat{\mu}_Q^2 + \widehat{\sigma}_Q^2)$

CF = Criterion Function = $\dfrac{[E(N) - \widehat{E}(N)]^2}{\widehat{E}(N)}$, $TCF = \sum_{t=1}^{21} CF_t$

variances, $\widehat{V}(\Delta N_t)$, of the trading variables are also very close to their sample counterparts, $V(\Delta N_t)$.

Also reported in Tables 14 and 15 are the $\widehat{\theta}$ values, which represent the degree of dependence of $\lambda(t)$ on $\lambda(t-1)$ from Equation 11. This is an equivalent measure of volatility persistence in GARCH models. On average, when the number of trades is used as the informational proxy, $\widehat{\theta} \simeq 0.05$ for INTEL, and $\widehat{\theta} \simeq 0.64$ for IBM. Similar results are obtained when the number of price changes is used as the informational proxy. In that case, $\widehat{\theta} \simeq 0.1$ for INTEL, and $\widehat{\theta} \simeq 0.64$ for IBM on average. In other words, the volatility persistence implied by our model is much smaller than those implied by the GARCH-type models.

To compare the persistence of GARCH-type models versus that of informational volatility models as in this chapter, we fit a GARCH(1,1) model on the same data sets. We compare the $\widehat{\theta}$ values listed in Tables 14 and 15 with the value of $\widehat{\alpha} + \widehat{\beta}$ reported in Table 16 below. We recall that Table 14 describes the models for the number of trades, whilst Table 15 describes the models for the number of price changes. In Table 14a, for INTEL, there are no values of $\widehat{\theta}$ greater than 0.5, and there are only three values greater than 0.1. Similarly, in Table 15a, there are only six values of $\widehat{\theta}$ greater than 0.1. However, for the GARCH(1,1) model for INTEL in Table 16, there are four values of $\widehat{\alpha} + \widehat{\beta}$ greater than 0.9, and 12 values greater than 0.5 out of the 21 days. Likewise, for IBM, there are no values of $\widehat{\theta}$ greater than 0.8 in either Table 14b or 15b. But, for the GARCH(1,1) model for IBM in Table 16, there are six values of $\widehat{\alpha} + \widehat{\beta}$ greater than 0.8. This indicates, to us at least, that the claimed persistence of volatility may be an artifact of the choice of model and does not reflect a market opportunity or a forecastable feature of the data.

Table 15a   Moments and persistence level of information arrival (NPC of INTEL).

Date	E(NPC)	V(NPC)	$\widehat{V}$ (NPC)	$\widehat{E}$(NPC) $= \widehat{E}(\lambda)$	$\widehat{V}(\lambda)$	$\widehat{\theta}$	CF
Jan/03/94	3.010	7.208	3.338	3.197	$1.417e - 001$	$1.665e - 004$	$1.0938e - 002$
Jan/04/94	3.123	6.869	3.094	3.093	$8.258e - 004$	$8.841e - 002$	$2.9098e - 004$
Jan/05/94	3.656	10.776	3.666	3.666	$1.049e - 005$	$9.184e - 002$	$2.7278e - 005$
Jan/06/94	3.203	8.650	3.945	3.391	$5.539e - 001$	$3.672e - 002$	$1.0423e - 002$
Jan/07/94	4.651	18.983	6.022	4.888	$1.134e + 000$	$5.615e - 002$	$1.1491e - 002$
Jan/10/94	4.472	10.111	4.490	4.474	$1.599e - 002$	$2.753e - 001$	$8.9405e - 007$
Jan/11/94	3.210	9.370	4.088	4.019	$6.868e - 002$	$1.844e - 004$	$1.6285e - 001$
Jan/12/94	5.382	38.401	5.302	5.291	$1.093e - 002$	$1.464e - 005$	$1.5651e - 003$
Jan/13/94	3.092	7.565	3.528	3.233	$2.950e - 001$	$2.212e - 002$	$6.1494e - 003$
Jan/14/94	4.028	12.156	3.989	3.984	$5.078e - 003$	$5.926e - 004$	$4.8594e - 004$
Jan/17/94	3.510	10.744	3.492	3.492	$1.188e - 004$	$3.322e - 001$	$9.2784e - 005$
Jan/18/94	4.818	12.967	4.809	4.803	$5.880e - 003$	$1.941e - 001$	$4.6846e - 005$
Jan/19/94	17.467	144.357	329.588	13.673	$3.159e + 002$	$8.409e - 002$	$1.0528e + 000$
Jan/20/94	6.785	60.792	15.638	6.729	$8.909e + 000$	$3.041e - 001$	$4.6604e - 004$
Jan/21/94	4.954	19.982	4.915	4.915	$7.154e - 006$	$3.686e - 002$	$3.0946e - 004$
Jan/24/94	4.123	11.383	4.118	4.116	$2.119e - 003$	$2.328e - 004$	$1.1905e - 005$
Jan/25/94	2.908	6.377	2.890	2.889	$7.848e - 004$	$3.398e - 001$	$1.2496e - 004$
Jan/26/94	3.933	12.448	4.617	4.189	$4.280e - 001$	$4.561e - 002$	$1.5645e - 002$
Jan/27/94	3.385	7.733	3.383	3.378	$5.064e - 003$	$1.579e - 001$	$1.4506e - 005$
Jan/28/94	2.777	6.148	3.065	2.993	$7.227e - 002$	$1.683e - 002$	$1.5588e - 002$
Jan/31/94	2.900	7.530	2.973	2.857	$1.163e - 001$	$2.698e - 002$	$6.4718e - 004$

| | | | | | | TCF | $1.2899e + 000$ |

E = Mean, V = Variance, $\widehat{E}$ = Estimated Mean, $\widehat{V}$ = Estimated Variance, $\widehat{\theta} = \beta(\widehat{\mu}_Q^2 + \widehat{\sigma}_Q^2)$

CF = Criterion Function $= \dfrac{[E(NPC) - \widehat{E}(NPC)]^2}{\widehat{E}(NPC)}$, $TCF = \sum_{t=1}^{21} CF_t$

Table 15b Moments and persistence level of information arrival (NPC of IBM).

Date	E(NPC)	VPC(NPC)	$\widehat{V}$ (NPC)	$\widehat{E}$(NPC) = $\widehat{E}(\lambda)$	$\widehat{V}(\lambda)$	$\widehat{\theta}$	CF
Jan/03/94	0.391	0.553	0.395	0.390	5.042e − 003	0.666	2.5641e − 006
Jan/04/94	0.253	0.339	0.265	0.261	3.802e − 003	0.641	2.4521e − 004
Jan/05/94	0.209	0.290	0.202	0.202	5.748e − 005	0.590	2.4257e − 004
Jan/06/94	0.328	0.387	0.333	0.332	1.339e − 003	0.662	4.8193e − 005
Jan/07/94	0.247	0.310	0.249	0.248	1.150e − 003	0.692	4.0323e − 006
Jan/10/94	0.303	0.361	0.302	0.301	6.543e − 004	0.650	1.3289e − 005
Jan/11/94	0.279	0.361	0.290	0.288	1.458e − 003	0.710	2.8125e − 004
Jan/12/94	0.252	0.292	0.256	0.256	2.260e − 004	0.662	6.2500e − 005
Jan/13/94	0.200	0.227	0.208	0.207	1.168e − 003	0.719	2.3671e − 004
Jan/14/94	0.190	0.236	0.201	0.198	2.424e − 003	0.653	3.2323e − 004
Jan/17/94	0.319	0.388	0.314	0.313	7.578e − 004	0.599	1.1502e − 004
Jan/18/94	0.349	0.495	0.356	0.349	6.080e − 003	0.566	0.0000e + 000
Jan/19/94	0.272	0.359	0.277	0.276	6.334e − 004	0.600	5.7971e − 005
Jan/20/94	0.331	0.371	0.335	0.334	2.980e − 004	0.667	2.6946e − 005
Jan/21/94	0.234	0.309	0.225	0.225	1.500e − 004	0.658	3.6000e − 004
Jan/24/94	0.607	0.971	0.595	0.595	2.023e − 006	0.659	2.4202e − 004
Jan/25/94	0.848	1.144	0.874	0.854	2.008e − 002	0.686	4.2155e − 005
Jan/26/94	0.420	0.523	0.424	0.411	1.300e − 002	0.512	1.9708e − 004
Jan/27/94	0.241	0.286	0.239	0.238	1.233e − 003	0.707	3.7815e − 005
Jan/28/94	0.285	0.328	0.283	0.280	3.275e − 003	0.614	8.9286e − 005
Jan/31/94	0.315	0.402	0.313	0.313	2.361e − 004	0.688	1.2780e − 005

$$TCF \quad 2.6406e − 003$$

E = Mean, V = Variance, $\widehat{E}$ = Estimated Mean, $\widehat{V}$ = Estimated Variance, $\widehat{\theta} = \beta(\widehat{\mu}_Q^2 + \widehat{\sigma}_Q^2)$, CF = Criterion

Function = $\dfrac{[E(NPC) - \widehat{E}(NPC)]^2}{\widehat{E}(NPC)}$, $TCF = \sum_{t=1}^{21} CF_t$

Table 16 Estimation results of GARCH(1, 1)[†].

	INTEL			IBM		
Date	$\widehat{\alpha}$	$\widehat{\beta}$	$\widehat{\alpha} + \widehat{\beta}$	$\widehat{\alpha}$	$\widehat{\beta}$	$\widehat{\alpha} + \widehat{\beta}$
Jan/03/94	0.09664	0.82548	0.92212	0.3665	0.1252	0.4917
	(3.28851)	(11.36881)		(4.7914)	(3.8129)[‡]	
Jan/04/94	0.13962	0.59413	0.73375	0.2045	0.4822	0.6867
	(6.86519)	(24.56781)		(5.1389)	(28.8343)	
Jan/05/94	0.11542	0.47626	0.59168	0.1017	0.5107	0.6124
	(3.05787)	(14.25865)		(3.6133)	(30.6564)	
Jan/06/94	0.15985	0.68766	0.84751	0.1506	0.5605	0.7111
	(6.31624)	(32.01800)		(5.0494)	(27.5990)	
Jan/07/94	0.03984	−0.17610	−0.13626	0.0572	0.8883	0.9455
	(0.62048)	(−3.08832)		(8.4115)	(188.5023)	
Jan/10/94	0.13667	0.23308	0.36975	0.0188	0.4938	0.5126
	(3.15266)	(7.25938)		(0.4940)	(1.6193)	

(continued overleaf)

Table 16   (*continued*).

Date	INTEL			IBM		
	$\widehat{\alpha}$	$\widehat{\beta}$	$\widehat{\alpha}+\widehat{\beta}$	$\widehat{\alpha}$	$\widehat{\beta}$	$\widehat{\alpha}+\widehat{\beta}$
Jan/11/94	0.12756	0.65105	0.77861	0.0848	0.8245	0.9093
	(4.28403)	(26.90697)		(7.5351)	(116.0896)	
Jan/12/94	0.34599	0.08378	0.42977	0.0758	0.7035	0.7793
	(7.54474)	(1.80773)		(4.1435)	(52.5527)	
Jan/13/94	0.02529	−0.91167	−0.88638	0.1824	0.5146	0.6970
	(1.05012)	(−12.03280)		(5.7604)	(29.6367)	
Jan/14/94	0.31604	−0.11722	0.19882	0.1104	0.8378	0.9481
	(3.55535)	(−1.52218)		(13.1450)	(194.2958)	
Jan/17/94	0.32243	0.10302	0.42545	0.2475	0.4167	0.6642
	(7.88337)	(2.12959)		(8.9954)	(17.9314)	
Jan/18/94	0.13544	0.50834	0.64378	0.3266	0.4013	0.7279
	(5.09211)	(28.72999)		(5.7305)	(17.8341)	
Jan/19/94	0.62457	0.33569	0.96026	0.0723	−0.1454	−0.0731
	(22.39771)	(17.95127)		(1.4920)	(−0.4893)	
Jan/20/94	0.10307	0.78258	0.88565	0.1321	0.3700	0.5021
	(7.73352)	(80.69002)		(3.6792)	(12.8733)	
Jan/21/94	−0.02205	−0.54658	−0.56863	0.0974	−0.1417	−0.0442
	(−0.94791)	(−7.26724)		(1.6897)	(−2.8914)	
Jan/24/94	0.07347	0.74165	0.81512	0.2565	0.7196	0.9760
	(9.96571)	(194.19238)		(21.5278)	(266.0425)	
Jan/25/94	0.42942	0.56253	0.99195	0.1222	0.8393	0.9616
	(37.31836)	(69.63233)		(27.1364)	(209.7340)	
Jan/26/94	0.14975	0.72163	0.87138	0.1611	0.6434	0.8045
	(7.07011)	(44.24845)		(6.7358)	(37.7690)	
Jan/27/94	0.05535	−0.04139	0.01396	0.1889	0.5634	0.7523
	(0.99949)	(−0.52909)		(6.6651)	(32.6528)	
Jan/28/94	0.15494	0.77262	0.92756	0.2110	0.1839	0.3949
	(3.81609)	(10.94175)		(3.1765)	(5.1117)	
Jan/31/94	0.03917	0.32467	0.36384	0.0673	−0.7187	−0.6514
	(0.75202)	(5.13231)		(2.5352)	(−6.6678)	

[†]GARCH(1,1) model: $\sigma_t^2 = a_0 + \widehat{\alpha}\varepsilon_{t-1}^2 + \widehat{\beta}\sigma_{t-1}^2$
[‡]Numbers in the parentheses are *t*-values

CONCLUSION

This chapter has had three objectives. They were (1) to compare different proxies for informational variables in high frequency equity data; (2) to model dynamic processes using doubly stochastic Poisson models; (3) to investigate intra-day volatility persistence. We find that the number of trades and the number of price changes seem to be the best choices for informational variables, volume being decidedly inferior. Secondly, we find that our model does seem to be estimable without undue difficulty and finally we find that persistence in volatility is much reduced when our model is used rather than GARCH(1,1). The use of informational variables seems to substantially eliminate much of the persistence. Since persistence in volatility is a stylized fact that seems somewhat flawed in terms of theoretical explanations, the results lead toward better modelling and understanding of intra-day volatility.

APPENDIX 1: LM TESTS

Our equation can be written as:

$$X(t) = \mu + \mu_Q \Delta N(t) + \varepsilon(t) \tag{1.1}$$

where $\varepsilon(t)$, conditional on $N(t)$, is $N(0, \sigma^2 + \sigma_Q^2 \Delta N(t))$. Let Y be a $(T \times 2)$ matrix $Y' = \begin{bmatrix} 1, & 1, & \cdots, & 1 \\ \Delta N_1, & \Delta N_2, & \cdots, & \Delta N_T \end{bmatrix}$, $\gamma' = [\mu, \mu_Q]$, $\beta' = [\sigma^2, \sigma_Q^2]$. Then the likelihood function L can be written as:

$$L = L(\gamma, \beta) = -\frac{1}{2}\sum \ln h_t - \frac{1}{2}\sum e_t^2/h_t \tag{1.2}$$

where $h_t = \beta' Y'_t$, Y_t is the t-th row of Y, $e_t = X_t - Y_{t\gamma}$, and the constant term is omitted. It follows that the first derivatives of the log-likelihood function are:

$$\frac{\partial L}{\partial \gamma} = \sum \frac{e_t Y_t}{h_t}$$

$$\frac{\partial L}{\partial \beta} = -\frac{1}{2}\sum \frac{Y_t}{h_t} + \frac{1}{2}\sum \frac{e_t^2 Y_t}{h_t^2} \tag{1.3}$$

The second derivatives follow immediately:

$$\frac{\partial^2 L}{\partial \gamma \partial \gamma'} = \sum \frac{Y'_t Y_t}{h_t}$$

$$\frac{\partial^2 L}{\partial \beta \partial \beta'} = \frac{1}{2}\sum \frac{Y'_t Y_t}{h_t^2} - \sum \frac{e_t^2 Y'_t Y_t}{h_t^3} \tag{1.4}$$

$$\frac{\partial^2 L}{\partial \gamma \partial \beta'} = -\sum \frac{e_t Y'_t Y_t}{h_t^2}$$

Given the above information, the Fisher's information matrix can be constructed as:

$$-\frac{\partial^2 L}{\partial\theta\partial\theta'} = \begin{bmatrix} \sum \frac{Y_t'Y_t}{h_t} & \sum \frac{e_t Y_t' Y_t}{h_t^2} \\ \sum \frac{e_t Y_t' Y_t}{h_t^2} & \sum \frac{e_t Y_t' Y_t}{h_t^3} - \frac{1}{2} \sum \frac{Y_t' Y_t}{h_t^2} \end{bmatrix} \qquad 1.5$$

We now calculate $\phi_{H_j} = E_{H_j}\left(-\frac{\partial^2 L}{\partial\theta\partial\theta'}\right), j = 1, 2, 3$ where $\theta' = [\gamma', \beta']$, that is,

$$\phi_{H_1} = \begin{bmatrix} \sum \frac{Y_t'Y_t}{h_t} & 0 \\ 0 & \frac{1}{2}\sum \frac{Y_t'Y_t}{h_t^2} \end{bmatrix}$$

$$\phi_{H_2} = \begin{bmatrix} \frac{1}{\sigma^2}(Y'Y) & 0 \\ 0 & \frac{1}{2\sigma^1}(Y'Y) \end{bmatrix} = \begin{bmatrix} \frac{1}{\sigma^2} & 0 \\ 0 & \frac{1}{2\sigma^4} \end{bmatrix} \otimes (Y'Y) \qquad 1.6$$

$$\phi_{H_3} = \phi_{H_2}$$

The score test for the hypothesis H_j, $j = 1, 2, 3$, is of the form $D'_{H_j}\phi_{H_j}^{-1}D_{H_j}$ which will be asymptotically distributed as $\chi^2(1)$ for $j = 1, 2$ and $\chi^2(2)$ for $j = 3$. In turn, from Equation 1.3:

$$D_{H_1} = \begin{bmatrix} 0 \\ \sum \frac{(x_t - \hat{u})\Delta N_t}{\hat{h}_t} \\ 0 \\ 0 \end{bmatrix} \qquad 1.7$$

where $\hat{h}_t$ is equal to $\hat{\beta}'Y_t$ (evaluated under H_0).

$$D_{H_2} = \begin{bmatrix} 0 \\ 0 \\ 0 \\ \frac{1}{2\hat{\sigma}^4}\sum(\hat{e}_t^2 - \hat{\sigma}^2)\Delta N_t \end{bmatrix} \qquad 1.8$$

where $\hat{e}_t = X_t - \hat{\mu} - \hat{\mu}_0\Delta N_t$ and $\hat{\sigma}^2 = \Sigma\hat{e}^2/T$, and

$$D_{H_3} = \begin{bmatrix} 0 \\ \frac{1}{\tilde{\sigma}^2}\sum\tilde{e}_t^2\Delta N_t \\ 0 \\ \frac{1}{2\tilde{\sigma}^4}\sum(\tilde{e}_t^2 - \tilde{\sigma}^2)\Delta N_t \end{bmatrix} \qquad 1.9$$

where $\tilde{e}_t = X_t - \hat{\mu}$ and $\hat{\sigma}^2 = \Sigma \tilde{e}_t^2 / T$.

We can compute $LM_j = D'_{H_j} \phi_{H_j}^{-1} D_{H_j}$ for $j = 1, 2, 3$ explicitly as follows:

$$LM_1 = \left(\sum \frac{(x_t - \hat{\mu}) \Delta N_t}{\hat{h}_t} \right)^2 \left(\sum \frac{\Delta N_t^2}{\hat{h}_t} - \left(\sum \frac{\Delta N_t}{\hat{h}_t} \right)^2 \left(\sum \frac{1}{\hat{h}_t} \right)^{-1} \right)^{-1}$$

where $\hat{h}_t = \hat{\sigma}^2 + \hat{\sigma}_Q^2 \Delta N_t$

$$LM_2 = LM_2(\hat{e}_t) = \frac{\left(\sum (\hat{e}_t^2 - \hat{\sigma}^2) \Delta N_t \right)^2}{2 \hat{\sigma}^4 \sum (\Delta N_t - \Delta \overline{N})^2} \quad \text{where } \hat{e}_t = x_t - \hat{\mu} - \hat{\mu}_Q \Delta N_t$$

$$LM_3 = LM_2(\tilde{e}_t) + \frac{1 \left(\sum \tilde{e}_t \Delta N_t \right)^2}{\hat{\sigma}^2 \sum \left(\Delta N_t - \Delta \overline{N} \right)^2} \quad \text{where } \tilde{e}_t = x_t - \hat{\mu}$$

1.10

APPENDIX 2: MOMENT GENERATING FUNCTION AND MOMENTS OF $\Delta N(t)$

$$\Delta N(t) | \lambda(t) \sim \text{Poisson } (\lambda(t))$$

2.1

$$E[\exp(s \cdot \Delta N(t)) | \lambda(t)] = \textit{mgf of a Poisson Process}$$

A Poisson distributed random variable x with density function $f(x)$

$$f(x) = \frac{\lambda^x e^{-\lambda}}{x!}, x = 0, 1, 2, \dots$$

2.2

has the following moment generating function:

$$E[e^{sx}] = e^{-\lambda} \sum_{x=0}^{\infty} \frac{(\lambda e^s)^x}{x!}$$

$$= e^{-\lambda} \exp(\lambda e^s)$$

2.3

$$= \exp(-\lambda(1 - e^s))$$

$$= \exp(\lambda(e^s - 1))$$

Therefore, $E[\exp(s \cdot \Delta N(t)) | \lambda(t)] = \exp(\lambda(t)(e^s - 1))$.

Now,

$$\lambda(t) = \frac{\beta \sigma^2}{1 - \theta} + \alpha \sum_{j=0}^{\infty} \theta^j v_{(t-j-1)}^2$$

2.4

which implies

$$E[\exp(q\lambda(t))] = \exp\left(q\frac{\beta\sigma^2}{1-\theta}\right) E\left[\exp\left(q\alpha\sum_{j=0}^{\infty}\theta^j v_{(t-j-1)}^2\right)\right] \qquad 2.5$$

Since $v_{(t-j-1)}^2 \sim \text{i.i.d. } \chi^2(1)$,

$$E\left[\exp\left(q\alpha\sum_{j=0}^{\infty}\theta^j v_{(t-j-1)}^2\right)\right] = \prod_{t=1}^{\infty} E[\exp(q\alpha\theta^j\chi^2(1))]$$

$$= \prod_{t=1}^{\infty}(1 - 2q\alpha\theta^j)^{-1/2} \qquad 2.6$$

Thus,

$$E[\exp(s \cdot \Delta N(t))] = E[\exp(\lambda(t)(e^s - 1))]$$

$$= \exp\left(\frac{\beta\sigma^2}{1-\theta}(e^s - 1)\right) \cdot \prod_{t=1}^{\infty}[1 - 2\alpha\theta^j(e^s - 1)]^{-1/2} \qquad 2.7$$

Based on this moment generating function, we can derive associated moments of $\Delta N(t)$ as the following:

$$E[\Delta N(t)|\lambda(t)] = \lambda(t)$$

$$E(\Delta N(t)) = E[\lambda(t)]$$

$$\text{Var}(\Delta N(t)) = E[\text{Var}(\Delta N(t)|\lambda(t))] + \text{Var}[E(\Delta N(t)|\lambda(t))] \qquad 2.8$$

$$= E[\lambda(t)] + \text{Var}[\lambda(t)]$$

where

$$E[\lambda(t)] = \frac{\beta\sigma^2 + \alpha}{1-\theta} \qquad 2.9$$

Define

$$M(q) = \ln E[\exp(q\lambda(t))]$$

$$= q\left(\frac{\beta\sigma^2}{1-\theta}\right) - \frac{1}{2}\sum\ln(1 - 2q\alpha\theta^j) \qquad 2.10$$

$$\frac{\partial M(q)}{\partial q} = \frac{\beta\sigma^2}{1-\theta} - \frac{1}{2}\sum_{j=0}^{\infty}\frac{-2\alpha\theta^j}{(1 - 2q\alpha\theta^j)} \qquad 2.11$$

It follows that

$$\text{Var}[\lambda(t)] = \frac{\partial}{\partial q} \left[\alpha \sum \frac{\theta^j}{(1 - 2q\alpha\theta^j)} \right]_{q=0}$$

$$= \alpha \sum \theta^j (-1)(1 - 2q\alpha\theta^j)^{-2}(-2\alpha\theta^j)|_{q=0} \qquad 2.12$$

$$= \frac{2\alpha^2}{1 - \theta^2}$$

Therefore,

$$E[\Delta N(t)] = \frac{\beta\sigma^2 + \alpha}{1 - \theta}$$

$$\qquad 2.13$$

$$\text{Var}[\Delta N(t)] = \frac{\beta\sigma^2 + \alpha}{1 - \theta} + \frac{2\alpha^2}{1 - \theta^2}$$

APPENDIX 3: MOMENT CONDITIONS OF $\Delta N(t)$, AND $X(t)$

From our model,

$$\text{Cov}(\Delta N(t), \Delta N(t-1))$$

$$= E_{I(t-1)}[\text{Cov}(\Delta N(t)|I(t-1)), \text{Cov}(\Delta N(t-1)|I(t-1))]$$

$$+ \text{Cov}_{I(t-1)}(E[\Delta N(t)|I(t-1)], E[\Delta N(t-1)|I(t-1)])$$

$$= \text{Cov}_{I(t-1)} \left(\alpha v^2(t-1) + \beta\sigma^2 + \theta\lambda(t-1), \lambda(t-1) \right)$$

$$= \theta\,\text{Cov}_{I(t-1)}(\lambda(t-1), \lambda(t-1)) = \theta\,\text{Var}_{I(t-1)}(\lambda(t-1))$$

$$= \frac{2\theta\alpha^2}{1 - \theta^2} \qquad 3.1$$

Then we derive the following recursively,

$$\text{Cov}(N(t), N(t-s)) = \frac{2\theta^s\alpha^2}{1 - \theta^2} \qquad 3.2$$

Finally, it follows that

$$\text{Corr}(N(t), N(t-s)) = \frac{\text{Cov}(N(t), N(t-s))}{\text{Var}(N(t))}$$

$$= \begin{cases} \dfrac{2\alpha^2\theta^s}{2\alpha^2 + (\beta\sigma^2 + \alpha)(1 + \theta)}, & \text{if } s = 1, 2, \ldots \\ 1, & \text{if } s = 0 \end{cases} \qquad 3.3$$

For the moments of $X(t)$,

$$X(t) = \mu + \sigma(z(t) - z(t-1)) + \sum_{i=1}^{\Delta N(t)} Q_i \qquad 3.4$$

it follows that

$$E[X(t)] = \mu + \mu_Q E[\lambda(t)] = \mu + \frac{\mu_Q(\beta\sigma^2 + \alpha)}{1 - \theta}$$

$$\text{Var}[X(t)] = \sigma^2 + (\mu_Q^2 + \sigma_Q^2)\frac{\beta\sigma^2 + \alpha}{1 - \theta} + \frac{2\alpha^2\mu_Q^2}{1 - \theta^2}$$

$$3.5$$

The correlation between $X(t)$ and $X(t-s)$ can be recursively derived by using $\text{Cov}(X(t), X(t-1))$. It is straightforward to show that

$$\text{Cov}(X(t), X(t-1))$$

$$= \text{Cov}\left(\sigma v(t) + \sum_{i=1}^{\Delta N(t)} Q_i, \sigma v(t-1) + \sum_{i=1}^{\Delta N(t-1)} Q_i\right) \qquad 3.6$$

$$= \sigma\,\text{Cov}\left(\sum_{i=1}^{\Delta N(t)} Q_i, v(t-1)\right) + \text{Cov}\left(\sum_{i=1}^{\Delta N(t)} Q_i, \sum_{i=1}^{\Delta N(t-1)} Q_i\right)$$

$$= E_{I(t-1)}\left[\text{Cov}\left(\sum_{i=1}^{\Delta N(t)} Q_i | I(t-1), \sum_{i=1}^{\Delta N(t-1)} Q_i | I(t-1)\right)\right]$$

$$+ \text{Cov}_{I(t-1)}\left(E\left[\sum_{i=1}^{\Delta N(t)} Q_i | I(t-1)\right], E\left[\sum_{i=1}^{\Delta N(t-1)} Q_i | I(t-1)\right]\right)$$

$$= \mu_Q^2\,\text{Cov}_{I(t-1)}(\Delta N(t), \Delta N(t-1)) = \mu_Q^2\,\text{Cov}(\lambda(t), \lambda(t-1))$$

$$= \mu_Q^2\frac{2\alpha^2\theta}{1 - \theta^2}$$

Then we derive the following recursively,

$$\text{Cov}(X(t), X(t-s)) = \frac{2\mu_Q^2\alpha^2\theta^s}{1 - \theta^2} \qquad 3.7$$

Finally, it follows that

$$\text{Corr}(X(t), X(t-s)) = \frac{\text{Cov}(X(t), X(t-s))}{\text{Var}(X(t))} \qquad\qquad 3.8$$

$$= \begin{cases} \dfrac{2\alpha^2 \mu_Q^2 \theta^s}{\sigma^2(1-\theta^2) + (\mu_Q^2 + \sigma_Q^2)(1+\theta)(\beta\sigma^2 + \alpha) + 2\alpha^2\mu_Q^2}, & \text{if } s = 1, 2, \dots \\ 1, & \text{if } s = 0 \end{cases}$$

NOTES

1. See also Karpoff (1987) for a survey of previous studies on the price-trading volume relationship.
2. This is probably due to the availability of data. As pointed out by Jones, Kaul and Lipson (1994), although trading volume for the NASDAQ securities have been available for many years, historical data on the number of transactions were not available until recent years.
3. To avoid getting negative variance estimates, we use NLS to obtain $\hat{\sigma}$, and $\hat{\sigma}_Q$. $\hat{\sigma}^2$, and $\hat{\sigma}_Q^2$ are then derived by δ-method.
4. A GARCH-type model would involve interpreting $v^2(t-1)$ as $\text{Var}(X(t-1)|I(t-2)) \times \Delta z^2(t)$ for $z(t) \sim$ i.i.d. $N(0,1)$. This complicates the model without adding to its explanatory power. We shall refer to this as GARCH-type effects, although the model in Equation 9 is closer to a stochastic volatility model.
5. We have assumed that $\Delta N(t)$ is stationary, an alternative expression can be calculated if we start from a fixed starting point.

BIBLIOGRAPHY

Andersen, T.G. (1996), "Return Volatility and Trading Volume: An Information Flow Interpretation of Stochastic Volatility", *Journal of Finance*, 51, 169–204.

Andersen, T.G. and Bollerslev, T. (1997), "Intraday Periodicity and Volatility Persistence in Financial Markets", *Journal of Empirical Finance*, 4, 115–158.

Bachelier, L. (1900), *Theorie de la Speculation*, Paris: Gauthier-Villars.

Bollerslev, T. and Domowitz, I. (1993), "Trading Patterns and Prices in the Interbank Foreign Exchange Market", *Journal of Finance*, 48, 1421–1443.

Breusch, T. and Pagan, A. (1980), "The Lagrange Multiplier Test and its Applications to Model Specification in Economics", *Review of Economic Studies*, 47, 239–253.

Brock, W., Dechert, W. and Sheinkman, J. (1986), "A Test for Independence Based on the Correlation Dimension", mimeo, University of Wisconsin, Madison.

Clark, P. (1973), "A Subordinated Stochastic Process Model With Finite Variance for Speculative Prices", *Econometrica*, 41, 135–155.

Engle, R.F. and Russell, J.R. (1994), "Forecasting Transaction Rates: The Autoregressive Conditional Duration Model", UCSD 94–27.

Engle, R.F. (1996), "The Econometrics of Ultra-High Frequency Data", NBER 5816.

Gallant, A., Rossi, P. and Tauchen, G. (1992), "Stock Prices and Volume", *Review of Financial Studies*, 5, 198–242.

Geman, H. and Ané, T. (1996), "Stochastic Subordination", *Risk*, 9, 145–149.

Goodhart, C.A. and Figliuoli, E. (1991), "Every Minute Counts in Financial Markets", *Journal of International Money and Finance*, 10, 23–52.

Goodhart, C.A.E. and O'Hara, M. (1997), "High Frequency Data in Financial Markets: Issues and Applications", *Journal of Empirical Finance*, 4, 73–114.

Gourieroux, C., Holly, A. and Monfort, A. (1982), "Likelihood Ratio Test, Wald Test, and Kuhn-Tucker Test in Linear with Inequality Constraints on the Regression Parameters", *Econometrica*, 50, 63–80.

Gourieroux, C., Jasiak, J. and LeFol, G. (1996), "Intra-day Market Activity", INSEE, No. 9633.

Harris, L. (1987), "Transaction Data Tests of the Mixture of Distributions Hypothesis", *Journal of Financial and Quantitative Analysis*, 22, 127–141.

Jones, C., Kaul, G. and Lipson, M. (1994), "Transactions, Volume and Volatility", *Review of Financial Studies*, 7, 631–651.

Judge, G., Hill, C., Griffiths, W., Lutkepohl, H. and Lee, T-C (1985), *The Theory of Econometrics*, John Wiley & Sons.

Karpoff, J. (1987), "The Relation Between Price Changes and Trading Volume: A Survey", *Journal of Financial and Quantitative Analysis*, 22, 109–126.

Lamoureux, C. and Lastrapes, W. (1990), "Heteroskedasticity in Stock Return Data: Volume versus GARCH Effects", *Journal of Finance*, 45, 7–38.

Lamoureux, C. and Lastrapes, W. (1994), "Endogenous Trading Volume and Momentum in Stock-Return Volatility", *Journal of Business and Economic Statistics*, 12, 253–260.

Locke, P.R. and Sayers, C.L. (1993), "Intra-day Futures Price Volatility: Information Effects and Variance Persistence", *Journal of Applied Econometrics*, 8, 15–30.

Madan, D. and Chang, E. (1997), "The Variance Gamma Option Pricing Model", mimeo.

Marsh, T. and Rock, K. (1986), "The Transactional Process and Rational Stock Price Dynamics", University of California at Berkeley.

Oldfield, G., Rogalski, R. and Jarrow, R. (1977), "An Autoregressive Jump Process for Common Stock Returns", *Journal of Financial Economics*, 5, 389–418.

Osborne, M. (1959), "Browning Motion and the Stock Market", *Operations Research*, 7, 145–173.

Rogers, A. (1986), "Modified Lagrange Multiplier Tests for Problems with One-Sided Alternatives", *Journal of Econometrics*, 31, 341–361.

Smaby, T. (1995), "An Examination of the Intraday Behavior of the Yen/Dollar Exchange Rate: The Relationship between Trading Activity and Returns Volatility", *Journal of Economics and Finance*, 19, 39–50.

Takezawa, N. (1995), "Note on Intraday Foreign Exchange Volatility and the Informational Role of Quote Arrivals", *Economics Letters*, 48, 399–404.

Zhou, B. (1996), "High-Frequency Data and Volatility in Foreign-Exchange Rates", *Journal of Business and Economic Statistics*, 14 (1), 45–52.

Chapter **3**

The Incremental Volatility Information in One Million Foreign Exchange Quotations

Stephen J. Taylor and Xinzhong Xu

Department of Accounting and Finance, Lancaster University, Monetary Markets and Instruments Division, Bank of England

INTRODUCTION

The volatility of a spot exchange rate S can be defined for many price models by the annualised standard deviation of the change in the logarithm of S during some time interval. For a diffusion process defined by $d(\ln S) = \mu dt + \Psi(t)dW$, with $\Psi(t)$ a deterministic function of time and $W(t)$ a standard Wiener process, the deterministic volatility $\sigma(0, T)$ from time 0 until time T is defined by

$$\sigma^2 = \frac{1}{T}\,\text{var}(\ln S(T) - \ln S(0))$$

Options traders make predictions of volatility for several values of T. These forecast horizons typically vary between a fortnight and a year and are defined by the times until expiration of the options traded. Insights into these predictions can be obtained by inverting an option pricing formula to produce implied volatility numbers for various values of T. Xu and Taylor (1994) show that these volatility expectations vary significantly for exchange rates, both across expiry times T and through time.

Options markets are often considered to be markets for trading volatility. It then follows that implied volatilities are likely to be good predictors of subsequent observed volatility if the options market is efficient. As options traders have more information than the historic record of asset prices it may also be expected that implied volatilities are better predictors than forecasts calculated from recent prices using ARCH models.

Day and Lewis (1992) investigate the information content of implied volatilities, calculated from call options on the S&P 100 index, within an

Printed with permission from *Journal of Empirical Finance*, 4, pp 317–340.

ARCH framework. They conclude that recent stock index levels contain incremental volatility information beyond that revealed by options prices. Lamoureux and Lastrapes (1993) report a similar conclusion for individual US stocks. Xu and Taylor (1995), however, use daily data to conclude that exchange rates do not contain incremental volatility information: implied volatility predictions cannot be improved by mixing them with conditional variances calculated from recent exchange rates alone. Jorion (1995) also finds that daily currency implieds are good predictors.

The superior efficiency of currency implieds relative to implieds calculated from spot equity indices has at least two credible explanations. First, there is the theoretical argument of Canina and Figlewski (1993) that efficiency will be enhanced when fast low-cost arbitrage trading is possible. S&P 100 index arbitrage, unlike forex arbitrage, is expensive because many stocks must be traded. Second, as Jorion (1995) observes, index option implieds can suffer from substantial measurement error because of the presence of some stale quotes in the index.

This paper extends the study of Xu and Taylor (1995), hereafter XT, by using high-frequency exchange rates to extract more volatility information from the historical record of exchange rates. From probability theory it is known that it may be possible to substantially improve volatility estimates by using very frequent observations. Nelson (1992) shows that it is theoretically possible for volatility estimates to be made as accurate as required for many diffusion models by using ARCH estimates and sufficiently frequent price measurements. As trading is not continuous and bid/ask spreads exist, there are, of course, limits to the benefits obtainable from high-frequency data.

The definition of implied volatility and the low-frequency results of XT are reviewed on pp 67 and 68. Our estimates of Deutschemark/dollar volatility obtained from the high-frequency dataset of Olsen & Associates are described on p 70. The results from estimating ARCH models when the conditional variance is a function of implied volatilities and/or high-frequency volatility estimates are presented on p 75. Further evidence about the incremental information content of options prices and the O&A quotations database is provided by evaluating the accuracy of volatility forecasts, see p 86. Our conclusions are summarised on p 89.

IMPLIED VOLATILITY

The implied volatilities used in this paper are calculated from the prices of nearest-the-money options on spot currency. These options are traded at the Philadelphia stock exchange (PHLX). Standard option pricing formulae assume the spot rate follows a geometric Brownian motion process. The appropriate European pricing formula for the price c of a call option is then a well-known function of the present spot rate S, the time until expiration T, the exercise price X, the domestic and foreign interest rates, respectively r and q and the volatility σ (see for example Hull, 1995). The Philadelphia options can be exercised early and consequently the accurate approximate formula of Barone-Adesi and Whaley (1987) is used to define the price C of an American call option. This price can be written as

$$C = \begin{cases} c + e, & S < S^*, \\ S - X, & S \geq S^*, \end{cases}$$

with e the early exercise premium and S^* the critical spot rate above which the option should be exercised immediately. The implied volatility is the number σ_I that equates an observed market price C_M with the theoretical price C:

$$C_M = C(S, T, X, r, q, \sigma_I).$$

There will be a unique solution to this equation when $C_M > S - X$. As $\partial C / \partial \sigma > 0$ when $S < S^*(\sigma)$, the solution can be found very quickly by an interval subdivision algorithm. Similar methods apply to put options. A typical matrix of currency implied volatilities calculated for various combinations of time-to-expiry T and exercise price X will display term structure effects as T varies for a fixed X near to the present spot price. These effects have been modelled by assuming mean reversion in implied volatilities (Xu and Taylor, 1994). Matrices of implieds also display smile effects as X varies for fixed T (Taylor and Xu, 1994).

Traders know that volatility is stochastic, nevertheless they make frequent use of implied estimates obtained from pricing models that assume a constant volatility. The implied volatility can be interpreted as a volatility forecast if we follow the analysis of Hull and White (1987) and make three assumptions: first that the price $S(t)$ and the stochastic volatility $\sigma(t)$ follow diffusion processes, second that volatility risk is not priced and third that spot price and volatility differentials are uncorrelated. The first and second assumptions are pragmatic and the third is consistent with the empirical estimates reported by XT. With these assumptions, let $\overline{V}_T$ be the average variance $(1/T) \int_0^T \sigma^2(t) dt$. Also, let $c(\sigma^2)$ represent the Black–Scholes, European valuation function for a constant level of volatility, σ. Then Hull and White (1987) show the fair European call price is the expectation $E[c(\overline{V}_T)]$, which is approximately $c(E[\overline{V}_T])$ when X is near S. Thus the theory can support a belief that the implied volatility for time-to-expiry T is approximately the square root of $E[\overline{V}_T]$. Traders might obtain efficient prices if they forecast the average variance and then insert its square root into a pricing formula that assumes constant volatility.

LOW-FREQUENCY RESULTS

The evidence for incremental volatility information can be assessed by making comparisons between the maximum likelihoods attained by different volatility models. An ARCH model for returns R_t based upon information sets Ω_t will specify a set of conditional variances h_t and hence conditional distributions $R_t|\Omega_{t-1}$, from which the likelihood of observed returns can be calculated. We consider information sets I_t, J_t and K_t respectively defined by (a) all returns up to time t, (b) implied volatilities up to time t and (c) the union of these two sets. We say that an information source has incremental information if it increases the log-likelihood of observed returns by a statistically significant amount.

The following maximum log-likelihoods are reported by Xu and Taylor (1995, Table 3) for a model defined below, for five years (1985–1989) of daily DM/$ returns from futures contracts:

$$I_t \qquad\qquad 4327.31$$

$$J_t \qquad\qquad 4349.64$$

$$K_t = I_t + J_t \quad 4349.65$$

Source J_t has incremental information because its addition to I_t adds 22 to the log-likelihood with only one extra parameter included in the ARCH model. This is significant at very low levels. Source I_t, however, does not contain incremental information because its addition to J_t only adds 0.01 to the log-likelihood. Thus, in this low-frequency example, there is only incremental information in options prices.

The models estimated in XT use daily conditional variances h_t that reflect higher levels of volatility for Monday and holiday returns. These seasonal effects are modelled by multiplicative seasonal parameters, respectively denoted by M and H. The quantity h_t^* represents the conditional variance with seasonality removed: it is defined by

$$h_t^* = \begin{cases} h_t & \text{if period } t \text{ ends 24 hours after period } t-1, \\ h_t/M & \text{if } t \text{ falls on a Monday and } t-1 \text{ on a Friday,} \\ h_t/H & \text{if a holiday occurs between the two prices.} \end{cases} \qquad 1$$

A general specification for h_t^* that incorporates information at time $t-1$ about daily returns R_{t-1}, implied volatilities i_{t-1} and their lagged values is given by

$$h_t^* = c + aR_{t-1}^2(h_{t-1}^*/h_{t-1}) + bh_{t-1}^* + di_{t-1}^2/(196 + 48M + 8H). \qquad 2$$

The quantity i_{t-1} here denotes the implied volatility for the nearest-the-money call option, for the shortest maturity with more than nine calendar days to expiration. Although i_{t-1} is an expectation for a period of at least ten days it is used as a proxy for the market's expectation for the single trading period t. The standard deviation measure i_{t-1} is an annualised quantity. It is converted to a variance for a 24-hour return in the above equation by assuming there are 48 Mondays, 8 holidays and 196 normal weekdays in a year.

An appropriate conditional distribution for daily returns from DM/\$ futures is the generalised error distribution (GED) that has a single shape parameter, called the thickness parameter v. The parameter vector for the general specification is then $\theta = (a, b, c, d, M, H, v)$. All conditional means are supposed to be zero.

The maximum likelihood for information sets I_t is obtained by assuming $d = 0$ followed by maximisation of the log-likelihood over the remaining parameters. This gives:

$$h_t = \mathrm{var}(R_t|I_{t-1}),$$

$$h_t^* = 2.5 \times 10^{-6} + 0.07R_{t-1}^2(h_{t-1}^*/h_{t-1}) + 0.88h_{t-1}^*, \qquad 3$$

$$v = 1.25, \quad M = 1.16, \quad H = 1.50.$$

The estimate of v has a standard error less than 0.1 and therefore fat-tailed conditional distributions describe returns more accurately than conditional normal distributions ($v = 2$), as has been shown in many other studies of daily exchange rates. The estimates of M and H are more than one but their standard errors, respectively 0.12 and 0.33, are substantial.

The maximum likelihood for options information J_t is obtained when a and b are constrained to be zero and all the other parameters are unconstrained. MLE then gives $c = 0$ and:

$$h_t = \mathrm{var}(R_t|J_{t-1}), \quad h_t^* = 0.97i_{t-1}^2/(196 + 48M + 8H), \quad v = 1.33. \qquad 4$$

The incremental importance of previous returns and options information is assessed by estimating the general specification without parameter constraints. The MLE estimates of a and c are zero, with b estimated as 0.04 (*t*-ratio 1.43) and d as 0.93 (*t*-ratio 3.11). Any conventional statistical tests accept the null hypotheses $a = 0$, $b = 0$, $c = 0$ and $d = 1$. They also reject $d = 0$ at very low significance levels.

XT conclude that all the relevant information for defining the next period's conditional variance is contained in the most recent implied volatility. This conclusion holds despite using a volatility expectation for at least a ten-day period as a proxy for the options market's expectation for the next trading period. XT also present results for volatility expectations for the next day calculated from a term structure model for implieds studied in Xu and Taylor (1994). These expectations are extrapolations ($T = 1$ day) from several implieds ($T \geq 10$ days). Such extrapolations provide both the same conclusions as short-maturity implieds and very similar maximum levels of the log-likelihood function. However, these extrapolations are biased.

Out-of-sample forecasts of realised volatility during four-week periods in 1990 and 1991 confirm the superiority of the options predictions compared with standard ARCH predictions based upon previous returns alone.

VOLATILITY ESTIMATES AND EXPECTATIONS

Intra-Day Data

Estimates of Deutschemark/dollar volatility have been obtained from the dataset of spot DM/$ quotations collected and distributed by Olsen & Associates. The dataset contains more than 1,400,000 quotations on the interbank Reuters network between Thursday 1 October 1992 and Thursday 30 September 1993 inclusive. It is our understanding that the dataset is an almost complete record of spot DM/$ quotations shown on Reuters FXFX page. The quotations are time stamped using GMT. We converted all times to US eastern time which required different clock adjustments for winter and summer.

Volatility estimates have been calculated for 24-hour weekday periods for comparison with daily observations of implied volatilities. The options market at the Philadelphia stock exchange closes at 14.30 US eastern time, which is 19.30 GMT in the winter and 18.30 GMT in the summer. A 24-hour estimate for a winter Tuesday is calculated from quotations made between 19.30 GMT on Monday until 19.30 GMT on Tuesday. We follow Andersen and Bollerslev (1997) and ignore the 48 hours from 21.00 GMT on Friday until 21.00 GMT on Sunday, because less than 0.1 percent of the quotations are made in this weekend period. Thus a 24-hour estimate for a winter Monday uses quotations from 19.30 to 21.00 GMT on the previous Friday and from 21.00 GMT on Sunday until 19.30 GMT on Monday.

Definition and Motivation of the Estimates

The realised volatility for day t is calculated from intra-day returns $R_{t,i}$ with i counting short periods during day t, in the following way:

$$v_t = \sqrt{m \sum_{i=1}^{n} R_{t,i}^2}. \qquad\qquad 5$$

Here m is a multiplicative constant that converts the variance for one trading day into an annual variance and v_t is an annualised measure of realised volatility. The number of short periods in one trading day is chosen to be $n = 288$ corresponding to five-minute returns.

We follow the methods of Andersen and Bollerslev (1997), hereafter AB, when five-minute returns are calculated. Their methods use averages of bid and ask quotations to define rates. They define the rate at any required time by a linear interpolation formula that uses two quotations that immediately precede and follow the required time. As in AB, suspect quotations are filtered out using the methods of Dacorogna *et al.* (1993). AB note that there is very little autocorrelation in the five-minute returns: the first-lag coefficient is −0.04. Negative dependence has previously been documented by Goodhart and Figliuoli (1991).

Some motivation for the above method of volatility estimation is provided by supposing that spot exchange rates $S(\tau)$ develop in calendar time τ according to a diffusion process described by

$$d(\ln S(\tau)) = \mu d\tau + s(\tau)\sigma(\tau)dW(\tau) \qquad\qquad 6$$

with $\sigma(\tau)$ an annualised stochastic quantity and $s(\tau)$ a deterministic quantity that reflects the strong intra-day seasonal pattern in volatility. This pattern has been investigated in detail by AB and has been described in earlier studies that include Bollerslev and Domowitz (1993) and Dacorogna *et al.* (1993). The square of the seasonal multiplier $s(\tau)$ averages one over a complete seasonal cycle, so if τ_1 and τ_2 denote the identical position in the cycle then $s(\tau_1) = s(\tau_2)$ and $\int_{\tau_1}^{\tau_2} s^2(\tau)d\tau = \tau_2 - \tau_1$.

When the volatility is constant during a one-day cycle, of length Δ years, and the multipliers are constants s_i during intra-day intervals, then

$$\sum_{i=1}^{n} \text{var}(R_{t,i}|\sigma(\tau)) = \Delta \frac{1}{n} \sum_{i=1}^{n} s_i^2 \sigma^2(\tau) = \Delta \sigma^2(\tau), \qquad\qquad 7$$

with τ the calendar time associated with trading period t. The quantity v_t^2 is the estimate of $\sigma^2(\tau)$ obtained by setting $m = 1/\Delta$ and using $R_{t,i}^2$ to estimate the above conditional variance of $R_{t,i}$. We set $m = 260$ which is appropriate when it can be assumed that there is no volatility during the weekend and a year contains exactly 52 weeks.

The estimate v_t will not be the optimal estimate of $\sigma(\tau)$ when volatility is constant within cycles. However, the estimate is consistent ($v_t \to \sigma(\tau)$ as $n \to \infty$) and it does not require estimation of intra-day seasonal volatility terms.

The Estimates from Intra-Day Quotations

Figure 1 is a time-series plot of the volatility estimates v_t for the 253 days that the PHLX was open between October 1, 1992 and September 30, 1993 inclusive. The average of these estimates is 12.5 percent and their standard deviation is 3.6 percent. Further descriptive statistics are presented in Table 1. The estimates have also been calculated for U.S. holidays and are smaller numbers as should be expected. The two extreme holiday estimates are 2.5 percent on Christmas Day and 1.9 percent on New Year's Day; the other six holiday estimates range from 6.7 to 10.5 percent.

The estimates are higher in October 1992 than in any other month, with the two highest estimates, 32 and 26 percent, respectively, calculated for Friday 2nd and Monday 5th October. The October average is 19.3 percent compared with 14.4 percent for November and 11.7 percent for the other ten months. The difference may be associated with events that followed the departure of Sterling from the EMS in September 1992.

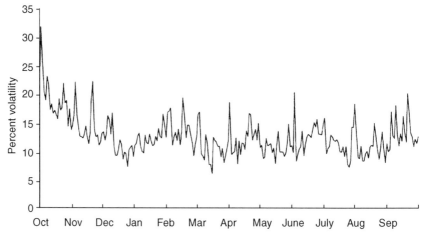

Figure 1   Volatility estimates from intra-day quotations.

Table 1 Summary statistics for volatility estimates v calculated from intra-day price quotations and implied volatilities i calculated from options prices.

	Intra-day estimates v		Implied volatilities i	
	Oct./Sept.	*Dec./Sept.*	*Oct./Sept.*	*Dec./Sept.*
Sample size	253	211	253	211
Mean	12.53	11.66	13.57	12.64
Standard deviation	3.57	2.61	2.68	1.27
Minimum	5.83	5.83	9.71	9.71
Lower quartile	10.30	9.76	11.92	11.81
Median	11.86	11.26	12.82	12.45
Upper quartile	13.90	12.81	13.90	13.36
Maximum	32.05	20.32	24.24	16.69
Monday mean	11.43	10.42	13.74	12.67
Tuesday mean	11.96	11.19	13.68	12.72
Wednesday mean	12.03	11.31	13.53	12.73
Thursday mean	13.14	12.26	13.53	12.66
Friday mean	14.12	13.09	13.36	12.42
p-value, ANOVA	0.001	0.000	0.966	0.816
Autocorrelation				
Lag 1	0.628	0.386	0.914	0.800
Lag 2	0.444	0.042	0.863	0.699
Lag 3	0.392	0.077	0.821	0.632
Lag 4	0.382	0.038	0.777	0.603
Lag 5	0.382	0.120	0.734	0.565
Partial autocorrelation				
Lag 2	0.083	0.184	0.169	0.165
Lag 3	0.140	0.150	0.067	0.094
Lag 4	0.123	0.119	0.001	0.127
Lag 5	0.109	0.172	−0.017	0.037

Summary statistics are calculated for the 12 months from October 1992 to September 1993 and for the 10 months commencing December 1992.

The estimates display a clear day-of-the-week effect. The average estimate increases monotonically as the week progresses, from 11.4 percent on Monday to 14.1 percent on Friday. This pattern reflects the predominance of important scheduled macroeconomic announcements on Fridays and less important announcements on Thursdays. Parametric (ANOVA) and non-parametric (Kruskal–Wallis) tests have p-values below 0.2 percent for tests of the null hypothesis that the distribution of the estimates is identical for the five days of the week. Removing the high volatility months of October and November reduces the mean estimate by about 1.0 percent for each day but the monotonic pattern and the low p-values remain.

The autocorrelations and partial autocorrelations of the volatility estimates are similar to those expected from an AR(1) process. The first-lag autocorrelation is 0.63 for all the estimates but it falls to 0.39 when October and November are excluded.

Implied Volatilities

Figure 2 is a time-series plot of implied volatility estimates i_t for the same days as are used to produce Figure 1. Each estimate is the average of two implied volatilities, one calculated from a nearest-the-money (NTM) call option price and the other from a NTM put option price. The last options prices before the PHLX close at 14.30 local time are used. These are the only useful options prices supplied to us by the PHLX: high and low options prices are supplied but they do not usually define high and low implied volatilities. The spot prices used for the calculations of the implieds are contemporaneous quotations supplied by the PHLX.

On each day, the shortest maturity options with more than nine calendar days to expiration are selected. The time to maturity of the options is always between 10 and 45 calendar days. We only use the estimates i_t to represent options information about volatility expectations. We do not seek shorter-term expectations from the term structure of implieds because this involves extrapolations that produced no statistical benefits in Xu and Taylor (1995).

The average of the estimates i_t is 13.6 percent, which is slightly more than the average of the intra-day estimates. Table 1 provides information for comparisons of the distributions of the implied and intra-day estimates.

Figure 2 Implied volatilities.

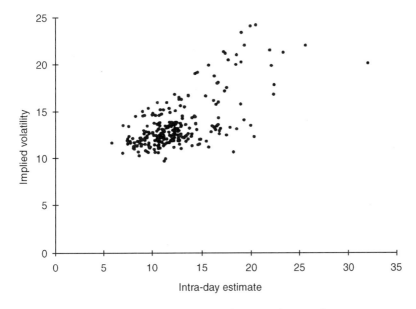

Figure 3 Comparison of implied volatilities and intra-day estimates.

Figure 2 shows that traders expected a higher level of volatility in October and November and thereafter had expectations that were within an unusually narrow band. There are no day-of-the-week effects because the implieds are expectations for long periods that average 25 calendar days. The implied estimates i_t are markedly less variable than the realised estimates v_t again because the implieds are a medium-term expectations measure. This also explains why the serial correlation in the implied volatilities is substantial: 0.91 at a lag of one-day, using all the data and 0.80 when the first two months are excluded.

The correlation between the implied volatilities and the intra-day volatility estimates is 0.66. These two volatility measurements are plotted against each other on Figure 3.

ARCH MODELS WITH VOLATILITY ESTIMATED FROM INTRA-DAY QUOTATIONS

Models and results are first discussed for daily returns and are subsequently discussed for hourly returns. Daily models are straightforward because they avoid estimation of intra-day, seasonal volatility patterns. Hourly models, however, are more incisive because of the much larger number of observed returns.

A General Model for Daily Returns

ARCH models are estimated for daily spot returns, $R_t = \ln(S_t/S_{t-1})$, obtained from rates when the PHLX closes. All the ARCH models are estimated using data for the set of PHLX trading days. Our set of 253 daily returns is small.

The results are unusual and only need to be discussed when the conditional distribution of returns is normal with mean zero and a conditional variance h_t that depends on the information K_{t-1}, given by combining the information from options trades with the set of five-minute returns up to time $t - 1$. The options information is summarised by the implied volatility term i_{t-1}. The volatility information provided by the five-minute returns is summarised by the estimate v_{t-1}.

The following model makes use of conditional variances h_t^* appropriate for 24-hour periods after removing multiplicative Monday and holiday effects, defined by Equation 1:

$$R_t|K_{t-1} \sim N(0, h_t), \qquad\qquad 8$$

$$h_t = h_t^*, Mh_t^* \text{ or } Hh_t^*, \qquad\qquad 9a$$

$$h_t^* = c + aR_{t-1}^2(h_{t-1}^*/h_{t-1}) + bh_{t-1}^* + dv_{t-1}^* + ei_{t-1}^*, \qquad 9b$$

$$v_{t-1}^* = v_{t-1}^2/f, \qquad\qquad 10a$$

$$i_{t-1}^* = i_{t-1}^2/f, \qquad\qquad 10b$$

$$f = 196 + 48M + 8H. \qquad\qquad 10c$$

The parameter vector is $\theta = (a, b, c, d, e, M, H)$. The terms v_{t-1}^2 and i_{t-1}^2 are divided by f to convert these annual quantities into quantities appropriate for a 24-hour period.

Results for Daily Returns

Table 2 presents results for the general model and seven special cases. When the history of five-minute returns contains all relevant information about future volatility, the options parameter e is zero. An estimation with this constraint produces a surprise, when the initial

Table 2 Parameter estimates for daily ARCH models that include intra-day volatility estimates and short-maturity implied volatilities.

$c \times 10^5$	a	b	d	e	*max.* $\ln(L)$
3.484 (3.55)			0.329 (2.01)		868.66
0.204 (1.95)		0.956 (45.87)	0.000		871.05
0.203 (1.94)	0.000	0.956 (45.78)			871.05
0.203 (1.89)	0.000	0.956 (44.38)	0.000		871.05
				1.000	870.95
0.897 (0.64)				0.683 (2.88)	873.04
0.897 (0.64)	0.000	0.000		0.683 (2.88)	873.04
0.897 (0.64)	0.000	0.000	0.000	0.683 (2.88)	873.04

The numbers in parentheses are t-statistics, estimated using the Hessian matrix and numerical second derivatives. t-statistics are not reported when an estimate is less than 10^{-6}. The 24-hour conditional variance h_t is the product of the 24-hour deseasonalised conditional variance h_t^* and a multiplier that is either 1, M (for Mondays) or H (for holidays). The deseasonalised conditional variance is defined by $h_t^* = c + aR_{t-1}^2(h_{t-1}^*/h_{t-1}) + bh_{t-1}^* + dv_{t-1}^* + ei_{t-1}^*$. The terms R_{t-1}, v_{t-1}^* and i_{t-1}^* are, respectively, daily returns, intra-day volatility estimates and the squares of scaled implied volatilities. All parameters are constrained to be non-negative. In the fifth row, e is constrained to equal one. The estimates of M and H for the most general model are 1.44 and 1.74, standard errors 0.34 and 0.89, respectively.

value h_0^* is an additional parameter. As $a = d = 0$, the conditional variances are deterministic, hence if the unconditional variance is $\mu_h = c/(1 - b)$ then:

$$h_t^* = \mu_h + b^t(h_0^* - \mu_h).$$ (11)

This result is less surprising when we recall the volatility estimates plotted on Figure 1. The twelve months begin with high volatility followed by a long period during which volatility does not change much. The above edge solution is unlikely to be estimated if the period of exceptionally high variance is anywhere other than at the beginning of the sample. Ex post, the selection of dates for the sample period is rather unfortunate!

The edge solution is a consequence of an unusual volatility pattern found in a small sample. Small samples can give more ordinary results, for example $a = 0.035$ and $b = 0.917$ for GARCH(1, 1) estimated from the daily DM/\$ rate from September 1994 to August 1995.

Next, consider models that make use of the information in implied volatilities. The specification

$$h_t^* = c + ei_{t-1}^*$$ (12)

has a maximum likelihood that is 1.99 above that of the edge solution. Estimation of the most general model simply produces the linear function of squared implied volatility above; the estimates of a, b and d are all zero.

The results are compatible with the hypothesis that there is *no* incremental volatility information in the dataset of five-minute returns, when calculating daily conditional variances. However, the hypothesis that there is no incremental volatility information in the implied volatilities is dubious.

Intra-Day Seasonal Multipliers

We now multiply the number of returns used to estimate models by 24. The much larger sample size provides a reasonable prospect of avoiding the unsatisfactory edge solutions found for daily returns. Before estimating conditional variances for hourly returns we must, however, produce estimates of the intra-day seasonal volatility pattern. We present simple estimates here. Our estimates ignore the effects of scheduled macroeconomic news announcements; we discuss the sensitivity of our conclusions to this omission on p 83. Andersen and Bollerslev (1997) provide different estimates based upon smooth harmonic and polynomial functions.

It may be helpful to review some notation before producing the seasonal estimates. The time t is an integer that counts weekdays, n is the number of five-minute returns in one day ($= 288$) and $R_{t,i}$ is a five-minute return; $i = 1$ identifies the return from 14.30 to 14.35 US eastern time (ET) on the previous day (i.e. $t - 1$) ... $i = 288$ is the return from 14.25 to 14.30 ET on day t. Returns over 24 hours and over 1 hour periods indexed by j are respectively given by

$$R_t = \sum_{i=1}^{n} R_{t,i} \text{ and } r_{t,j} = \sum_{i=12(j-1)+1}^{12j} R_{t,i} \qquad 13$$

Sums of squared returns provide simple estimates of price variability and averages across similar time periods can be used to estimate the seasonal volatility pattern. Let N be the number of days in the sample. It would be convenient if the seasonal pattern could be described by 24 one-hour, multiplicative, seasonal variance factors s_j^2, with $\sum_{j=1}^{24} s_j^2 = 24$. A natural estimate of the variance multiplier for hour j is given by

$$\hat{s}_j^2 = \frac{24 \sum_{t=1}^{N} \sum_{i=12(j-1)+1}^{12j} R_{t,i}^2}{\sum_{t=1}^{N} \sum_{i=1}^{n} R_{t,i}^2} \qquad 14$$

However, the seasonal pattern varies by day of the week, as might be expected from Table 1 and thus it appears preferable to estimate 120 multiplicative factors that average one over a complete week.

A second way to estimate variance multipliers takes account of the day of the week. Let S_t be the set of all daily time indices that share the same day-of-the-week as time index t. Let N_t be the number of time indices to be found in S_t. Then a set of 120 factors are given by:

$$\hat{s}_{t,j}^2 = \frac{24N}{N_t} \frac{\sum_{s \in S_t} \sum_{i=12(j-1)+1}^{12j} R_{s,i}^2}{\sum_{s=1}^{N} \sum_{i=1}^{n} R_{s,i}^2} \qquad 15$$

Figure 4 is a plot of standard deviation multipliers, $\hat{s}_{t,j}$. The final hourly interval, $j = 24$, is the hour ending at 14.30 ET (19.30 GMT, winter) when the options market closes. The first interval, $j = 1$, is the hour beginning after the previous day's options close.

The multipliers are generally higher for intervals 13 to 24, corresponding to 07.30 until 19.30 local time in London, with the highest levels in intervals 18 to 23 when both US and European dealers are active. The Thursday and Friday spikes, at interval $j = 19$, reflect the additional volatility when many US macroeconomic news reports are released in the hour commencing at 08.30 ET. Ederington and Lee (1993, 1995) provide detailed documentation of this link with macroeconomic news. The lower local maximum, at $j = 13$, occurs when trade accelerates in Europe in the hour commencing at 07.30 local time in London. The Monday spike earlier in the day, at $j = 6$, is the start of a new week in the Far East markets.

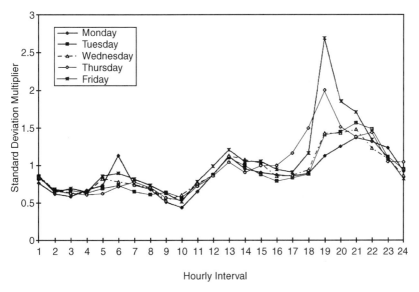

Figure 4 DM/$ intra-day standard deviation multipliers.

A Model for Hourly Returns

An ARCH specification for hourly returns that is similar to that considered for the daily returns involves hourly returns $r_{t,j}$, information sets $K_{t,j-1}$, recent five-minute returns $R_{t,i}$, one-hour realised variances $V_{t,j}$, one-hour conditional variances $h_{t,j}$, one-hour deseasonalised conditional variances $h_{t,j}^*$ and the multipliers $\hat{s}_{t,j}$. The specification also incorporates the annualised implied volatility i_{t-1} calculated at the previous close; hourly implieds are not available to us, although we would not expect them to contribute much because the implieds change slowly. The information set $K_{t,j-1}$ is defined to be all relevant variables known at the end of hour $j-1$ on day t, namely the implieds $i_{t-1}, i_{t-2}, \ldots$, the latest five-minute return $R_{t,12(j-1)}$ and all previous five-minute returns.

The most general ARCH model that has been estimated for hourly returns is:

$$r_{t,j}|K_{t,j-1} \sim D_\nu(m_{t,j}, h_{t,j}), \tag{16a}$$

$$m_{t,j} = \phi r_{t,j-1}, \tag{16b}$$

$$h_{t,j} = \hat{s}_{t,j}^2 h_{t,j}^*, \tag{16c}$$

$$h_{t,j}^* = c + ar_{t,j-1}^2/\hat{s}_{t,j-1}^2 + bh_{t,j-1}^* + dV_{t,j-1}/\hat{s}_{t,j-1}^2 + ei_{t-1}^*, \tag{16d}$$

$$V_{t,j-1} = \sum_{i=12(j-2)+1}^{12(j-1)} R_{t,i}^2, \tag{16e}$$

$$i_{t-1}^* = i_{t-1}^2/f, \tag{16f}$$

for some number f that does not need to be estimated; we set f equal to the number of annual hourly returns (24×252). The subscript pair t, i refers to the time interval $t-1$, $n-i$ whenever i is not positive. The distribution $D_\nu(m_{t,j}, h_{t,j})$ is GED with thickness parameter ν, mean $m_{t,j}$ and variance $h_{t,j}$. The parameter vector is $\theta = (a, b, c, d, e, \phi, \nu)$. As the autoregressive, mean parameter ϕ is always insignificant, we only discuss results when ϕ is constrained to be zero.

Equation 16d contains terms, with coefficients a and d, that are both measures of hourly return variability. Both measures are included to permit comparisons of the information content of five-minute and hourly returns.

Results for Hourly Returns

Table 3 presents results for 6049 hourly returns when 120 seasonal volatility multipliers are included in the models. The maximum

Table 3 Parameter estimates for ARCH models of hourly returns with 120 seasonal terms.

$c \times 10^5$	a	b	d	e	v	max. $ln(L)$
Panel A: normal distribution						
0.1321			0.2875		2	31848.67
(27.29)			(13.38)			
0.0012		0.9490	0.0352		2	31963.41
(2.35)		(115.84)	(6.49)			
0.0012	0.0196	0.9743			2	31933.21
(3.24)	(5.58)	(197.49)				
0.0012	0.0045	0.9480	0.0319		2	31964.09
(2.44)	(1.14)	(110.71)	(5.38)			
				0.6528	2	31945.15
				(54.99)		
0.0000				0.6528	2	31945.15
				(54.88)		
0.0000	0.1046	0.2926		0.3935	2	31999.55
	(6.98)	(3.78)		(8.20)		
0.0000		0.1766	0.1437	0.4141	2	31997.85
		(1.70)	(7.01)	(6.76)		
0.0000	0.0713	0.1812	0.0876	0.4127	2	32011.87
	(4.51)	(2.14)	(4.22)	(8.30)		
Panel B: GED distribution						
0.1232			0.3197		1.1025	32193.31
(19.12)			(10.68)		(42.42)	
0.0008		0.9434	0.0408		1.1460	32253.21
(1.25)		(89.55)	(5.53)		(41.90)	
0.0013	0.0227	0.9707			1.1376	32230.24
(2.38)	(4.45)	(136.35)			(41.88)	
0.0009	0.0028	0.9431	0.0387		1.1463	32253.36
(1.31)	(0.52)	(87.44)	(4.65)		(41.89)	
				0.6482	1.1418	32231.90
				(39.05)	(41.58)	
0.0000				0.6482	1.1458	32231.90
				(38.98)	(41.58)	
0.0000	0.1221	0.2590		0.4034	1.1598	32266.90
	(5.74)	(2.66)		(6.71)	(41.40)	
0.0000		0.2212	0.1678	0.3641	1.1594	32268.01
		(1.88)	(5.96)	(5.38)	(41.51)	
0.0000	0.0808	0.1801	0.1099	0.3887	1.1638	32277.00
	(3.64)	(1.83)	(3.87)	(6.71)	(41.45)	

The numbers in parentheses are t-statistics, estimated using the hessian matrix and numerical second derivatives. All parameters are constrained to be non-negative. t-statistics are not reported when an estimate is less than 10^{-6}.

The one-hour conditional variance is defined by $h_{t,j} = \hat{s}^2_{t,j} h^*_{t,j}$, $h^*_{t,j} = c + ar^2_{t,j-1}/\hat{s}^2_{t,j-1} + bh^*_{t,j-1} + d(\sum_{i=12(j-2)+1}^{12(j-1)} R^2_{t,i})/\hat{s}^2_{t,j-1} + ei^*_{t-1}$.

The terms $r_{t,j-1}$, $R_{t,i}$ and i^*_{t-1} are, respectively, one-hour returns, five-minute returns and the squares of scaled implied volatilities. The conditional distributions are normal distributions in panel A and are generalised error distributions, with thickness parameter v, in panel B.

log-likelihood increases substantially when 120 day-of-the-week multipliers replace 24 hourly multipliers, typically by about 65 for conditional normal distributions and by about 22 for conditional GED distributions. Consequently, our discussion of the results is based upon models with 120 intra-day seasonal multipliers. All our observations and conclusions are also supported by numbers in a further table, available upon request, for models that have only 24 seasonal multipliers.

The lower panel of Table 3 shows that the conditional distribution of the hourly returns is certainly fat-tailed. The GED thickness parameter is estimated to be near 1.15 with a standard error less than 0.03. Conditional normal distributions are rejected for the most general specification and all the special cases. The log-likelihood ratio test statistic is 130.26 for the general specification with the null distribution being χ_1^2. A thickness parameter of 1 defines double negative-exponential distributions so the hourly returns have conditional distributions that are far more peaked and fat-tailed than the normal.

Our assumption of the GED for the conditional distributions does not ensure consistent parameter estimates and standard errors if the assumption is false. The quasi-ML estimates in the upper panel of Table 3 are consistent although they are not efficient.

The results in the lower panel of Table 3 fall into three major categories, and are discussed separately. The conclusions are the same if we focus on the upper panel for normal distributions.

First, consider models that only make use of returns information. The models that incorporate information more than one-hour old, through parameter b, have significant parameters for both recent information (the last hour, through a and d) and old information. This is the usual situation when ARCH models are estimated and so we no longer have the curious edge solutions discussed for the daily returns at p 77. When five-minute returns are used, but hourly returns are not ($a = 0$; $b, d > 0$), the maximum of $\ln(L)$ is 23 more than the maximum when only hourly returns are used ($d = 0$; $a, b > 0$). There is thus more relevant volatility information in five-minute returns than in hourly returns. This information comes from more than twelve five-minute returns, as expected, because the maximum of $\ln(L)$ decreases by 60 when older information is excluded ($a = b = 0$; $d > 0$). When all the returns variables are included in the model, a is insignificant and much smaller than d. The persistence estimates, given by the sum $a + b + d$, are between 0.984 and 0.993 when old information is included ($b > 0$).

Second, consider models that only make use of daily implied volatilities. The variable i_{t-1}^* is biased because estimates of the multiplier e are significantly smaller than 1. Some of this bias is presumably due to an unsuitable choice for the constant f that converts annual variances into hourly variances. When e and f are unconstrained the maximum of $\ln(L)$ is 21 less than the maximum when spot price quotations alone are used. This shows that five-minute returns are more informative than implied volatilities, at least when estimating hourly conditional variances.

Third, consider models that make use of five-minute returns, hourly returns and daily implied volatilities. The most general model in the final row of Table 3 is estimated to have a zero intercept c and the parameters a, d and e have t-ratios above 3.5 and thus are significant at very low levels. Deleting the implied volatility contribution from the most general model would reduce the maximum of $\ln(L)$ by 24. Alternatively, deleting the quotations terms would give a reduction of 45. It is concluded that both the quotations and the implied volatilities contain a significant amount of incremental information.

Results When Scheduled News is Incorporated

The hourly seasonal volatility multipliers are particularly high in the hour commencing at 08.30 ET when many US macroeconomic news reports are released. This effect is most prominent on Fridays. The volatility multipliers used in the preceding analyses are, for example, the same for all Friday hours commencing at 8:30 regardless of any news releases. This methodology might induce systematic mis-measurements of the volatility process. We have assessed the importance of this issue by comparing the results when there are 120 volatility multipliers with further results when either 121 or 144 multipliers are used.

Our first set of 121 multipliers contains two numbers for Friday 08.30 to 09.30 ET: one multiplier for those Fridays that have a relevant report and another multiplier for the remaining Fridays. Our first set of 144 multipliers contains two numbers for each of the 24 hours from Thursday 14.30 to Friday 14.30 ET, one used when there is a relevant report and the other when there is not. We have defined a relevant report as a news announcement about one or more of the six significant macroeconomic variables listed by Ederington and Lee (1993, p1189): employment, merchandise trade, PPI, durable goods orders, GNP and retail sales. These reports were issued on 25 of the Fridays in our sample.

We find that the maximum of the log-likelihood function increases by similar amounts when there are more multipliers whichever model is estimated. Consider the nine log-likelihood values reported in Table 3, panel B, for nine specifications with 120 multipliers. These values increase by between 6.6 and 8.6 when 121 multipliers are used and by between 16.7 and 19.6 when 144 are used. Consequently, as our conclusions depend on substantial log-likelihood differences across specifications these conclusions do not change when the additional multipliers are used.

It may be objected that the Fridays have been partitioned by announcements rather than by the impact of unexpected news. Second sets of 121 and 144 multipliers have been calculated by separating the 25 Fridays having the highest realised volatility from 08.30 to 09.30 from the remaining Fridays. The results are then similar, as 19 of the 25 high-volatility hours include a relevant announcement. The increases in the log-likelihoods from the values reported in Table 3, Panel B are now in the ranges 8.4 to 10.7 and 9.3 to 11.7, respectively, for 121 and 144 multipliers. We note that the first, second, fourth and fifth Fridays in the ranked list coincide with employment reports but the third ranked Friday has no relevant announcements.

The estimates of the parameters a, b, d and e change very little when the number of multipliers is increased above 120. The magnitudes of the changes are all less than 0.03 when the most general model is estimated. When the general model is constrained by ignoring the options information ($e = 0$), the persistence measure $a + b + d$ is always between 0.984 and 0.985.

Results for Quarterly Subperiods

It could be possible that some of the conclusions are only supported by the data during part of the year studied. The higher than average realised volatility during the first quarter, from October to December 1992, might be an unusual period whose exclusion would reverse some of the conclusions.

The models whose parameter estimates have been given in the lower panel of Table 3 for the whole year in the datasets have been re-estimated for the four quarters of the year commencing in October 1992 and in January, April and July 1993. The same 120 seasonal multipliers are used for the whole year and for each of the four quarters. All the conclusions for the whole year are supported by each quarter of the data: (1) when quotations alone are considered, five-minute returns have more volatility information than hourly returns and the relevant information is not all in the most recent hour (likelihood-ratio tests, 5 percent significance level), (2) five-minute returns are more informative than implied volatilities when estimating hourly conditional variances and (3) there is significant incremental information in both the quotations and the implied volatilities (likelihood-ratio tests, 5 percent significance level).

The reductions in the maximum of the log-likelihood when the quotations information is removed from the most general model are 14.7 for

Table 4   Parameter estimates for the most general ARCH model of hourly returns.

Sample	$c \times 10^5$	a	b	d	e	v	max. $ln(L)$
Full	0.0000	0.0808	0.1801	0.1099	0.3887	1.1638	32277.00
		(3.64)	(1.83)	(3.87)	(6.71)	(41.45)	
Q1	0.0000	0.0775	0.0000	0.1591	0.4841	1.1621	7726.38
		(1.78)		(2.54)	(11.01)	(20.94)	
Q2	0.0000	0.0435	0.2391	0.0995	0.3797	1.2155	8622.58
		(1.19)	(1.05)	(1.84)	(2.82)	(21.04)	
Q3	0.0164	0.1071	0.0000	0.0877	0.4334	1.1480	7676.79
	(0.32)	(2.06)		(1.53)	(2.05)	(20.05)	
Q4	0.0000	0.0750	0.4420	0.1185	0.2120	1.1421	8255.79
		(1.47)	(2.33)	(2.50)	(2.18)	(20.65)	

The general model has conditional variances defined in Table 3. There are 120 seasonal multipliers and the conditional distributions are generalised error distributions. The estimates are for the full year (October 1992 to September 1993) and for the four quarters that commence in October 1992, January 1993, April 1993 and July 1993. The numbers in parentheses are *t*-statistics.

the first quarter, 8.0 for the second quarter, 8.4 for the third quarter and 17.3 for the fourth quarter. The incremental information in the quotations information is thus of a similar order of magnitude in all the quarters and the first quarter is not clearly different to the other three quarters. The reductions in the maximum of the log-likelihood when the information in implied volatilities is removed from the most general model are 4.2 for the first quarter, 4.4 for the second quarter, 2.4 for the third quarter and 2.1 for the fourth quarter. These reductions are much smaller and are similar across quarters.

Table 4 presents the quarterly parameter estimates for the most general model. The estimates change little from quarter to quarter. The sum of the maximum log-likelihoods for the four quarters is only 4.54 more than the maximum when the same parameters are used for the whole year. Twice this increase in the log-likelihood is less than the number of extra parameters when four quarterly models are estimated compared with one annual model. There is no statistical evidence, therefore, that the parameters of the general model changed during the year. The variations in estimated parameters, by quarter, are minor relative to their estimated standard errors.

Residual Diagnostic Statistics and Tests

A time series of standardised residuals from our most general model for hourly returns is defined by:

$$z_T = r_{t,j}/\sqrt{h_{t,j}}, \quad T = 24t + j. \qquad\qquad 17$$

The conditional variances are calculated using the maximum likelihood estimates of the model parameters for the whole year. In the unlikely event of our model being perfect we would expect the standardised residuals to be approximately independent and identically distributed observations from a zero-mean and unit-variance distribution.

There are 6049 numbers in the time series $\{z_T\}$. Their mean is 0.005 and their standard deviation is 1.004. Their skewness is -0.01 and their kurtosis is 5.30, both of which are close to the values expected from a generalised error distribution with thickness parameter v near one (skewness = 0 for all v, and kurtosis = 6 when $v = 1$). A histogram of the z_T shows fat tails and a substantial peak around zero, which is a feature of the GED when v is near one. Twenty of the standardised residuals are outside ± 4 although all of them are inside ± 5.5.

The autocorrelations of z_T, $|z_T|$ and z_T^2, from lags 1 to 10, are all within $\pm 0.025 = \pm 1.96/\sqrt{6049}$ and therefore provide no evidence against the i.i.d. hypothesis, since all 30 tests accept this null hypothesis at the 5 percent level. The first-lag autocorrelations of the three series are 0.003, 0.007 and -0.007. Statistically significant dependence is found at lags that are multiples of 24: for z_T at lag 96 (correlation = 0.056), for $|z_T|$ at lags 24, 48, 72, 96 and 120 (the correlations are 0.045, 0.042, 0.049, 0.056 and 0.026) and for z_T^2 at lags 24, 72 and 96 (correlations 0.032, 0.022 and 0.062). These correlations show that the model is not perfect, presumably because of estimation errors in the hourly seasonal multipliers. Nevertheless, with all autocorrelation estimates within ± 0.07 the model is considered a satisfactory approximation to the process that generates hourly returns.

Estimates of spectral density functions, calculated from the autocorrelations at lags 1 to 240 of z_T, $|z_T|$ and z_T^2, confirm this conclusion. No statistical evidence against the i.i.d. hypothesis can be found in the estimates at frequencies corresponding to either 24-hour or 120-hour cycles. There is a significant spectral peak at zero frequency for the series $|z_T|$ (t-statistic = 3.49) that may simply reflect very small positive dependence at several lags.

FORECASTS OF REALISED VOLATILITY

A comparison of volatility forecasts can provide further evidence about incremental information. We divide the whole year of data into an in-sample period from which ARCH parameters and intra-day seasonal volatility multipliers are estimated and an out-of-sample period for which the accuracy of forecasts of hourly realised volatility is evaluated. We split the year into a nine-month in-sample period followed by a three-month out-of-sample period. Relative accuracy measures for five forecasting methods are calculated using 120 seasonal volatility multipliers. The relative measures are not sensitive to the treatment of Friday macroeconomic announcements. Using our first set of 121 or 144 multipliers, defined at p 83, has no effect on the rankings of the forecasts.

Two measures of hourly realised volatility are forecast, defined first by

$$a_{t,j,1} = \sum_{i=12(j-1)+1}^{12j} R_{t,j}^2 \qquad\qquad 18$$

and second by the same quantity adjusted for intra-day seasonality using 120 volatility multipliers:

$$a_{t,j,2} = a_{t,j,1}/\hat{s}_{t,j}^2 \qquad\qquad 19$$

Three forecasts of $a_{t,j,l}$ are defined by conditional variances $h_{t,j}$ obtained from variations on the most general ARCH model for hourly returns defined in Section 5.4. The first forecast excludes all quotations information by imposing the restriction $a = b = d = 0$ on the ARCH model. The second forecast excludes the options information by requiring $e = 0$ in the ARCH model. The third forecast is calculated from the general model without any parameter restrictions. These three forecasts are denoted $f_{t,j,1,l}$, $l = 1, 2, 3$. A fourth forecast, $f_{t,j,1,4}$, is defined by $\hat{s}_{t,j}^2$ multiplied by the in-sample average of the quantities $a_{t,j,2}$. Four forecasts $f_{t,j,2,l}$ of $a_{t,j,2}$ are defined in a similar way. The first three of these forecasts are now defined by deseasonalised conditional variances $h_{t,j}^*$ for the three ARCH specifications and the fourth forecast is the in-sample average of $a_{t,j,2}$.

The accuracy of a set of forecasts $f_{t,j,k,l}$ of the outcomes, $a_{t,j,k}$ is reported here relative to the accuracy of a reference forecast given by the previous realised volatility

$$f_{t,j,1,5} = a_{t,j-1,2}\hat{s}_{t,j}^2, \quad f_{t,j,2,5} = a_{t,j-1,2} \qquad\qquad 20$$

Table 5 presents values of the relative accuracy measures

$$F_{k,l,p} = \frac{\sum |a_{t,j,k} - f_{t,j,k,l}|^p}{\sum |a_{t,j,k} - f_{t,j,k,5}|^p} \qquad\qquad 21$$

Table 5   Measures of relative forecast errors when forecasting hourly realised volatility out-of-sample.

Forecast	Error metric Seasonal adjustment	Absolute No	Absolute Yes	Square No	Square Yes
1	options only	0.767	0.772	0.807	0.795
2	quotations only	0.781	0.769	0.812	0.783
3	options and quotations	0.731	0.731	0.797	0.776
4	in-sample average	1.055	1.080	0.821	0.803
5	lagged realized volatility	1	1	1	1

The accuracy of forecasts is measured by either the absolute forecast error or the squared forecast error.
Hourly realized volatility is forecast, either without or with a seasonal adjustment.
Nine months are used for in-sample calculations and then three months for out-of-sample evaluations.
The numbers tabulated are $\sum |a - f_l|^p / \sum |a - f_5|^p$ with a the realized volatility number. f_l forecast l and p either 1 or 2.

for powers $p = 1, 2$. The summations are over all hours in the out-of-sample period. The best of a set of five forecasts $f_{t,j,k,l}$, $l = 1, \ldots, 5$, has the least value of F. The least value of F is considered for each of the four columns in Table 5. The columns are defined by all combinations of p (1 or 2) and k (1 or 2).

When accuracy is measured by absolute forecast errors, so $p = 1$, the best forecasts come from the general ARCH specification for both realised measures ($k = 1, 2$). This is further evidence that there is incremental volatility information in both the spot quotations and the options prices. The average absolute forecast error from the general specification is 5 percent less than that from the next best specification. The second best set of forecasts are from quotations alone when the quantity forecast is adjusted for seasonality, but are from options prices alone when the quantity forecast is not adjusted, although the differences between the accuracies of the second and third best forecasts are small.

The results are similar but less decisive when accuracy is measured by squared forecast errors ($p = 2$). The most general ARCH specification again gives the best out-of-sample forecasts. However, the average of the squared forecast errors for the best forecasts are only slightly less than for the next best forecasts. This may be attributed to the marked skewness to the right of the distribution of the quantities to be forecast: this inevitably produces some outliers in the forecast errors whose impact is magnified when they are squared.

Concluding Remarks

The evidence from estimating ARCH models using one year of exchange rate quotations for one exchange rate supports two conclusions. First, five-minute returns cannot be shown to contain any incremental volatility information when estimating daily conditional variances. This negative result may simply be a consequence of the small number of daily returns available for this study. Second, when estimating hourly conditional variances there is a significant amount of information in five-minute returns that is incremental to the options information. Furthermore, the quotations information then appears to be more informative than the options information. Thus there is significant incremental volatility information in one million foreign exchange quotations. This conclusion is confirmed by out-of-sample comparisons of volatility forecasts. Forecasts of hourly realised volatility are more accurate when the quotations information is used in addition to options information.

Acknowledgements

The authors thank the two referees and the editor for their very helpful reports. This manuscript is a revised and extended version of a paper prepared for the Conference on High Frequency Data in Finance, sponsored by Olsen & Associates and held in March 1995. The authors thank participants at the O&A conference, the 1995 European Finance Association conference and the Aarhus Mathematical Finance conference for their comments. They also thank participants at seminars held at the Isaac Newton Institute Cambridge, City University London, Lancaster University, Liverpool University, Warwick University and the University of Cergy-Pontoise.

Bibliography

Andersen, T.G. and Bollerslev, T. (1997), "Intraday Periodicity and Volatility Persistence in Financial Markets", *Journal of Empirical Finance*, 4, 115–158.
Barone-Adesi, G. and Whaley, R.E. (1987), "Efficient Analytic Approximation of American Option Values", *Journal of Finance*, 42, 301–320.

Bollerslev, T. and Domowitz, I. (1993), "Trading Patterns and Prices in the Interbank Foreign Exchange Market", *Journal of Finance*, 48, 1421–1443.

Canina, L. and Figlewski, S. (1993), "The Informational Content of Implied Volatility", *Review of Financial Studies*, 6, 659–681.

Dacorogna, M.M., Müller, U.A., Nagler, R.J., Olsen, R.B. and Pictet, O.V. (1993), "A Geographical Model for the Daily and Weekly Seasonal Volatility in the FX Market", *Journal of International Money and Finance*, 12, 413–438.

Day, T.E. and Lewis, C.M. (1992), "Stock Market Volatility and the Information Content of Stock Index Options", *Journal of Econometrics*, 52, 289–311.

Ederington, L.H. and Lee, J.H. (1993), "How Markets Process Information: News Releases and Volatility", *Journal of Finance*, 49, 1161–1191.

Ederington, L.H. and Lee, J.H. (1995), "The Short-run Dynamics of the Price-Adjustment to New Information", *Journal of Financial and Quantitative Analysis*, 30, 117–134.

Goodhart, C.A.E. and Figliuoli, L. (1991), "Every Minute Counts in Financial Markets", *Journal of International Money and Finance*, 10, 23–52.

Hull, J. (1995), *Introduction to Futures and Options Markets*, 2nd edn., Prentice-Hall, Englewood Cliffs, NJ.

Hull, J. and White, A. (1987), "The Pricing of Options on Assets with Stochastic Volatilities", *Journal of Finance*, 42, 281–300.

Jorion, P. (1995), "Predicting Volatility in the Foreign Exchange Market", *Journal of Finance*, 50, 507–528.

Lamoureux, C.B. and Lastrapes, W.D. (1993), "Forecasting Stock Return Variance: Toward an Understanding of Stochastic Implied Volatilities", *Review of Financial Studies*, 6, 293–326.

Nelson, D.B. (1992), "Filtering and Forecasting with Misspecified ARCH models I: Getting the Right Variance with the Wrong Model", *Journal of Econometrics*, 52, 61–90.

Taylor, S.J. and Xu, X. (1994), "The Magnitude of Implied Volatility Smiles: Theory and Empirical Evidence for Exchange Rates", *Review of Futures Markets*, 13, 355–380.

Xu, X. and Taylor, S.J. (1994), "The Term Structure of Volatility Implied by Foreign Exchange Options", *Journal of Financial and Quantitative Analysis*, 29, 57–74.

Xu, X. and Taylor, S.J. (1995), "Conditional Volatility and the Informational Efficiency of the PHLX Currency Options Market", *Journal of Banking and Finance*, 19, 803–821.

Chapter **4**

Correlation of High-Frequency Financial Time Series

Mark Lundin, Michel M. Dacorogna and Ulrich A. Müller

Olsen and Associates, Research Institute for Applied Economics, Zürich

PREFACE

This chapter addresses three problematic issues concerning the application of the linear correlation coefficient in the high-frequency financial data domain. First, correlation of intra-day, homogeneous time series derived from unevenly spaced tick-by-tick data deserves careful treatment if a data bias resulting from the classical missing value problem is to be avoided. We propose a simple and easy to use method which corrects for frequency differentials and data gaps by updating the linear correlation coefficient calculation with the aid of co-volatility weights. We view the method as a bi-variate alternative to time scale transformations which treat heteroscedasticity by expanding periods of higher volatility while contracting periods of lower volatility. Secondly, it is generally recognized that correlations between financial time series are unstable, and we probe the stability of correlation as a function of time for seven years of high-frequency foreign exchange rate, implied forward interest rate and stock index data. Correlations estimated over time in turn allow for estimations of the memory that correlations have for their past values. Third, previous authors have demonstrated a dramatic decrease in correlation as data frequency enters the intra-hour level (the "Epps effect"). We characterize the Epps effect for correlations between a number of financial time series and suggest a possible relation between correlation attenuation and activity rates.

INTRODUCTION

The estimation of dependence between financial time series is of increasing interest to those concerned with multivariate decision formation.

Dependence is often characterized numerically using the linear correlation coefficient.[1] The popularity of this estimation technique stems from its simple definition, practical ease of use and from its straightforward results which are easily interpreted, unitless and directly comparable. Despite the relative simplicity of its definition, there exist a number of unresolved issues regarding sample estimation and interpretation of results in the high-frequency data domain.

- The data input for the correlation coefficient calculation are two time series with equal, usually homogeneous, spacing between observations or data. This necessity is easily satisfied where low frequency ($\leq$ one tick per week) data is concerned. However, formulation of intra-day, homogeneous time series deserves more careful treatment if a resulting estimation bias is to be avoided. This is especially the case when the original time series of unevenly spaced tick-by-tick data occur at different frequencies or opening (overlap) hours. We propose a simple and easily applied normalization method which corrects for differences in observation frequencies and for data gaps. This alternative approach updates the correlation calculation only when data exist and not when there is none, ensuring that there is no estimation bias resulting from the missing value problem (Krzanowski and Marriott, 1994, 1995) and when time series with largely different characteristics are correlated. In addition this approach remains scale free and straightforward to implement and interpret. We view the method as a bi-variate alternative to time scale transformations which treat conditional heteroscedasticity by expanding periods of higher volatility while contracting periods of lower volatility.

- The calculation of the linear correlation coefficient does not account for variability of variances or covariances over time. The variances of two time series and their covariance are defined either with the assumption that they are stationary in time, or as a type of average value if these are recognized as exhibiting non-stationarity. It has been generally accepted that estimations of correlation between financial time series are unstable (Longin and Solnik, 1995) and even subject to correlation "breakdown" or large changes in correlation during critical periods. In the discussion that follows, we probe the stability of correlation estimates as a function of time, for a number of financial instruments, in order to determine the relevance of high-frequency financial data on such statistical measurements. We go on to investigate the form in which sample correlation values depend on their past values (auto-correlation of correlations). A parametric model for the "self memory of correlation" is proposed as the basis for the formulation of a long term correlation forecast.

- For any given financial distribution, the role of the frequency of time series data on the estimation of correlation should be clearly established. This is especially relevant as higher frequency data become more widely available and more often used in order to boost statistics. Previous authors have demonstrated a dramatic decrease in correlation estimations as data frequency enters the intra-hour level, for both stock (Epps, 1979) and foreign exchange returns (Guillaume *et al*, 1994, Low *et al*, 1996). We follow the suggestion of Low *et al*, (1996) by referring to this phenomenon as the "Epps" (Epps, 1979) effect. In this discussion, an attempt is made to characterize and investigate more deeply the Epps effect in a number of financial time series through the examination of seven years of high-frequency financial returns.

The discussion which follows will cover the following points. First the characteristics of the financial data used for the study are specified. Next, a covolatility normalized method of adjusting the standard correlation coefficient for differences in data frequency between time series and as a compensation mechanism for data gaps or non-overlapping periods is described. Monte Carlo and high-frequency financial data are used to illustrate the characteristic features of this alternative methodology. Estimation of the relative time dependent variance of correlations between a number of instruments is then considered and the dependence of these correlations on their past values is determined. A simple parameterization of correlation self memory, tested on various financial instruments, is proposed. This is followed by the estimation of correlation as a function of varying data frequency; the previously mentioned Epps effect is examined in detail. A relation is drawn between the attenuation of correlation in financial time series and the activities of the correlation constituents. Finally, conclusions are drawn regarding the correlation of high-financial time series.

SPECIFICATION OF THE DATA USED IN THE STUDY

Starting with an observed, non-equally spaced tick-by-tick time series, we use linear interpolation to construct an equally spaced times series with time between observations equal to Δt. Linear interpolation may introduce some form of undesirable dependence in the data and a correction method applicable for estimation of correlation will be discussed later. We address three types of different intra-day price time series in this discussion. Foreign exchange prices are reported in terms of the bid-ask spread and we define the logarithmic middle price (Guillaume *et al*, 1994), $x(t_i)$, as the arithmetic mean of the logarithmic bid and ask quotations (p_{bid} and p_{ask} respectively) as given in Equation 1:

$$x(t_i) \equiv x(\Delta t; t_i) \equiv [\ln p_{ask}(t_i) + \ln p_{bid}(t_i)]/2 \qquad 1$$

where Δt is the duration of a fixed time interval and $x(t_i)$ is the sequence of equally spaced (by Δt), logarithmic prices. Stock index data arrives in terms of a simple price which we transform as:

$$x(t_i) \equiv x(\Delta t; t_i) \equiv \ln p(t_i) \qquad 2$$

Defining a time series of forward interest rates is less straightforward. As a basis, we use interest rate futures (Eurofutures) with fixed expiry dates which represent the forward interest rate starting at the expiry date and ending after a fixed period. A time series of prices coming from a single Eurofutures contract is not large enough to allow for a serious study, therefore it is necessary to join contracts together in an appropriate way. A suitable continuous-time series that can be derived from Eurofutures is the series of forward interest rates. Here the beginning of the forward interest period (which we choose to be of three months) is always at a fixed time interval, e.g. six months, from the quotation time. Sometimes, when the expiry of a 3-month Eurofutures contract happens to be six months in the future (in the aforementioned example), the resulting forward interest rate coincides with the interest rate implied by that Eurofutures contract. For a time t_i where this is the case, the logarithmic forward interest rate x is defined as follows:

$$x(t_i) \equiv x(\Delta t; t_i) \equiv \ln \left[1 + \left(1 - \frac{f(t_i)}{100\%}\right)\right] \qquad 3$$

where f is the Eurofutures quote and $(1 - f/100\%)$ is the annualized implied forward interest rate (which could be multiplied by 100 percent to obtain the usual form of an interest rate). In all other cases, the forward period to be taken overlaps with the forward periods of more than one Eurofutures contract, so we need an empirical method to compute the forward interest rate from several contracts. A number of such methods exist and typically attempt to simulate what a trader does when holding a contract and switching (rolling over) to another, some time before the expiry of a contract. Other methods try to obtain the best estimate of the true forward interest rate through linear or non-linear interpolation of implied interest rates of Eurofutures contracts. The method used here belongs to the latter type and is described by Müller, (1996). However, the choice of this method is not the focus of this paper; other methods may be suitable. The final forward interest rate is in logarithmic form as shown in Equation 3.

In the following study, we are less interested in the (logarithmic) prices of these instruments than in their returns (Guillaume *et al*, 1994) which we define as:

$$\Delta x_i \equiv r_i \equiv r(\Delta t; t_i) \equiv [x(t_i) - x(t_i - \Delta t)] \qquad 4$$

The discussion which follows involves the use of intra-day foreign exchange, stock index and implied forward interest rate return values ranging from January 9, 1990 to January 7, 1997. Correlations between the following financial instruments were considered:

- USD/DEM—USD/NLG
- USD/DEM—USD/GBP
- USD/DEM—USD/ITL
- DEM/GBP—USD/GBP
- USD/FRF—USD/GBP
- USD/JPY—DEM/JPY
- Dow Jones Industrial Average (DJIA)—American Stock Exchange Index (Amex)
- USD 3 to 6 month implied forward interest rate—DEM 3 to 6 month implied forward interest rate
- DEM 3 to 6 month implied forward interest rate—DEM 9 to 12 month implied forward interest rate

USD implied forward interest rate data consisted of transactions at the Chicago Mercantile Exchange (CME) and DEM implied forward interest rate data describe transactions at the London International Financial Futures and Options Exchange (LIFFE). Further characteristics of these implied interest rate data is described in Ballocchi *et al*, (1998). For the sake of comparison, we negate the returns from the "cable" cross rate GBP/USD. Thus they are reported as USD/GBP instead. The cross rate GBP/DEM was converted to DEM/GBP in the same manner. The correlations between instruments of fundamentally different financial natures are not discussed in this study since they were observed to be largely uncorrelated, making them less interesting for the purposes of this discussion. Tick activity averages for the instruments used in this discussion are shown in Table 1. These relative numbers are not actual volume figures, but the mean number of price quotations observed per day (including weekends and holidays) and for the database which was

Table 1   Activity (in terms of the average number of quotations per day) for the financial instruments considered in this study. The sampling period was from January 9, 1990 to January 7, 1997 (2,555 days).

Financial instrument	Mean price quotations per day	Mean price quotes per business day
USD/DEM	3390	4715
USD/JPY	1492	2060
USD/GBP	1217	1697
USD/FRF	708	991
USD/NLG	594	831
USD/ITL	432	604
DJIA	385	539
DEM/JPY	328	454
Amex	319	446
DEM/GBP	280	390
DEM 3–6m IR	156	218
USD 3–6m IR	97	136
DEM 9–12m IR	89	125

used. For some instruments, multiple data sources were merged to form more populated time series while for others only one source was used.

All foreign exchange (FX), stock index and implied forward interest rate returns were obtained in physical time unless otherwise stated and included weekdays as well as weekends and any holidays. A relatively reliable set of data filters were also applied to the data, removing two to three percent of the data as obviously false outliers.

COVOLATILITY WEIGHTING IN THE CORRELATION CALCULATION

Estimation of the correlation coefficient is straightforward but some inconvenience is introduced via its simple definition. The usual definition of the sample correlation requires two equally spaced stationary time series as input. This necessity is easily satisfied when low frequency ($\leq$ one tick per week) data are concerned. However, the problem requires more careful treatment for higher data frequencies and where one cannot dictate the observations times or number of observations (Müller *et al*, 1990).

One often faces two main problems when estimating correlation between two high-frequency financial time series. First, the two observed time series usually have completely different frequencies. If both time series happen to occur at completely regular time grids but with different frequencies, one might want to generate from them two equally spaced time series with equal frequency, just by taking the time grid with the smaller frequency as the joint time grid for both series. However, this easily satisfied situation does not occur very often in practice. More frequently, one is faced with time series such as the USD/DEM foreign exchange rate, which can vary from one thousand or more quotes per hour (from a single data supplier) to tens of quotes per hour, sometimes within a 24-hour period. What is then a reasonable way to statistically measure or estimate the dependence between this foreign exchange rate, with its associated varying arrival times, and another one which is perhaps less active or with activity peaks and valleys at completely different times of the day or week? Ideally, one would prefer to update the correlation estimation more often when more information exists and less often when no or little information is available. Formulating two equal but unevenly spaced time series grids for both instruments would be a possible solution. In fact, a time scale transformation which treats seasonal heteroscedasticity, known in the literature as ϑ("theta")-time (Dacorogna *et al*, 1993), has already been demonstrated for high-frequency foreign exchange data. This time scale models the intra-daily deterministic seasonal patterns of the volatility caused by the geographical dispersion of market agents. Weekends and holidays are also accounted for. One of its characteristics consists of compressing physical time periods of inactivity while expanding periods of greater activity. Although this method has proven useful for a number of applications, its implementation is time consuming in practice. A multivariate formulation of ϑ-time even increases the complexity of the situation. In addition, one of the characteristics of ϑ-time is to remove seasonalities in order to measure more subtle underlying effects. However, deseasonalizing is not necessarily suitable for estimating correlation; one risks to eliminate pertinent information from the time series.

A second problem one faces when estimating correlation between two high-frequency financial time series is that of missing values or data gaps. Large data gaps are actually a border case of the first problem (varying and non-matching data arrival frequencies) but there is no harm in discussing them separately for purposes of motivation. Despite one's best efforts, data gaps sometimes occur due to failure in the data acquisition chain. One can only make an educated guess about the correlation between two time series when such a gap occurs, it cannot be estimated empirically. More commonly, there exist financial instruments whose time series exhibit regular and large data gaps by virtue of their definition. Consider, for example, attempting to estimate the correlation between an exchange reported stock index such as the Dow Jones Industrial average, which exists for 6.5 hours per day, five days per week (usually), and another instrument which exists for a similar amount of time each day but with a relatively large time shift (perhaps the Financial Times 100 index). There are a number of different schools of thought regarding the correlation between two financial instruments when one or both are not actually active. One solution might be to carry out the estimation with the derivative of an instrument as an input proxy for the underlying, but these are often significantly different in character and a number of application-limiting assumptions would be involved. Another possible solution might involve estimation of intra-day correlation using all available data, but after applying a simple time shift to one of the geographically offset markets so that, for example, the closing price in New York occurs at the same time as the closing price in London. However, this is actually a form of time lagged correlation estimation and we consider it a different issue entirely. When confronted with varying activity rates and data gaps, it often seems convenient to use some form of data interpolation to solve ones problems. Unfortunately, the experience of many practitioners has not been reassuring (Press *et al*, 1992).

There exist a number of methods for approximation of an equally spaced time series from an irregularly spaced, tick-by-tick data set. Most of these methods involve some form of data imputation. Methods of imputing data vary in complexity and effectiveness; most have been found to be beneficial under at least some set of conditions and assumptions. However, all forms of imputation rely on a model and a standard supposition is that characteristics of the data do not change between in-sample and out-of-sample periods. There is always the possibility that imputation will introduce a bias into variance and co-variance estimations but nevertheless it is difficult to avoid some form of it in cases where data is not of an infinitely high-frequency. Some useful attempts have been made to circumvent imputation altogether. One interesting and recent example is described in De Jong and Nijman (1997). This work builds primarily on efforts described in Cohen *et al*. (1983), and Lo and MacKinlay, (1990a,b). The authors develop a covariance estimator which uses irregularly spaced data whenever and wherever it exists in either of two time series. However, methods such as this one rely on the assumption that process generating transaction times and prices themselves are independent. This assumption may be well-suited, depending on the instruments and application being considered. However, testing for this independence is rarely trivial and we prefer to avoid the assumption altogether. Instead we develop what we see as a complementary technique.

In this discussion, we propose and illustrate a simple estimate of correlation which avoids imputation based on data models that are constructed from out of sample data or on distributional assumptions. Although the inputs for this alternative estimator are equally spaced time series derived through simple linear interpolation, the method filters out any underestimation of variances and co-variances caused by the lack of sampling variation which results from the over-interpolation of data. In addition, rather than making the strong assumption that prices and transaction times are independent, this method makes use of arrival times in order to compensate for the (sometimes large) differences in the observation frequencies of financial time series. Data gaps of varying size are common and we avoid any discussion of whether correlation actually exists during this period, since in any case we cannot estimate it directly. Our goal is rather to develop a statistical measure of dependence (correlation) when information exists and to avoid updating this estimation when data are not available. This should be recalled when it the time comes to interpret results. This approach implies that a lower data frequency or data gap in one time series may limit the use of another one. The unavoidable price to pay for such a methodology is the loss of statistics in the estimation. However, this method is specifically meant for estimation of correlation at higher data frequencies where computational statistics become less of a constraint on accuracy.

Formulation of an Adjusted Correlation Estimation

The standard linear correlation coefficient is an estimator of the correlation between two time series, Δx_i and Δy_i whose definition is given in Equation 5:

$$\varrho(\Delta x, \Delta y) \equiv \frac{\sum_{i=1}^{n} (\Delta x_i - \overline{\Delta x})(\Delta y_i - \overline{\Delta y})}{\sqrt{\sum_{i=1}^{n} (\Delta x_i - \overline{\Delta x})^2 \sum_{i=1}^{n} (\Delta y_i - \overline{\Delta y})^2}} \qquad 5$$

where

$$\overline{\Delta x} \equiv \frac{\sum_{i=1}^{n} \Delta x_i}{n} \quad \text{and} \quad \overline{\Delta y} \equiv \frac{\sum_{i=1}^{n} \Delta y_i}{n} \qquad 6$$

The sample is of size T with $n = T/\Delta t$ equally spaced observations. Correlation values are unitless and may range from -1 (completely anti-correlated) to 1 (completely correlated). A value of zero is indicative of no correlation between the two time series.

An estimate of the *local* sample covolatility[2] for each of these regions is defined by further dividing each time interval of length Δt (on which Δx_i and Δy_i are evaluated) into m disjoint subintervals of equal length $\Delta \tilde{t} = \Delta t / m$, and we may obtain sub-return values, $\Delta \tilde{x}_j$ and $\Delta \tilde{y}_j$, $j = 1, \ldots, m$ in the usual way. This refined time series now consists of $\tilde{n} = T / \Delta \tilde{t}$ equally spaced (via linear interpolation) observations on returns.

$$\tilde{x}(\tilde{t}_j) \equiv \tilde{x}(\Delta \tilde{t}; \tilde{t}_j) \equiv [\ln p_{\text{ask}}(\tilde{t}_j) + \ln p_{\text{bid}}(\tilde{t}_j)]/2 \qquad 7$$

Then for each of the periods $[t_{i-1}, t_i]$ with corresponding coarse returns, Δx_i (as for Δy_i), we can define an estimator of the covolatility between the two refined time series of returns:

$$\omega_i(\Delta \tilde{x}; \Delta \tilde{y}; \Delta \tilde{t}) \equiv \sum_{j=1}^{m} \left(|\Delta \tilde{x}_{i \cdot m - j} - \overline{\Delta \tilde{x}_{i \cdot m}}| \cdot |\Delta \tilde{y}_{i \cdot m - j} - \overline{\Delta \tilde{y}_{i \cdot m}}| \right)^\alpha \qquad 8$$

where

$$\overline{\Delta \tilde{x}_{i \cdot m}} = \frac{\sum_{j=1}^{m} \Delta \tilde{x}_{i \cdot m - j}}{m} \quad \text{and} \quad \overline{\Delta \tilde{y}_{i \cdot m}} = \frac{\sum_{j=1}^{m} \Delta \tilde{y}_{i \cdot m - j}}{m} \qquad 9$$

The most obvious choice for α is 0.5, though the choice of the value of α can be studied as a way to magnify or demagnify the weight given to farther outlying return values. A value of 0.5 is used in all cases described in the discussions which follow.

Equation 8 defines covolatility around the mean rather than around zero and $\omega_i = 0$ for the case of returns derived from two linearly interpolated prices existing outside of our region of interest, Δt. This follows from the fact that each of the j sub-return values would be equal to each other and also equal to their mean value. The difference between these is equal to zero and the sum of the products of zero and any other quantity will also be equal to zero.[3] These covolatility estimates can be inserted as weights into the sample variances and covariances to obtain an estimator of correlation:

$$\varrho(\Delta x, \Delta y, \omega) \equiv \frac{\sum_{i=1}^{T/\Delta t} [(\Delta x_i - \overline{\Delta x})(\Delta y_i - \overline{\Delta y})\omega_i]}{\sqrt{\sum_{i=1}^{T/\Delta t} [(\Delta x_i - \overline{\Delta x})^2 \omega_i]} \sqrt{\sum_{i=1}^{T/\Delta t} [(\Delta y_i - \overline{\Delta y})^2 \omega_i]}} \qquad 10$$

Notice that Δx_i and Δy_i in Equations 10 and 5 are the same since they are taken over the same time period, $[t_{i-1}, t_i]$. The return values on the coarser grid with span Δt can then be defined as the sum of the return values on the refined grid with span $\tilde{\Delta} t$:

$$\Delta x_i \equiv \sum_{j=1}^{m} \Delta \tilde{x}_{i \cdot m - j} \qquad 11$$

There are two sums left in Equation 10 which are updated with linearly interpolated returns even in cases when no actual information exists: $\overline{\Delta y}$, $\overline{\Delta x}$. That is the case if we define them according to Equation 6. One would rather prefer that mean values, $\overline{\Delta y}$ and $\overline{\Delta x}$, be calculated again in a weighted fashion so that true return values are input to the calculation where they exist and not where they do not exist. In addition, there should be assurance that weighted means are calculated over the same data sample used for the rest of the correlation calculation. Therefore we define weighted mean values for both time series which are also covolatility weighted:

$$\overline{\Delta x} \equiv \frac{\sum_{i=1}^{T/\Delta t} (\Delta x_i \cdot \omega_i)}{\sum_{i=1}^{T/\Delta t} \omega_i} \quad \text{and} \quad \overline{\Delta y} \equiv \frac{\sum_{i=1}^{T/\Delta t} (\Delta y_i \cdot \omega_i)}{\sum_{i=1}^{T/\Delta t} \omega_i} \qquad 12$$

Equation 12 then defines mean values which are unbiased by ω_i if all Δx_i (or Δy_i) are equal. The weights correctly adjust for periods of lower or higher activity and in periods when data does not exist the mean value is numerically equal to the usual mean value calculation but with data gaps removed.

It was already noted that Equation 8 is formulated in such a way that $\omega_i = 0$ for the case of returns derived from two linearly interpolated prices existing outside of our region of interest, Δt, and in that case the summations of Equations 10 and 12 are not updated. The covolatility adjusted estimation of correlation described by Equation 10 also retains the desirable characteristics of the original, standard linear correlation coefficient; it is scale free, invariant and completely different estimations are directly comparable. In addition, this alternative method is only slightly more complicated to implement than the standard linear correlation coefficient and can easily be implemented on any personal computer.

As will be applied later, this statistical correlation measure also fits easily into the framework of autocorrelation analysis. Given a time series of correlations $\tilde{\varrho}_t$, it can be correlated with a copy of itself but with different time lags (τ) between the two, as shown in Equation 13:

$$R(\tilde{\varrho}(\Delta x, \Delta y, \omega), \tau) = \frac{\displaystyle\sum_{t=\tau+1}^{n} (\tilde{\varrho}_t - \overline{\tilde{\varrho}_1})(\tilde{\varrho}_{t-\tau} - \overline{\tilde{\varrho}_2})}{\left[\displaystyle\sum_{t=\tau+1}^{n} (\tilde{\varrho}_t - \overline{\tilde{\varrho}_1})^2 \sum_{t=\tau+1}^{n} (\tilde{\varrho}_{t-\tau} - \overline{\tilde{\varrho}_2})^2\right]^{1/2}} \qquad 13$$

for $\tau > 0$ and where

$$\overline{\tilde{\varrho}_1} = \frac{1}{n-\tau} \sum_{t=\tau+1}^{n} \tilde{\varrho}_t \quad \text{and} \quad \overline{\tilde{\varrho}_2} = \frac{1}{n-\tau} \sum_{t=\tau+1}^{n} \tilde{\varrho}_{t-\tau} \qquad 14$$

For the discussions which now follow, we estimate correlation using the covolatility adjusted method described by Equation 10, unless otherwise stated and always with $m = 6$ and $\alpha = 0.5$ (see Equation 8). Any subsequent use of the commonly recognized linear correlation coefficient (Equation 5) will be referred to as the "standard" method.

Tests of the Method with Monte Carlo and Financial Data

Various tests were performed with the adjusted correlation estimator in order to test its effect on data gaps and on time series of differing frequencies. Monte Carlo data were used to illustrate the covolatility adjusted correlation method's effectiveness on sections of missing data.

Two separate (uncorrelated), normally distributed, random data sets, A_i, B_i, were produced with zero mean, with standard deviation $\sigma = 0.01$ and length $m = 10,000$. A third distribution, C_i, was then formed as a linear combination of the previous two, according to relation 15.

$$C_{i=1}^{m} \equiv kA_{i=1}^{m} + (1-k)B_{i=1}^{m} \qquad 15$$

where the constant k is selected such that $0 \leq k \leq 1$. In this way, the new distribution C_i was formed with a controllable correlation to one of the original distributions, A_i.

The pseudo return distribution, C_i, was then used to create a pseudo price distribution, P_i, with starting value $P_1 = 10$ and length $m + 1 = 10,001$. Subsequent prices were generated by the return distribution, C_i, according to relation 16.

$$P_{i=2}^{m+1} \equiv e^{\ln(P_{i-1}) + C_{i-1}} \qquad 16$$

Repeated sections of fixed length equal to 50 price values were then deleted in the price distribution P_i and replaced with prices linearly interpolated from the previous and next actual prices. The distance between these induced data gaps was also of length equal to 50, creating an alternating series of original data patches following by data gaps filled with linearly interpolated prices. Finally, a return distribution, D_i, was created from this altered price distribution containing periodic patches of linearly interpolated data as prescribed by Equation 4. Equation 10 was then used to estimate the correlation between one of the original return distributions, A_i, and the manipulated return distribution, D_i, given various values of the constant multiplier k. Results are shown in comparison to the standard linear correlation calculation in Table 2.

Comparison of columns two ($\varrho(A, C)$) and four ($\tilde{\varrho}(A, D)$) shows that the covolatility adjusted correlation estimator described by Equation 10 well approximates the original, coarse, standard linear correlation between distributions A and C before missing data patches were induced and replaced with linearly interpolated values. Any small deviations which exist are within the bounds dictated by statistical error ($\sim$2%) for these tests. This simple example illustrates one of the original design goals of the covolatility adjusted linear correlation estimator; correlation is statistically measured when data exists and the calculation is not updated when data does not exist.

Tests were also performed to exemplify the effect of the covolatility adjusted correlation estimator on time series of differing frequencies. High-frequency USD/DEM 3 minute interval, absolute return values were produced in both normal, physical time and through the de-seasonalizing time scale transformation ϑ-time. The absolute value of USD/DEM returns were used since they are known to have autocorrelations of greater magnitude than with actual returns. The USD/DEM foreign exchange rate is one

Table 2 Monte Carlo comparison of the standard linear correlation between two related pseudo return distributions and the covolatility adjusted linear correlation method described in the text.

multiplier k Equation (15)	$\varrho(A_i, C_i)$ Equation (5)	$\varrho(A_i, D_i)$ Equation (5)	$\tilde{\varrho}(A_i, D_i)$ Equation (10)
0.0	0.00	0.00	0.00
0.1	0.12	0.10	0.12
0.2	0.23	0.15	0.22
0.3	0.38	0.28	0.38
0.4	0.52	0.40	0.51
0.5	0.69	0.51	0.69
0.6	0.83	0.62	0.82
0.7	0.92	0.67	0.91
0.8	0.97	0.72	0.95
0.9	0.99	0.74	0.97
1.0	1.00	0.74	0.99

of the more active (see Table 1) but is also characterized by large intra-day and intra-week activity fluctuations (Dacorogna *et al*, 1993). Autocorrelations (Equation 5) of the absolute returns of this exchange rate were performed in order to demonstrate the effect that correlation estimators have on time series whose activity at any given time differs. First, estimation using the standard method of correlation was performed on a time series with 18 minutes between data points, where linear interpolation to closest tick values was used to form a homogeneous time series from an unevenly spaced tick-by-tick data set. In addition, the standard correlation method was applied to a time series of 18 minute ϑ-time USD/DEM return values. Finally, correlation estimation using the alternative method described by Equation 10 was performed on the homogeneous times series with 3 minute data intervals and with $m = 6$ (Equation 8), therefore the final granularity of all correlation estimations was the same. Results of these estimations are shown in Figure 1. A total data period of six months was used, ranging from January 1, 1996 to July 1, 1996.

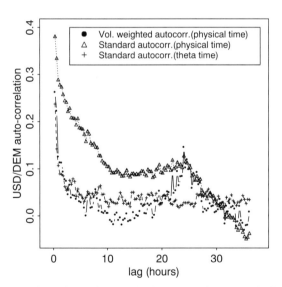

The triangles refer to the standard autocorrelation method applied to the return time series. Darkened circles refer to covolatility adjusted autocorrelation estimation. Crosses refer to the standard autocorrelation estimations but applied to USD/DEM return values measured in ϑ-time. The sample period used was January 1, 1996 to July 1, 1996.

Figure 1 Autocorrelation of the absolute value of USD/DEM returns as a function of lag time.

The covolatility adjusted correlation values (darkened circles) are significantly less than autocorrelation values using the standard method of estimation (triangles). We ascribe this difference to the fact that periods of higher combined or coactivity are given more weight in the correlation calculation than periods of lower coactivity. This amounts to the same as expanding the time scale during periods of higher activity and compressing the time scale during periods of lower activity. The exception to this difference is at a lag equal to 24 hours where the two methods result in largely the same correlation values. In addition, it is noted that the covolatility adjusted correlation estimations largely reproduce correlation estimations calculated with the standard method but with data measured in ϑ-time. The ϑ time scale is itself a statistical measure of activity since it is designed to compress periods of inactivity while expanding periods of higher activity, thus the two results are largely the same. The exception again occurs at the peak in covolatility adjusted correlation at a lag of 24 hours. The ϑ time scale is also designed to remove intra-day and intra-week seasonalities. For correlation studies this is not always desirable and we find the covolatility adjusted correlation estimation to be a more suitable method for many applications. In addition, the simplicity of this methodology lends itself to wider use.

STABILITY OF FINANCIAL TIME SERIES RETURN CORRELATIONS

When correlation is calculated between two time series, the implication is that this quantity does not vary itself over time. For the case of financial time series this is seldom the case, although variance of the correlation coefficient over time can sometimes be small. This issue is critical for portfolio pricing and risk management where hedging techniques can become worthless when they are most needed; during periods known as correlation "breakdown", or relatively rapid change. As demonstrated in Boyer *et al*, (1997), detection of correlation breakdown or other structural breaks by splitting a return distribution into a number of quantiles can yield misleading results. We used high-frequency data to estimate correlations literally as a function of time for a number of different financial time series in an effort to better understand the level of change which can occur. These high-frequency correlation estimations are contrasted with lower frequency, lower time resolution estimates for the same sample periods. The "memory" that correlation coefficients have for their past values was also estimated for a number of examples using a simple and appropriate parameterization. Such estimations can be applied to long term correlation forecasting which is required, for example, in order to price or hedge financial options involving multiple assets (Gibson and Boyer, 1997).

Correlation Variations Over Time

The general stability of correlation coefficients were examined using various correlation calculation intervals and data frequencies. This involved examination of a fixed historical data set of horizon or period T. The temporal set of returns $(r(t_i))$ was then divided into N subsets of equal size in time (T/N) from which correlation coefficients are computed according to Equation 5. This was performed on our data set ranging from January 7, 1990 to January 5, 1997. Four values of N were selected, while the total period, T, always remained constant. A number of returns, n, were then obtained via linear interpolation from inside the period T/N. The frequency (or resolution) of data involved in each correlation calculation, $f = (n \times N)/T$, was adjusted throughout the four sets in order to maintain nearly uniform statistics, as shown in Table 3. Results from these calculations are shown in Figures 2 to 7, where correlations versus time are displayed as circular data points and dashed lines above and below zero correlation are 95 percent confidence intervals assuming normally distributed random distributions. The confidence limits are slightly non-uniform due to small sample-to-sample variations in statistics. Although exactly matching homogeneous data grids were used for each sample, the correlation calculated is not updated if a weight, ω_i, from Equation 8 is equal to zero. Statistics were increased by one in all other cases.

Table 3   The various calculation periods and frequencies selected in order to maintain nearly uniform statistical confidence for the study of linear correlation coefficient variation over time. The total sampling period, T, was from January 7, 1990 to January 5, 1997.

Correlation calculation period T/N	Data frequency (quotes/day) $f = (n \times N)/T$	Number of points n	95% Confidence limit $1.96/\sqrt{n}$
365 days	1	365	0.10
128 days	3	384	0.10
32 days	12	384	0.10
7 days	72	504	0.09

Correlation coefficient mean values and variances are given for each pair of financial instruments and for each of the four calculation frequencies in Table 4. Having virtually the same statistical significance for all correlation calculations shown in Figures 2–7, one can make a number of observations about correlation stability. The highly correlated USD/DEM—USD/NLG FX returns shown in Figure 2 appear largely constant over the total sample period of seven years. As the sub period width for correlation calculation decreases (and the number of correlation calculations inside the total period increases) more structure becomes apparent. This additional structure is reflected in a changing variance (see Table 4).

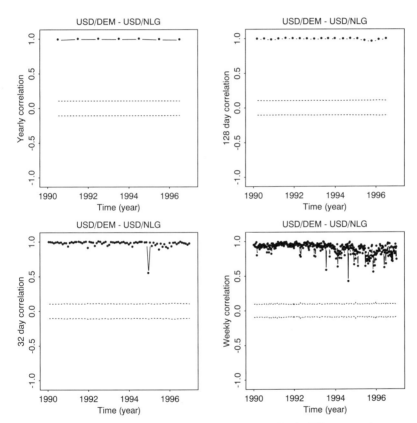

$T/N = $ (365 days, 128 days, 32 days and 7 days), for the FX return pair USD/DEM — USD/NLG. The dashed lines above and below zero correlation are 95% confidence intervals assuming normal, random distributions.

Figure 2 Linear correlation coefficients calculated using increasingly small subintervals.

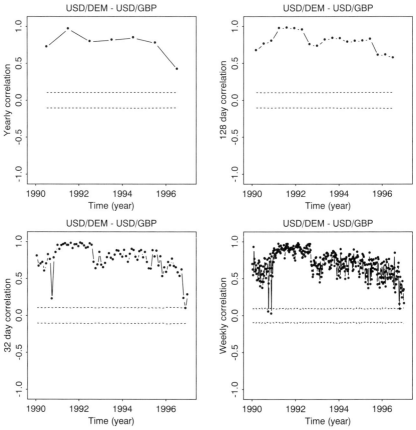

T/N = (365 days, 128 days, 32 days and 7 days), for the FX return pair
USD/DEM – USD/GBP. The dashed lines above and below zero correlation
are 95% confidence intervals assuming normal, random distributions.

Figure 3   Linear correlation coefficients calculated using increasingly
small sub-intervals.

In addition, correlations calculated with lower data frequency are
not simply an average of those calculated with higher quotation
frequencies (revealing more structure); Table 4 shows the mean value for
USD/DEM—USD/NLG correlations moving steadily downward with
increasing correlation resolution (a −11 percent change between yearly
data resolution and weekly resolution). This can be partially explained
by considering that systematic error estimates for correlation calculations
are not symmetric where coefficients are not zero. However, such drops

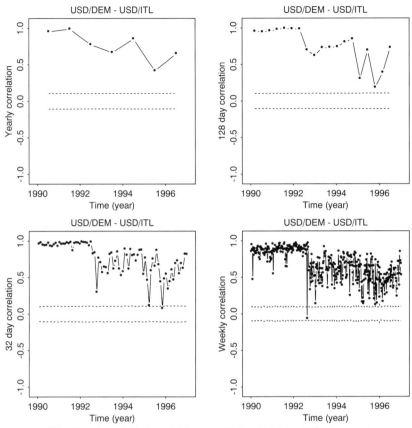

T/N = (365 days, 128 days, 32 days and 7 days), for the FX return pair USD/DEM – USD/ITL. The dashed lines above and below zero correlation are 95% confidence intervals assuming normal, random distributions.

Figure 4 Linear correlation coefficients calculated using increasingly small sub-intervals.

in correlation with higher data frequency as can be observed with the DJIA—Amex pair point to a stronger effect which will be addressed in more detail later in this chapter.

Figures 3 and 4 (correlations for USD/DEM—USD/GBP and USD/DEM—USD/ITL respectively) both exhibit fast and large drops in correlations (nearly a factor of two decrease within a two week period) during the 2nd and 3rd weeks September 1992. Presumably, this directly reflects the turmoil leading to and resulting from GBP and ITL breaks

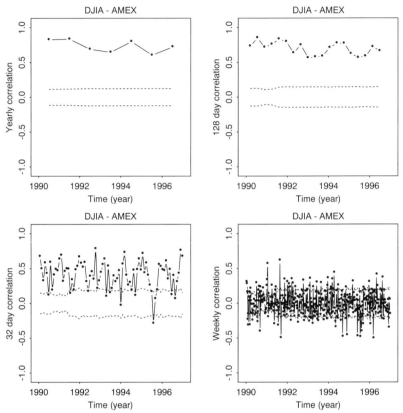

T/N = (365 days, 128 days, 32 days and 7 days), for the stock index pair DJIA – Amex. The dashed lines above and below zero correlation are 95% confidence intervals assuming normal, random distributions.

Figure 5   Linear correlation coefficients calculated using increasingly small sub-intervals.

with the European Monetary System (EMS) during that time and appears to be a clear example of correlation breakdown.

Recapitulating the major points made so far, correlation stability was examined as a function of time for a number of different examples. Comparisons were achieved by considering a relatively long, fixed time frame of data. This time frame of seven years was then divided in four different ways using subperiods of 365, 128, 32 and 7 days. The number of sub-periods over the total seven year period was then 6, 17, 68 and 312 respectively. The object of this exercise was to determine, for these

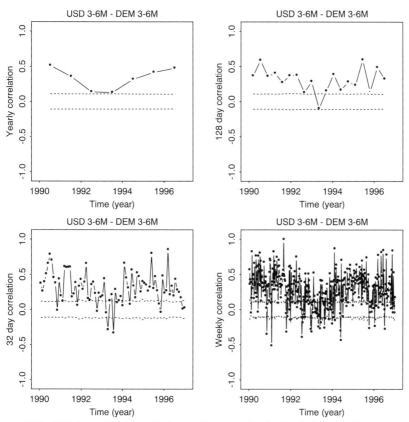

T/N = (365 days, 128 days, 32 days and 7 days), for the implied forward interest rate pair USD 3–6 months – DEM 3–6 months. The dashed lines above and below zero correlation are 95% confidence intervals assuming normal, random distributions.

Figure 6 Linear correlation coefficients calculated using increasingly small sub-intervals.

examples, the structure of correlations over time. In an attempt to make these comparisons in a statistically equal manner, the frequency of data used in correlation calculations was varied inversely as the subperiod size; if a period of 365 days was divided into 52 correlation subperiods of one week each, the frequency of data was increased by roughly the same factor. In this way the statistical significance of correlation calculations was maintained on the same level throughout and more valid comparisons could be made in searches for correlation structure.

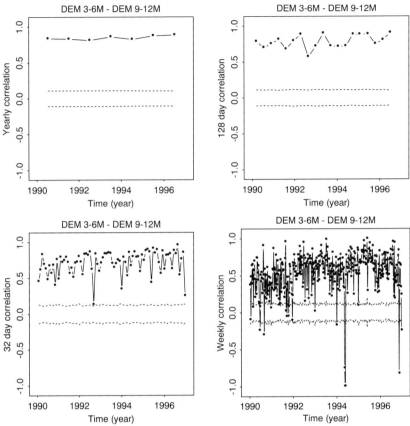

T/N = (365 days, 128 days, 32 days and 7 days), for the implied forward interest rate pair DEM 3–6 months – DEM 9–12 months. The dashed lines above and below zero correlation are 95% confidence intervals assuming normal, random distributions.

Figure 7 Linear correlation coefficients calculated using increasingly small sub-intervals.

The correlation between some financial instruments can be described as relatively stable. However, brief but large breaks can be observed in almost all cases and the additional statistics provided by higher frequency time series is essential to detecting such occurrences. In addition, we observed moderate decreases in the absolute values of all correlations we examined when going to higher data frequencies. This will be discussed further later in this chapter.

Table 4 Mean values, variances, minima and maxima (calculated from the data in Figures 2 through 7) of linear correlation coefficients calculated using increasingly small sub-intervals for the financial instruments return pairs described in the text. The total sampling period, T, was from January 7, 1990 to January 5, 1997.

instrument pair	correlation period	mean value	variance (σ^2)	max.	min.
USD/DEM—USD/NLG	1 year	0.99	0.000026	0.99	0.98
USD/DEM—USD/NLG	128 day	0.99	0.00012	1.00	0.95
USD/DEM—USD/NLG	32 day	0.96	0.0029	1.00	0.54
USD/DEM—USD/NLG	7 day	0.88	0.0067	0.98	0.41
USD/DEM—USD/GBP	1 year	0.76	0.029	0.96	0.42
USD/DEM—USD/GBP	128 day	0.79	0.015	0.98	0.57
USD/DEM—USD/GBP	32 day	0.76	0.031	0.98	0.09
USD/DEM—USD/GBP	7 day	0.69	0.030	0.97	0.20
USD/DEM—USD/ITL	1 year	0.76	0.040	0.99	0.41
USD/DEM—USD/ITL	128 day	0.75	0.057	0.99	0.18
USD/DEM—USD/ITL	32 day	0.76	0.044	0.99	0.07
USD/DEM—USD/ITL	7 day	0.68	0.044	0.97	0.07
DJIA—Amex	1 year	0.73	0.0083	0.84	0.60
DJIA—Amex	128 day	0.70	0.0087	0.85	0.57
DJIA—Amex	32 day	0.41	0.041	0.78	−0.29
DJIA—Amex	7 day	−0.01	0.030	0.62	−0.50
DEM 3–6m-DEM 9–12m	1 year	0.84	0.00074	0.88	0.81
DEM 3–6m-DEM 9–12m	128 day	0.78	0.0084	0.90	0.57
DEM 3–6m-DEM 9–12m	32 day	0.71	0.025	0.96	0.13
DEM 3–6m-DEM 9–12m	7 day	0.54	0.074	1.00	−1.00
USD 3–6m-DEM 3–6m	1 year	0.33	0.024	0.51	0.13
USD 3–6m-DEM 3–6m	128 day	0.30	0.028	0.59	−0.10
USD 3–6m-DEM 3–6m	32 day	0.30	0.051	0.85	−0.34
USD 3–6m-DEM 3–6m	7 day	0.28	0.066	1.00	−0.52

The Exponential Memory of Financial Time Series Return Correlations

Figures 2 through 7 show a general tendency towards the revelation of increased correlation structure as correlation resolution increases. In a search for potential seasonalities, and in order to gauge the memory of each correlation pair for past values, autocorrelations were performed on each of the one week correlation series shown in Figures 2 through 7 (lower-right plots). Following these autocorrelation estimations, a parameterization is presented which might form the basis for a correlation forecast.

Autocorrelation analysis using different time lags (τ) was performed on the time dependent series of correlation coefficients, $\varrho(t_i)$, by application of Equation 13. Results of these calculations are shown in Figure 8. Shown along with each autocorrelation curve are the 95 percent confidence limits for a normally distributed random process. The differences in autocorrelations of the six correlation pairs is striking. The long term autocorrelation of foreign exchange rate correlations is significant for 50 to 100 weeks. The autocorrelations of correlations between implied forward interest rates tended to remain above this significance level for lags corresponding to three to four months while the same quantity for the Dow Jones and Amex stock index pair dives below the same significance level in the first (one week) lag. Figure 8 also shows that autocorrelation values for each of the six correlation pairs decline roughly exponentially but with markedly different attenuation rates.

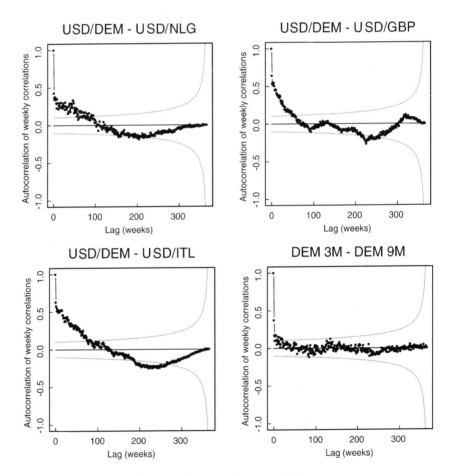

Figure 8   Autocorrelations of correlation coefficients.

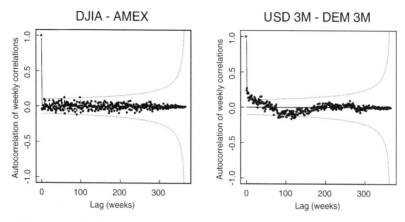

The auto correlations (points joined by solid lines) are calculated from the finest (7 day) sub-interval (T/N) using the linear correlation coefficient data shown in the lower-right plots of Figures 2 through 7, and for the return pairs described in the text. Also shown are the 95% confidence intervals corresponding to normally distributed random distributions (dotted lines). The total sampling period, T, was from January 7, 1990 to January 5, 1997.

Figure 8   (*continued*).

In order to better gauge the difference in autocorrelation attenuation for these correlation pairs, the autocorrelations shown in Figure 8 were fitted to a simple exponential function as given in Equation 17:

$$Y \equiv Ae^{-x/\lambda} \qquad\qquad 17$$

where λ is an exponential attenuation length and A is a simple weight. A smaller attenuation length refers to a faster, exponential attenuation. Each autocorrelation curve was fitted starting with the first lag (neglecting the zero*th* lag which is equal to one by definition) and only to the point where data autocorrelation data fell below the 68 percent confidence limit (1σ); the character of autocorrelations varies from the exponential parameterization near that point. An example of one such fit to the autocorrelation of USD/DEM—USD/GBP correlations is shown in Figure 9 and fit results for all of the autocorrelation of correlation data shown in Figure 8 are given in Table 5. A fit to DJIA—Amex data was not made since the autocorrelation of its weekly correlation values is almost immediately insignificant at the level of our statistics. This is not simply due to a lack of correlation between the two stock indices, but rather to the fact that correlations estimated using a data interval of 20 minutes are highly subject to the Epps effect which will be discussed later in this chapter.

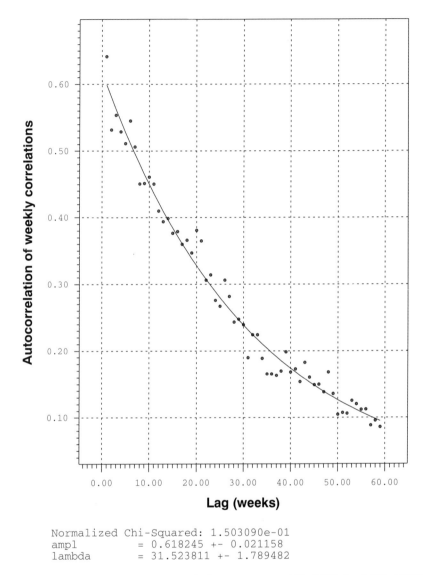

```
Normalized Chi-Squared: 1.503090e-01
ampl          = 0.618245 +- 0.021158
lambda        = 31.523811 +- 1.789482
```

Figure 9 Fit of an exponential function to USD/DEM—USD/GBP weekly correlation coefficients.

Goodness of fits of the data to Equation 17 can be judged for each case curve from their individual χ^2 per degree of freedom values shown in Table 5. These values of χ^2 were obtained after performing fits where individual data points were assigned symmetric errors corresponding to

Table 5 Results of fits of the autocorrelation of correlation data shown in Figure 8 to the parameterization given in Equation 17, for the correlation pairs described in the text. The large values for λ indicate correlation self-memories which decay exponentially over very long periods.

Instrument	A	λ (weeks)	$\chi^2/D.O.F$
USD/DEM—USD/NLG	0.35 ± 0.01	80.9 ± 7.1	0.65
USD/DEM—USD/GBP	0.62 ± 0.02	31.5 ± 1.8	0.15
USD/DEM—USD/ITL	0.61 ± 0.02	59.8 ± 3.0	0.34
DEM 3–6m-DEM 9–12m	0.27 ± 0.04	10.0 ± 2.6	1.30
USD 3–6m-DEM 3–6m	0.23 ± 0.03	21.8 ± 5.4	0.41

$1\sigma = 1/\sqrt{N}$, where N is the total number of correlation points considered when calculating an individual autocorrelation value. In all cases $\chi^2/D.O.F.$ values were below one indicating the function describes the data relatively well. Adding a second exponential function to Equation 17 did not significantly improve the goodness of fit in all cases unless the $0th$ lag data point (defined as being equal to one) was added to the data set.

The weighting factor A is an estimation of the initial (1 week) strength of correlation self-memory and can be at most equal to one (or negative one). The component λ from Equation 17 can be referred to as an attenuation length which has actual units (in this case time in terms of weeks); the exact attenuation length then refers to the time required for a $1/e$ drop in auto-correlation. A larger (smaller) λ component describes a less (more) rapid exponential attenuation. For example, the fit to USD/DEM—USD/NLG auto-correlation data reveals the correlation between these cross rates to have correlation self memory which is very long lived, being reduced by an exponential factor in just over one and a half years. This autocorrelation parameterization gives the basis for a correlation forecast and in addition the λ values reported here point to the possibility for a forecast accurate in the long term (> six months depending on the instruments involved).

CORRELATION CHANGES TOWARDS HIGHER DATA FREQUENCIES

Previous authors have observed a dramatic decrease in correlation as data frequency enters the intra-hour level, for both stock (Epps, 1979) and FX returns (Guillaume *et al*, 1994, Low *et al*, 1996). We follow the suggestion of Low *et al*. (1996) by referring to this phenomenon as the Epps effect after the first identifiable author (Epps, 1979) to thoroughly document it. In this discussion, the Epps effect is characterized and investigated for a number of foreign exchange rates, stock indices and implied forward interest rate pairs through the examination of the same seven years of high-frequency return values as has been described previously.

High-frequency returns for the pairs of financial instruments given in Table 1 were used as the basis for formation of equally spaced time series with varying data time intervals or data frequencies. Linear interpolation between points was used in order to insure precise time alignment of data from one time series to another. 1,377 equally spaced time series were assembled in this way; 500 time series were formed with data time intervals varying from 1 data point per 5 minutes of time to 1 data point per 2,500 minutes, this with an interval of 5 minutes. Another 877 time series were formed to have data time intervals ranging from one data per 2,530 minutes to one data per 28,810 minutes (20 days), going by steps of 30 minutes of time interval. Various calculations were performed with the times series, including the calculation of their variances and the covariances and correlations between different financial return time series with the same data time intervals. Diminution of correlations when performing calculations with higher frequency (intra-day) data can be observed in Figure 10. A rapid decline to zero is noted as data frequency increases (or data time interval decreases). This is better viewed in Figure 11, where the same data is shown with a logarithmic horizontal scale and where the data point farthest to the left (highest data frequency or smallest shown interval between data points) corresponds to correlations calculated using linearly interpolated, homogeneous time series with five minutes between data points. Table 6 gives the minimum and maximum values for the linear correlation coefficient data shown in Figure 10. Also given are the time intervals at which maximums occurred. We noted several problems with taking the maximum value of a given correlation vs. time interval distribution. None of the correlation values reach a true stabilization value, even at very large time intervals (>10 days). This can be the result of correlations rising asymptotically to unity with data intervals approaching infinity but is certainly also a result of the inevitable increased spread in correlation data arising from the gradual loss of statistics moving toward greater data intervals. In an attempt to more accurately characterize Epps effect drops, Table 6 also reports the arithmetic mean value of correlation calculations for correlation values whose time interval was between one and two days. These calculations involved 224 data points for each of the correlation pairs. The correlation value of relevance for a particular situation depends entirely on the time horizon one is interested in; there is no best correlation value for the general case, only for a particular case. However, this mean

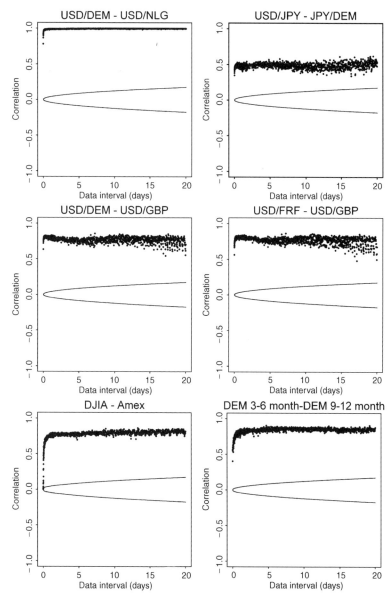

For all calculations the total sampling period remained constant (from January 9, 1990 to January 7, 1997), causing the 95% confidence intervals to be small at high data frequencies and larger as data time interval decreases. Rapid declines in correlation at higher data frequencies are noted in all cases.

Figure 10   Linear correlation coefficients calculated for six example correlation pairs as a function of return data time interval.

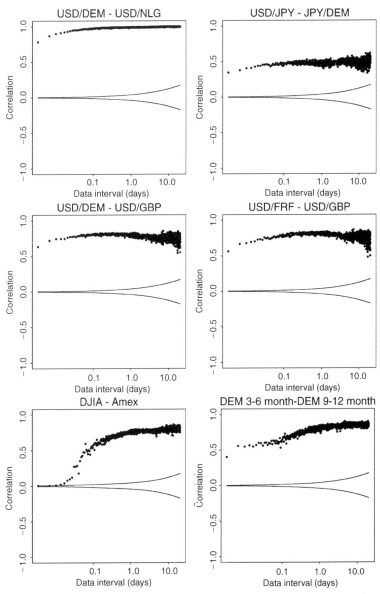

This is the same data as in Figure 10 but shown with logarithmic horizontal axes. Rapid declines in correlation are noted in all cases for higher return frequencies.

Figure 11   Linear correlation coefficients calculated for six example correlation pairs as a function of date time interval (inverse frequency) used in the calculation.

Table 6 Minimum and maximum values for the linear correlation coefficient data shown in Figures 10 and 11. Also given are the time intervals at which maximums occurred and the mean values of correlations for data intervals between one and two days. In addition, the time intervals at which mean values occurred and the data intervals at which correlation coefficients rose to at least 90% of the mean value—a nominal stabilization point—are reported. The sampling period was from January 9, 1990 to January 7, 1997.

Instrument pair	Min. corr.	Max. corr.	Max. point (days)	mean correlation (1–2 days)	90% of mean	90% point (minutes)
USD/DEM—USD/GBP	0.55	0.86	7.2	0.79	0.71	10
USD/DEM—USD/NLG	0.78	1.00	14.0	0.99	0.89	15
USD/FRF—USD/ITL	0.49	0.86	12.0	0.79	0.71	25
USD/NLG—USD/FRF	0.69	0.99	16.9	0.97	0.87	25
USD/FRF—USD/GBP	0.48	0.86	7.2	0.80	0.72	30
USD/JPY—DEM/JPY	0.34	0.62	19.4	0.48	0.43	30
USD/GBP—USD/GBP	0.23	0.75	17.0	0.45	0.41	170
DJIA—Amex	0.00	0.86	13.3	0.77	0.69	320
DEM 3–6M-DEM 9–12M	0.40	0.90	19.2	0.82	0.74	340

value is considered as a less arbitrary (though still imperfect) estimate of correlation maximum (a true maximum value or stabilization point being difficult to estimate in most cases). The data time intervals at which correlations reach 90 percent of the means are also shown in Table 6. This estimation for the correlation stabilization point has the advantage that it can be uniformly applied to all cases but it does not deliver obviously misleading stabilization intervals as would be observed by taking the point at which correlations drop to 90 percent of an absolute maximum value. We conclude from this data that even currency pairs which are highly correlated in the long term, become much less correlated in the intra-hour data frequency range. The authors of Müller *et al*, 1997 propose a hypothesis of heterogeneous markets where the market agents differ in their perception of the market, have differing risk profiles and operate under different institutional constraints. This diversity of agents causes volatilities of different time horizons to behave differently. If the financial markets are indeed composed of heterogeneous agents with different time horizons of interest, then the Epps effect drop in correlation estimations could be interpreted as a horizon cut-off level. As time intervals decrease below this horizon cut-off, fewer and fewer actors are present to take actions rapidly enough to result in significant correlation between instruments.

The data in Table 6 were examined for a relation between the position of Epps effect drops in correlation and tick activities of the financial time series involved. Standard correlation was estimated between the two

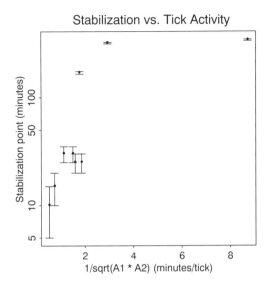

Figure 12   Correlation stabilization points as a function of the inverse square root of the product of tick activity rates.

individual activities involved for the instrument pairs described in Table 6. Mean business day activities were used for this and were taken from Table 1. The greater of the two activities for each pair was estimated to have −0.59 (standard) correlation with the 90 percent point of 1–2 day mean values (Table 6, column 4). The same quantity estimated between the lesser of the two activities in each pair and the 90 percent points was −0.65. These values are significant to 92 percent and 95 percent confidence levels respectively, assuming a normal random distribution. Therefore we conclude that, to a reasonable level of confidence, both of the activities play a substantial role in the Epps effect drop in correlations and that they are inversely related. This can be seen graphically in Figure 12 where the point of 90 percent correlation drops are plotted versus the inverse square root of the product of activities. The data points towards a stabilization point of zero in the time axis when the activities of both time series are infinite. However, at very low activities, a plateau in the correlation stabilization point appears to exist at a data interval of 300 to 400 minutes. This would lead to an indication that the Epps effect does not play a substantial role in attenuating correlation values beyond five to six hour data intervals. This even if the instruments involved are very inactive (<100 data updates per business day). It should be stated that these are indicative and preliminary results and an enhanced study with greater statistics is called for.

CONCLUSIONS

The problems associated with estimation of correlation at higher data frequencies ($<$ one week) have been discussed and illustrated using examples. An easy to use covolatility adjusted correlation estimator which correctly accounts for missing or non existent data and which also compensates for formulation of time series comovements when data frequencies between time series differ has been proposed. The effect of this new formulation is to estimate correlation when data exists, and to make no update to the correlation calculation when data does not exist. The method takes as input linearly interpolated data which is automatically corrected to filter out any bias which is introduced when and if over-interpolation occurs. Since the estimator is adjusted by co-volatility, some of the information from the more frequent of the two time series involved will not be fully utilized and statistical significance can be degraded. However this proposed statistical measure, being complementary to others mentioned here, is specifically meant for estimation of correlation at higher data frequencies, where computational statistics become less of a constraint on accuracy. We view the method as a bi-variate alternative to time scale transformations which treat conditional heteroscedasticity by expanding periods of higher volatility while contracting periods of lower volatility.

The issue of correlation coefficient stability in a number of financial time series has been addressed. Correlation stability over time would appear to be completely instrument dependent. Some return correlations have demonstrated wide fluctuations from week to week, while others may be very stable over a period of many years. It was observed that long term historical stability is not a guarantee of future correlation stability. This was evidenced through the examination of USD/ITL and USD/GBP FX return correlations with the USD/DEM rate. The crisis of 1992 which led to suspension of involvement for ITL and GBP rates from the EMS was directly reflected in a dramatic and rapid change in their correlations with other currencies thereafter. Correlation calculated over a long data sample has an averaging effect and increased structure in correlations has been observed when correlations are calculated over smaller periods (weeks) as opposed to larger periods (years). Depending on the time horizon of interest, there is pertinent information to be gained when calculations are performed over smaller periods using high-frequency data.

The self-memories of return correlations have been parameterized through estimation of the autocorrelation of linear correlation coefficients; the understanding of such correlation self-memory is a first step towards more accurate forecasting. Rate-to-rate variations in the manner of exponential attenuations of autocorrelations has been estimated. In general, correlation values for financial instruments have memories for their past values that extend for years rather than only days or weeks.

The Epps effect has been investigated for the case of a number of correlation pairs of financial return time series. Dramatic attenuations in all non-zero correlations were noted. This is equally the case with negatively correlated pairs. There exist measurable differences in the rates of rise in correlation coefficients (when moving towards lower data frequencies), depending on the currency pair being considered. The location (in terms of data interval) of the correlation stabilization point also varied depending on the correlation pair being considered. The characteristic rapid decline in correlations towards higher data frequencies has also been observed in the components of the correlation coefficient calculation; covariance and individual variances. The relative strength of the Epps effect in a particular case is related to the way in which these quantities interact; neither covariance nor a single variance could be identified as a lone mechanism behind the effect.

There is no evident statistical reason for correlations to drop beginning at data frequencies which are $\sim$100 times the average market activity rate. There is, however, some preliminary evidence of an inverse relationship between the rate of correlation attenuation and the activities of both of the instruments involved. The Epps effect data shown here would appear to be the result of a real and physical characteristic of financial time series: returns are likely to be uncorrelated or only slightly correlated in the very short term (on the order of minutes), even if they are very highly correlated on the longer term (hours and above). If the financial markets are composed of heterogeneous agents with different time horizons of interest (Müller *et al*, 1997), then a possible interpretation of the Epps effect might be as a time horizon of interest cut-off level. As time intervals decrease below this horizon cut-off, fewer and fewer actors are present to take actions rapidly enough to result in significant correlation between instruments. There would appear to be no true or "best" time interval for measuring correlation. Rather it is important to consider which time horizon is most pertinent when determining the most relevant data frequency for a specific application.

NOTES

1. The use of the linear correlation coefficient is appropriate not only for multivariate normal joint distributions but also for multivariate elliptical joint distributions. Many financial joint return distributions have been observed to fall into or close to this latter category.

The linear correlation coefficient is, to a significant extent, a useful and relevant statistical measure of association between fat tailed return distributions. Only the interpretation of results and more specifically determination of accurate confidence limits is problematic. The same cannot always be said about correlations of the square of return values of fat tailed distributions

2. We use the term "covolatility" in order to make a distinction from sample covariance whose usual definition involves normalizing by the number of sample observations.

3. In practice computers often give a non-zero value for the difference between two seemingly equal real numbers. These non-zero values are small, usually on the order of machine accuracy. The weight, ω_i, in this case may have a minuscule value. This hardly affects the final estimator, but in any case we programmed a threshold (typically a factor of 10,000 under the smallest return values) below which the real number differences in Equation 8 were set equal to integer zero. This insured that weights were mathematically equal to zero in our computations for the case of drastic over-interpolation of data.

ACKNOWLEDGMENTS

The authors gratefully acknowledge discussions with Tim Bollerslev whose insights motivated the development of a special method for treating differing activity rates of financial markets. In addition we are thankful for comments received from the editor, Pierre Lequeux, and also for comments provided by Thomas Mikosch and Frank de Jong.

BIBLIOGRAPHY

Ballocchi, G., Dacorogna, M.M., Hopman, C.M. and Müller, U.A. (1998), *The Multivariate Volatility Structure in the Interest Rate Futures Market*, Paper presented at the second High Frequency Data in Finance Conference (HFDF), Zürich, April 1–3, 1998.

Boyer, B.H., Gibson, M.S. and Loretan, M. (1997), *Pitfalls in Tests for Changes in Correlations*, Federal Reserve Board International Finance Discussion Paper Series, 1997-597, 1–11.

Cohen, K., Hawawimi, G., Maier, S., Schwartz, R. and Whitcomb, D. (1983), "Friction in the Trading Process and the Estimation of Systematic Risk", *Journal of Financial Economics*, 12, 263–278.

Dacorogna, M.M., Müller, U.A., Nagler, R.J., Olsen, R.B. and Pictet, O.V. (1993), "A Geographical Model for the Daily and Weekly Seasonal Volatility in the FX Market", *Journal of International Money and Finance*, 12(4), 413–438.

De Jong, F. and Nijman, T. (1997), "High Frequency Analysis of Lead-lag Relationships between Financial Markets", *Journal of Empirical Finance*, 4(2–3), 259–277.

Epps, T. (1979), "Comovements in Stock Prices in the Very Short Run", *Journal of the American Statistical Association*, 74(366), 291–298.

Gibson, M.S. and Boyer, B.H. (1997), *Evaluating Forecasts of Correlation Using Option Pricing*, Federal Reserve Board International Finance Discussion Paper Series, 1997-600, 1–46.

Guillaume, D.M., Dacorogna, M.M., Davé, R.D., Müller, U.A., Olsen, R.B. and Pictet, O.V. (1994), *From the Bird's Eye to the Microscope: A Survey of New Stylized Facts of the Intra-daily Foreign Exchange Markets*, Internal document DMG. 1994-04-06, Olsen and Associates, Seefeldstrasse 233, 8008 Zürich, Switzerland.

Krzanowski, W.J. and Marriott, F.H.C. (1994), *Multivariate Analysis, Distributions, Ordination and Inference*, Vol. 1 of Kendall's Library of Statistics, Edward Arnold, London, 1st edition.

Krzanowski, W.J. and Marriott, F.H.C. (1995), *Multivariate Analysis, Classification, Covariance Structures and Repeated Measurements*, Vol. 2 of Kendall's Library of Statistics, Edward Arnold, London, 1st edition.

Lo, A.W. and MacKinlay, A.C. (1990a), "An Econometric Analysis of Nonsynchronous Trading", *Journal of Econometrics*, 45, 181–211.

Lo, A.W. and MacKinlay, A.C. (1990b), "When are Contrarian Profits due to Stock Market Overreaction?", *Review of Financial Studies*, 3, 175–205.

Longin, F. and Solnik, B. (1995), "Is the Correlation in International Equity Returns Constant: 1960-1990?", *Journal of International Money and Finance*, 14(1), 3–26.

Low, A., Muthuswamy, J. and Sarkar, S. (1996), *Time Variation in the Correlation Structure of Exchange Rates: High Frequency Analyses*, Proceedings of the Third International Conference on Forecasting Financial Markets, London, England, March 27–29, 1996, 1, 1–24.

Müller, U.A. (1996), *Generating a Time Series of Fixed-period Spot Interest Rates from Interest Rate Futures*, Internal document UAM. 1996-04-19, Olsen and Associates, Seefeldstrasse 233, 8008 Zürich, Switzerland.

Müller, U.A., Dacorogna, M.M., Davé, R.D., Olsen, R.B., Pictet, O.V. and von Weizsäcker, J.E. (1997), "Volatilities of Different Time Resolutions—Analyzing the Dynamics of Market Components", *Journal of Empirical Finance*, 4(2–3), 213–239.

Müller, U.A., Dacorogna, M.M., Olsen, R.B., Pictet, O.V., Schwarz, M. and Morgenegg, C. (1990), "Statistical Study of Foreign Exchange rates, Empirical Evidence of a Price Change Scaling Law, and Intraday Analysis", *Journal of Banking and Finance*, 14, 1189–1208.

Press, W.H., Teukolsky, S.A., Vetterling, W.T. and Flannery, B.P. (1992), *Numerical Recipes in C. The Art of Scientific Computing*, Cambridge University Press, Cambridge.

Chapter **5**

Highs and Lows: Times of the Day in the Currency CME Market

Emmanuel Acar and Robert Toffel

Dresdner Kleinwort Benson, Imperial College London

INTRODUCTION

As a trader watches prices move, he is, of course, forecasting their direction and seeking the optimal time range to execute a trade he is considering. Trivially, the optimal time to execute a trade is at the bottom of the day when one buys and at its top when one sells. This is especially true for intra-day traders who take positions solely inside the trading day and have to square their positions at the close of the market. Therefore, an informed trader will want to know at which moments extreme prices are more likely to occur in order to take actions corresponding to their risk appetite.

Although there is a quite extensive literature on the stochastic properties of extreme prices (Garman and Klass, 1980), very little is known on the probability of observing an extreme price during a given time interval. With the increasing power of computers, it is natural to collect and analyse data at ever higher frequencies. The ultimate in high frequency data collection records every transaction. At each recorded transaction there is some probability that the quoted price is the high or low of the day. Detecting at which time a high or low might happen is of primordial importance for an intra-day trader who does not perceive all the times of the day with equal importance. It may be argued that forecasting the time of the day an extreme occurs is far less important than forecasting its magnitude.

There is one fundamental reason why forecasting the magnitude of extreme prices is not sufficient on its own and why timing cannot be ignored: volumes and volatility are not equally distributed inside the day.

Financial Markets Tick by Tick
Edited by Pierre Lequeux. © 1999 John Wiley & Sons Ltd

There are huge disparities inside the trading session. An implication of unequal distribution of volume inside the day is that an extreme price observation, let's say at lunch time, might not be filled the same way as an extreme price occurring at the close or open, just for liquidity reasons. Then any information on extreme prices to be exploitable by traders and investors must include both magnitude and timing.

This chapter concentrates on the second aspect: timing. More specifically, this chapter seeks to develop a model which measures and forecasts the time at which extreme prices are more likely to occur. We will treat the time at which extremes occur as a stochastic time varying process. Such a measure is closely related to measures of volatility but may be particularly useful for trading. The times at which highs and lows are triggered will be observed in the currency futures markets and compared with their theoretical expectations.

It is first assumed that the asset returns follow a Brownian Random Walk with drift and establishes the probability that a high or low falls inside a given time interval. The special case of no drift will be detailed since it gives especially simple and practical formulae. The intra-day statistics of the currency futures contracts traded on the Chicago Mercantile Exchange (CME) are described at p 133. New stylized facts of extreme clustering in that market are discovered at p 139. Our findings are compared with previous research in the FTSE futures markets at p 144. This chapter is summarized and concluded at p 146.

TIMING OF EXTREME PRICES UNDER THE BROWNIAN RANDOM WALK ASSUMPTION

This section establishes the probability of observing an extreme price during a given time interval when the underlying returns follow a Brownian random walk. Let us define our notations and assumptions. The time will be counted from opening to close. Therefore, the price at time zero is the opening price, and the price at time T is the closing price where T is the length of the trading session. Let us note:

- O the opening price, C the closing price, P_t the price of the asset at time t

- H_T the maximum price between open and close, L_T the minimum price between open and close, T_H the time at which the maximum price occurs, T_L the time at which the minimum price occurs. $0 \leq T_H \leq T$, $0 \leq T_L \leq T$

- $W_t = \text{Ln}(P_t/O)$ the logarithmic return since opening
- $M_{[r;s]} = \underset{r<t<s}{\text{Max}}(W_t)$ the cumulative maximum return over the time interval $[r;s]$
- $m_{[r;s]} = \underset{r<t<s}{\text{Min}}(W_t)$ the cumulative minimum return over the time interval $[r;s]$
- $f_r(x)$ the probability density function of a zero-mean normal variable $N(0, r)$
- $\Phi_r(x)$ the cumulative distribution function at x.

Proposition 1

If we assume that the process which drives logarithmic returns is a Brownian random walk without drift, the probability that a high (or low) occurs after a time $t = r$ out of a trading session of length T is given by:

$$P_{r,T} = \text{Prob}[T_H > r] = \text{Prob}[T_L > r]$$

$$= \frac{2}{\pi} \text{Arctg}\left(\frac{\sqrt{T-r}}{\sqrt{r}}\right) \text{ with } 0 \leq r \leq T \qquad 1$$

The marginal density function is then given by:

$$f(r) = \frac{1}{\pi\sqrt{T-r}\sqrt{r}}$$

Proofs.

$$P_{r,T} = \text{Prob}[T_H > r] = \text{Prob}[\underset{0<t<r}{\text{Max}}(W_t) < \underset{r<t<T}{\text{Max}}(W_t)]$$

$$= \text{Prob}[\underset{0<t<r}{\text{Min}}(-W_t) > \underset{r<t<T}{\text{Min}}(-W_r)] = \text{Prob}[T_L > r]$$

This formulation shows that when there is no drift, $P_{r,T}$ does not depend on the underlying volatility of the Brownian random walk. Therefore, we will assume in what follows that the underlying volatility has been standardized to 1. Using symmetry arguments $\text{Prob}[\underset{0<t<r}{\text{Max}}(W_t) < \underset{r<t<T}{\text{Max}}(W_t)] = \text{Prob}[\underset{0<t<r}{\text{Max}}(W_t) < \underset{0<u<T-r}{\text{Max}}(V_u)]$ where V_u is a Brownian random walk independent on W_t.

Therefore, $P_{r,T} = \text{Prob}[M_{[0;r]} < \tilde{M}_{[0;T-r]}]$ where $M_{[0;r]}$ and $\tilde{M}_{[0;T-r]}$ are the maximums of two independent Brownian random walks. Duffie (1988) recalls that the maximum $M_{[0;r]}$ follows the same law as the absolute value of a normal variable $N(0, r)$.

Therefore,

$$\text{Prob}[M_{[0;r]} < x] = \text{Prob}[|W_r| < x] = 2\left[\Phi_r(x) - \tfrac{1}{2}\right] \text{ and}$$

$$\text{Prob}[\tilde{M}_{[0;T-r]} < y] = 2\left[\Phi_{T-r}(y) - \tfrac{1}{2}\right]$$

Since $M_{[0;r]}$ and $\tilde{M}_{[0;T-r]}$ are the maximums of two independent Brownian random walks:

$$P_{r,T} = \text{Prob}[M_{[0;r]} < \tilde{M}_{[0;T-r]}] = \int_0^{+\infty} 4f_{T-r}(y)\left[\int_0^y f_r(x)dx\right]dy$$

To solve this integral, we can apply the usual polar change of variables given by:

$$A = \text{Exp}\left(-\frac{X^2 + Y^2}{2}\right), \quad B = \frac{1}{2\pi}\text{Arctg}\left(\frac{Y}{X}\right)$$

Since the Jacobian of the transformation

$$a(x,y) = \text{Exp}\left[-\frac{x^2+y^2}{2}\right], \quad b(x,y) = \frac{1}{2\pi}\text{Arctg}\left(\frac{y}{x}\right) \text{ is } |J| = \frac{1}{2\pi}\text{Exp}\left[-\frac{x^2+y^2}{2}\right]$$

it follows that:

$$P_{r,T} = \text{Prob}[M_{[0;r]} < \tilde{M}_{[0;T-r]}]$$

$$= 4\int_0^1 \int_0^{\frac{1}{2\pi}\text{Arctg}\left(\frac{\sqrt{T-r}}{\sqrt{r}}\right)} da\, db = \frac{2}{\pi}\text{Arctg}\left(\frac{\sqrt{T-r}}{\sqrt{r}}\right)$$

This result is not new and relates to the arcsine law for the position of the maximum developed by Feller (1951). Other authors such as Ferger (1995) established the joint distribution of the running maximum and its location. They, however, assumed paths for which $W_0 = W_T = 0$. Under these assumptions, the marginal densities for the location of the maximum of a Brownian bridge is given by $f(r) = 1/T$. As we have shown here, relaxing the assumption that $W_T = 0$ tremendously affects the density function. Figure 1 highlights formulae 1 by sampling a total day of $T = 400$ minutes in 20-minutes bar charts. Contrary to intuition, an extreme price is much more likely to occur towards the very beginning or the very end of the trading day than somewhere in the middle.

Proposition 2

If we assume that the process which drives logarithmic returns is a Brownian random walk with drift $W_t \approx N(\mu t, \sigma^2 t)$, the probability that

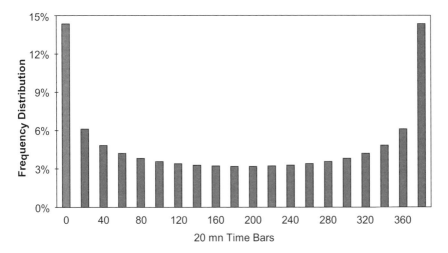

Figure 1 Timing of extreme prices under the Brownian random walk without drift assumption.

a high occurs after a time $t = r$ out of a trading session of length T is given by:

$$P_{r,T} = \text{Prob}[T_H > r] = \int_0^{+\infty} \int_0^y g_{T-r}(x)g_r(y)dx\,dy$$

Where $g_t(x) = \Phi\left(\dfrac{x - \mu t}{\sigma\sqrt{t}}\right) - \exp\left(\dfrac{2\mu t}{\sigma^2}\right)\Phi\left(\dfrac{-x - \mu t}{\sigma\sqrt{t}}\right)$

$$q_{r,T} = \text{Prob}[T_L > r] = \int_0^{+\infty} \int_0^y h_{T-r}(x)h_r(y)dx\,dy$$

Where $h_t(x) = \Phi\left(\dfrac{x + \mu t}{\sigma\sqrt{t}}\right) - \exp\left(\dfrac{-2\mu t}{\sigma^2}\right)\Phi\left(\dfrac{-x + \mu t}{\sigma\sqrt{t}}\right)$

Proofs. $P_{r,T} = \text{Prob}[T_H > r] = \text{Prob}[\underset{0<t<r}{\text{Max}}(W_t) < \underset{r<t<T}{\text{Max}}(W_t)]$. Using symmetry arguments $\text{Prob}[\underset{0<t<r}{\text{Max}}(W_t) < \underset{r<t<T}{\text{Max}}(W_t)] = \text{Prob}[\underset{0<t<r}{\text{Max}}(W_t) < \underset{0<u<T-r}{\text{Max}}(V_u)]$ where V_u is a Brownian random walk independent on W_t. Therefore, $P_{r,T} = \text{Prob}[M_{[0,r]} < \tilde{M}_{[0,T-r]}]$ where $M_{[0,r]}$ and $\tilde{M}_{[0;T-r]}$ are the maximum of two independent Brownian Random Walks. The law of the maximum $M_{[0,r]}$ is well known and can be found in Duffie (1988). Its probability density function is given by:

$$g_r(x) = \Phi\left(\dfrac{x - \mu r}{\sigma\sqrt{r}}\right) - \exp\left(\dfrac{2\mu r}{\sigma^2}\right)\Phi\left(\dfrac{-x - \mu r}{\sigma\sqrt{r}}\right)$$

Since $M_{[0;r]}$ and $\tilde{M}_{[0;T-r]}$ are the maximums of two independent Brownian random walks:

$$P_{r;T} = \text{Prob}[T_H > r] = \int_0^{+\infty} \int_0^y g_{T-r}(x)g_r(y)\,dx\,dy$$

The probability that a low occurs after time r is easily deduced using symmetry arguments:

$$P_{r,T} = \text{Prob}[T_H > r] = \text{Prob}[\underset{0<t<r}{\text{Max}}(W_t) < \underset{r<t<T}{\text{Max}}(W_t)]$$

$$= \text{Prob}[\underset{0<t<r}{\text{Min}}(-W_t) > \underset{r<t<T}{\text{Min}}(-W_t)] = \text{Prob}[T_L^* > r]$$

where T_L^* is the time of occurrence of a low price assuming that the underlying process follows a Brownian random walk $N(-\mu t, \sigma^2 t)$.

Contrary to the case without drift, there is no simple analytical formulae to establish the probability of an extreme price falling inside a given time interval. Therefore, to assess the effect of a drift in the time series, we have performed a number of Monte-Carlo simulations. Ten thousand samples of four hundred 1-minute returns were simulated and the occurrence of high and low prices were noted. Figures 2 and 3 illustrate the influence of a positive drift equal to 15 percent on an annualized basis, for varied volatility levels from 5 to 30 percent on an annualized basis, using steps

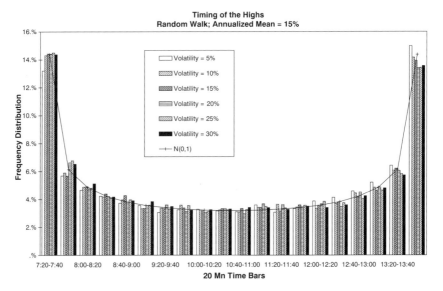

Figure 2   Frequency distribution of high time.

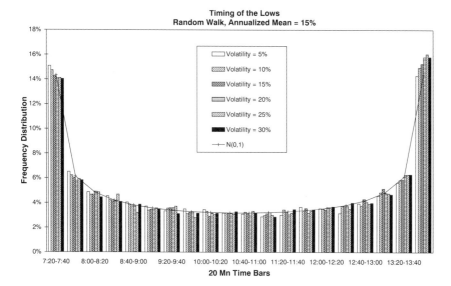

Figure 3   Frequency distribution of low time.

of 5 percent. The biggest departure from the random walk without drift occurs when the ratio mean divided by volatility is the biggest. In this case, that is for a mean equal to 15 percent and a volatility equal to 5 percent. But even in this case, deviations are very small. We might have expected with a positive drift a shift towards more highs at the end of the day and more lows at the beginning of the day. This means that even when drifts are significant on a yearly basis, they are not likely to impact the positions of intra-day highs and lows.

INTRA-DAY STATISTICS OF THE CURRENCY FUTURES MARKET

Having established the theoretical distributions of high and low times, a natural concern is to test the adequacy of the model in financial markets. To do so, we have chosen the currency contracts traded on the Chicago Mercantile Exchange (CME) for which high frequency data are available. The transactions records come straight from the tick by tick database provided by the exchange. The period under study runs from the October 4, 1988 to June 30, 1995. This encompasses a period of 1,629 uniform trading sessions[1] from 7:20 to 14:00 Chicago time for all three contracts considered in this chapter: German Mark (Dem), Swiss Franc (Chf) and Japanese Yen (Yen). This chapter considers intra-day prices involving the same maturity, that is the front month contract up to the penultimate trading day. Since we only measure variations from open to close, we do not face rollover problems. Figures 4 to 6 plot the cumulative intra-day returns for the Dem, Chf and Yen contracts. This is the open to close variation ignoring any overnight appreciation/depreciation of the dollar. Overall, the dollar depreciated intra-day against all three currencies during the periods studied. Consequently, all three contracts being quoted in foreign currencies appreciated between March 1988 and June 1995.

Rates have been sampled every 20 minutes from a trading session of 400 minutes starting at 7:20 to finish at 14:00. Each day $j = 1, N$ includes, therefore, 21 prices $P_{i,j}$ where $i = 0, 20$ denotes the time index: $7 : 20, 7 : 40, \ldots, 14 : 00$. Logarithmic returns over a 20 minute period have been calculated as $X_{i,j} = Ln(P_{i,j}/P_{i-1,j})$, $i = 1, 20$ for each of the 20-minute times

Table 1   Open to close variations; October 1988—June 1995.

	Dem	Chf	Yen
Annualised* Average	10.16%	9.58%	5.42%
Annualised Volatility	9.08%	10.35%	7.51%
Skewness	−0.149	−0.061	−0.117
Kurtosis	1.768	1.849	6.689

* Assuming 250 working days.

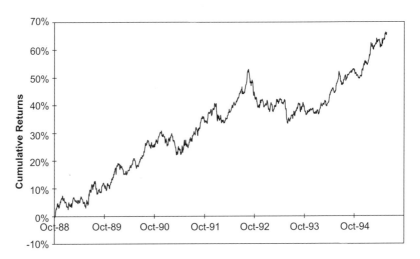

Figure 4   Dem intra-day cumulative returns.

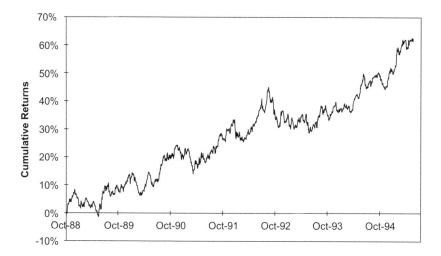

Figure 5 Chf intra-day cumulative returns.

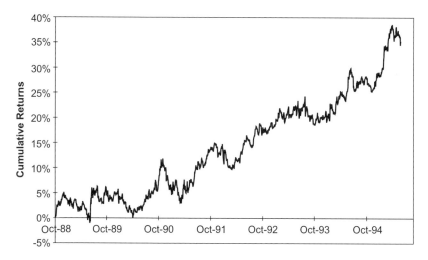

Figure 6 Yen intra-day cumulative returns.

bars. The volatility of a given time interval i is nothing else than the standard deviation of 20-minute returns over the total number of N days:

$$\sigma_i^2 = \frac{1}{N-1} \sum_{j=1}^{N} \left(X_{i,j} - \frac{1}{N} \sum_{j=1}^{N} X_{i,j} \right)^2$$

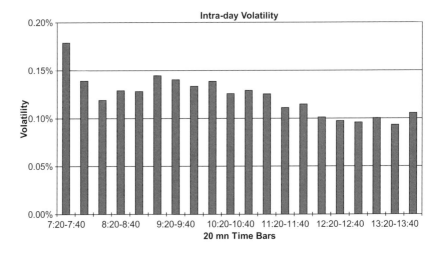

Figure 7 Dem intra-day volatility.

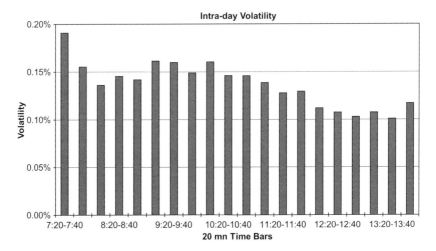

Figure 8 Chf intra-day volatility.

Figures 7 to 9 exhibit the intra-day volatility for each of the contracts, as calculated by the standard deviation of each 20-minute variation during a given time interval over the whole period. The opening of the market is the most volatile time of the day whereas the penultimate 20 minutes is the least volatile time of the day. The ratio is almost equal to two for the Chf contract. The peak of volatility during the first 20 minutes is mainly due to the intense market activity caused by the opening of the

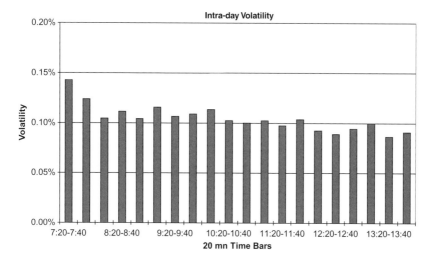

Figure 9 Yen intra-day volatility.

Treasury bond markets and more significantly the release of US figures. We observe a relative peak of volatility towards 10:00 corresponding to the close of the European Cash market. Thereafter, volatility decreases almost continuously for both the Chf and Dem. The Yen volatility exhibits a much more uniform distribution. The close of the market shows some slight resurgence of volatility.

For all three currencies, volatility exhibits a L-shape rather than a U-shape. This may be due to the release of the US figures at 7.30 which has no other equivalent during the rest of the day. Contrary to most other futures markets, currency traders can hedge their exposure after the close of the session through the 24-hour OTC market. This might explain why volatility doesn't jump towards the close of Chicago.

Higher moments have been established to denote departures from the normal assumption. Twenty minute returns can be positively or negatively skewed (Figure 10). However, there are no clear consistent patterns across different currencies and different times of the day.

Figure 11 indicates the amount of kurtosis. All returns distributions are massively leptokurtic: positive kurtosis indicates that the curve is steep at the centre and has fat tails. This is a feature of high frequency data (Müller *et al.*, 1990). They include many zero returns, no price change, and a few large moves. These results, namely stochastic volatility and leptokurtosis, suggest that the Brownian random walk assumption may not be adequate to predict time occurrence of extreme prices. The next section investigates this issue in more detail.

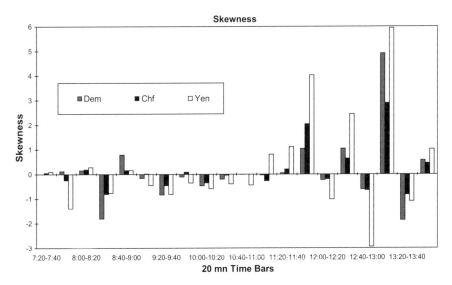

Figure 10   Skewness coefficient 20 mn time series.

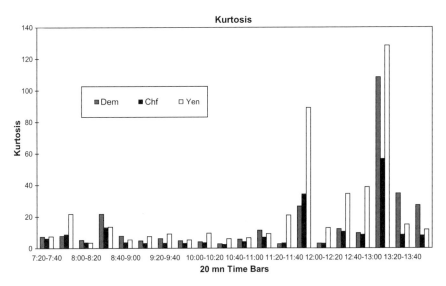

Figure 11   Kurtosis coefficient 20 mn time series.

Timing of Extreme Prices, an Empirical Application to the CME Markets

We now observe the timing of extreme prices in the three currency Futures contracts previously described. Then results are compared with those expected from a random walk.

Although the assumption of continuous markets is now well accepted, it must be recognised that there are a few cases for which extreme values could be attained repeatedly. Strictly speaking, we should distinguish between the first and last extreme. In theory, the results are practically the same (Feller, 1951). Empirical findings concerning occurrence of last extreme are also given here for purpose of completeness.

Given the relatively high number of observations, more than seven years of tick by tick data, time bars of twenty minutes have been chosen. As can be seen from Figures 12 to 17, differences between first and last extreme are very small indeed. We have used as theoretical expectation the frequency of high and low times of the day under the Brownian random walk without drift assumption. This is given by the continuous line. To formally measure the adequation of observed frequencies with their expectations, we have used a simple Chi-square test (Table 2). Overall, the normal random walk hypothesis is not compatible with the times of the day at which highs and lows occur. This is not a surprising result given the

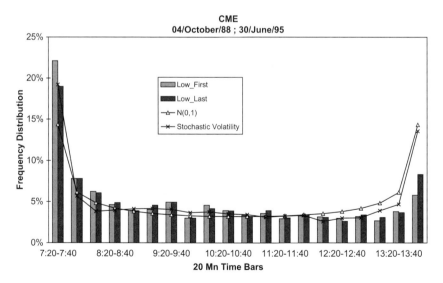

Figure 12 Dem, frequency distribution of low time.

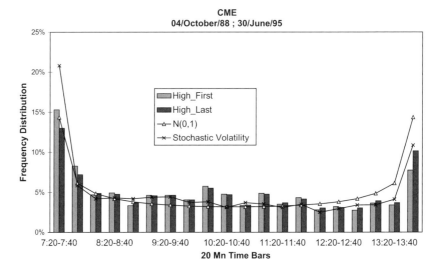

Figure 13 Dem, frequency distribution of high time.

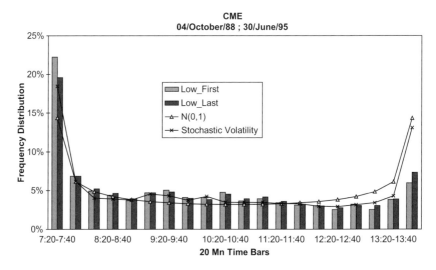

Figure 14 Chf, frequency distribution of low time.

many departures from a zero-centred normal distribution we observed
in the previous section. Possible causes are, among others: positive drift,
stochastic volatility and leptokurtosis. We now review the influence of
each of these variables on the timing of extremes in the currency CME
market.

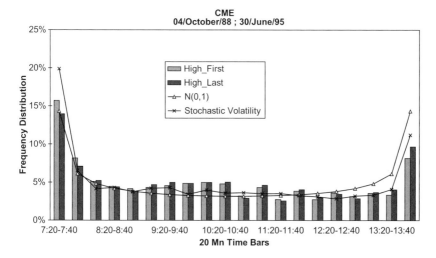

Figure 15   Chf, frequency distribution of high time.

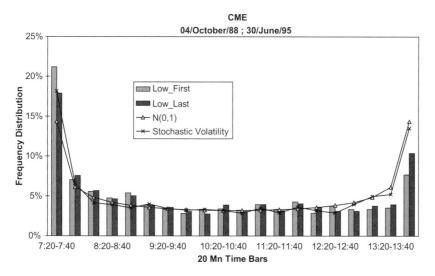

Figure 16   Yen, frequency distribution of low time.

First, one should note the dollar depreciated against all three currencies during the period. Consequently, all three contracts being quoted in foreign currencies appreciated between 1988 and 1995. A positive drift might explain the bigger than expected number of low prices on the opening of the market than at the close. But if the drift was the sole

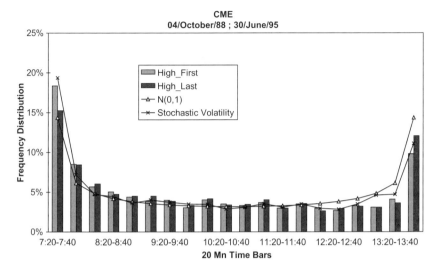

Figure 17   Yen, frequency distribution of high time.

explanation, we should note more high prices at the end of the day than expected from a driftless random walk. Or if this is not the case, we note in fact far less high prices towards the close of the market than anticipated. This tends to confirm a finding of Section 1: the presence of a long-term drift is not likely to impact the timing of intra-day high and low prices.

The relative lack of interest by market participants towards the closing of Chicago time might be the most surprising discovery of this study. One reason might be the lesser market participants due to the earlier closing of Europe. Indeed, Figures 12 to 17 show an abnormally active mid-market session corresponding to the time zone when both Europe and US are open. Then once the London market has closed, the activity level decreases and with it the likelihood to observe a new extreme. On most futures markets, both volume and volatility are positively correlated and both follow a U-shape. This would explain why new highs and lows are more likely to occur during volatile periods when volumes are large. The relationship between volume and volatility is now well known and has been well documented (see Karpov, 1987 for a survey).

Since a homoskedatic normal random walk cannot explain the timing of extreme prices, it is natural to investigate more realistic models. In particular, Figures 7 to 9 show that volatility varies inside the day. To test the assumption that increased volatility triggers more extremes,

Table 2 Chi-square test of adequation.

	DEM				CHF				YEN			
	H_N(0,1)	L_N(0,1)	H_Stoc	L_Stoc	H_N(0,1)	L_N(0,1)	H_Stoc	L_Stoc	H_N(0,1)	L_N(0,1)	H_Stoc	L_Stoc
7:20–7:40	0.04	45.66*	49.46*	27.97*	0.28	50.99*	36.36*	20.29*	7.11*	31.79*	29.61*	17.27
7:40–8:00	7.26*	7.80*	0.21	0.53	6.24*	1.51	0.41	0.01	15.35*	3.84	3.15	0.65
8:00–8:20	0.01	5.90*	1.42	3.71	0.38	0.20	1.61	2.23	3.74	2.23	0.05	1.70
8:20–8:40	1.67	1.24	0.06	0.21	0.21	0.41	0.06	0.34	1.98	0.99	0.26	0.31
8:40–9:00	0.40	0.03	0.66	0.38	0.13	0.00	0.01	0.01	1.83	8.80*	0.14	0.37
9:00–9:20	5.13*	2.64	3.23	1.73	4.30*	6.04*	2.03	4.61*	1.87	0.36	0.94	0.85
9:20–9:40	7.62*	11.68*	5.32*	2.18	9.55*	11.68*	4.06*	4.24*	1.40	0.02	0.54	0.00
9:40–10:00	2.98	0.46	1.05	0.71	12.92*	2.98	0.10	1.01	0.04	0.66	0.23	0.02
10:00–10:20	30.73*	6.98*	1.84	1.54	16.48*	2.88	3.21	5.39*	4.14*	0.16	0.38	0.04
10:20–10:40	12.57*	2.71	0.03	0.55	16.16*	11.17*	0.82	0.45	0.40	1.07	0.51	0.00
10:40–11:00	0.18	0.05	1.45	0.31	0.06	1.89	1.19	0.37	0.24	0.01	0.05	0.65
11:00–11:20	13.36*	1.50	0.54	0.04	8.48*	3.61	0.47	0.28	2.24	2.66	0.54	0.33
11:20–11:40	0.52	0.46	0.17	0.01	2.00	0.21	0.35	0.00	0.46	0.01	0.17	0.79
11:40–12:00	3.64	0.02	0.05	0.02	1.56	0.27	0.09	0.07	0.11	2.93	0.05	0.22
12:00–12:20	1.93	0.88	5.35*	4.38*	2.30	1.43	1.00	1.82	2.71	0.47	1.65	0.72
12:20–12:40	1.88	4.48*	3.36	2.83	0.32	6.19*	4.09*	3.67	4.48*	0.66	4.26*	3.92*
12:40–13:00	6.81*	3.18	2.52	5.26*	5.63*	4.57*	3.89*	4.38*	3.61	3.84	1.92	0.25
13:00–13:20	3.90*	13.16*	6.96*	2.95	5.07*	14.81*	8.09*	7.16*	10.51	5.84*	0.16	0.06
13:20–13:40	18.50*	15.67*	11.32*	5.66*	16.45*	14.53*	11.43*	9.49*	14.16*	16.06*	5.43*	2.29
13:40–14:00	34.79*	63.10*	14.44*	0.70	35.17*	70.41*	11.83*	1.85	13.88*	33.67*	12.44*	0.87
Chisquare	153.92*	187.61*	109.43*	61.70*	143.69*	205.77*	91.11*	67.66*	90.27*	116.06*	62.48*	31.30

*significantly different from expected frequency at the critical threshold of 1%.

we considered a model allowing for heteroskedastic volatility. Again Monte-Carlo simulations have been used and performed as follows:

1. Simulate 400 minute per minute returns from 7:20 to 14:00. The first 20 returns are drawn from a normal distribution $N(0, \sigma_1/\sqrt{20})$ where σ_1 is the volatility of the first twenty minutes time bar (7:20;7:40). The next 20 returns are drawn from a normal distribution $N(0, \sigma_2/\sqrt{20})$ where σ_2 is the volatility of the second time bar (7:40;8:00) and so on.

2. Build a cumulative returns series from open to close.

3. Detect the times at which high and low cumulative returns are reached

4. Replicate the process 10,000 times

5. Establish the distribution of extreme times inside the day

By doing so, we obtain the stochastic volatility lines in Figures 12 to 14. Overall, the fitness with empirical observations has increased compared with the homoskedastic random walk. Such a model allows a much better explanation for the larger number of extrema on the opening and the smaller number towards the close of the London market. This still overestimates the number of extrema at the close of Chicago. Although there has been a clear improvement in the use of a model including stochastic volatility, there remain however two main drawbacks. First, it uses ex-post volatility and therefore assumes that volatility can be precisely predicted. Secondly, the fitness with empirical observations, although better, is far from perfect. The Chi-square values are still very large as indicated by Table 2.

   Clearly, further research is needed. The massive amount of leptokurtosis indicated by Figure 11 cannot be ignored. Models taking into account higher moments will have to be considered.

A COMPARISON WITH THE FTSE LIFFE MARKET

The results of this study can be compared with those found in the FTSE Futures market (Acar *et al.*, 1996). In that market highs and lows occur also most often at the beginning of the day while the mid-session is exceptionally quiet (Figure 18). The number of extreme prices towards the close of the market is neither more nor less than would be expected from the random walk without drift. The big difference between the FTSE and the currency CME contracts lies in the fact that the former can be

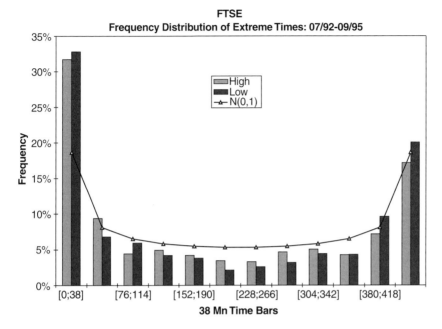

Figure 18 Frequency distribution of extreme times for the FTSE.

considered as a local market and the latter as a global and continuous market.

Volume of transactions reaches its peak on the opening of both LIFFE and CME markets. For the FTSE, investors want to adjust their positions following overnight movements in the US and Japanese stock markets. For currency contracts, the peak of volatility during the first 20 minutes is mainly due to the intense market activity caused by the opening of the Treasury bond markets and more significantly the release of US figures. Both factors affect the UK stock market far less. Volume grows towards the close of the LIFFE market because this is the last opportunity for market participants to hedge their book or trigger an overnight position. This is less the case on the CME markets. Currency exposure can still be hedged after the close of the market through the 24 hours OTC market. Indeed, currency markets can be fairly thin on the close of Chicago. Bid/Ask spreads widen as the liquidity decreases. Consequently, hedging might be better achieved through the cash market either a couple of hours later on the opening of Tokyo or during the European day time. This might indeed explain the relative lack of interest of currency players in the close of Chicago.

CONCLUSION

It is well known that deviations with the normal assumption are numerous such as skewness, kurtosis and heteroskedasticity. It is however unknown to what extent such deviations might change the timing of extreme prices. This study has shown that the impact of the drift on the timing of intra-day extrema is negligible. Heteroskedasticity seems to affect timing of extremes more significantly. New highs and lows are more likely to occur during volatile periods when volumes are large.

New stylized facts of extreme clustering have been discovered for the CME currency contracts. A striking question would be: does volume cause extreme prices or vice-versa? Both hypotheses could be defended. One may argue that volume on CME is higher at the opening of the market because of the ex-ante higher probability of observing extreme prices. On the other hand, it could be said that rising volume may cause increased trends in futures contracts and therefore increase the probability of observing extreme prices. Clearly, more theoretical and empirical work is needed to gain insight on the relationship between volume, volatility and extreme price.

NOTE

1. The data traded on the 24 hours Globex market has not been included in this study because of its too short history.

BIBLIOGRAPHY

Acar, E., Lequeux, P. and Ritz, S. (1996), "Timing the Highs and Lows of the Day", *Liffe Equity Products Review, 2nd Quarter*.

Duffie, D. (1988), *"Security Markets, Stochastic Models"*, Academic Press., San Diego.

Feller, W. (1951), *"An Introduction to Probability Theory and Its Applications"*, John Wiley & Sons.

Ferger, D. (1995), "The Joint Distribution of the Running Maximum and its Location of D-valued Markov Processes", *Journal of Applied Probability* (32), 842–845.

Garman, M. and Klass, M. (1980), "On the Estimation of Security Price Volatilities from Historical Data", *Journal of Business* (53), 67–78.

Karpoff, J.M. (1987), "The Relationship between Price Changes and Trading Volume: A Survey", *Journal of Financial and Quantitative Analysis* (3), 169–176

Müller, U.A., Dacorogna, M.M., Olsen, R.B., Pictet, O.V., Schwarz, M. and Morgenegg, C. (1990), "Statistical Study of Foreign Exchange Rates, Empirical Evidence of a Price Change Scaling Law and Intra-day Analysis", *Journal of Banking and Finance* (14), 1189–1208.

Part II

Statistical Features of High Frequency Financial Series and Forecasting

Chapter **6**

The Intra-day Behaviour of Key Market Variables for LIFFE Derivatives

Owain ap Gwilym, Mike Buckle and Stephen Thomas

Department of Management, University of Southampton, European Business Management School, University of Wales, UK, corresponding author

INTRODUCTION

Research interest in financial market microstructure has increased recently as numerous transaction datasets for different markets have become available. Empirical analysis of high frequency financial market data has yielded a number of interesting statistical regularities that have proved challenging to economic theorists. Much of this evidence involves US data, focusing on the intraday behaviour of several aspects of market activity, such as bid-ask spreads, returns, returns volatility, traded volume and price reversals. This chapter examines the behaviour of these variables using data on UK futures and options contracts traded on the London International Financial Futures and Options Exchange (LIFFE) and also investigates the impact of UK and US macroeconomic announcements.

LIFFE has grown considerably in recent years and is currently the second largest futures and options exchange in the world, having traded over 100 million contracts in the first half of 1997. The exchange is strategically important in terms of maintaining London's position as an international financial centre. However, the level of published research into the contracts traded at the exchange does not begin to reflect this elevated position, especially given the more complete price data available from LIFFE compared to the US futures exchanges.

This chapter extends our understanding of intraday empirical regularities in a number of ways. It offers further insight into the intraday behaviour observed in the US markets by using European data; it

Financial Markets Tick by Tick
Edited by Pierre Lequeux. © 1999 John Wiley & Sons Ltd

compares intraday aspects of numerous futures and options contracts; and finds some notable parallels and divergences which require further explanation. The key features of high opening volatility, so prevalent in US studies of futures markets and "explained" by removing the effects of scheduled macroeconomic announcements, remains in our data. This latter feature is important since many of the theories regarding trading volume and returns volatility predict the U-shape mentioned above, with market closure being an important factor in such models. Further, US studies cannot examine the reaction of equity futures contracts to the main US macroeconomic announcements at 08:30 EST since the market opens for trading after the announcement time.

We first discuss the relevant theoretical literature and then describe the datasets and methodology used. The results of empirical work on various futures and options contracts are presented at p 158, and this chapter is concluded at p 186.

THEORETICAL BACKGROUND FOR INTRA-DAY VARIATIONS IN KEY MARKET VARIABLES

This section considers the theories which aim to predict the intra-day behaviour of key market variables, and examines some of the published empirical evidence.

Returns, Returns Volatility and Traded Volume

A number of empirical regularities have been identified using US data. It is now well established that stock returns and the variance of returns (across days) follow a familiar U-shaped intraday pattern (Wood *et al.* 1985, Harris 1986). Returns on stock indices tend to be positive near both the open and close of trading, though Harris (1986) finds negative returns near the Monday open. Jain and Joh (1988) also find U-shaped intraday patterns in hourly returns and volatility for the S&P500 index. Ekman (1992) extends the analysis to the S&P500 index futures contracts, examining 15-minute returns, returns volatility, the number of recorded transactions, percentage price reversals, and the autocorrelation of 1-minute returns. The intra-day patterns in volatility and volume are approximately U-shaped, while the returns are similar in shape to those observed in NYSE index returns by Harris (1986). However, Ederington and Lee (1993) find an L-shape pattern in intra-day volatility for US Treasury Bond, Eurodollar and Deutschmark futures markets, with a peak in volatility early in the day followed by reasonably flat volatility for the rest of the day. However, they find that this peak is not at the open of the market but 10 minutes later, coinciding with the release of macroeconomic announcements.

There are a number of theories seeking to explain these intra-day patterns, usually involving the interaction of privately informed traders, liquidity traders and market makers. Admati and Pfleiderer (1988) explain the intra-day patterns within a game-theoretic model involving informed traders and liquidity traders whose activities lead to concentrations in volume and volatility at the open and close of trading. In a similar vein, Foster and Viswanathan (1990) further develop the work of Admati and Pfleiderer (1988) to provide a game-theoretic model to explain patterns in returns volatility both across weekdays and intra-day. In this model, liquidity traders can delay trades, and hence choose times when there is less private information and choose securities for which there is more efficient public information production. In particular, if weekends feature little public information, liquidity traders will prefer not to trade on Mondays.

Reversals

Reversals are an indicator of the level of autocorrelation in returns data. The intra-day pattern for autocorrelation in returns is explained by Glosten and Milgrom (1985) in terms of information trading. In their model, the existence of bid-ask spreads will lead to negative serial correlation between successive price changes as prices oscillate between bid and ask prices. As the level of information trading increases, the bid-ask spread will increase as market makers attempt to capture gains from uninformed traders. A larger spread increases the possibility of trades taking place between the bid and ask prices thus reducing the bid-ask bounce effect and hence increasing the autocorrelation coefficient (towards zero). McInish and Wood (1990) find U-shaped intra-day patterns in 1-minute index returns autocorrelation and attempt to distinguish whether this is due to non-synchronous trading or information arrival. They favour the latter as returns variance also has a similar pattern (which they consider a proxy for information arrival). Gosnell (1995) examines the intra-day patterns of the percentage of transaction price reversals, which is a proxy for transactions returns autocorrelations. This rises quickly for NYSE stocks early in the day and then stabilizes, unlike the U-shaped findings for the autocorrelation of returns in McInish and Wood (1990). Gosnell (1995) examines the price change reversals pattern for individual US stocks, and finds that intra-day reversal patterns vary systematically between stocks, across each day, and between days. In particular, there is a lower concentration of reversals during the opening 90 minutes of trading than during the rest of the day. Evidence on intra-day transactions price change continuations and reversals is important when studying the impact of new information on security prices, and the pattern of such variables around an event is informative about the speed of price adjustment to new information.

Bid-ask Spreads

It is convenient to consider three main approaches to explaining the intra-day behaviour of bid-ask spreads (e.g. see O'Hara (1995), and Chan, Chung and Johnson (1995)). The first approach considers the institutional structure of a market, in particular the degree of market power of participants; a single "specialist" will have more market power than competing market-makers. The other approaches focus on the role of inventories and information asymmetries.

Market Structure.   There is a clear theoretical and empirical distinction between the intra-day behaviour of bid-ask spreads in markets occupied by a monopolistic specialist (e.g. NYSE) versus those with competing market-makers (e.g. CBOE and National Association of Securities Dealers Automated Quotation (NASDAQ)). Brock and Kleidon (1992), McInish and Wood (1992), Lee *et al.* (1993) and Chan, Chung and Johnson (1995) show that the spreads in the NYSE follow a U-shaped pattern throughout the day, whereas Chan, Christie and Schultz (1995) find that spreads in the NASDAQ market are relatively stable through the day but narrow significantly near the close. Chan, Chung and Johnson (1995) find that spreads for actively traded CBOE options on stock decline sharply after the open and then level off.

The difference in the intra-day behaviour of spreads can be explained by the different structure of the markets. Brock and Kleidon (1992) develop a model where a single specialist has monopolistic power and is faced with a fairly inelastic transactions demand at the open and close of trading due to the overnight accumulation of information prior to opening and the immediacy of the non-trading period after the close. The specialist can price discriminate during these crucial periods of inelastic demand and can extract monopolistic profits, particularly if he has access to any opening order imbalances. Price volatility will thus ensue (see Stoll and

Whaley (1990)). Consequently, with a market served by a single specialist we would expect high price volatility, volume and bid-ask spreads near the open and close of trading. In contrast, in markets with competing market makers we would not expect to observe the U-shaped intra-day pattern if the specialist's monopolistic power is an important influence on such behaviour.

Inventory Models. Bid-ask spreads exist as a reward to market-makers for bearing the risk of holding inventories. Amihud and Mendelson (1980) develop a model for specialists whereby spreads are widened as inventory imbalances accumulate. Lee *et al.* (1993) find evidence linking spreads to inventory control costs; in particular, higher trading volume is associated with wide spreads. Consequently, the high volumes observed at the open and close of many markets (e.g. NYSE) would be accompanied by wide spreads. Hence, for a specialist structure, such as NYSE, a U-shaped intraday pattern of spreads is predicted as a single market maker may be forced to accumulate unwanted inventories during peak trading volumes, whereas competing market makers will be (individually) less likely to accumulate such positions. Further, Chan, Chung and Johnson (1995) suggest that specialists and competing market makers may differ in their ability to manage imbalances by using their bid and ask quotes; in maintaining a fair and orderly market specialists cannot execute orders on only one side of the spread, in contrast to competing market makers who can set bid and ask quotes to attract trades on only one side of the spread (and thus enhance their ability to avoid unwanted inventories). Inventory based models thus suggest that specialists will widen spreads during periods of high volume, i.e. at the open and close. This theory does not explain the occurrence of high volumes at these times; for this we turn to the information models.

Information Models: the Adverse Selection Problem. A number of recent contributions to the literature concentrate on information asymmetries, (e.g. Glosten and Milgrom (1985), Admati and Pfleiderer (1988), and Foster and Viswanathan (1990, 1994)). In these models, the following agents are active in the market: market makers, informed traders, and liquidity traders. In some models, a distinction is made between liquidity traders who are forced to trade at a given time of day regardless of cost and discretionary liquidity traders. The market maker is at an informational disadvantage relative to informed traders, and this is termed the adverse selection problem. Spreads must therefore be wide enough to ensure that the gains from trading with the uninformed agents exceed the losses associated with trading with the informed agents. Admati and Pfleiderer (1988) predict narrow spreads when volume is high and prices are more volatile, while Foster and Viswanathan (1990) predict narrow spreads when volume is high and prices are less volatile. However, in a model of strategic trading between two asymmetrically informed traders, Foster and Viswanathan (1994) predict high volume, high variance and wide spreads near the open.

Discriminating Between Competing Explanations. Early intra-day studies of derivatives markets (e.g. Ekman (1992)) involved detailed description of returns, returns volatility, volume and price reversals for various financial instruments, but there was little discussion of competing theories of the intraday patterns. However, the distinction between specialist and multiple market maker institutional structures has provided one possible way of improving our ability to discriminate between competing theories. Chan, Chung and Johnson (1995) compare the intra-day behaviour of volume, volatility and spreads for a sample of NYSE stocks and their associated options traded on the CBOE. The former is a specialist market while the latter involves multiple market makers; further, information (whether public or private) affecting a stock will also influence the associated call and put options. Consequently, the authors can attempt to distinguish between the influence of market structure, adverse selection and inventory control for the intra-day patterns. They conclude that higher uncertainty at the opening of both markets can explain the wide spreads observed, but that information cannot then explain wide stock spreads and narrow option spreads at the close. The narrow option spreads are therefore likely to arise from a differing market structure.

The Impact of Macroeconomic Announcements

There is a growing literature relating intra-day patterns in futures data to the impact of scheduled macroeconomic news announcements. For example, Ederington and Lee (1993) find that these announcements are responsible for most of the observed time-of-day and day-of-the-week volatility patterns in US interest rate and foreign currency futures markets. In particular, they find that returns volatility early in the day, found in studies such as Ekman (1992), does not occur at the opening of trading if more finely timed aggregated data is used (at 5-minute intervals). Volatility is then found to occur during the third 5-minute interval (08:30–08:35 EST) thus coinciding with macroeconomic announcements released to the market at 08:30 EST. Removing the effect of these announcements is found to remove most of this volatility.

A number of papers document the volatility of UK futures prices around UK and US macroeconomic announcements. Becker *et al.* (1993, 1995) find that returns volatility in the FTSE100 and Long Gilt futures markets responds to the release of economic data in the UK and US. This chapter extends this to cover intra-day returns, volume and reversals.

DATA AND METHODOLOGY

The futures data used consists of every quote, transaction and associated volume for the UK stock index (FTSE100), 3-month interest rate (Short Sterling), and government bond (Long Gilt) futures contracts. The data is potentially far more informative than that used in many previous US studies, because "time and sales" data from US futures exchanges, e.g. Chicago Mercantile Exchange (CME) and Chicago Board of Trade (CBOT), only contain bid and ask quotes if the bid quote exceeds or if the ask quote is below the previously recorded transaction price. Also, trades are only recorded if they involve a change in price from the last trade.

The futures contracts examined are primarily traded by open outcry followed by evening screen trading sessions. The floor trading time of the Long Gilt futures market was 08:30–16:15 GMT until July 31, 1994, when opening was brought forward to 08:00 GMT. Floor trading times for the FTSE100 and Short Sterling are 08:35–16:10 GMT and 08:05–16:05 GMT respectively. The analysis focuses on the most heavily traded contracts. For the Long Gilt and Short Sterling contracts, trading tends to be concentrated in the nearest expiry month until the turn of the expiry month, e.g. March contracts trade most heavily until the end of February when trading switches to the June contract. For the FTSE100 contract, trading is concentrated in the front month contract right up to the expiry date.

Index options are traded by open outcry at LIFFE from 08:35–16:10 GMT. The options data sample consists of all trades and quotes for American-style FTSE100 index options at LIFFE from January 4, 1993 to March 31, 1994. The database contains the time of the quote, exercise style, expiry month, exercise price, call or put, matched bid and ask quotes, and the current level of the underlying asset. Only at-the-money and near-maturity contracts are considered here.

Intraday behaviour is examined by partitioning the trading day as appropriate for the frequency of the data and calculating mean values for each interval across the days in the sample. In order to examine the statistical significance of any observed intra-day patterns, regressions of the following form are estimated:

$$X_{i,j,n} = \alpha_i + \sum_{t=1}^{k} \beta_{i,t} D_{i,t} + \varepsilon_{i,j,n} \qquad\qquad 1$$

where $X_{i,j,n}$ is the value taken by the variable of interest i ($i =$ return, return volatility, traded volume, price reversal or bid-ask spread) for the interval j on day n, and $(0,1)$ dummy variables are included as necessary for the k intervals of the day and/or days of the week under investigation. A positive (negative) coefficient on one of the dummy variables indicates higher (lower) levels of the variable of interest during that interval (day) than the average across the rest of the day (week). The estimation uses Hansen's (1982) Generalized Method of Moments (GMM) to ensure robustness to returns autocorrelation and heteroscedastic errors, both of which are common in this type of data. Since the system is just identified, the GMM estimates are identical to those from Ordinary Least Squares (OLS) although their standard errors differ. This methodology is commonly used in the US literature on the intra-day behaviour of financial markets, e.g. Chan, Christie and Schultz (1995) and Chan, Chung and Johnson (1995).

EMPIRICAL EVIDENCE

The empirical evidence is presented as follows. The behaviour of returns, volatility, volume and reversals for the FTSE100 and Short Sterling futures contracts is examined at p 159. The following section presents evidence on intra-day volatility and volume in the Long Gilt futures market. Both sections consider the impact of scheduled UK and US macroeconomic announcements The following nine scheduled UK macroeconomic announcements are included: the Public Sector Borrowing Requirement, Labour Market Statistics, Retail Price Index, Retail Sales, Gross Domestic Product, Balance of Payments, Confederation of British Industry Survey of Industrial Trends, Producer Price Index, and Monetary Statistics. These have been chosen largely to reflect our a priori view of which announcements are most likely to move the futures markets. These variables broadly correspond with the US data which is released at 08:30 EST as documented in Ederington and Lee (1993), and these are the US announcements we consider. The intra-day behaviour of bid-ask spreads, returns and volatility for FTSE100 stock index options is discussed at p 175.

The Intra-day Behaviour of the FTSE100 Stock Index and Short Sterling Interest Rate Futures Contracts

For more detail on the analysis in this sub-section, see Buckle *et al.* (1998). Transactions data is used for the period from November 1, 1992 to October 31, 1993. Returns, returns volatility, traded volume and percentage of price reversals are examined over 5-minute intervals. All the UK announcements considered in this section are released at 11:30 GMT.[1,2] In addition to these regular announcements, we also examined the effect of interest rate changes on the markets. During the sample period there were two UK base rate changes on November 12, 1992 and January 26, 1993, both of which were announced at 09:50 GMT. Further, we examine how market closure and different days of the week impact on the variables of interest.

Returns and Volatility for FTSE100 and Short Sterling Futures Contracts. Returns are calculated as the logarithm of the last transactions price in the current 5-minute interval minus the logarithm of the last transactions price in the preceding interval. The results for the 5-minute mean returns for the Short Sterling and FTSE100 contracts are reported in Figures 1 and 2. The theoretical literature generally has little to say about intra-day returns behaviour. Figures 1 and 2 show very noisy patterns in returns with no clear intra-day behaviour emerging. Mean returns at the open and close are negative for Short Sterling while positive for the FTSE100 contract. Positive and relatively large returns are found at the timing of interest rate changes (09:55 GMT), but no clear pattern occurs at times of UK nor US macroeconomic announcements (11:35 and 13:35 GMT).

Table 1 presents the results of regression Equation 1 for returns, which are consistent with the observations from the Figures. No significant coefficients are reported for the intra-day effects for either contract, though a large positive coefficient exists on the dummy for interest rate changes. In terms of days of the week, the only significant coefficient is for Mondays for Short Sterling and it is negative. This indicates that returns on the Short Sterling contract tend to be lower on Mondays than the mean across the rest of the week.

Returns volatility is initially calculated as the standard deviation of log returns across days for a given interval and the intra-day patterns are presented in Figures 3 and 4. It is observed from these figures that both the Short Sterling and FTSE100 returns are highly variable at the open but less so at the close. However, for US bond, interest rate, and exchange rate futures contracts, Ederington and Lee (1993) find that it is the third 5-minute interval of the day (when US announcements are released) that is associated with high volatility rather than the opening.

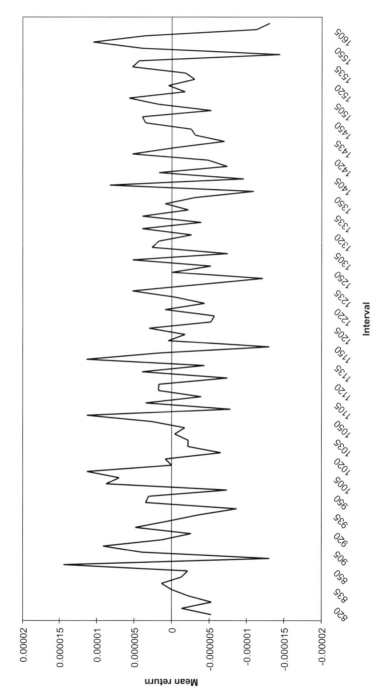

Figure 1 Intra-day 5-minute mean returns for Short Sterling futures contract.

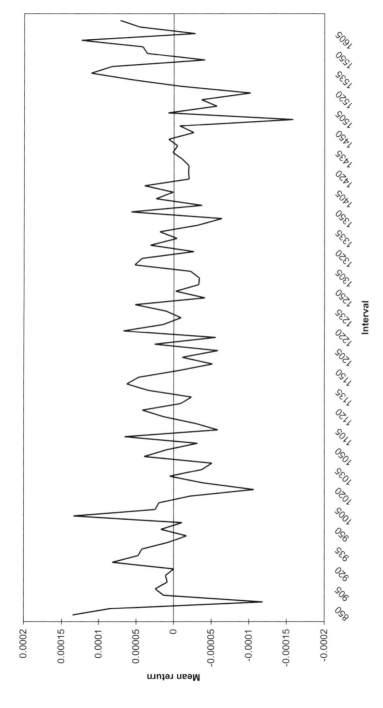

Figure 2   Intra-day 5-minute mean returns for FTSE100 futures contract.

Table 1   Regression tests of the intra-day behaviour of Short Sterling and FTSE100 futures returns.

$$R_{j,n} = \alpha + \sum_{t=1}^{9} \beta_t D_t + \varepsilon_{j,n}$$

The table presents the results of the following regression:

where $R_{j,n}$ is the return during interval j on day n, D_1 is equal to 1 during the opening interval of the day and 0 otherwise, D_2 equals 1 during the interval 09:50–09:55 GMT on days of UK interest rate changes and 0 otherwise, D_3 equals 1 during the interval 11:30–11:35 GMT on days of scheduled UK macroeconomic announcements and 0 otherwise, D_4 equals 1 during the interval 13:30–13:35 GMT on days of scheduled major US macroeconomic announcements and 0 otherwise, and D_5 equals 1 in the closing interval of the day and 0 otherwise. For days of the week, D_6 equals 1 on Mondays and 0 otherwise, D_7 equals 1 on Tuesdays and 0 otherwise, D_8 equals 1 on Thursdays and 0 otherwise, and D_9 equals 1 on Fridays and 0 otherwise. All coefficients are multiplied by 10^6.

	Short Sterling	*FTSE100*
	Coefficient (t-statistic)	*Coefficient (t-statistic)*
á	−0.67(−0.72)	−2.28(−0.21)
D_1	−4.52(−0.36)	133.23(1.41)
D_2	2026.88(1.49)	6611.86(1.59)
D_3	34.65(0.89)	106.54(0.75)
D_4	6.69(0.55)	−49.25(−0.41)
D_5	−12.30(−1.75)	70.58(1.29)
D_6	−2.77(−2.08)[b]	20.47(1.31)
D_7	1.47(0.95)	−5.82(−0.38)
D_8	−0.88(−0.65)	−2.34(−0.16)
D_9	1.47(1.10)	7.66(0.50)

[b]significant at 5%

There are two further clear spikes in Short Sterling volatility. The first peak is higher than the opening volatility and occurs at the interval 9:50–9:55 GMT. It is driven by an unexpected interest rate change on January 26, 1993.[3] The second occurs over the interval 11:30–11:35 GMT, the timing for UK macroeconomic data releases. For the FTSE100 contract, peaks in volatility at the above times are also apparent but not as pronounced. There is a third peak at the timing of US macroeconomic announcements (13:30–13:35 GMT), and it therefore appears that these have more impact on the stock index futures volatility than the interest rate futures volatility.

In Figures 3 and 4 there is a crude L-shaped pattern in volatility i.e. higher volatility at the open and close than through the day, though less pronounced at the close. This is in contrast to the U-shaped pattern that has been well documented for stock markets, e.g. Harris (1986), Admati and

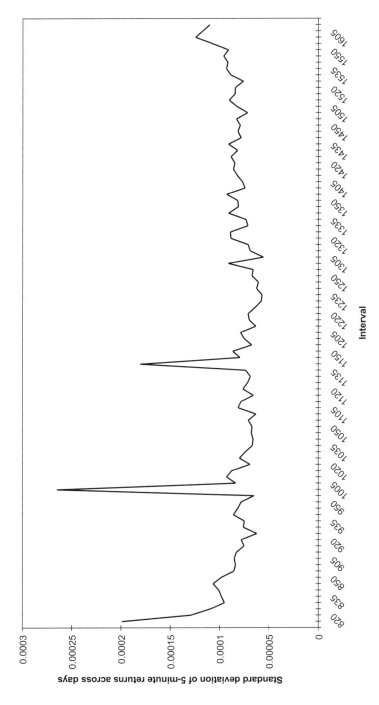

Figure 3 Intra-day standard deviation of 5-minute returns for Short Sterling futures contract.

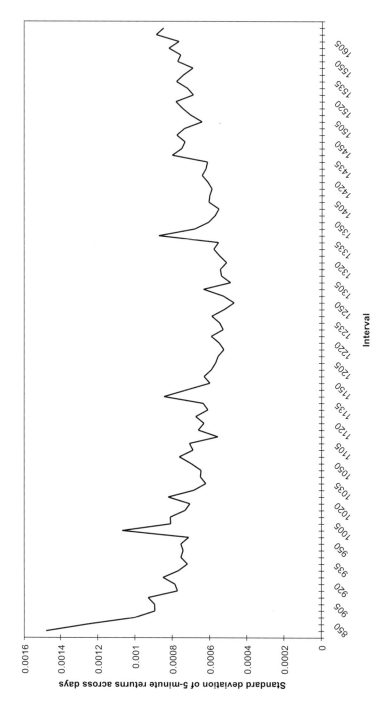

Figure 4   Intra-day standard deviation of 5-minute returns for FTSE100 futures contract.

Table 2 Regression tests of the intra-day behaviour of the volatility of returns on Short Sterling and FTSE100 futures contracts.

$$AR_{j,n} = \alpha + \sum_{t=1}^{9} \beta_t D_t + \varepsilon_{j,n}$$

The table presents the results of the following regression:

where $AR_{j,n}$ is the absolute value of the difference between the actual return $R_{j,n}$ for the 5 minute interval j on day n and the mean return R_j^* for interval j across all the days in the sample. D_t are defined as at Table 1. All coefficients multiplied by 10^6.

	Short Sterling	FTSE100
	Coefficient (t-statistic)	*Coefficient (t-statistic)*
á	46.96(23.38)[a]	522.70(37.01)[a]
D_1	76.59(7.91)[a]	672.85(11.80)[a]
D_2	1969.41(1.45)	5972.30(1.43)
D_3	153.91(5.15)[a]	394.19(4.45)[a]
D_4	11.71(1.26)	147.59(1.69)
D_5	35.00(7.66)[a]	138.55(3.95)[a]
D_6	−7.00(−2.28)[b]	−46.19(−2.24)[b]
D_7	−2.74(−0.91)	−45.23(−2.63)[b]
D_8	5.00(1.66)	−1.77(−0.10)
D_9	2.24(0.72)	−0.94(−0.05)

[a]significant at 1%; [b]significant at 5%

Pfleiderer (1988), Berry and Howe (1994). However, it is similar to Ekman (1992) who finds for the S&P500 futures contract that volatility is three times higher than average at the open and two times higher at the close.

Table 2 presents regression tests of volatility based on Equation 1. In contrast to the returns results, some statistically significant patterns emerge which are broadly consistent for both contracts. Both Short Sterling and the FTSE100 contract have significantly higher volatility at the market open (D1) and close (D5). However, the size of the open coefficient is larger than the close coefficient, confirming the pattern observed in Figures 3 and 4. For the news release dummies, the only one which is statistically significant is at the 11:30–11:35 GMT UK macroeconomic announcement time. The other announcement coefficients are positive but insignificant at the 5 percent level. Volatility on Mondays is significantly lower in both markets, and Tuesday volatility is also lower than the rest of the week for the FTSE100 case.

Traded Volume for FTSE100 and Short Sterling Futures Contracts.
Figures 5 and 6 report the mean traded volume in both contracts over each interval. There is a U-shaped pattern for both but, like volatility, it is not

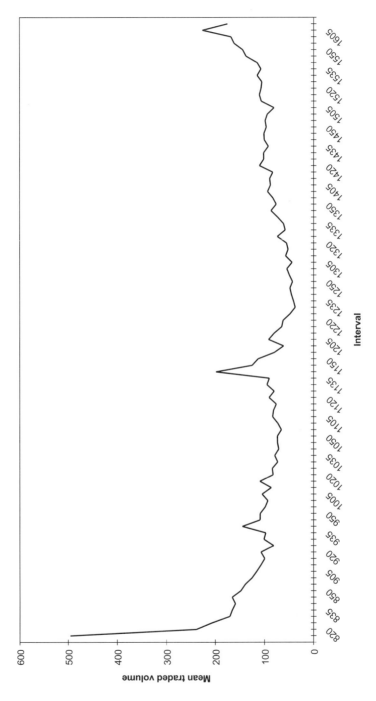

Figure 5 Intra-day 5-minute mean traded volume for Short Sterling futures contract.

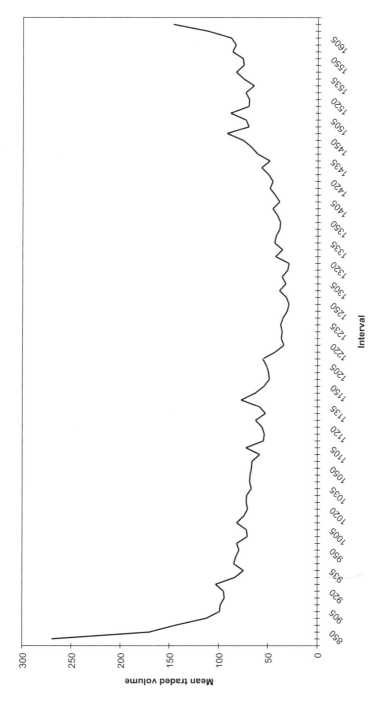

Figure 6 Intra-day 5-minute mean traded volume for FTSE100 futures contract.

symmetric in that volume is higher at the start than the end of the day. The high traded volume at the open is consistent with Berry and Howe (1994) who find a positive relationship between public information and trading volume. In Figure 5 for Short Sterling, the main deviation from a relatively smooth pattern is a definite peak at 11:30–11:35 GMT, the timing of UK announcements. There is a much less pronounced peak at this time for the FTSE100 contract in Figure 6. There are no obvious peaks in volume at the times of interest rate changes nor US macroeconomic announcements for either contract.

Table 3 presents the results of applying Equation 1 to the volume data, which are consistent with Figures 5 and 6. Both contracts show similar patterns with significantly higher volume at the open and close and also in the interval 11:30–11:35 GMT. Volume is not significantly higher on days of interest rate changes and is lower at times of US macroeconomic announcements (significantly lower for Short Sterling). Volume in both markets is significantly lower on Mondays than across the rest of the week, which is a common result for stock markets, and is consistent with the predictions of Foster and Viswanathan (1990). This corresponds with significantly lower volatility on Mondays as reported in the previous section.

Hence the intra-day pattern in both volatility and volume are essentially similar to each other, with higher levels at the open and close, but higher

Table 3 Regression tests of the intra-day behaviour of traded volume in Short Sterling and FTSE100 futures contracts.

$$V_{j,n} = \alpha + \sum_{t=1}^{9} \beta_t D_t + \varepsilon_{j,n}$$

The table presents the results of the following regression:
where $V_{j,n}$ is traded volume during interval j on day n, and D_t are defined as at Table 1.

	Short Sterling Coefficient (t-statistic)	FTSE100 Coefficient (t-statistic)
á	102.97(12.10)[a]	68.49(17.16)[a]
D_1	398.21(19.33)[a]	205.37(10.38)[a]
D_2	310.52(1.29)	53.59(0.77)
D_3	356.57(4.88)[a]	58.01(5.11)[a]
D_4	−27.43(−2.15)[b]	−10.68(−1.36)
D_5	77.80(5.94)[a]	82.39(14.68)[a]
D_6	−25.35(−2.48)[b]	−13.70(−2.69)[a]
D_7	−10.77(−1.00)	−3.69(−0.71)
D_8	8.79(0.76)	−2.47(−0.51)
D_9	−1.17(−0.10)	−1.66(−0.32)

[a]significant at 1%; [b]significant at 5%

at the open than the close. This contrasts with the more symmetric pattern found for these two variables for stock markets but is similar to that found by Ekman (1992) for the S&P500 futures market. The positive correlation between volume and volatility suggested in the above results is consistent with empirical studies of this relationship, as summarized in Karpoff (1987). The results are also consistent with Admati and Pfleiderer (1988) with volatility and volume being higher at open and close compared to the rest of the day.

The differing intra-day pattern compared to some stock market evidence may reflect different trading arrangements. One important difference is that trading at LIFFE and major US futures markets occurs in pits with a number of traders known as scalpers present. Scalpers trade a small number of contracts, holding positions for very short periods of time (often just a few minutes) and generally do not hold positions overnight. High volatility at the close in futures markets could therefore be explained by scalpers and day traders closing out their positions before the close.

Price Reversals for FTSE100 and Short Sterling Futures Contracts. A price reversal is defined as a price change that is in the opposite direction to the previous price change. A price change in the same direction as the previous price change is termed a continuation. For consistency with US studies, the data examined in this section uses price change transactions only, i.e. all non-price change transactions were excluded. Thus, every observation is either a reversal or a continuation. Reversal price changes are generally a consequence of the random arrival of buy and sell orders that are executed at stationary bid and ask prices. The price change transaction series will then display a sequence of up and down movements between the bid and ask prices. Continuations, on the other hand, are usually associated with information arriving into the market that causes an imbalance between supply and demand for the security at the current price level. Traders will then revise their view of the value of the security and if this new value lies outside the current bid-ask spread there will be an imbalance of buy and sell orders until the spread changes to capture the new security value. Under these conditions, we will observe a series of continuation price changes as the price adjusts to its new equilibrium. Thus, a low level of reversals (i.e. a high level of continuations) is typically a consequence of new information arriving into the market.

For this analysis we calculate the percentage of price change transactions which are reversals using 15-minute intervals across the day. The interval means of percentage reversals are displayed graphically in Figures 7 and 8. Short Sterling reversals vary between 73 percent and 100 percent, while those for the FTSE100 contract range between 64 percent and 72 percent.

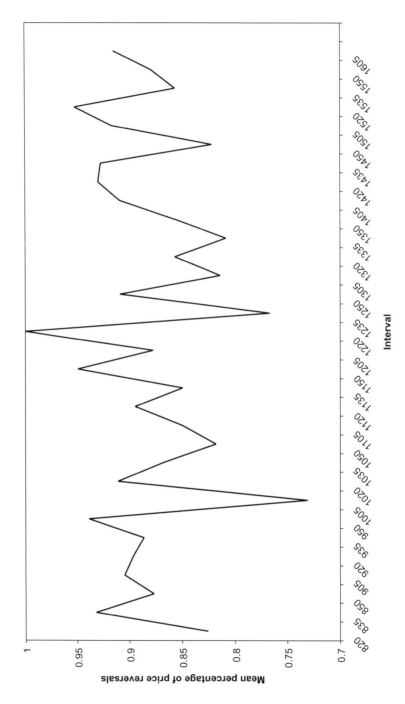

Figure 7   Intra-day mean percentage of price reversals at 15-minute intervals for Short Sterling futures contract.

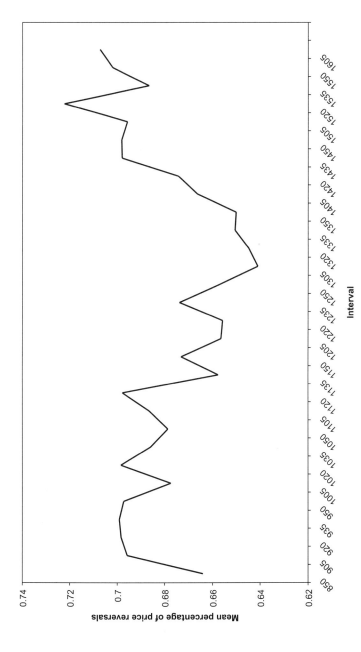

Figure 8   Intra-day mean percentage of price reversals at 15-minute intervals for FTSE100 futures contract.

The higher level of reversals for Short Sterling may reflect relatively fewer information events affecting that market.

Figure 7 for Short Sterling shows a very noisy plot for reversals, with no clear pattern emerging. Reversals are relatively low at the open, suggestive of information arrival, and relatively high at the close. The lowest point in the plot is for the interval following 09:50 GMT, the timing of interest rate changes. There are many intervals with a very high level of reversals, reflecting a predominance of prices bouncing between bid and ask and relatively few information events to cause continuations. Figure 8 shows a different pattern for the FTSE100 contract with reversals generally at a lower level. Consistent with Short Sterling, reversals are relatively low at the open and relatively high at the close. Reversals are also relatively low from 11:30–14:00 GMT, suggestive of information arrival.

Table 4 presents regression results from Equation 1 for reversals. For Short Sterling, reversals are significantly lower than average at the open.

Table 4 Regression tests of the intra-day behaviour of price reversals for Short Sterling and FTSE100 futures contracts.

$$REV_{j,n} = \alpha + \sum_{t=1}^{9} \beta_t D_t + \varepsilon_{j,n}$$

The table presents the results of the following regression:
where $REV_{j,n}$ is the percentage of price changes which are reversals during the 15-minute interval j on day n. D_1 is equal to 1 during the opening interval of the day and 0 otherwise, D_2 equals 1 during the interval from 09:50 GMT on days of UK interest rate changes and 0 otherwise, D_3 equals 1 during the interval from 11:30 GMT on days of scheduled UK macroeconomic announcements and 0 otherwise, D_4 equals 1 during the interval from 13:30 GMT on days of scheduled major US macroeconomic announcements and 0 otherwise, and D_5 equals 1 in the closing interval of the day and 0 otherwise. For days of the week, D_6 to D_9 are defined as at Table 1.

	Short Sterling	FTSE100
	Coefficient (t-statistic)	Coefficient (t-statistic)
á	0.89(57.09)[a]	0.69(97.45)[a]
D_1	−0.06(−2.87)[a]	−0.02 (−2.16)[b]
D_2	−0.41(−1.65)	−0.40(−1.95)
D_3	−0.07(−1.48)	−0.04(−1.57)
D_4	0.03(0.31)	−0.08(−1.99)[b]
D_5	0.03(1.03)	0.03(2.92)[a]
D_6	0.03(1.45)	−0.01(−1.35)
D_7	0.02(0.95)	0.01(1.21)
D_8	0.01(0.32)	−0.00(−0.03)
D_9	0.02(0.77)	−0.01(−1.11)

[a]significant at 1%; [b]significant at 5%

Despite a large negative coefficient on the interest rate dummy, it is only significant at the 10 percent level. All other coefficients on the dummy variables are insignificantly different from zero. For the FTSE100 contract, reversals are again significantly lower at the open. Reversals are lower than average at each announcement time, but only significantly so at 13:35 GMT (US announcements). Further, there is a significantly higher level of reversals at the close. As for Short Sterling, no day of the week effects appear for reversals.

The significantly lower level of reversals at the open is suggestive of information arrival and supports the results of previous sections showing higher volume and volatility at the open. The higher level of reversals at the close (significant for the FTSE100 contract), suggests that higher volume and volatility at the close is not a result of information arrival. This supports the hypothesis in the previous section that scalpers and day traders are an important factor in the behaviour of these variables near the close of futures markets.

Intra-day Volatility and Volume for the Long Gilt Futures Contract

In this section, data from the period January 24, 1992 to July 31, 1994 is used to measure volatility and volume at 5-minute intervals. The end of the sample is determined by a change in opening hours at that date. In this sample there are 93 intra-day intervals for 614 days (57,102 observations). The analysis covers a period when the release time for UK macroeconomic announcements changed from 11:30 GMT to 09:30 GMT (as discussed in endnote 1), therefore both times need to be examined. For analysis of returns, volatility, volume and autocorrelation for the German and Italian bond futures contracts at LIFFE, see apGwilym *et al.* (1996).

Figure 9 presents the volatility and volume patterns for the Long Gilt contract. Notable peaks occur at 11:30–11:35 GMT and 13:30–13:35 GMT. In Table 5, the regression results for volatility show a significant coefficient for each of the dummy variables, indicating that volatility is significantly higher for the opening and closing intervals of the day and for the intervals of UK and US economic data releases. Table 5 also presents the results for Equation 1 for traded volume. Significantly higher traded volume is observed near the open and close, and following US data releases and UK announcements at 09:30 GMT. The UK announcements at 11:30 GMT do not induce significantly higher traded volume in the following five minutes. These results suggest a positive correlation between volatility and volume across the trading day, although macroeconomic announcements seem to have a greater effect on volatility than on volume.

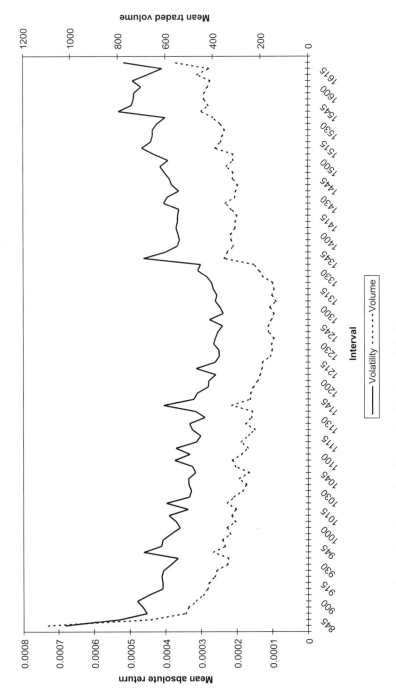

Figure 9 Intra-day volatility and volume for the Long Gilt futures contract.

Table 5 Regression results for volatility and volume for the Long Gilt futures contract.

$$X_{j,n} = \alpha + \sum_{t=1}^{5} \beta_t D_t + \varepsilon_{j,n}$$

The table presents the results of the following regression:

where $X_{j,n}$ is the absolute return or traded volume for the 5-minute interval j on day n, D_1 is a dummy variable taking the value 1 during the first interval of the day and 0 otherwise, D_2 takes the value 1 during the 09:30–09:35 GMT interval and 0 otherwise, D_3 takes the value 1 during the 11:30–11:35 GMT interval and 0 otherwise, D_4 takes the value 1 during the 13:30–13:35 GMT interval and 0 otherwise, and D_5 takes the value 1 during the last interval of the day and 0 otherwise. Coefficients are multiplied by 10^4 in the case of absolute returns (volatility).

	Volatility		Volume	
	Coefficient	t-stat	Coefficient	t-stat
á	3.61	164.3[a]	303.30	122.1[a]
D_1	3.21	11.1[a]	790.03	23.1[a]
D_2	3.73	5.7[a]	333.79	7.9[a]
D_3	0.61	2.1[b]	19.33	1.0
D_4	0.98	4.3[a]	48.48	2.6[a]
D_5	1.54	5.9[a]	255.57	14.3[a]

[a]significant at 1%; [b]significant at 5%

The Intra-day Behaviour of Bid-ask Spreads, Returns, and Volatility for FTSE100 Stock Index Options

The options data sample used is described at p 157. For more detail on the analysis in this section, see ap Gwilym *et al.* (1997).

Bid-ask Spreads on FTSE100 Index Options. Figure 10 presents the intra-day pattern in mean absolute and percentage spreads for 15-minute intervals across all days for at-the-money, near-maturity contracts. Both calls and puts demonstrate higher levels of absolute spreads at the market open which quickly decrease to the level around which they fluctuate for much of the rest of the day. However, there is also a fall in the level of spreads towards the end of the day. Percentage spreads for calls follow the pattern in absolute spreads but this is not the case for puts.[4] This pattern in spreads contrasts with the U-shaped pattern across the day which has been frequently documented in previous research. However, Chan, Christie and Schultz (1995) and Chan, Chung and Johnson (1995) report decreasing spreads near the close in markets with competing

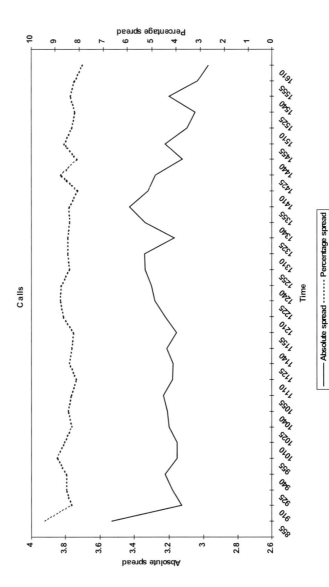

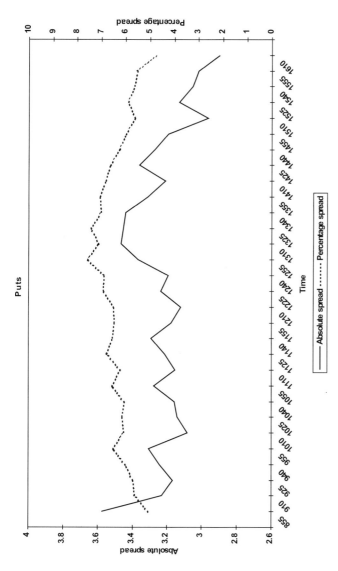

Figure 10 Mean absolute and mean percentage spreads at 15 minute intervals for American-style FTSE100 index options.

market-makers, and suggest that market structure influences the intra-day behaviour of spreads.

Regression results for spreads appear in Table 6, where for both calls and puts, the absolute spread is significantly positive in interval 1, insignificant in interval 2 and significantly negative in the final two intervals of the day. This observation of significantly wider spreads near the market open and significantly narrower spreads near the close is consistent with Figure 10. The narrower spreads at the close contrasts with the U-shape reported for markets such as the NYSE. While the specialist at the NYSE may use its monopolist position to widen spreads to take advantage of inelastic demand near the close, market makers at LIFFE may quote aggressively on one side of the spread as a means of controlling overnight inventory. For further analysis of the bid-ask spread on FTSE100 index options, see ap Gwilym *et al.* (1998).

Table 6 Regression results for the bid-ask spread on FTSE100 index options. The table presents the results of the following regression:

$$S_{j,n} = \alpha + \sum_{t=1}^{4} \beta_t D_t + \varepsilon_{j,n}$$

where $S_{j,n}$ is the absolute spread for interval j on day n, D_1 is a dummy variable taking the value 1 during the first 15-minute interval of the day and 0 otherwise, D_2 takes the value 1 during the second 15-minute interval of the day and 0 otherwise, D_3 takes the value 1 during the penultimate 15-minute interval of the day and 0 otherwise, and D_4 takes the value 1 during the final 15-minute interval of the day and 0 otherwise. A significant positive coefficient on a dummy variable indicates wider spreads than average occur during that interval and a significant negative coefficient indicates narrower spreads than average. There are 19,181 observations for calls and 17,869 for puts.

	Coefficient	t-statistic
CALLS		
á	3.209	232.58[a]
D_1 (0835–0855)	0.326	7.72[a]
D_2 (0855–0910)	−0.082	−1.68
D_3 (1540–1555)	−0.175	−3.08[a]
D_4 (1555–1610)	−0.235	−5.01[a]
PUTS		
á	3.211	213.46[a]
D_1 (0835–0855)	0.365	7.52[a]
D_2 (0855–0910)	0.021	0.37
D_3 (1540–1555)	−0.190	−3.21[a]
D_4 (1555–1610)	−0.312	−6.21[a]

[a]significant at 1%

Returns on FTSE100 Index Options. For options, the returns calculation must use prices from contracts with identical maturity, exercise price, and exercise style (American or European for LIFFE index options), and both must be either calls or puts. Even with high-frequency data, this imposes a restriction on the time interval over which returns can be calculated. Tracking observations which satisfy the above conditions at a suitably high frequency requires the use of at-the-money, near-maturity contracts.[5] We conduct analysis of hourly returns (as in Sheikh and Ronn (1994) for US options) calculated from the midpoints of bid and ask quotes. The trading day was split as follows: Interval 1: 08:35–09:10, Intervals 2–8: Hourly from 09:11 to 16:10. Intervals of equal length back from the close are used, with the remaining time at the open treated as the overnight return. The price for an interval is taken as the last observation before the end of that interval. A further issue is encountered when the exercise price which is at-the-money changes between intervals. A return based on contracts with differing exercise prices is meaningless, therefore it is also necessary to track the previously at-the-money contract.[6]

For returns, Figure 11 presents our results for calls, and mean returns do not show a consistent pattern across days. The mean overnight return is negative across all days and for each day except Tuesday. A larger negative mean return on Monday open is notable. Figure 12 presents the results for puts, and a lack of distinct patterns is again observed. However, mean overnight returns are negative and relatively large for each day of the week.

Table 7 presents the coefficients for returns based on Equation 1. The results for calls demonstrate no significant (at the 5 percent level) coefficients on the dummy variables. This indicates that the call returns near the open and close are not significantly different from returns across the rest of the day, which is consistent with Figure 11. For puts, insignificant coefficients appear for intervals 2, 7 and 8, but a highly significant negative coefficient is observed for the opening interval of the day. This demonstrates that the consistently negative overnight returns in Figure 12 are significantly lower than those during the rest of the day.

The reason for consistently negative overnight put returns is not clear, though we now offer some suggestions. The time value of options naturally decreases as time passes and this could be a contributing factor, as calls also exhibit smaller negative overnight returns for each day except Tuesdays. Due to the derivative nature of options, if the underlying market is rising call prices will tend to increase while puts will tend to lose value. Over the sample period used, the underlying market rose by 7.6 percent, which may indicate that the fair expected overnight put return would tend to be negative. The result could also be due to a mispricing in the options market whereby puts lost money because they were systematically overpriced.

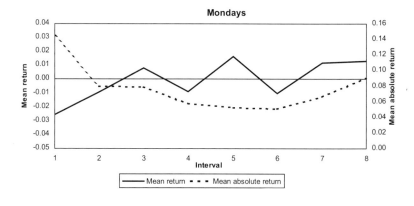

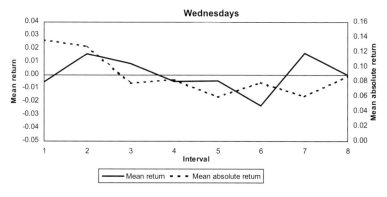

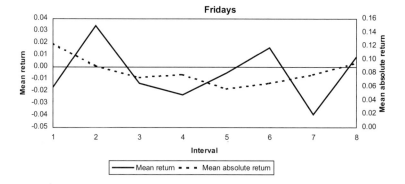

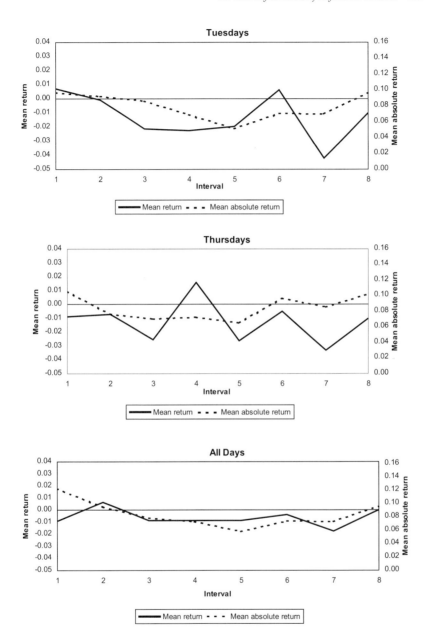

Figure 11   Mean returns and mean absolute returns for at-the-money, near-maturity American-style FTSE100 index call options.

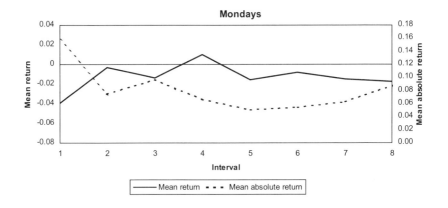

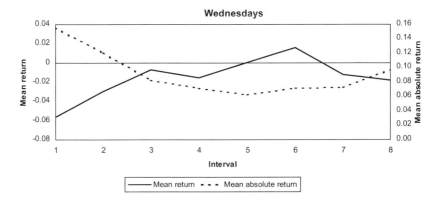

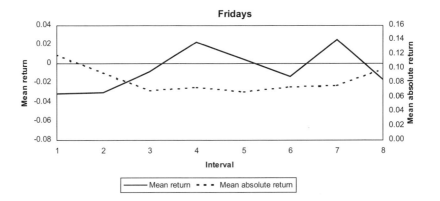

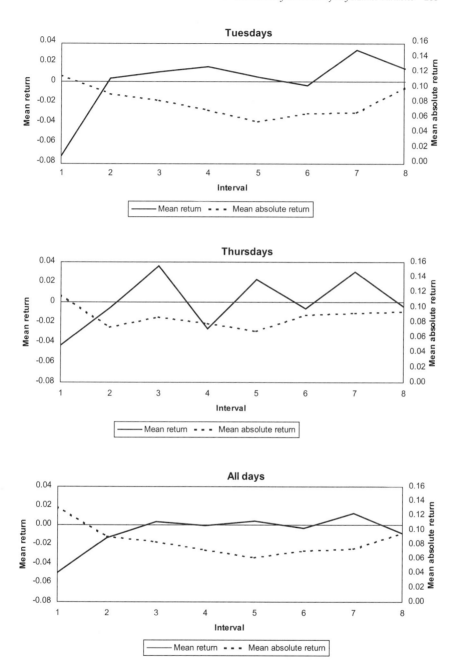

Figure 12 Mean returns and mean absolute returns for at-the-money, near-maturity American-style FTSE100 index put options.

Table 7   Regression results for returns on FTSE100 index options.

$$R_{j,n} = \alpha + \sum_{t=1}^{4} \beta_t D_t + \varepsilon_{j,n}$$

The table presents the results of the following regression:

where $R_{j,n}$ is the return for interval j on day n, D_1 is a dummy variable taking the value 1 during the first interval of the day and 0 otherwise, D_2 takes the value 1 during the second interval of the day and 0 otherwise, D_3 takes the value 1 during penultimate interval of the day and 0 otherwise, and D_4 takes the value 1 during the final interval of the day and 0 otherwise. A significant positive coefficient on a dummy variable indicates that larger returns than average occur during that interval and a significant negative coefficient indicates lower returns than average. There are 2,520 observations for both calls and puts.

	Coefficient	t-statistic
CALLS		
á	−0.006	−2.65[a]
D_1 (0835−0910)	−0.002	−0.26
D_2 (0910−1010)	0.013	1.74
D_3 (1410−1510)	−0.010	−1.69
D_4 (1510−1610)	0.006	0.88
PUTS		
á	0.001	0.41
D_1 (0835−0910)	−0.048	−4.98[a]
D_2 (0910−1010)	−0.014	−1.89
D_3 (1410−1510)	0.010	1.69
D_4 (1510−1610)	−0.009	−1.23

[a]significant at 1%

The profitability of a trading strategy based on this observation remains a subject for future research, though further comments appear in the next sub-section.

From the above analysis, no clear pattern emerges in intra-day option returns. The most consistent observation is the negative mean return overnight for each day except Tuesdays for calls. Mean overnight returns for puts are consistently negative and significantly lower than returns across the rest of the day.

Volatility of Returns on FTSE100 Index Options. The price formation models of Admati and Pfleiderer (1988) and Foster and Viswanathan (1990) indicate patterns to be expected in the volatility of intra-day returns. It is suggested that discretionary liquidity traders will play a role in accentuating intra-day variations in volatility because they adjust their transactions to avoid times when trading costs are highest. Periods of high volume are also times when informed traders choose to trade, hence prices are expected to be most informative and variable in such periods. The empirical evidence on the volatility of intra-day returns has primarily been based on US markets, and options markets have received little attention relative to stock markets. For US stock markets, Wood *et al.* (1985), Harris (1986), and others report a U-shape in returns volatility across the trading day, with the highest volatility at the market open and close. Foster and Viswanathan (1993) also report high returns volatility at the market open.

For options markets, the two most relevant studies are Peterson (1990) and Sheikh and Ronn (1994), both examining US equity options. Peterson reports that the highest volatility occurs at the start and end of the trading day for stocks, calls and puts. Sheikh and Ronn find the same U-shaped pattern not only for stocks, calls and puts, but also for adjusted call and put returns which are independent of stock returns. The U-shaped pattern in variances is similar to patterns in volume and spreads previously reported for stock and futures markets.

Table 8 Regression results for FTSE100 index options returns volatility.

$$AR_{j,n} = \alpha + \sum_{t=1}^{4} \beta_t D_t + \varepsilon_{j,n}$$

The table presents the results of the following regression:

where $AR_{j,n}$ is the absolute return for interval j on day n, and the dummy variables are defined as in Table 7. A significant positive coefficient on a dummy variable indicates larger absolute returns (volatility) than average occur during that interval and a significant negative coefficient indicates lower returns (volatility) than average. There are 2,520 observations for both calls and puts.

	Coefficient	t-statistic
CALLS		
á	0.061	33.21[a]
D_1 (0835–0910)	0.051	8.65[a]
D_2 (0910–1010)	0.028	5.73[a]
D_3 (1410–1510)	0.006	1.45
D_4 (1510–1610)	0.029	5.79[a]
PUTS		
á	0.063	33.21[a]
D_1 (0835–0910)	0.061	8.83[a]
D_2 (0910–1010)	0.025	5.13[a]
D_3 (1410–1510)	0.006	1.37
D_4 (1510–1610)	0.029	5.74[a]

[a]significant at 1%

We now test whether intra-day returns volatility in the UK index option market is significantly higher near the open and close of the market relative to the rest of the day. Figures 11 and 12 present the results for mean absolute returns for calls and puts respectively. Each day in both figures demonstrates a crude U-shape in volatility with high volatility at the market open and an increase in volatility at the close. The pattern is also observed for the "all days" case.

The results for absolute returns based on Equation 1 appear in Table 8. Absolute returns are found to have significantly positive coefficients (at the 1 percent level) for the opening two intervals and the closing interval, as would be expected from the U-shape in Figures 11 and 12. Interval 7 has an insignificant coefficient in both cases. Volatility is thus significantly higher near the open and close than in other intervals of the day for both calls and puts. The observation of significantly higher returns volatility in the opening interval of the day indicates that attempts to exploit the statistically significant negative overnight returns in puts reported above would entail a high degree of risk.

CONCLUSIONS

This chapter investigates the intra-day pattern of key variables relating to futures and options contracts traded on LIFFE. The dataset is superior to those commonly used in studies of US futures markets in that it contains all quotes and transactions rather than only those which involve a change in price, and in addition its use in this context provides an independent check of intra-day patterns observed in US markets.

For UK futures markets, the familiar U-shape is found for intra-day trading volume and volatility but these variables are higher at the open than the close. The finding of low reversals at the open suggests that the high volatility and volume found at this time is the result of information trading, thus supporting the model of Admati and Pfleiderer (1988). However, the higher volume and volatility at the close (though not as high as at the open) is associated with high reversals and therefore cannot be explained by information trading. One possible explanation for the high volume and volatility at the close for futures markets is the existence of scalpers who trade to close out their positions before the market closes. Public information in the form of UK and US macroeconomic announcements are found to increase volume and volatility.

For FTSE100 index options, bid-ask spreads for both calls and puts demonstrate significantly higher levels at the market open, which then quickly decrease, and there is also a significant decrease in the level of spreads near the close. The fall in the level of spreads near the market close is inconsistent with the pattern in trading activity, and is unrelated to intra-day volatility. However, it is consistent with the hypothesis suggested by Chan, Christie and Schultz (1995) that dealers reduce spreads in order to attract trades and avoid holding inventory overnight. The spread results are consistent with Chan, Christie and Schultz (1995) and Chan, Chung and Johnson (1995) and support their hypotheses that market structure affects spreads behaviour. Specifically, markets with competing market makers experience narrower spreads near the market close while specialist markets have wider spreads at that time. No consistent pattern emerges in intra-day FTSE100 index option returns, but a U-shaped curve for intra-day returns volatility is observed which is consistent with the futures contracts results.

AKNOWLEDGEMENT

Many of the results in this chapter stem from a research project on the intra-day behaviour of LIFFE derivatives which was supported by the Leverhulme Trust (Grant F391/I). We alone are responsible for any errors or omissions.

NOTES

1. During the sample period used for this chapter, both the Central Statistical Office (CSO) and the Bank of England changed the release time for the main macroeconomic announcements from 11:30 GMT to 09:30 GMT. For consistency, days with 09:30 GMT announcements were omitted from the sample. All the main CSO releases were at 09:30 GMT from the first announcement day after August 23, 1993. The monetary statistics released by the Bank of England changed to a 09:30 GMT release time from September 3, 1993. Labour market statistics were released at 09:30 GMT from November 18, 1993 and hence were unaffected for our sample. Accounting for days where more than one announcement is made provides a sample of 84 separate announcement days.
2. The release procedures for the Central Statistical Office (CSO) and Employment Department announcements is through a fax system, with data faxed to subscribers of the service at 11:30 GMT precisely. For the monetary statistics released by the Bank of England, the release is distributed to reporters at the Bank prior to the release time, but reporters cannot leave the room or use the telephone until the scheduled release time. These strict release procedures leave very little scope for leakage of information prior to the release time.
3. The *Financial Times* of January 27, 1993 reported, *"The cut to 6 percent, which took senior ministers and the markets by surprise, ..."*.
4. It is curious why percentage spreads for puts are low in the first 15-minute interval of the day, but on inspection of results based on 5-minute intervals, the first 5-minute interval

of the day is actually found to have high percentage spreads and the next intervals have relatively low values.

5. A further restriction imposed is that the option must have at least five trading days to expiry to avoid well-documented price effects as expiry approaches. It is also necessary to eliminate the overnight return when the expiry month switches to the next month.

6. To illustrate, if the underlying price is at 2830 for the last observation of interval 1, then for the American-style options the 2850 contract is at-the-money. However, if the underlying price changes to 2820 during interval 2, it will be the 2800 contract which is at-the-money. At the end of interval 2 it is necessary to find the most recent observations for both the 2800 and 2850 contracts with appropriate expiry date.

BIBLIOGRAPHY

Admati, A.R. and Pfleiderer, P. (1988), "A Theory of Intra-day Patterns: Volume and Price Variability", *Review of Financial Studies*, 1(1), 3–40.

Amihud, Y. and Mendelson, H. (1980), "Dealership Markets: Market-making with Inventory", *Journal of Financial Economics*, 8, 31–53.

ap Gwilym, O., Buckle, M., Foord, T. and Thomas, S. (1996), "The Intra-day Behaviour of European Bond Futures", *Journal of Fixed Income*, 6(2), 49–66.

ap Gwilym, O., Buckle, M. and Thomas, S. (1997), "The Intra-day Behaviour of Bid-Ask Spreads, Returns and Volatility for FTSE100 Stock Index Options", *Journal of Derivatives*, 4(4), 20–32.

ap Gwilym, O., Clare, A. and Thomas, S. (1998), "The Bid-Ask Spread on Stock Index Options: An Ordered Probit Analysis", *Journal of Futures Markets*, 18(4), 467–485.

Becker, K.G., Finnerty, J.E. and Kopecky, K.J. (1993), "Economic News and Intra-day Volatility in International Bond Markets", *Financial Analysts Journal*, 49, (May/June), 81–86.

Becker, K.G., Finnerty, J.E. and Friedman, J. (1995), "Economic News and Equity Market Linkages Between the US and UK", *Journal of Banking and Finance*, 19, 1191–1210.

Berry, T.D. and Howe, K.M. (1994), "Public Information Arrival", *Journal of Finance*, 49(4), 1331–1346.

Brock, W. and Kleidon, A. (1992), "Periodic Market Closure and Trading Volume: A Model of Intra-day Bids and Asks", *Journal of Economic Dynamics and Control*, 16, 451–489.

Buckle, M., ap Gwilym, O., Thomas, S. and Woodhams, M. (1998), *Intra-day Empirical Regularities in Interest Rate and Equity Index Futures Markets, and the Effect of Macroeconomic Announcements, Journal of Business Finance and Accounting, forthcoming.*

Chan, K.C., Christie, W.G. and Schultz, P.H. (1995), "Market Structure and the Intra-day Pattern of Bid-Ask Spreads for NASDAQ Securities", *Journal of Business*, 68, 35–60.

Chan, K., Chung, Y.P. and Johnson, H. (1995), "The Intra-day Behaviour of Bid-Ask Spreads for NYSE Stocks and CBOE Options", *Journal of Financial and Quantitative Analysis*, 30, 329–346.

Ederington, L.H. and Lee, J.H. (1993), ''How Markets Process Information: News Releases and Volatility'', *Journal of Finance*, 48(4), 1161–1191.

Ekman, P.D. (1992), ''Intra-day Patterns in the S&P500 Index Futures Markets'', *Journal of Futures Markets*, 12(4), 365–381.

Foster, F. and Viswanathan, S. (1990), ''A Theory of the Intra-day Variations in Volume, Variance, and Trading Costs in Securities Markets'', *Review of Financial Studies*, 3, 593–624.

Foster, F. and Viswanathan, S. (1993), ''Variations in Trading Volume, Return Volatility, and Trading Costs: Evidence on Recent Price Formation Models'', *Journal of Finance*, 48, 187–211.

Foster, F. and Viswanathan, S. (1994), ''Strategic Trading with Asymmetrically Informed Traders and Long-Lived Information'', *Journal of Financial and Quantitative Analysis*, 29, 499–518.

Glosten, L.R. and Milgrom, P.R. (1985), ''Bid, Ask and Transaction Prices in a Specialist Market with Heterogeneously Informed Traders'', *Journal of Financial Economics*, 14, 71–100.

Gosnell, T.F. (1995), ''The Distribution of Reversals and Continuations and Tests for Intra-day Market Efficiency'', *Journal of Business Finance and Accounting*, 22(2), 225–243.

Hansen, L.P. (1982), ''Large Sample Properties of Generalized Method of Moments Estimators'', *Econometrica*, 50, 1029–1054.

Harris, L. (1986), ''A Transaction Data Survey of Weekly and Intra-daily Patterns in Stock Returns'', *Journal of Financial Economics*, 16, 99–117.

Jain, P.J. and Joh, G. (1988), ''The Dependence between Hourly Prices and Trading Volume'', *Journal of Financial and Quantitative Analysis*, 23, 269–283.

Karpoff, J.M. (1987), ''The Relation Between Price Changes and Trading Volume: A Survey'', *Journal of Financial and Quantitative Analysis*, 22, 109–126.

Lee, C., Mucklow, B. and Ready, M. (1993), ''Spreads, Depths, and the Impact of Earnings Information: An Intra-day Analysis'', *Review of Financial Studies*, 6, 345–374.

McInish, T.H. and Wood, R.A. (1990), ''Autocorrelation of Daily Index Returns: Intra-day-to-Intra-day versus Close-to-Close Intervals'', *Journal of Banking and Finance*, 15, 193–206.

McInish, T.H. and Wood, R.A. (1992), ''An Analysis of Intra-day Patterns in Bid/Ask Spreads for NYSE Stocks'', *Journal of Finance*, 47, 753–764.

O'Hara, M. (1995), *Market microstructure theory*, Blackwell, Oxford, UK.

Peterson, D.R. (1990), ''A Transaction Data Study of Day-of-the-Week and Intra-day Patterns in Option Returns'', *Journal of Financial Research*, 13, (Summer), 117–132.

Sheikh, A.M. and Ronn, E.I. (1994), ''A Characterization of the Daily and Intra-day Behaviour of Returns on Options'', *Journal of Finance*, 49, 557–579.

Stoll, H. and Whaley, R.E. (1990), ''Stock Market Structure and Volatility'', *Review of Financial Studies*, 3, 37–71.

Wood, R.A., McInish, T.H. and Ord, J.K. (1985), ''An Investigation of Transaction Data for NYSE Stocks'', *Journal of Finance*, 40, 723–741.

Chapter **7**

Price Discovery and Market Integration in European Government Bond Markets

Allison Holland

UK Debt Management Office

This chapter examines the relationship between the four major European government bonds and their associated futures contracts. In common with many financial futures markets, price discovery occurs in the futures markets with prices in the spot market following with a lag. Over short time horizons, arbitrage activity appears to be limited by the presence of market frictions. In the case of dually traded futures, the importance of spread trading is highlighted. In contrast to each cash-futures pair, dually traded futures contracts are highly integrated reflecting very active arbitrage between the markets.

INTRODUCTION

Futures markets have formally existed since 1848.[1] Futures markets have two key functions: (1) to allow the transferral of price risk[2] and (2) to facilitate price discovery. This chapter focuses on the second of these.

In common with many other derivatives products, the initial capital outlay required to trade futures contracts is small relative to the cost of the underlying asset.[3] So if new information on the value of the underlying asset becomes known to investors, many rational investors will choose to trade on the futures market first because less capital is required immediately to trade in it. This may reflect the presence of market frictions; for instance, investors may have to search to arrange financing and/or may only have limited access to immediate funds. The result of this is that the "news" will be reflected first in futures prices and then, through the actions of arbitrageurs, in spot prices. Empirically this is reflected in the observation that spot prices lag futures prices. Many studies have investigated this price leadership feature of futures markets, including Garbade and Silber (1982), Kawaller, Koch and Koch (1987), Stoll and Whaley (1990) and de Jong and Nijman (1997). This chapter investigates this relationship as it applies to the four major European bond and futures markets; i.e. the UK gilt market, the French OAT market, the German Bund market and the Italian BTP market . It also considers how this relationship is affected by the existence of a dually traded futures contract in the case of the German Bund and the Italian BTP.

The results show that the futures price leads the cash price in each of the four markets studied. Hence, price discovery occurs in the futures markets. The results also show that the futures and cash markets remain to some extent segmented, with mispricing between the two markets persisting over (short) time horizons. By contrast, dually traded futures contracts are very integrated suggesting active arbitrage between the two markets. The results also show clearly that the foreign BTP futures contract (the LIFFE contract) leads the domestic contract but that the domestically traded Bund contract (the DTB) leads the foreign one. These results are borne out when the three variable system, including the two futures contracts and the cash bond, is considered.

The chapter is set out as follows. The standard methodology used to examine this relationship is described at p 191. A discussion follows on how this can be extended to cover the case of dually traded futures contracts. The data and the necessary data transformations are discussed at p 196. The results of the estimation of the model are reported at p 198 and some of the implications are drawn out. The chapter concludes with some thoughts for future work at p 203.

METHODOLOGY

Arbitrage pricing theory allows us to determine the price of a futures contract in perfect capital markets. Theory says that the price of the futures contract should equal the spot price adjusted for financing costs; i.e. as the payoff of being long a futures contract is the same as that from buying the asset now and holding it for the duration of the futures contract, then the cost of both these options should be the same. Explicitly

$$f_t = s_t(1 + r)^{T-t} \qquad\qquad 1$$

where T is the expiry date of the contract, t is the date on which the futures contract is traded and r is the relevent interest rate.

This can be rearranged to give the *theoretical* or spot equivalent futures price

$$f'_t = s_t = \frac{f_t}{(1+r)^{T-t}} \qquad 2$$

In the presence of market frictions such as transactions costs Equation 2 may not always hold; however, once prices deviate sufficiently from this equilibrium, an opportunity for profit opens up and arbitrageurs will enter the market. Their actions will cause prices to come back into line with each other, thus restoring the equilibrium.

Equation 2 is a specific form of a cointegrating relationship[4]

$$\Gamma_t = f'_t - \mu - \tau s_t \qquad 3$$

with $\mu = 0$ and $\tau = 1$.[5]

Garbade and Silber (1982) exploited this equilibrium relationship and set up the following model to describe how prices evolve in the spot and futures market:

$$\begin{bmatrix} s_t \\ f'_t \end{bmatrix} = \begin{bmatrix} \alpha_s \\ \alpha_f \end{bmatrix} + \begin{bmatrix} 1-\gamma_s & \gamma_s \\ \gamma_f & 1-\gamma_f \end{bmatrix} \begin{bmatrix} s_{t-1} \\ f'_{t-1} \end{bmatrix} + \begin{bmatrix} \varepsilon_{s,t} \\ \varepsilon_{f,t} \end{bmatrix} \qquad 4$$

where $\varepsilon_{s,t} \varepsilon_{f,t}$ are unpredictable white noise disturbances and α_s and α_f take account of any potential trends in the series.

Rearranging gives the dynamic specification

$$\Delta s_t = \alpha_s + \gamma_s(f'_{t-1} - s_{t-1}) + \varepsilon_{s,t}$$
$$\Delta f'_t = \alpha_f + \gamma_f(s_{t-1} - f'_{t-1}) + \varepsilon_{f,t} \qquad 5$$

The parameters γ_s and γ_f measure how much each market adjusts in this time period to last period's deviation from 2.[6] If both γ_s and γ_f are zero then the two markets are completely independent of each other and the futures market will be unable to fulfill its risk transferral function. The continued existence of the futures market would then be called into question. If one of γ_s or γ_f is zero then that market is completely independent from the other. Conversely, if one of the γ_s or γ_f is unity, then that market is a pure satellite of the other, simply tracking prices in the other market. We define θ as the relative adjustment of one market to the mispricing described by the error correction term $(f'_{t-1} - s_{t-1})$; i.e. $\theta_s = (|\gamma_s|)/(|\gamma_s| + |\gamma_f|)$. It can be interpreted as a measure of price discovery. Note that θ_s will lie in the interval $[0,1]$. If $\theta_s > 0.5$, then the spot market does the majority of the adjustment and can be thought of as the price follower, i.e. if new information is revealed first in the futures market, resulting in a deviation from 2, then the spot market adjusts in the next period to re-establish 2, thereby reflecting the new information.

In equilibrium we know that $f'_{t-1} - s_{t-1} = 0$, so if we construct and examine this difference we see that

$$f'_t - s_t = (\alpha_f - \alpha_s) + (1 - \gamma_s - \gamma_f)(f'_{t-1} - s_{t-1}) + (\varepsilon_{f,t} - \varepsilon_{f,t}) \qquad 6$$

This is an autoregressive (AR) process in the mispricing term $(f'_t - s_t)$. We can then define δ as the parameter of persistence $(1 - \gamma_s - \gamma_f)$. This parameter captures the intensity of arbitrage between the two markets. Values of δ close to unity indicate that most of the mispricing persists into the next period, suggesting that arbitrage activity is not very intense over one time period; values close to zero indicate that the market is very actively arbitraged.

In estimation, 5 is usually augmented to a general vector error correction model (VECM) as follows:[7]

$$\Delta s_t = \alpha_s + \sum_{i=1}^{k} \beta_{ss,i} \Delta s_{t-i} + \sum_{j=1}^{k} \beta_{sf,j} \Delta f'_{t-j} + \gamma_s \Gamma_{t-1} + \varepsilon_{s,t}$$

$$\Delta f'_t = \alpha_f + \sum_{i=1}^{k} \beta_{fs,i} \Delta s_{t-i} + \sum_{j=1}^{k} \beta_{ff,j} \Delta f'_{t-j} + \gamma_f \Gamma_{t-1} + \varepsilon_{f,t} \qquad 7$$

The inclusion of lags of the dependent and independent variables will capture the short run dynamics in the system. For example, the short run terms will capture any temporary price changes which might arise from uninformed noise trading.

The model 4 can be further extended to cover the multivariate case. If we consider a dually traded futures contract and the associated bond, then 2 should hold for each of the futures contracts individually and the two futures contracts should also be cointegrated with each other; i.e. we should be able to define

$$\Gamma_{1,t} = f'_{df,t} - \mu_1 - \tau_1 s_t$$

$$\Gamma_{2,t} = f'_{ff,t} - \mu_2 - \tau_2 s_t \qquad 8$$

$$\Gamma_3 = f'_{ff,t} - \mu_3 - \tau_3 f'_{df,t}$$

where the subscripts df and ff indicate the futures contract traded on the domestic exchange and on LIFFE (the foreign exchange) respectively and the restrictions $\mu_1 = \mu_2 = \mu_3 = 0$ and $\tau_1 = \tau_2 = \tau_3 = 1$ apply. Note, however, that these three equations will be linearly dependent and that in this three variable system there will be only two linearly independent cointegrating vectors.

Now 4 becomes

$$
\begin{bmatrix} s_t \\ df'_t \\ ff'_t \end{bmatrix} = \begin{bmatrix} \alpha_s \\ \alpha_{df} \\ \alpha_{ff} \end{bmatrix} + \begin{bmatrix} 1 - \gamma_{sdf} - \gamma_{sff} & \gamma_{sdf} & \gamma_{sff} \\ \gamma_{dfs} & 1 - \gamma_{dfs} - \gamma_{dfff} & \gamma_{dfff} \\ \gamma_{ffs} & \gamma_{ffdf} & 1 - \gamma_{ffs} - \gamma_{ffdf} \end{bmatrix}
$$

$$
\begin{bmatrix} s_{t-1} \\ df'_{t-1} \\ ff'_{t-1} \end{bmatrix} + \begin{bmatrix} \varepsilon_{s,t} \\ \varepsilon_{df,t} \\ \varepsilon_{ff,t} \end{bmatrix} \tag{9}
$$

which can be rearranged to give

$$
\Delta s_t = \alpha_s + \gamma_{sdf}(df'_{t-1} - s_{t-1}) + \gamma_{sff}(ff'_{t-1} - s_{t-1}) + \varepsilon_{s,t}
$$

$$
\Delta df'_t = \alpha_{df} + \gamma_{dfs}(s_{t-1} - df'_{t-1}) + \gamma_{dfff}(ff'_{t-1} - df'_{t-1}) + \varepsilon_{df,t} \tag{10}
$$

$$
\Delta ff'_t = \alpha_{ff} + \gamma_{ffs}(s_{t-1} - ff'_{t-1}) + \gamma_{ffdf}(df'_{t-1} - ff'_{t-1}) + \varepsilon_{ff,t}
$$

As noted above, these three error correction terms $(df'_{t-1} - s_{t-1})$, $(ff'_{t-1} - s_{t-1})$ and $(ff'_{t-1} - df'_{t-1})$ are linearly dependent. This means we can rewrite 10 in terms of just two of these vectors. Here, I will use $\Gamma_2 = (ff'_{t-1} - s_{t-1})$ and $\Gamma_3 = (ff'_{t-1} - df'_{t-1})$. So 10 becomes

$$
\Delta s_t = \alpha_s + \gamma_s^* \Gamma_{2,t-1} - \gamma_{sdf} \Gamma_{3,t-1} + \varepsilon_{s,t}
$$

$$
\Delta df'_t = \alpha_{df} - \gamma_{dfs} \Gamma_{2,t-1} + \gamma_{df}^* \Gamma_{3,t-1} + \varepsilon_{df,t} \tag{10a}
$$

$$
\Delta ff'_t = \alpha_{ff} - \gamma_{ffs} \Gamma_{2,t-1} - \gamma_{ffdf} \Gamma_{3,t-1} + \varepsilon_{ff,t}
$$

where $\gamma_s^* = \gamma_{sdf} + \gamma_{sff}$ and $\gamma_{df}^* = \gamma_{dfff} + \gamma_{dfs}$.[8] This is similar to the procedure followed by Harris, *et al.* (1995).

Again, augmenting 10a with lags of the dependent and independent variables will capture the short run dynamics of the system and so the following VECM is estimated

$$
\Delta s_t = \alpha_s + \sum_{i=1}^{k} \beta_{ss,i} \Delta s_{t-i} + \sum_{j=1}^{k} \beta_{sdf,j} \Delta df'_{t-j} + \sum_{l=1}^{k} \beta_{sff,l} \Delta ff'_{t-l}
$$

$$
+ \gamma_s^* \Gamma_{2,t-1} - \gamma_{sdf} \Gamma_{3,t-1} + \varepsilon_{s,t} \tag{10b}
$$

$$
\Delta df'_t = \alpha_{df} + \sum_{i=1}^{k} \beta_{dfs,i} \Delta s_{t-i} + \sum_{j=1}^{k} \beta_{dfdf,j} \Delta df'_{t-j} + \sum_{l=1}^{k} \beta_{dfff,l} \Delta ff'_{t-l}
$$

$$
- \gamma_{dfs} \Gamma_{2,t-1} + \gamma_{df}^* \Gamma_{3,t-1} + \varepsilon_{df,t}
$$

$$\Delta ff_t' = \alpha_{ff} + \sum_{i=1}^{k} \beta_{ffs,i} \Delta s_{t-i} + \sum_{j=1}^{k} \beta_{ffdf,j} \Delta df_{t-j}' + \sum_{l=1}^{k} \beta_{ffff,l} \Delta ff_{t-l}' \qquad \text{10b}$$

$$- \gamma_{ffs} \Gamma_{2,t-1} - \gamma_{ffdf} \Gamma_{3,t-1} + \varepsilon_{ff,t}$$

The multivariate counterpart to θ can be calculated from the estimated coefficients. The disequilibrium in the system is described by the two error correction terms. Again the γ parameters capture each market's adjustment to the disequilibrium and the sum of the γs captures the systems total adjustment to the disequilibrium, so each market i's relative adjustment is captured by the sum of its $\gamma_{i\_}$'s relative to the total sum; for example $\theta_s = (|\gamma_s^*| + |\gamma_{sff}|)/(|\gamma^*s| + |\gamma_{sff}| + |\gamma_{dfs}| + |\gamma_{df}^*| + |\gamma_{ffdf}| + |\gamma_{ffs}|)$. Again θ_s lies in the interval [0,1] with values close to zero indicating price leadership of the spot market and values close to unity suggesting that the spot market is a price follower.

Unfortunately, there is no simple counterpart to δ in the multivariate case. In equilibrium we know that $s_t = df_t' = ff_t'$ so taking each pair we can express this period's partial disequilibrium in terms of last period's disequilibrium. Therefore, taking differences and calculating this period's partial disequilibrium we get (after some manipulation)

$$(df_t' - s_t) = (\alpha_{df} - \alpha_s) + (1 - \gamma_{dfs} - \gamma_s^*)\Gamma_{2,t-1} + (\gamma_{df}^* + \gamma_{sdf} - 1)\Gamma_{3,t-1}$$

$$(ff_t' - s_t) = (\alpha_{ff} - \alpha_s) + (1 - \gamma_{ffs} - \gamma_s^*)\Gamma_{2,t-1}(\gamma_{sdf} - \gamma_{ffdf})\Gamma_{3,t-1} \qquad \text{11}$$

$$(ff_t' - df_t') = (\alpha_{ff} - \alpha_{df}) + (\gamma_{dfs} - \gamma_{ffs})\Gamma_{2,t-1} + (1 - \gamma_{df}^* - \gamma_{ffdf})\Gamma_{3,t-1}$$

From this, define six scalars δ_{12}, δ_{13}, δ_{32}, δ_{23}, δ_{32} and δ_{33} as follows:

	$\delta_{\_2}$	$\delta_{\_3}$
$\delta_{1\_}$	$1 - \gamma_{dfs} - \gamma_s^*$	$\gamma_{df}^* + \gamma_{sdf} - 1$
$\delta_{2\_}$	$1 - \gamma_{ffs} - \gamma_s^*$	$\gamma_{sdf} - \gamma_{ffdf}$
$\delta_{3\_}$	$\gamma_{dfs} - \gamma_{ffs}$	$1 - \gamma_{ffdf} - \gamma_{df}^*$

In order for the system to be stable, these six coefficients should lie within the unit circle. If all the coefficients are close to zero then this would suggest that there is little persistence in the system and the markets are actively arbitraged; conversely, if they are all close to unity, this would suggest a high degree of persistence of the disequilibrium and relatively little arbitrage between the markets. Similarly, if the coefficients in any one row are small, for example if $\delta_{3,2}$ and $\delta_{3,3}$ are close to zero, then this would suggest that the foreign futures and domestic futures markets are well integrated.

DATA

The dataset consists of transactions prices collected *via* a REUTERS feed for the December 1996 futures contract traded on each futures exchange and for the underlying bonds in the basket of deliverables traded over the period September 30 to October 30, 1996.[9] We use one month repo rates at a daily frequency for each country to enable us to calculate the *theoretical futures prices*.

For each futures contract, the "cheapest to deliver" (CTD) bond in each basket of deliverables is identified using daily closing prices for the bonds and their respective price factors (supplied by the futures exchanges).[10]

Choice of Time Interval

Next, the most appropriate time interval to use in the econometric analysis is considered. As transactions prices are characterized by unequal intervals between observation—which invalidates the econometric specification–researchers typically construct prices for k-minute intervals. This is done by choosing a k-minute interval and recording only the last available price in each kth minute. If no trade took place in a particular interval, the previous interval's observation is used. In doing so, we are effectively assuming that the price process remains constant in the kth interval, which may *not* reflect the true price dynamics. Hence, researchers need to consider the trade-off between losing the high frequency dynamics (high k) and creating a large number of no-trade intervals (low k).[11] Table A shows the percentage of missing observations which result from constructing one, five, 10 and 15 minute intervals for each of the six futures contracts under consideration and the identified CTD bonds.

Based on the results outlined in Table 1, I choose a 5-minute time interval for all series except the French data. For the French data, I use a

Table 1 Proportion of missing observations.

| *Fineness of grid* | Gilts | | Bunds | | | BTPs | | | | OATs | | |
| | *Future* | *CTD* | *Future* | | | *Future* | | | | *Future* | *CTD* | *MFT** |
			LIFFE	*DTB*	*CTD*	*LIFFE*	*MIF*	*CTD*	*MFT**			
1-minute	30%	69%	6%	12%	38%	7%	20%	94%	44%	10%	98%	90%
5-minute	5%	15%	0%	0%	0%	1%	3%	77%	13%	1%	94%	63%
10-minute	2%	3%	0%	0%	0%	0%	0%	62%	9%	0%	90%	44%
15-minute	0%	2%	0%	0%	0%	0%	0%	50%	7%	0%	85%	32%

*MFT is the most frequently traded bond in the basket of deliverables.

15-minute time interval. Also I use the most frequently traded (MFT) BTP and OAT instead of the "cheapest-to-deliver" for the sample period.

Overnight Returns

It is well documented that the variance of overnight returns is different from that observed intra-day.[12] Reasons for this include the fact that public information arrival tends to be concentrated during trading hours and that private information (which is only revealed through the trading process) cannot be incorporated into prices outside of trading hours, so the first price of the day will reflect the cumulation of private information since the previous day's close and is not just the next observation in the price series. So, in the econometric analysis that follows, overnight returns are excluded by the inclusion of suitable dummy variables.

Financing Costs

Equation 2 shows that the theoretical futures price and the spot price should be cointegrated with coefficient 1. Also, the model of Garbade and Silber uses the theoretical price in its specification. So we transform the observed futures prices into their theoretical equivalents as follows:

Recall the theoretical futures price $f'_t = (f_t)/((1 + r_d)^{D-d})$ where r_d is the implied daily repo rate and $D - d$ is the number of days to expiry of the contract.[13] Given that the introduction of a new variable, the interest rate, introduces a further source of measurement error, is this adjustment entirely necessary?

The aim of this study is to examine how "news" is transmitted across markets. News arrival is generally proxied by unpredictable innovations in prices. If we restrict ourselves to simply examining the short-run dynamics of the system 7, ignoring the long-run equilibrium embodied in the cointegrating vector, we could simply use the observed futures prices, with their relevant price factors, and avoid this extra measurement error.[14] However, the level of the cointegrating vector will be affected by the adjustment for financing costs and so, if we are interested in the adjustment toward equilibrium (captured by our price leadership and market integration measures, θ and δ), we do need to take into account the relevant financing costs.[15]

The resulting theoretical futures prices are more volatile than the original series but, given that interest rates were quite stable over the sample period, the effect is not excessive.[16]

Table 2 Long-run relationships: $f'_t = \mu + \tau s_t$.

Cash and futures pairs $f'_t = \mu + \tau s_t$	No. of cointegrating vectors	τ
Gilt futures and gilt	1	1.02
OAT futures and OAT	1	1.04
Bund futures on DTB and Bund	1	0.98
Bund futures on LIFFE and Bund	1	0.98
BTP futures on MIF and BTP	1	0.98
BTP futures on LIFFE and BTP	1	0.98
Dually traded futures $ff'_t = \mu + \tau df'_t$		
Bund futures on LIFFE and Bund futures on DTB	1	1.00
BTP futures on LIFFE and BTP futures on MIF	1	1.00

Long-run Relationships

The natural logarithim of each series, cash and futures, was then taken. Augmented Dickey-Fuller tests were carried out to check each series for stationarity. Each series was found to be I(1) in levels but I(0) in first differences. Given that levels of the series are non-stationary, we can test for cointegration between pairs of the series (see Table 2). In line with expectations, one cointegrating vector was found between each pair. The restriction $\tau = 1$ was also tested; the restriction was rejected in each cash-futures pair with the exception of the two BTP cash-futures pairs. Given that there are a number of different bonds in the basket of deliverables, and that arbitrageurs will also concentrate on the second cheapest-to-deliver bond, it is not surprising that the restriction was largely rejected. In the case of the dually traded futures pairs the restriction holds, as one would expect given that the futures contracts are (almost) perfect substitutes.

EMPIRICAL RESULTS

The lag lengths were chosen, using the Schwarz and Akaike information criteria, to ensure that the vectors of errors were uncorrelated with each other. This allows the VECM to be estimated consistently and efficiently equation by equation.[17] Each equation was further augmented to a GARCH(1,1) specification to capture the well documented time varying nature of volatility in financial time series.[18]

Bivariate Specification

The bivariate model 7 was estimated and standard Granger causality tests were carried out by testing the joint significance of groups of variables. Table 3 tabulates the results. Model 7 was also estimated for the two pairs of dually traded futures contracts. Similar Granger causality tests were carried out and the results are reported in the lower panel.

Table 3 shows that for each spot-futures pair, the joint test of the β and γ coefficients is significant when the spot price is the dependent variable and the futures price is the explanatory variable (F $\rightarrow$ S). So the futures price leads the spot price. In only one case (namely the gilt market) is there some evidence of bidirectional causality.

From the results for the dually traded contracts, it is clear that the LIFFE BTP futures contract leads the domestically traded futures contract (FF $\rightarrow$ DF). This is consistent with the relative market shares of the two contracts; over the sample period, LIFFE's share of the market was around 85 percent. In contrast, even though the equilibrating mechanism, represented by the cointegrating vector, is important in both cases, overall it is difficult to distinguish which futures contract leads. This is in line with past findings on the Bund contract.[19]

The price leadership statistics, θ, clearly establish that in each cash-futures pair the futures price leads. The measure shows that over 80 percent of the adjustment to the mispricing embodied in the error correction term is done by the cash market. In the case of the dually traded futures contracts, LIFFE is clearly the price leader in the BTP market. However, in the Bund market, these results clearly indicate that it does the majority of the adjustment to the mispricing, suggesting it is the price follower and that the error correction process is stronger in the LIFFE market. This is in contrast with the earlier Granger causality results. These results might suggest that traders on the DTB may have an informational advantage, with respect to information on the state of the German macro economy, relative to traders on LIFFE.

Finally, the persistence parameters δ indicate that the majority of the mispricing between each cash-futures pair persists into the next period. The high values suggest the presence of market frictions which are strong enough to delay arbitrage beyond one time period.

As one might expect, given that they are almost perfect substitutes, each pair of dually traded futures contracts is highly integrated and actively arbitraged ($\delta = 0.10$ in both cases).

Table 3　Bivariate specification.

$$\Delta Y_t = \alpha + \sum_{i=1}^{m} \beta_{X,i} \Delta X_{t-i} + \sum_{j=1}^{m} \beta_{Y,j} \Delta Y_{t-j} + \gamma \Gamma_{t-1} + \varepsilon_t$$

(where $\Gamma_t = f_t' - \mu - \tau s_t$ or $\Gamma_t = f\!f_t' - \mu - \tau df_t'$)

Domestic futures and spot			Lags	Point estimate	Significance tests (F-tests) associated probabilities		
	Y	X	m	γ	$\beta_{X,i}$	γ	$\beta_{X,i}\&\gamma$
Gilt	spot	futures	3	0.18	0.00*	0.00*	0.00*
	futures	spot	3	−0.01	0.16	0.55	0.05*
OAT	spot	futures	2	0.05	0.06	0.00*	0.00*
	futures	spot	2	−0.01	0.56	0.31	0.62
BTP	spot	futures	1	0.07	0.00*	0.00*	0.00*
	futures	spot	1	−0.00	0.61	0.65	0.77
Bund	spot	futures	4	0.19	0.00*	0.01*	0.00*
	futures	spot	4	−0.01	0.17	0.62	0.15

Foreign futures and spot			Lag	Point estimate	Significance tests (F-tests) associated probabilities		
	Y	X	m	γ	$\beta_{X,i}$	γ	$\beta_{X,i}\&\gamma$
BTP	spot	futures	1	0.07	0.01*	0.00*	0.00*
	futures	spot	1	−0.01	0.82	0.75	0.92
Bund	spot	futures	5	0.16	0.00*	0.04*	0.00*
	futures	spot	5	−0.01	0.35	0.53	0.29

Foreign and domestic futures			Lag	Point estimate	Significance tests (F-tests) associated probabilities		
	Y	X	m	γ	$\beta_{X,i}$	γ	$\beta_{X,i}\&\gamma$
BTP	foreign futures	domestic futures	1	−0.23	0.98	0.33	0.46
	domestic futures	foreign futures	1	0.67	0.89	0.00*	0.00*
Bund	foreign futures	domestic futures	1	−0.69	0.49	0.00*	0.00*
	domestic futures	foreign futures	1	0.21	0.15	0.06	0.00*

Notes: Table 3 reports the probabilities associated with F-tests of the joint significance of the specified sets of coefficients. *Indicates that the result was significant at the 5% level.

Table 3   Summary.

Domestic features and spot	Short term price dynamics	Long term relationship	θ	δ
Gilt	Futures leads	Futures leads	0.95	0.81
OAT	Futures leads	Futures leads	0.83	0.94
BTP	Futures leads	Futures leads	0.88	0.92
Bund	Futures leads	Futures leads	0.95	0.80
Foreign futures and spot			θ	δ
BTP	Futures leads	Futures leads	0.88	0.92
Bund	Futures leads	Futures leads	0.94	0.83
Foreign and domestic features			θ^a	δ
BTP	None	Foreign leads	0.26	0.10
Bund	None	Bidirectional	0.77	0.10

[a]I report $\theta_{FF} = |\gamma_{FF}|/(|\gamma_{FF}| + |\gamma_{DF}|)$; it has the same significance as θ_s in that it measures the foreign exchange's, i.e. LIFFE's adjustment to the mispricing relative to that of the domestic exchange.

Multivariate Specification

Table 4 reports the results from the estimation of model (10b). Again, Granger causality tests similar to those in the bivariate case are carried out. Here the γ coefficients refer to the error correction terms $\Gamma_{2,t-1}(\gamma_1)$ and $\Gamma_{3,t-1}(\gamma_2)$; β_1 and β_2 refer to the first and second independent variables listed respectively.

When we look at the results for the BTP contract, we first observe that changes in the price of the LIFFE futures contract are independent of the two explanatory variables tested here. Both the spot market and the domestic futures market adjust to mispricing errors between themselves and the LIFFE contract rather than those between each other.[20] This supports the findings in the bivariate case that it is the price leader in this market.

The importance of spread trading between the two futures contracts is highlighted by the δ coefficients. Mispricing between the two futures markets tends not to persist into the next period ($\delta_{32} = 0.02$ and $\delta_{33} = 0.08$), which is consistent with the bivariate results of Table 3.

In contrast, the futures-spot mispricing tends to persist, although the majority of this reflects the partial disequilibrium between the foreign futures contract and the spot market ($\delta_{12} = 0.91$ and $\delta_{22} = 0.93$) rather than that between the futures-futures pair ($\delta_{13} = -0.11$ and $\delta_{23} = -0.03$).

Table 4 Multivariate specification.

$$\Delta Y_t = \alpha + \sum_{i=1}^{m} \beta_{X_1,j} \Delta X_{1,t-i} + \sum_{i=1}^{m} \beta_{X_2,i} \Delta X_{2,t-i} + \sum_{j=1}^{m} \beta_{Y,j} \Delta Y_{t-j} + \gamma_1 \Gamma_{2,t-1} + \gamma_2 \Gamma_{3,t-1} + \varepsilon_t$$

(where $\Gamma_{2,t} = ff'_t - \mu_2 - \tau_2 s_t$ and $\Gamma_{3,t} = ff'_t - \mu_3 - \tau_3 df'_t$)

				Lags	Point estimate		Significance tests (F-tests)				
							associated probabilities				
	Y	X_1	X_2	m	γ_1	γ_2	β_{X_1}	β_{X_2}	γ_1	γ_2	All
BTP	S	FF	DF	1	0.07	−0.20	0.19	0.93	0.00*	0.48	0.00*
	DF	S	FF	1	−0.01	0.69	0.73	0.87	0.35	0.00*	0.00*
	FF	S	DF	1	0.00	0.23	0.99	0.98	0.98	0.34	0.17
Bund	S	FF	DF	5	0.17	−0.34	0.46	0.92	0.05*	0.65	0.00*
	DF	S	FF	5	−0.01	0.19	0.29	0.34	0.46	0.27	0.00*
	FF	S	DF	5	−0.00	−0.52	0.30	0.26	0.97	0.00*	0.00*

Notes: See Table 3.

Table 4 Summary.

	θ_S	θ_{DF}	θ_{FF}
BTP	0.22	0.59	0.18
Bund	0.43	0.17	0.42

	δ_{12}	δ_{13}	δ_{22}	δ_{23}	δ_{32}	δ_{33}
BTP	0.91	−0.11	0.93	−0.03	0.02	0.08
Bund	0.81	−0.47	0.83	−0.19	0.00	0.28

Finally, the θ coefficients also indicate that price discovery is initiated in the foreign futures market. Surprisingly, however, the results suggest that the domestic futures market adjusts more than the spot market ($\theta_{FF} < \theta_S < \theta_{DF}$), i.e. it is more of a price follower *vis á vis* the futures market than the spot market. This reflects the strength of the foreign-domestic futures link in the system. The domestic futures contract adjusts rapidly and substantially in order to re-establish equilibrium between itself and the foreign market ($|\gamma^*_{df}| \gg |\gamma^*_s|$).

The results for the Bund contract are very similar except that the dominant futures contract in this case is the domestically traded one. Again, significance tests indicate that the spot market adjusts to mispricing errors between itself and the LIFFE contract but in this case it is the DTB contract which is independent of the other two markets, clearly marking it as the price leader. These results suggest that while foreign futures lead spot prices, both futures influence each other, so that both spot-futures and futures-futures arbitrage are important in maintaining the long-run equilibrium between the three markets

Consider the δ coefficients. As in the BTP case, the two futures markets are highly integrated, reflecting little of last period's disequilibrium ($\delta_{32} = 0.00$ and $\delta_{33} = 0.28$). Again, the futures-spot pairs are more segmented.

Next, consider the measure of price leadership, θ. Here (similar with the BTP case) the spot market plays a strong role and is equal price follower with LIFFE. The apparent subordinate role played by LIFFE again reflects the strength of its adjustment back to the futures-futures equilibrium ($\gamma_{ffaf} = 0.52$).

Taken together, our results point to the importance of inter-futures markets arbitrage. The pair of futures markets is the driving force in each system. Equilibrium is first restored along the futures-futures axis and then the spot-futures pairs come into line. We cannot, however, establish in general that either the domestic or the foreign futures market has a natural advantage in terms of price discovery.[21] Although, the domestic contract has the advantage in the Bund market; the price of a BTP futures contract on LIFFE appears to reflect more information than its Italian counterpart. Our results seem to be contract-specific.

Conclusions

Consistent with other studies, the results of this study show that the futures price leads the cash price in each of the four markets studied here. Hence, price discovery occurs first in the futures markets, with the cash markets merely acting as satellites. However, the futures and cash markets remain to some extent segmented, with mispricing between the two persisting over (short) time horizons. By contrast, dually traded futures contracts are very integrated suggesting active arbitrage between the two markets. When we consider the two futures contracts and the cash bond together we find that, in the case of the BTP, the LIFFE futures contract dominates price discovery, while in the Bund it appears to be the domestic futures contract which leads.

The econometric framework outlined at p 191 could also be used to address broader questions of market integration. For instance, given the anecdotal evidence of cross hedging of European bond positions, one might expect some common elements to run through the yields on two different European bonds. Again, one could examine the question of whether prices are determined simultaneously in both markets or whether one market leads. If the markets *are* interrelated then arbitrage between pairs of markets must be possible. One could then use the same methodology to examine the intensity of arbitrage between these markets. The analysis would indicate whether European markets remain segmented or whether they are converging towards some common base.[22] I intend to investigate these questions in future work.

APPENDIX

Specification of Futures Contracts[23] and Bonds Selected for Analysis.

		Gilt	OAT	BTP	Bund
Future	Nominal value	£50,000	FFr500,000	ITL200,000,000	DM250,000
	Notional coupon	9%	10%	12%	6%
	Maturity range of deliverables	10–15 years	7–10 years	$8-10\frac{1}{2}$ years	$8\frac{1}{2}-10$ years
Underlying	Selected bond	8.5% Treasury 2007	7.5% OAT 2005	9.5% BTP 2006	6% Bund 2006

NOTES

Note: This research was undertaken while the author was employed by the Bank of England. The views expressed in this paper are those of the author and not necessarily those of either the Debt Management Office or of the Bank of England. I am grateful to Ian Bond, Andy Brookes, Joe Ganley, Richard Payne, Victoria Saporta, John Spicer, Anne Vila and Ingrid Werner for their helpful suggestions. I have also benefited from comments made by seminar participants at the Bank of England and the London School of Economics. I would also like to thank Ravi Pindoria for his able research assistance. Any remaining errors are mine.

1. The Chicago Mercantile Exchange was established in 1848 and is generally taken to be the oldest futures exchange.
2. The first futures contracts were largely based on agricultural commodities, allowing farmers to offset their price risk by guaranteeing them a price for their produce in advance of the harvest. Today financial futures contracts make up the bulk of trading but they offer a similar guarantee to investors who are required to hold a financial asset for a certain length of time.

3. For instance, if an investor believed that the price of a stock was going to rise s/he could either buy the stock today or buy a futures contract on that stock. Although the initial outlays for both strategies are very different (the full price of the stock versus the initial margin on the futures contract), the payoffs are similar.

4. Two series are said to be cointegrated if each series is individually non-stationary but a linear combination of the two exists which is stationary. See Engle and Granger (1987) for further details on cointegration.

5. In the case of a bond futures contract, where there are multiple deliverables, the restriction $\tau = 1$ may not hold.

6. If the system is stable both γ coefficients should lie within the unit circle.

7. See, for example, Shyy and Lee (1995) or Kofman and Moser (1996). Schwarz and Szakmary (1994) discuss more fully how the GS model is a special case of the general VECM.

8. Given estimates of the transformed parameters γ_s^* and γ_{df}^* it is possible to recover estimates of the original parameters.

9. Futures data came from the London International Financial Futures Exchange (LIFFE), the Deutsche Terminborse (DTB), the Mercato Italiano dei futures e options su titoli di stato (MIF) and the Marche A Terme International de France (MATIF). We used OTC data on the underlying bonds in the gilt and Bund market, data supplied by the French stock exchange, SBF Bourse, for the underlying OATs and data from the Mercato in Titoli di Stato (MTS) for the underlying BTPs. Note: Given the nature of the bond markets involved, the coverage of the data cannot be guaranteed to be 100%.

10. While a number of bonds are deliverable into the futures contract, i.e. they have a remaining maturity in line with the contract's specification, one will be the cheapest to deliver. The prices of all the bonds are adjusted by a price factor, which attempts to standardise the bonds, bringing them into line with the notional bond on which the futures contract is based. See *Government Bond Futures*, LIFFE, 1995 for further details.

11. See de Jong and Nijman (1997) for a fuller discussion of this problem.

12. See French and Roll (1986) for a discussion of this.

13. In the case of bonds, the theoretical futures price should also be adjusted for the accrued interest on the bond. This will change across each bond in the basket of deliverables. As the accrued interest element carries no information and is relatively small in magnitude, for reasons of simplicity, I ignore it.

14. Intra-day, there is no difference between actual and theoretical returns and overnight returns are excluded from the analysis.

15. Note, the results of the econometric analysis are largely robust to the choice of actual or theoretical prices.

16. Italian interest rates were the most volatile with a variance of 6 basis points; all other interest rates used had a variance of less than $\frac{1}{4}$ of a basis point.

17. See Charemza and Deadman (1992, 183).

18. See Bollerslev, *et al.* (1992) or Sandmann and Vila (1996) for a fuller discussion of modelling time varying or stochastic volatility in financial markets.

19. See Kofman and Moser (1996) and Breedon and Holland (1998).

20. The coefficients on both the level of and differences in the domestic futures price in the spot equation were insignificant and *vice versa* in the domestic futures equation.

21. Neither is it related to whether the exchange has the first mover advantage or not; in both cases LIFFE was the first exchange to list the contract.

22. Similar questions were addressed by Booth, Martikainen and Tse (1997) in their study of Scandinavian stock markets.

23. For full details of the contract specifications contact the individual futures exchanges.

BIBLIOGRAPHY

Booth, G.G, Martikainen, T. and Tse, Y. (1997), "Price and Volatility Spillovers in Scandinavian Stock Markets", *Journal of Banking and Finance*, 21, 811–23.

Bollerslev, T, Chow, R. and Kroner, K. (1992), 'Arch Modelling in Finance: A Review of the Theory and Empirical Evidence', *Journal of Econometrics*, 52, 5–59.

Breedon, F. and Holland, A. (1998), "Electronic versus Open Outcry Markets: The Case of the Bund Futures Contract", *Bank of England*, Working Paper series No. 76.

Charemza, W.W. and Deadman, D.F. (1992), *New Directions in Econometric Practice*.

De Jong, F. and Nijman, T. (1997), "High Frequency Analysis of Lead-lag Relationships between Financial Markets", *Journal of Empirical Finance*, 4, 259–77.

Engle, R. and Granger, C. (1987), "Cointegration and Error Correction: Representation, Estimation and Testing", *Econometrica*, 55, 2215–76.

French, K.R. and Roll, R. (1986), "Stock Return Variances: The Arrival of Information and the Reaction of Traders", *Journal of Financial Economics*, 17, 5–26.

Garbarde, K.D. and Silber, W.L. (1982), "Movements and Price Discovery in Futures and Cash Markets", *Reviews of Economic Statistics*, 64, 289–97.

Government Bond Futures, LIFFE, 1995.

Harris, F.H, McInish, T.H, Shoesmith, G.L. and Wood, R.A. (1995), "Cointegration, Error Correction, and Price Discovery on Informationally Linked Security Markets", *Journal of Financial and Quantitative Analysis*, 30, 563–79.

Kawaller, I.G, Koch, P.D. and Koch, T.W. (1987), "The Temporal Relationship between S&P 500 Futures and the S&P 500 Index", *The Journal of Finance*, 42, 1309–29.

Kofman, P. and Moser, J. (1996), "Spreads, Information Flows and Transparency across Trading Systems", mimeo, Monash University.

Sandmann, G. and Vila, A. (1996), "Stochastic Volatility, Error Correction and Dual Listing in Futures Markets", mimeo, London School of Economics.

Schwarz, T.V. and Szakmary, A.C. (1994), "Price Discovery in Petroleum Markets: Arbitrage, Cointegration, and the Time Interval of Analysis", *The Journal of Futures Markets*, 14, 147–67.

Shyy, G. and Lee, J. (1995), "Price Transmission and Information Asymmetry in Bund Futures Markets: LIFFE vs. DTB", *Journal of Futures Markets*, 15, 87–99.

Stoll, H.R. and Whaley, R.E. (1990), "The Dynamics of Stock Index and Stock Index Futures Returns", *Journal of Financial and Quantitative Analysis*, 25, 441–68.

Chapter **8**

A Practical Approach to Information Spillover at High Frequency: Empirical Study of the Gilt and FTSE LIFFE Contracts

Pierre Lequeux

Banque Nationale de Paris, London

INTRODUCTION

The interaction of financial prices within the global market is emphasized by the correlation of their returns. The changing degree of this is generally felt more obviously during time of high volatility. Whereas the instantaneous relationship of financial markets remains an important feature in terms of risk diversification for the portfolio manager, it is not of a great added value for a trader who concentrates upon an individual market and trades a single financial instrument. As a rational "investor" the trader tries to forecast the direction of his/her market. Consequently, the trader is interested in the information embedded in the markets cross-correlation at a lag different from zero because this can improve his/her chances of making the right directional forecast. Spillover of information from one market to another implies possible opportunities of profit through arbitrage or directional trades. Academics and market practitioners (Amaro and Van Norden, 1995; Kaufman 1987, Frances *et al.* 1995) have extensively reported on relationships that may exist between related markets. The research has been concentrating mainly on the analysis of high frequency lead-lag relationships between derivatives and cash markets within the same instrument (Stoll and Waley, 1990; Kawaler *et al.*, 1987) or between different exchanges and the same financial instrument (Frances *et al.*, 1995; Breedon, 1996; Breedon and Holland, 1998;), little has been produced on high frequency inter-markets relationships.

Financial Markets Tick by Tick
Edited by Pierre Lequeux. © 1999 John Wiley & Sons Ltd

Most of the work produced tends to be clustered onto fundamental and econometric theories which address time horizons varying from daily to longer term. Whereas this is undoubtedly a strong contribution which might be of use to a fund manager or a hedger, this does not plainly address the microstructure of markets and is of no great help to the intra-day trader that relies on the "market noise" to generate profits. "Noise traders" are known not to rely on fundamental analysis (Menkhoff, 1997). They use other types of analysis such as technical analysis and statistical analysis of price behaviour to formalise their decision to buy or sell a financial instrument (Acar and Lequeux, 1995). Their approach might not seem fully rational to a long term investor, but its economic value has been proven by the high performance of arbitrage teams that concentrate on short term inefficiencies. The lack of research in this field is quite surprising since market practitioners have been looking at inter-markets relationships for a long time to refine their decision process when trading. Amongst lead lag relationships that are followed by markets practitioners are: possible relation between copper prices and Australian dollar, crude oil and Japanese yen, Eurodollar futures contracts and S&P500 to name only a few. One of the most commonly experienced lead-lag relationship by market practitioners is the interaction between interest rates and stock index (Sutcliffe, 1997), as underlined by the following quotes extracted from the *LIFFE Yearbook* 1995 and 1996:

> 07 Jul 95, Sep FTSE 100 Index future gained 74 ticks to 3491 the index's biggest one day gain in 11 months following unexpected US rate cut, leading to optimism on UK rates.

> 6 Oct 95, Stronger than expected UK manufacturing and US jobs report reduced chances for a UK rate cut and the FTSE 100 fell by 19 index points.

> 13 Oct 95, Dec FTSE 100 Index future fell by 54 points to 3500 pulling Gilts down following news of US durable order much higher than expected.

> 18 Jan 96, The UK benchmark stock index, the FTSE 100 100, soared to an all time high after the bank of England announced a cut of 0.25% in its base lending rate.

In the following, we investigate a practical methodology to detect the occurrence of intraday information spillover between financial instruments. Though we only evaluate such an approach empirically on the LIFFE Gilts and FTSE 100 contracts it could be applied to numerous other markets.

THE DATA AND METHODOLOGY

The data we used in this research was extracted from a database of historical prices that the LIFFE supplied on CD-ROM. We sampled data from January 2, 1987 to March 25, 1997 at an interval of 15-minutes from 9:00 GMT to 16:00 GMT (synchronous trading time). We concentrate on the first available contract which is rolled onto the next delivery on the last day of the month preceding the delivery month. This allows us to conduct the study on the most liquid contracts. There was a total of 73,051 prices per contract for the period studied. Missing values were interpolated linearly. For each contract we then constructed 15-minute logarithmic returns series. Because the intervals are quite large and the trading of the contracts is high enough to generate prices for most of the time segments, non-trading and non-synchronous trading problems that might arise in some research (De Jong and Nijman, 1994) is of little effect in our sample. Unrealistically high probabilities of non-trading period are required to generate cross-autocorrelation of high magnitudes (Campbell *et al.*, 1997). Since the study concentrates on intra-day features there is no need to simulate overnight returns or to adjust for any rollover of contract deliveries. Because both of the contracts are denominated in GBP, our analysis is not affected by spurious currency effects when calculating covariance. The characteristics of the contracts are shown in Table 1 and the summary statistics of the 15-minute returns are shown in Tables 2 to 5.

Though the returns of the FTSE 100 contract are on average positive at the opening and close of the trading session in agreement with previous research (Buckle *et al.* 1995), there is no significant pattern in the mean of the 15-minute returns for both contracts over the whole sample (Tables 2 to 5). The standard deviation (Figures 1 and 2) of the 15-minute returns series exhibits the well known "U-Shape" for both contracts. This clustering of volatility at the open and at the close of

Table 1 Summary of futures contracts.

	Long Gilt	FT-SE 100
Nominal value	£ 50,000 nominal value notional Gilt with 9% coupon	Valued at £ 10 per index point
Quotation	1/32	0.5
Delivery	March, June, September, December	March, June, September, December
Tick value	£ 15.625	£ 5.00
Trading hours	8:00–16:15	8:35–16:10

Table 2 Gilt 15-minutes returns 9:00 to 12:30.

	91500	93000	94500	100000	101500	103000	104500
Mean	−0.00003	0.00003	0.00002	0.00005*	0.00001	0.00000	0.00002
Standard deviation	0.00091	0.00080	0.00086	0.00075	0.00077	0.00066	0.00065
Kurtosis	2.55	2.96	3.87	4.09	4.08	4.73	3.16
Skewness	−0.21	0.25	−0.14	0.10	0.12	−0.10	0.22
Range	0.00946	0.00869	0.00896	0.00908	0.00904	0.00868	0.00772
Minimum	−0.00476	−0.00382	−0.00431	−0.00458	−0.00440	−0.00382	−0.00338
Maximum	0.00470	0.00487	0.00465	0.00450	0.00464	0.00486	0.00434
Sum	−0.07050	0.07563	0.06103	0.11473	0.02756	−0.00796	0.04229
Count	2517	2517	2517	2517	2517	2517	2517

	110000	111500	113000	114500	120000	121500	123000
Mean	0.00000	−0.00001	0.00003	−0.00003	0.00001	−0.00001	0.00000
Standard devlation	0.00067	0.00064	0.00065	0.00086	0.00060	0.00060	0.00057
Kurtosis	4.75	4.10	4.29	6.66	4.75	8.61	7.92
Skewness	−0.68	−0.38	0.07	−0.43	0.45	−0.56	0.05
Range	0.00771	0.00768	0.00827	0.00948	0.00677	0.00824	0.00895
Minimum	−0.00469	−0.00385	−0.00383	−0.00486	−0.00269	−0.00491	−0.00406
Maximum	0.00302	0.00384	0.00444	0.00462	0.00408	0.00333	0.00489
Sum	0.00406	−0.02694	0.07288	−0.07544	0.03405	−0.03257	0.00805
Count	2517	2517	2517	2517	2517	2517	2517

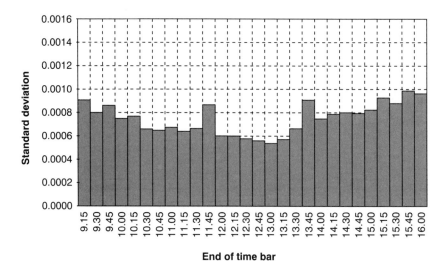

Figure 1 Standard deviation of 15-minute Gilt returns.

Table 3 Gilt 15-minutes returns 12:30 to 16:00.

	124500	130000	131500	133000	134500	140000	141500
Mean	0.00002	0.00002	−0.00001	−0.00004*	−0.00002	−0.00006*	−0.00003
Standard deviation	0.00056	0.00053	0.00056	0.00065	0.00090	0.00075	0.00078
Kurtosis	9.65	9.84	7.90	3.36	3.94	3.56	4.20
Skewness	0.29	−0.53	−0.18	−0.13	0.03	−0.29	0.03
Range	0.00913	0.00792	0.00891	0.00712	0.00943	0.00829	0.00961
Minimum	−0.00438	−0.00466	−0.00498	−0.00369	−0.00445	−0.00437	−0.00462
Maximum	0.00475	0.00325	0.00392	0.00343	0.00498	0.00392	0.00499
Sum	0.03945	0.04513	−0.02975	−0.08946	−0.04896	−0.14233	−0.06441
Count	2517	2517	2517	2517	2517	2517	2517

	143000	144500	150000	151500	153000	154500	160000
Mean	−0.00002	0.00000	−0.00003	−0.00002	0.00008*	0.00002	0.00001
Standard deviation	0.00080	0.00079	0.00082	0.00092	0.00088	0.00099	0.00096
Kurtosis	3.05	2.47	2.23	2.81	2.59	2.19	2.50
Skewness	−0.25	−0.11	−0.11	−0.11	0.18	−0.08	−0.13
Range	0.00973	0.00863	0.00879	0.00964	0.00963	0.00866	0.00965
Minimum	−0.00476	−0.00427	−0.00438	−0.00499	−0.00497	−0.00436	−0.00468
Maximum	0.00498	0.00436	0.00441	0.00465	0.00466	0.00430	0.00497
Sum	−0.04368	0.00230	−0.06845	−0.05253	0.21125	0.06216	0.03331
Count	2517	2517	2517	2517	2517	2517	2517

*significant at the critical threshold of 5%

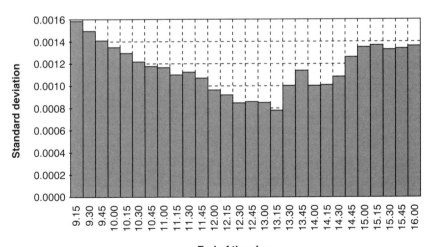

Figure 2 Standard deviation of 15-minute FTSE 100 returns.

Table 4   FTSE 100 15-minutes returns 9:00 to 12:30.

	91500	93000	94500	100000	101500	103000	104500
Mean	0.00005	0.00004	0.00004	0.00004	−0.00002	−0.00003	0.00004
Standard deviation	0.00159	0.00150	0.00141	0.00135	0.00129	0.00122	0.00118
Kurtosis	0.45	0.63	0.83	0.81	1.21	1.06	1.85
Skewness	−0.01	−0.15	−0.03	−0.04	−0.18	−0.05	−0.08
Range	0.00994	0.00994	0.00994	0.00973	0.00978	0.00951	0.00987
Minimum	−0.00500	−0.00499	−0.00496	−0.00486	−0.00494	−0.00464	−0.00488
Maximum	0.00494	0.00496	0.00498	0.00487	0.00485	0.00487	0.00499
Sum	0.12897	0.09469	0.09612	0.10760	−0.03906	−0.06468	0.09443
Count	2517	2517	2517	2517	2517	2517	2517

	110000	111500	113000	114500	120000	121500	123000
Mean	−0.00002	−0.00001	−0.00002	0.00000	0.00001	−0.00002	0.00003
Standard deviation	0.00117	0.00110	0.00112	0.00107	0.00096	0.00092	0.00085
Kurtosis	1.59	1.42	1.89	2.17	2.40	3.24	4.02
Skewness	−0.11	0.01	−0.14	−0.16	−0.17	−0.19	0.04
Range	0.00976	0.00942	0.00957	0.00966	0.00924	0.00935	0.00943
Minimum	−0.00496	−0.00462	−0.00493	−0.00474	−0.00437	−0.00443	−0.00462
Maximum	0.00480	0.00480	0.00463	0.00492	0.00487	0.00492	0.00481
Sum	−0.05406	−0.01682	−0.04421	−0.00777	0.02747	−0.05383	0.06690
Count	2517	2517	2517	2517	2517	2517	2517

the trading session has been described extensively by the academic literature for a large number of markets (Buckle *et al.* 1995). This is also found in the intra-daily distribution of the trading volume (Jain and Joh, 1988; Lequeux, 1996). This pattern can be explained by stock adjustment theory, the use for risk of a trader is not the same depending if he is holding a position over a trading or non-trading period, consequently traders adjust their positions to reflect this utility for risk (and potential reward) at the open and close of market session. This burst of activity and volume increases the standard deviation in the price return at the opening and close of the trading session. The study of market volatility is paramount for a trader, not only because it expresses the risk of the market but also because of the market inefficiencies it might reflect.

The coefficient of Kurtosis is a measure of the peakedness or flatness of a distribution relative to a normal distribution. For a normal distribution the kurtosis coefficient would be zero.[1] A negative coefficient indicates a distribution that is relatively flat with short tails. A positive coefficient is an indication of a curve very steep at the centre with relatively long

Table 5 Summary statistics of the FTSE 100 15-minutes returns 12:30 to 16:00.

	124500	130000	131500	133000	134500	140000	141500
Mean	0.00001	−0.00001	−0.00002	−0.00002	0.00003	−0.00003	0.00000
Standard deviation	0.00085	0.00084	0.00078	0.00099	0.00114	0.00100	0.00101
Kurtosis	4.98	5.51	3.68	3.65	2.23	3.00	2.14
Skewness	−0.21	0.01	−0.11	0.05	0.08	0.05	−0.09
Range	0.00929	0.00991	0.00893	0.00989	0.00972	0.00928	0.00902
Minimum	−0.00447	−0.00499	−0.00494	−0.00499	−0.00491	−0.00453	−0.00414
Maximum	0.00482	0.00492	0.00399	0.00490	0.00482	0.00475	0.00488
Sum	0.03560	−0.01546	−0.04131	−0.04208	0.07928	−0.07360	−0.01021
Count	2517	2517	2517	2517	2517	2517	2517

	143000	144500	150000	151500	153000	154500	160000
Mean	−0.00003	−0.00007	−0.00014*	−0.00010*	0.00004	0.00006	0.00003
Standard deviation	0.00107	0.00126	0.00134	0.00136	0.00132	0.00134	0.00136
Kurtosis	1.96	1.26	1.03	1.02	1.24	1.32	1.16
Skewness	−0.15	0.03	−0.04	−0.04	−0.10	−0.06	−0.11
Range	0.00954	0.00960	0.00986	0.00989	0.00952	0.00977	0.00961
Minimum	−0.00484	−0.00462	−0.00498	−0.00491	−0.00456	−0.00488	−0.00480
Maximum	0.00470	0.00498	0.00487	0.00499	0.00497	0.00489	0.00482
Sum	−0.07849	−0.16518	−0.36457	−0.26061	0.09050	0.15232	0.08712
Count	2517	2517	2517	2517	2517	2517	2517

*significant at the critical threshold of 5%

tails. Financial time price series usually have highly positive kurtosis which indicates extreme observations that are not expected under a normal distribution (Taylor, 1986). The presence of extreme values can be explained by the sudden reaction of market participants to unexpected clusters of information. Figures 3 and 4 show the coefficient of kurtosis for each 15 minutes of a trading session for each working day. Extreme price moves are not evenly distributed during the day. The kurtosis surges at midsession for both contracts and the shape is pretty much an inverted V-shape. It would seem that the less volatile the return the more kurtosis and vice-versae. This could be explained by the frequency of trading during this part of the day; since there is little volume going through, there is a higher probability to observe zero returns for this part of the day than at any other time. High kurtosis can be explained by a distribution of returns with numerous zero values and only a few non-zero returns (Acar and Satchell, 1998).

The correlation between the 15-minute variations of the FTSE 100 and the Gilt contract (Figure 5) tends to increase in the afternoon. This change

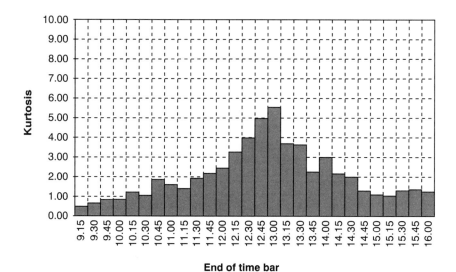

Figure 3 Kurtosis for the FTSE 100 15-minute returns.

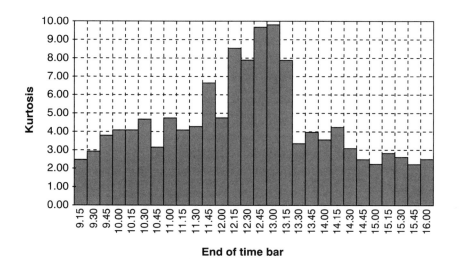

Figure 4 Kurtosis for the 15-minute Gilt returns.

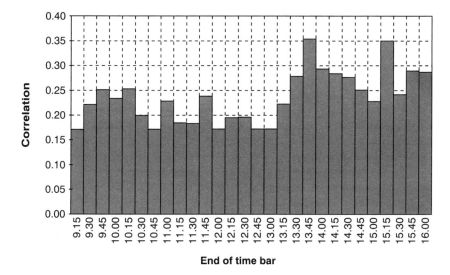

Figure 5   FTSE 100 and Gilt 15-minute returns correlation.

in behaviour can be explained by the opening of the US-T bond market that "kicks in" at 13:20 GMT and the NYSE at 14:30 GMT. The price process of the contracts might be more receptive to the economic figures and flow of information originating from the US rather than from the UK. The changing intensity of the relationship between the Gilt and FTSE 100 contracts underlines the non-normality of these markets and is coherent with previous results (Lequeux and Acar, 1996; Lequeux, 1997).

Correlation analysis is generally one of the first calculations done when analysing two variables. Correlation measures the relative degree of agreement or disagreement between two variables by giving a measure of how the means of the two series move together. Instantaneous correlation is a must when trying to implement a better risk management and analysis but becomes quite redundant within a forecasting context. There is no specific advantage in knowing that Gilt and FTSE 100 move alike when one wants to predict the next period move. For a forecasting purpose we would like to know, for example how the variation in the Gilt price from 9:00 to 9:15 is correlated with the variation in the FTSE 100 price from 9:15 to 9:30. If highly correlated this might help us in making an early decision about when to buy or sell the FTSE 100. Though instantaneous correlation is of little help within a forecasting context it is thought that high instantaneous correlation gives a higher likelihood of information spillover between series. Säfvenblad (1997) notes that securities with highly correlated return processes have relatively stronger correlation of their prior valuations, therefore lead-lag effects are stronger between strongly correlated securities. Lead-lag relationships are usually expected to be bi-directional (Säfvenblad, 1997), and can possibly be attributed to liquidity and transactions costs that makes arbitrageurs react more or less quickly to clusters of market information. In the following, we investigate how the use of a simple cross-autocorrelation function can help an intraday trader to detect short term price anomalies. The methodology concentrates on the study of cross-correlation matrix at various time lags and is described as follows.

X_t and Y_t being two series of logarithmic returns x_{it} and y_{it} each of same length N for which we try to evaluate the relationship at high frequency. Each return is indexed by i which denotes the day in which the logarithmic return occurred and t which represent the linear time clock at which the return x_i ended. Values of t are equally spaced at a discrete interval of length τ which will depend on the granularity required for the analysis.

A correlation matrix 1 is calculated out of non overlapping periods of n days. The number of days used depends on the definition required.

$$M = \{\rho(x_i, y_j), \{i = 1, t\}, \{j = 1, t\}\} \qquad\qquad 1$$

Each matrix of correlation can be broken down into three sub-areas A, B and C (see Table 7). Each of the areas characterises the relationship between the two instruments. We define each area A, B and C as being the

Table 6 Example of a data series with $\tau = 15$ minutes.

	9:15	9:30	$\cdots$	t
2-Jan-87	0.000276	0.002484	$\cdots$	0.000276
5-Jan-87	−0.00055	0.001912	$\cdots$	−0.00027
6-Jan-87	0.002199	0.000275	$\cdots$	0.000549
12-Jan-87	−0.00054	−0.00108	$\cdots$	−0.00135
$\cdots$	$\cdots$	$\cdots$	$\cdots$	$\cdots$
I	$\Delta x_{(i,9:15)}$	$\Delta x_{(i,9:30)}$	$\Delta x_{(i,\ldots)}$	$\Delta x_{(i,t)}$

Table 7 Cross-correlation matrix.

Top right area of the matrix (A)

$\rho(x,y)$	9:15	....	T
9:15	$\rho(x_{9:15}, y_{9:15})$	$\rho(x_{9:15}, y_{\ldots})$	$\rho(x_{9:15}, y_t)$
...	$\rho(x_{\ldots}, y_{9:15})$	$\rho(x_{\ldots}, y_{\ldots})$	$\rho(x_{\ldots}, y_t)$
t	$\rho(x_t, y_{9:15})$	$\rho(x_t, y_{\ldots})$	$\rho(x_t, y_t)$

Bottom left area of the matrix (B)

Central area of the matrix (C)

arithmetic average of their respective coefficients 2.

$$A = \left[\sum_{\substack{j=1 \\ i=2}}^{\substack{j=t-\tau \\ i=t}} \rho(x_i, y_j) \right] \Bigg/ \left(\frac{t^2 - t}{2} \right) \qquad B = \left[\sum_{\substack{j=2 \\ i=1}}^{\substack{j=t \\ i=t-\tau}} \rho(x_i, y_j) \right] \Bigg/ \left(\frac{t^2 - t}{2} \right)$$

For all τ with $i > j$ \qquad\qquad For all τ with $i < j$

$$C = \left[\sum_{\substack{j=1 \\ i=1}}^{\substack{j=t \\ i=t}} \rho(x_i, y_j) \right] \Bigg/ t \qquad\qquad\qquad 2$$

For all τ with $i = j$

The contour plot of the matrix (Figure 6) helps to illustrate the strength of the relation between two contracts X and Y at various times of the day. The contour plot is divided into two surfaces A and B by a dotted line C. C represents the instaneous correlation between the two instruments and consequently is of little use for evaluating the direction of the spillover of information if any, except that we have a higher likelihood to detect lead-lag effects for high values of C (Säfvenblad, 1997). A shift of the central contour toward the upper/lower side of the graph indicates spillover from one contract toward the other (from instrument X to instrument Y in Figure 6, i.e. instrument X is a predictor of instrument Y, and this particularly around 11:00 AM).

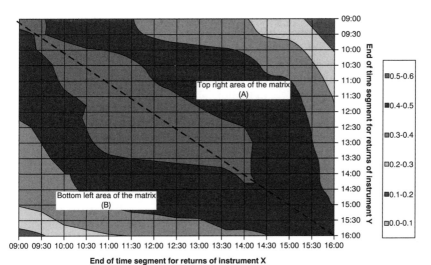

Figure 6   Contour plot of the cross-correlation matrix.

Table 8 Interpretation of A, B and C statistics.

Case	Interpretation
A ≅ B	no transfer of information between X and Y
A > B	Y is predictor of X
B > A	X is predictor of Y
C High	Possible Lead-Lag relationship

The statistics A, B and C can be interpreted as shown in Table 8.

We will also look at the average values for each diagonal vector 4 of the matrix to evaluate the time horizon of the lead-lag relationship if any. Of course, since we are dealing with a non-continuous market far values will have a lot less weight than near values due to the number of observations involved. The diagonal vectors are defined as follows:

$$Diag(\tau) = \frac{\sum_{\substack{i=1 \\ j=1}}^{\substack{i=t \\ j=t}} \rho(x_i, y_j)}{|t - \tau|} \qquad 3$$

For all i, j where $(i - j) = \tau$

EMPIRICAL RESULTS

In the following, we calculated the previously described A, B and C statistics for 119 non-overlapping 15-minute returns sub-samples of 21 days. Average values of the diagonal vectors for all possible lags were also calculated. We use Gilt as X and FTSE-100 as Y. The instantaneous correlation (C) changed quite considerably through time (Figure 7). From a near to zero correlation in the late eighties it went to a higher level from 1993 onward. So if we accept the hypothesis put forward by Säfvenblad (1997) we might find more significant lead-lag relationships toward the end of the sample than at the beginning. This change in correlation between the two instruments might come from a change occurring in the trading pattern of market participants after the 1992 currency crisis.

We spliced our original sample into two sub-samples, one covering the first half of the synchronous session (9:00 to 12:30) and the other (12:30 to 16:00). In this way, we can investigate if the economic information released by the UK authorities has a greater impact than the economic figures released by the US authorities on the two series. All the UK figures are released before 12:30 GMT whereas the afternoon is principally dominated by the announcement of US economic figures.

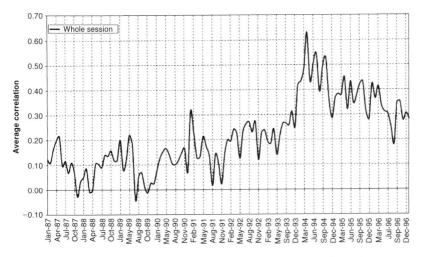

Figure 7 Average instantaneous correlation between Gilt and FTSE-100 returns (C statistic).

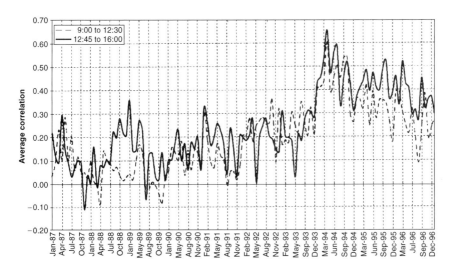

Figure 8 Average instantaneous correlation between Gilt and FTSE-100 returns (C statistic) for first and second part of the trading session.

Figure 8 shows that there is a difference between the average level of correlation noted in the morning and the average level of correlation observed in the afternoon. This has been more obvious from 1995 onwards. The differences seems to be persistently for higher values in

Table 8 Summary statistics of correlation differences.

	Differences between PM and AM
Mean	0.04681*
Standard Deviation	0.10725
Kurtosis	−0.04586
Skewness	−0.37653
Range	0.55546
Minimum	−0.23913
Maximum	0.31632
Sum	5.57051
Count	119

*significant at the critical threshold level of 5%

the afternoon (Table 8). This might indicate a higher likelihood to find lead-lag relationships in the afternoon.

The cumulative average value for the A and B statistics show a bias. The B statistic is generally higher than the A statistic and this since April 1991 (Figure 9). This might underline the presence of some kind of information transfer from the Gilts toward the FTSE.

When we discriminate between afternoon and morning (Figures 10 and 11) we observe a more pronounced bias between the two cumulative averages in the afternoon rather than in the morning. The information released in the morning affects Gilt and FTSE in an equal fashion. More interesting is the stronger evidence of lead lag relationship in the afternoon when the correlation, as seen in the previous section, is at its highest for the day.

Other important information for a trader is the time horizon of the spillover that governs the relationship between the two instruments. This can be deducted from the matrix of cross-autocorrelation using Equation 4. Figure 12 shows all the average cross-autocorrelation at various time lags. We note again a higher level of correlation in the afternoon than in the morning and also more pronounced values at Lag −1.

Figure 13 shows the cumulative average value with a centred origin at lag 0 (the value at lag 0 is forced to zero). An interesting pattern emerges, there is a confirmation that the Gilt tends to lead the FTSE-100, but also that this effect tends to have a life cycle of between 15 minutes to 45 minutes.

FINAL REMARKS

In this analysis we observed a lead-lag relationship between Gilt and FTSE, the Gilt variable being a predictor of the FTSE returns at various lags. This

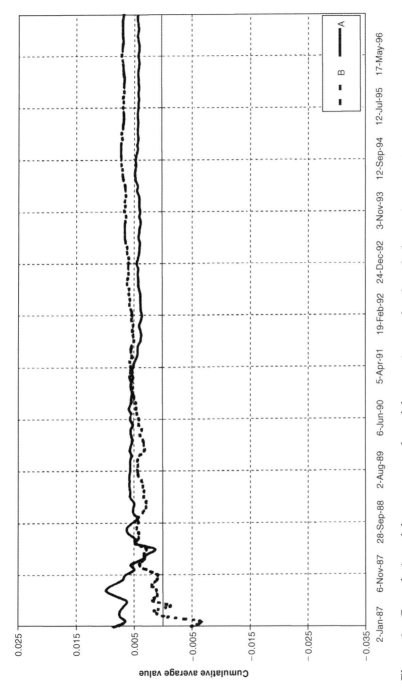

Figure 9 Cumulative of the average value of the matrix area for the whole session.

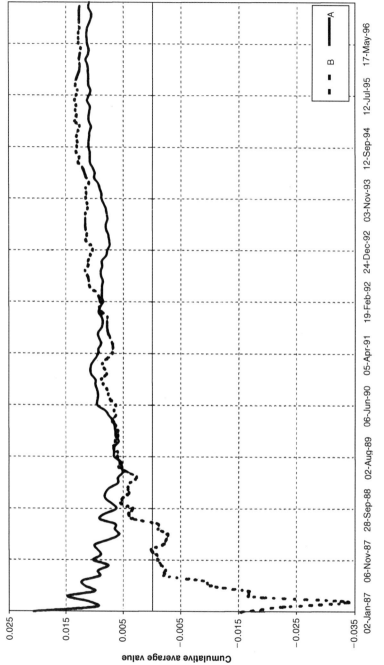

Figure 10   Cumulative of the average value of the matrix area for the first part of the session.

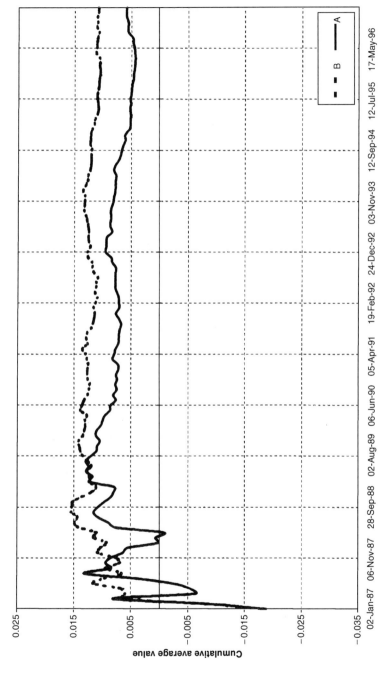

Figure 11 Cumulative of the average value of the matrix area for second part of the session.

4 Pierre Lequeux

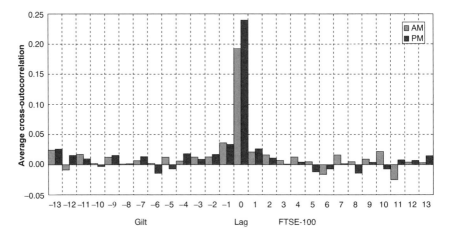

Figure 12   Average cross-autocorrelation at various lags.

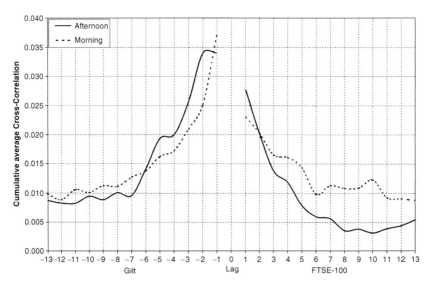

Figure 13   Cumulative average cross-autocorrelation from the origin (lag 0 forced at 0).

relationship is more pronounced in the afternoon than in the morning probably due to the different information flow. Finally, we found that the Gilt tends to lead the FTSE by 15 to 45 minutes. Though there is an obvious lead-lag relationship between the two contracts due to the high frequency of the time horizon, it might be difficult to exploit due to the transaction cost that would be incurred. This information could probably help a system trader in the designing of his/her trading program or a pit trader that trades spreads. We tried to illustrate how simple statistics and high frequency data allows traders to pinpoint and verify price patterns and ultimately improve forecasting and risk analysis.

NOTES

1. When centred by $\left[\frac{-(3(n-1)2)}{(n-2)(n-3)} \right]$ with n = number of observations.

BIBLIOGRAPHY

Acar, E. and Lequeux, P. (1995), "Dynamic Strategies: A Correlation Study", *Presentation at the International Conference Sponsored by Chemical Bank and Imperial College*, March 1995, in London.

Acar, E. and Satchell, S. (1998), "The Portfolio Distribution of Directional Strategies", *Advanced Trading Rules*, Butterworth Heinemann.

Amaro, R. and Van Norden, S. (1995), "Exchange Rates and Oil Prices", *Working paper* 95–8, Bank of Canada.

Breedon, F. (1996), "Why do Liffe and DTB Bund Futures Contracts Trade at Different Prices?", *Bank of England Working Paper* Series No. 57.

Breedon, F. and Holland, A. (1998), "Electronic versus Open Outcry Markets: The Case of the Bund Futures Contract", *Bank of England Working Paper* Series No. 76.

Buckle, S.H. and Woodhams, M.S. "Intraday Empirical Regularities in Liffe Data". Presentation at the International Conference "Forecasting Financial Markets" sponsored by Chemical Bank and Imperial College, London, March 1995.

Campbell, J., Lo, W. and MacKinlay, C. (1997), *The Econometrics of Financial Markets*, Princeton University Press.

De Jong, F. and Nijman, T. (1994), "Information Flows Between Financial Markets: An Analysis of Irregularly Spaced Data", *First International Conference on High Frequency Data in Finance*, March 1995, Zurich Switzerland.

Frances, P.H., Van Ieperen, R., Martens, M., Menkveld, B. and Kofman, P. (1995), "Volatility patterns and spillovers in bund futures", *First International Conference on High Frequency Data in Finance*, March 1995, Zurich Switzerland.

Jain, P.C. and Joh, G.H. (1988), "The Dependence between Hourly Prices and Trading Volume", *Journal of Financial and Quantitative Analysis*, 23, 269–283.

Kaufman P.J. (1987), *The New Commodity Trading Systems and Methods*, John Wiley & Sons, New York.

Kawaler, I.G., Koch, P.D. and Koch, T.W. (1987), "The Temporal Price Relationship between S&P500 Futures and the S&P500 Index", *Journal of Finance* 42, 1309–1329.

Lequeux, P. and Acar, E. (1996), "An Hourly Study: the Bunds and BTP Markets on the Liffe" *Liffe Bond Review*, October 1996.

Lequeux, P. and Acar, E. (1996), "Tick Data for a Closer Look at Cross Currency Spread Trading: An Empirical Study on the BTP and Bund Liffe Contracts", *Liffe Smart Spreads Newsletter*, June.

Lequeux, P. (1997), "Empirical Evidences of Information Spillover, The Gilts FTSE 100 Relationship", *Liffe Equity Product Review* 1st quarter 1997.

Lequeux, P. (1996), "The Volume Price Relationship in Short Sterling", *Liffe Money Market Review* September.

Menkhoff, L. (1997), "The Noise Trading Approach—Questionnaire Evidence from Foreign Exchange", *Dept of Economics, Aachen University of Technology*.

Stoll, H.R. and Waley, R.E. (1990), "The Dynamic of Stock Index and Stock Index Futures Returns" *Journal of Financial and Quantitative Analysis*, No. 25, 441–468.

Sutcliffe, C. (1997), *Stock Index Futures*, International Thompson Business Press.

Säfvenblad, P. (1997), "Lead-Lag Effects When Prices Reveal Cross-Security Information" *Stockholm School of Economics Department of Finance* September 1, 1997.

Taylor, S.J. (1986), *Modelling Financial Time Series*, John Wiley & Sons, Chichester, UK.

Chapter **9**

High-Frequency Random Walks?

Michael Gavridis, Raphael N. Markellos and Terence C. Mills

Banque Nationale de Paris, London, Department of Economics, Loughborough University

INTRODUCTION

Despite the importance of random walks and market efficiency in finance, these concepts are often misunderstood. For example, contrary to popular belief, random walks are not necessarily completely unpredictable and certainly do not imply that markets cannot be *beaten* (see, for example, Granger, 1970). If the daily prices of stock AAA follow a random walk then, abstracting from dividend payments, AAA stock returns are indeed unpredictable on the basis of past AAA stock returns. However, historical information on some other economic variable or on stock BBB may allow some predictability of future AAA returns. Similarly, the efficient market hypothesis, at least in its informational-efficiency version (Grossman and Stiglitz, 1976), does not say that investing in high-frequency data, sophisticated statistical and trading techniques, analytical software, investment advisors, is futile. It simply states that *free lunches* do not exist, either for long or for long enough, and that a price has to be paid to obtain average returns in excess of the risk-free rate. Within the context of opportunity costs, this price can be viewed in terms of *risk* (e.g. the beta of a stock, junk bond default risk, the risk of illegal insider trading), *liquidity* (e.g. the ability to sell thinly traded stock, the right to withdraw investment from a foreign country), *money* (e.g. investment in tick data sets, consultants and seminars), *time* (e.g. time spent reading this chapter, CPU time) or even *psychological factors* (e.g. stress and/or pleasure from investment activities and research).

Formal finance theory began in 1900 with Louis Bachelier's brilliant doctoral dissertation, *Théorie de la Spéculation*, in which he developed the mathematical theory of Brownian motion—a random walk in continuous time—to describe the unpredictable evolution of stock prices and used it to build the first option pricing model.[1] After that, random walks were completely forgotten in finance for many years, although they played a fundamental role in physics and mathematics through the research of Einstein, Wiener and Kolmogorov. In 1959, independently of Bachelier, Osborne also used Brownian motion to model the unpredictability of stock prices (Osborne, 1959). By the mid-1960s, Samuelson (1965) and Fama (1965) had again placed random walks at the centre of theoretical finance through the efficient market hypothesis paradigm.

The major implication of the random walk hypothesis of asset prices is that it allows us to invoke the central limit theorem and characterize asset returns as normally distributed. This is extremely important since expected returns and risks in a multivariate-normal financial world can be fully described probabilistically using means, variances and covariances, as in the Markowitz portfolio model, for example. Most of the analysis in applied and theoretical finance, such as option pricing, risk management, and portfolio optimisation, relies heavily on the validity of the market efficiency and/or random walk hypotheses. Although an enormous empirical literature exists on these issues, results have unfortunately been largely inconclusive and/or conflicting.

Vast advances in information technology in the 1990s have allowed and motivated the collection of financial data at very high frequencies. These developments have opened a new chapter in empirical finance and for the random walk saga (for an excellent review of research with high-frequency data, see Goodhart and O'Hara, 1997). From a broader point of view, as discussed by Granger (1998), the availability of huge high-frequency data sets is changing the science and practice of statistics, econometrics and decision making in many different ways. "Business intelligence"—the collection, management, analysis, utilization and distribution of data—is emerging as one of the key strategic functions of a company and relevant operations are predicted to have a world market worth $70 billion by the end of the century.[2]

The present study is concerned with some of the violations of the random walk hypothesis that characterize high-frequency exchange rate data. We argue that these violations have significant implications for currency risk management and trading at short-term horizons and that analysis of high-frequency data is strongly justified for certain groups of investors. Our methodology and research objectives can be summarised under two broad perspectives, namely, with respect first, to the unconditional probabilities and secondly, to the conditional probabilities.

Unconditional probabilities. If Gaussian random walks provide a poor description of financial prices then the validity of any analysis based on the assumption of Gaussian return distributions is questionable (e.g. in option pricing, hedging, value-at-risk, portfolio optimisation). We are interested in two questions. First, what are the characteristics of high-frequency unconditional return distributions? Secondly, which stochastic processes are consistent with the behaviour of the data and could thus be used as working alternatives to the Gaussian assumption?

Conditional probabilities. If contemporaneous information flows have time-of-day conditional regularities, then intra-day investors require high-frequency data to estimate the effective systematic risks that correspond to their individual *trading epoch.* At the same time, short- and long-run dynamics in high-frequency data could be translated into improved forecasting and trading performance. Analysing such dynamics is also important because they may introduce significant biases into statistical estimates. Here we are interested in two questions: first, do correlations and principal components of returns change systematically throughout the trading day and secondly, does significant evidence of inefficiencies, delayed information flows and long-run dynamic relationships (cointegration between levels) exist in high-frequency data?

METHODOLOGY

The methodology used in this chapter is outlined below, with further details given in the remainder of this section. In the present study, we first analyse the unconditional distribution[3] by examining the behaviour of the tails of the distribution (by fitting Stable and GARCH processes) and the central part of the distributions (by means of Truncated Lévy flights). Secondly, we analyse the conditional distribution by examining the contemporaneous information flows (by means of correlation and Principal Component Analysis) and inefficiencies and dynamics (by means of cointegration analysis).

Unconditional Distribution Analysis

Tail Behaviour Analysis—Stable and GARCH Processes. Since the seminal work of Benoit Mandelbrot (1963a, 1963b, 1997), the *stable family of distributions* (also known as Paretian, Pareto-Lévy, Lévy flights and products of anomalous diffusion) has been a popular choice among researchers for capturing the *leptokurtosis*—the fat tails and high peaks[4]—that characterizes most financial return distributions. Other non-normal distributions that have been considered in the literature include the Student-*t* and mixtures of normals.[5]

The *symmetric about zero* stable class of distributions is characterized by two parameters, a scale factor and the characteristic exponent, which indexes the distribution. (We restrict attention to symmetric about zero stable distributions so that we may more easily focus on the behaviour of the tails of the distributions. Allowing asymmetry about a non-zero location measure introduces two further parameters that merely complicate matters for the purpose at hand). Most attention is focused on the characteristic exponent because, since closed-form density functions do not exist for most stable distributions, they are usually defined by their characteristic functions, which always exist.

Suppose $\{X_t\}_1^T$ is an independent and identically distributed (iid) zero mean process with probability distribution $F(X) = P(X < x)$. The characteristic function of X is defined as the Fourier transform of $F(X)$:

$$\varphi(\zeta) = \int_{-\infty}^{+\infty} \exp(i\zeta x) dF(X)$$

where ζ is real. The symmetric (about zero) stable characteristic function has the form:

$$\varphi(\zeta) = \exp(-\sigma^\alpha |\zeta|^\alpha) \qquad\qquad 1$$

where $0 < \alpha \le 2$ is the characteristic exponent, which determines the peakedness of the distribution about zero and the amount of probability in the tails (the fatness) and σ is a scale parameter. The $N(0, 2)$ distribution is obtained when $\alpha = 2$ and the Cauchy distribution is obtained when $\alpha = 1$. If $\alpha < 2$ all moments greater than α are infinite, and this property produces the fat-tailed (relative to the normal) behaviour of stable distributions. A necessary and sufficient condition for a distribution to be fat-tailed is that of *regular variation at infinity*. Stable distributions have this property, which implies a power declining tail, $X^{-\alpha}$, rather than an exponential decline as is the case with the normal.

Despite the empirical evidence in favour of stable distributions, the statistical framework underlying these distributions is relatively complicated and financial applications that employ stable assumptions have been sparse.[6] Indeed, once lower frequency returns are considered, of around a month, the empirical evidence in support of stable distributions usually disappears. The implication of infinite moments, especially the variance, that is made by stable distributions is unappealing both analytically and intuitively for finance (but see Mandelbrot, 1997). However, stable distributions do offer important advantages over alternative non-Gaussian distributions. For example, stable distributions are the limiting class of distributions in the most general version of the Central Limit Theorem, which applies to scaled sums of iid random variables with infinite variances. Stable distributions also have the property of *invariance under addition*, something that is very important for financial data, which are usually produced as the result of time aggregation. Moreover, moving averages of stable random variables are also stable, as long as certain conditions on the coefficients are satisfied (Samorodnitsky and Taqqu, 1994). We are therefore not restricted to analysing uncorrelated series, and correlated series can be filtered in usual ways, e.g. by fitting autoregressions. Correlated stable variables may thus be able to explain the *volatility clustering* that is so prevalent in financial data.

A stochastic process that has been widely applied in finance and can also generate fat-tailed distributions and volatility clustering is the *GARCH* (Generalized Autoregressive Conditionally Heteroskedastic) family of models.[7] It is interesting to note the overlap between GARCH and stable processes: for example, de Haan *et al.* (1989) consider the "ARCH(1) with normal innovations" process for X_t:

$$X_t = \varepsilon_t \sigma_t, \quad \varepsilon_t \sim \text{iid } N(0, 1) \tag{2}$$

and

$$\sigma^2 = \omega + \beta X_{t-1} \tag{3}$$

De Haan *et al.* show that this process can generate X_ts with a fat-tailed distribution and a tail index ζ defined implicitly by the equation:

$$\Gamma \left(\frac{\zeta + 1}{2} \right) = \pi^{0.5} (2\beta)^{-0.5\zeta} \tag{4}$$

where Γ is the gamma function.[8]

Following Groenendijk *et al.* (1995, Figure 1) and Mills (1996a), we can show that ARCH and stable processes overlap in terms of their tail-behaviour and that ζ can help in discriminating between the two in the regions where they do not overlap. For a stable distribution, the tail index ζ *is* the characteristic exponent α. However, as we have seen, ζ may be defined for distributions other than the stable, and for these it will not equal the characteristic component, although it will determine the maximal finite component, i.e. the tail index ζ is such that $E\left(|X|^k\right) < \infty$ for all $0 \le k < \zeta$. If $\zeta \ge 2$, the variance of X is finite, but the distribution is not necessarily normal and may thus still have fat tails: for example, it may be Student-t, in which case ζ defines the degrees of freedom. Distributions such as the normal and the power exponential possess all moments and for these ζ is infinite and they may be described as being thin-tailed. The

Table 1   Tail indices (ζ) for distinguishing between stable and non-stable processes.

Tail index	Distribution	Variance
$\zeta < 2$	Fat-tails, stable distribution with $\alpha = \zeta$	Infinite
$\zeta \geq 2$	Possibly non-normal distribution with fat tails (e.g. Student-t with ζ degrees of freedom)	Finite
$\zeta \to \infty$	Thin tailed (e.g., Normal, power exponential)	Finite

most interesting cases that can be discriminated with respect to values of ζ are summarized in Table 1.

While a number of different methods exists for estimating tail indices, in this study we adopt the order statistics procedure of Loretan and Phillips (1994), which estimates ζ as:

$$\hat{\zeta}_s = \left(s^{-1} \sum_{j=1}^{s} (\ln X_{(T-j+1)} - \ln X_{(T-s)}) \right)^{-1} \qquad 5$$

where $X_{(1)} \leq X_{(2)} \leq \ldots \leq X_{(T)}$ are the order statistics of $\{X_t\}_1^T$ in ascending order and s is the tail truncation lag.

The Central Part of Distributions—Truncated Lévy Flights. Researchers on return distributions, especially those that study stable distributions, have concentrated on the tails and said little about the central, high-peaked part. This is because tail observations are relatively more important from both statistical (e.g. for assessing normality and dispersion, and for regression and Monte Carlo analysis) and financial (e.g. for risk, probability of ruin and option pricing) viewpoints.

In a recent sequence of papers, Mantegna and Stanley (1994, 1995, 1997) take an alternative approach and analyse the central part of distributions rather than the tails. More specifically, they study scaling behaviour with respect to a new class of models: the truncated stable distributions or *truncated Lévy flights* (TLFs). TLFs have central parts that behave according to a stable distribution, while the tails decline exponentially, as in a normal distribution, rather than according to a power law. In this simple, yet appealing way, we can maintain all the advantages of the stable distribution in the central part while avoiding the problems of an infinite variance and higher moments. The very interesting property of TLF processes is that after some interval they converge to a Gaussian distribution. Mantegna and Stanley (1994) and Matacz (1997) have found evidence of a TLF process in high-frequency equity data in which the point where the distribution converges to a normal is around one month. This is consistent with previous studies in the literature which find that returns at intervals longer than one month have distributions that are very close to the Gaussian.

Mantegna and Stanley employ a straightforward method to estimate the characteristic exponent α of the TLF, which is based on the fact that the scaling behaviour of the probability of a return to the origin scales as Δt^{α}. More specifically, this methodology can be performed using the following three steps:

1. Calculate logarithmic returns at different frequencies Δt. The lowest frequency of data that is calculated must be well below the point after which it is suspected that the distribution of returns becomes normal. Since for financial data this point is around a month, only data from tick to say a few days-intervals should be considered.

2. Estimate the probability that returns for each of the intervals Δt equals the mean (origin), i.e., $P(X = \mu_x, \Delta t)$ where μ_x is the mean value of X. In practice, X *equals* the mean if it is within a range of values close to the origin, say, $\pm 5\% \mu_x$.

3. Regress the logarithms of the probabilities $P(X = \mu_x, \Delta t)$ on the logarithms of Δt; the inverse of the slope estimate from this regression provides an estimate of the characteristic exponent α .

CONDITIONAL DISTRIBUTION ANALYSIS

Contemporaneous Information Flows—Correlation and Principal Component Analysis

The majority of research in financial markets and portfolio theory assumes efficient markets, i.e., prices fully, correctly and instantaneously reflect all publicly available information. This justifies a simple and elegant analysis of investment based on contemporaneous correlation or regression coefficients (e.g. the correlations used in the Markowitz model, the single regression beta used in the CAPM, and the multiple regression betas estimated in multi-index models). An alternative approach that can be used to study contemporaneous relationships is Principal Component analysis (PCA).[9] Broadly speaking, PCA is similar to factor analysis and can be thought of as a sophisticated way of summarising and representing a correlation matrix. The method of principal components constructs from a set of variables, Y, a new set of orthogonal variables, P, the principal components. Each of these components absorbs and accounts for the maximum possible proportion of the variation in the variables Y. One of the most obvious implications of PCA is that if the variation in the returns of a set of financial assets is explained by relatively few principal components, then the conclusion may be drawn that the assets are highly integrated and that opportunities for risk diversification are relatively limited.[10]

Inefficiencies and Dynamics—Cointegration Analysis

Cointegration provides a consistent approach to testing and modelling long-run dynamic relationships between trending financial time series.[11] Essentially, as argued by Markellos and Mills (1998b), cointegration can be thought as a generalization and formalization of financial ratio analysis. In the long-run cointegrated variables will not drift apart and an error-correction mechanism will correct short-run disequilibrium movements. The prices of cointegrated assets will be driven by common factors around some shared trend and therefore, the degree of independent variation and diversification will be limited. In the presence of cointegration, static measures of association, such as correlation coefficients, will underestimate the strength of the relationship between cointegrated assets and may cause significant biases in estimation and inference.[12] Cointegration also has important implications for forecasting, since the existence of cointegration between levels implies (some) predictability for the underlying series of returns through error-correction modelling. It should be emphasized, however, that although cointegration implies forecasting ability, this is not necessarily inconsistent with the existence of random walks since cointegration utilises multivariate information.

In a single-equation framework, if two series, x_t and y_t, are both nonstationary, ($I(1)$), then, in general, the linear combination:[13]

$$z_t = y_t - bx_t \qquad\qquad 6$$

will also be $I(1)$. In the case where z_t is stationary, ($I(0)$), x_t and y_t are said to be cointegrated. In practical terms this means that if we run a linear regression on two trending variables and the residuals from this regression have "no trend", then these two variables have a common linear trend, i.e. they are cointegrated. Tests of cointegration involve assessing the stationarity of residuals or the eigenvalue-stability of systems. If a set of variables is cointegrated then, according to *Granger's Representation Theorem* (Engle and Granger, 1987), an error-correction model can be used to forecast the differenced series. For the bivariate case, a linear error-correction model can be written as:

$$\Delta x_t = \rho_1 \cdot z_{t-1} + \rho_2 \cdot W_{t-\tau} + \varepsilon_t \qquad\qquad 7$$

where $W_{t-\tau}$ is a vector that contains lagged differences of x_t and y_t.

AN APPLICATION USING HIGH-FREQUENCY FX RATES

The data set to be analysed consists of 13 spot exchange rates against the dollar for the following currencies: British pound (GBP), Deutsche mark (DEM), Swiss franc (CHF), French franc (FRF), Dutch guilder (NLG), Belgium franc (BEF), Italian lira (ITL), Spanish peseta (ESP), Danish krone (DKK), Finish markka (FIM), Swedish krona (SEK), European Currency Unit (ECU) and Japanese yen (JPY).

The data for each currency, as collected by the *Olsen and Associates* group, includes the closest bid and ask rates before and after all 17,546 half-hour intervals throughout 1996. The bid and ask prices that surround each half-hour interval, four prices for each interval, were averaged and then transformed to a logarithmic level and return, respectively. The final pairs of series, referred to hereafter as simply levels and returns, contained a few obvious spikes, which were removed using a simple filter rule.

The descriptive statistics of returns, given in Table 2, suggest that all the distributions are strongly non-Gaussian with a high degree of kurtosis and in most cases, negative skewness. We also find that conditional heteroskedasticity characterizes all series.

Similar inferences were drawn from observing empirical densities and the cumulative distributions of returns. These densities were computed as

Table 2 Descriptive statistics of tick FX data.

	Return	*Volatility*	*Skewness*	*Kurtosis*	*JB*	*ARCH*
GBP	−9.03	7.62	0.09	16.22	127,923	537
DEM	7.81	7.94	−0.31	13.25	77,282	223
CHF	16.12	9.93	−0.10	13.33	78,107	234
FRF	6.35	8.02	−0.19	12.58	67,277	202
NLG	7.72	8.73	−0.15	13.12	75,116	374
BEF	8.26	8.24	−0.30	13.69	83,860	248
ITL	−3.51	9.19	0.08	9.53	31,205	453
ESP	7.14	10.48	0.07	15.49	114,185	511
DKK	6.77	8.09	−0.16	11.39	51,607	282
FIM	5.92	10.07	−0.24	10.30	39,232	384
SEK	4.53	11.33	0.00	8.84	24,944	316
ECU	3.14	8.19	−0.17	13.35	78,533	237
JPY	3.01	9.13	0.07	9.70	32,870	245

Return and volatility are expressed as percentages per annum; volatility has been calculated from the standard deviation of exchange rate logarithmic returns; JB is the Jarque-Bera normality test statistic and ARCH gives the F-statistic at 4 lags for the LM test for autoregressive conditional heteroskedasticity (for descriptions, see Mills 1993, 143–145). All test statistics are significant at much less than the 1% level.

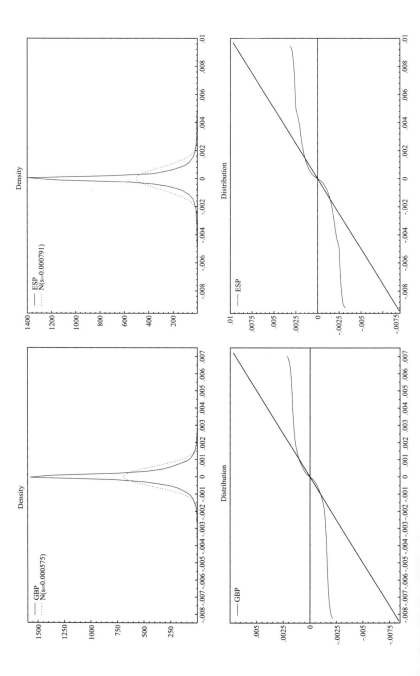

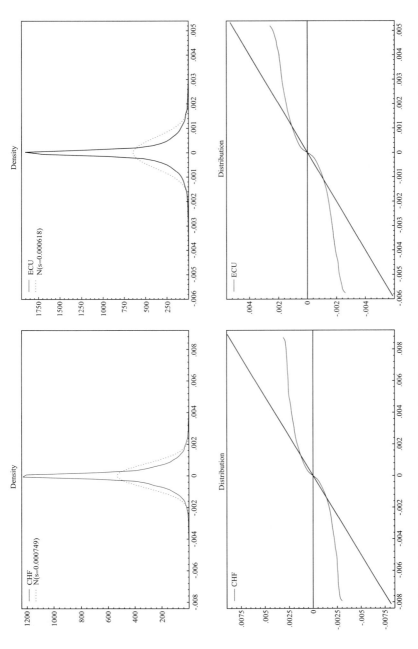

Figure 1 Empirical densities and cumulative distributions compared to those given by normal distributions for GBP, ESP, CHF and ECU returns.

smoothed versions of the histogram of each series using a normal kernel (see Silverman, 1986, chapter 6).

Figure 1 shows the empirical densities and cumulative distributions for four of the currencies; the results obtained for the remaining nine series of returns were very similar and are omitted. It is clear that, in all cases, the unconditional Gaussian distributions that are implied by the mean and variance of the data cannot capture the high peak and fat tails of the empirical densities. Both the descriptive statistics and estimated densities suggest that some non-Gaussian leptokurtotic distribution should be considered.

Unconditional Distribution Analysis: Tails and Central Parts

We begin with the analysis of the unconditional distribution tails and apply the methodology of Loretan and Phillips (1994) to estimate the tail index ζ. From the results, given in Table 3, two main conclusions can be drawn, namely that:

- All return distributions appear to have heavy tails (ζ estimates are less than three) and some slight, but insignificant, asymmetry.

- Some weak evidence of an infinite variance (ζ significantly less than two) is found for the smaller (in terms of trading volume) currencies studied. The most conclusive evidence exists for the ESP, where we find that all three tail index estimates take values well below two.

Since values of ζ larger than two may be consistent with a normal distribution if the tail index does not converge to a finite value, we also estimated ζ's for several different truncation lags and confirmed that tail indices remain reasonably stable.[14] Time-of-day seasonalities were ignored since they have been found not to affect the estimates of tail estimators (Abhyankar *et al.*, 1995).

The results we report here are in accordance with previous findings in the literature. More specifically, the general conclusion from a number of studies on exchange rate returns (Koedijk *et al.*, 1990; Hols and de Vries, 1991; Koedijk *et al.* 1992; Loretan and Phillips, 1994; Abhyankar *et al.*, 1995; Mills, 1996a) is that distributions are heavy-tailed with tail index values ranging between two and four during floating rate regimes and between one and two during fixed regimes. The existence of an infinite variance during fixed rate regimes has been interpreted as being the result of abrupt corrections to inefficiently determined rates. Our results are consistent with this argument since we find evidence of an infinite variance only for the smaller currencies, which can intuitively be considered to be the least efficiently traded.

Table 3 Estimates of tail indices $\hat{\zeta}$ for the unconditional return distributions.

	Left tail index	Right tail index	Index from both tails
GBP	2.215	2.277	2.651
	(0.061)	(0.063)	(0.074)
DEM	2.237	2.030	2.207
	(0.060)	(0.056)	(0.056)
CHF	2.212	2.168	2.543
	(0.055)	(0.057)	(0.071)
FRF	2.155	**1.916**	2.102
	(0.057)	(0.053)	(0.052)
NLG	**1.748**	2.007	2.213
	(0.041)	(0.051)	(0.061)
BEF	**1.747**	**1.822**	2.480
	(0.044)	(0.051)	(0.069)
ITL	2.398	2.021	2.774
	(0.067)	(0.053)	(0.073)
ESP	**1.512**	**1.430**	**1.797**
	(0.030)	(0.028)	(0.033)
DKK	2.514	**1.895**	2.444
	(0.070)	(0.053)	(0.064)
FIM	2.018	2.046	2.699
	(0.049)	(0.055)	(0.075)
SEK	**1.853**	2.096	2.292
	(0.042)	(2.096)	(0.052)
ECU	2.136	**1.816**	2.501
	(0.056)	(0.050)	(0.062)
JPY	2.542	2.411	2.526
	(0.071)	(0.067)	(0.063)

The values in brackets give the Hall (1982) asymptotic standard errors. The tail indices were calculated using the "optimal" truncation lag adopted by Phillips *et al.* (1996). Tail indices ζ with values under 2 are underlined and indicate an infinite variance stable distribution with characteristic exponent $\alpha = \zeta$. Normal distributions have tail indices tending to infinity, while distributions with $\zeta > 2$ (e.g. Student-t, GARCH) are characterized by finite variances and possibly fat-tails. The average ζ's across currencies for the left, right and both tails respectively are 2.104, 1.990 and 2.402.

We now analyse the central part of the distributions using the methodology of Mantegna and Stanley. The results, given in Table 4, indicate that all the distributions, except three (BEF, ITL and DKK), have central parts that exhibit significant scaling behaviour. Combined with the results obtained previously, we thus conclude that the behaviour of most distributions is consistent with the existence of a truncated Lévy flight process: although central parts behave according to a stable distribution, analysis of the tails suggests that variances are finite, although not Gaussian.

Table 4   Stable distribution characteristic exponents ($\hat{\alpha}$) estimated from the central part of the unconditional distributions.

	GBP	DEM	CHF	FRF	NLG	BEF	ITL	ESP	DKK	FIM	SEK	ECU	JPY
$\hat{\alpha}$	1.550	1.503	1.489	1.595	1.229	2.205	2.117	1.817	2.058	1.146	1.344	1.865	1.391
R^2	89%	94%	85%	94%	85%	75%	78%	86%	67%	87%	82%	89%	85%

R^2 gives the percentage of variation explained by the log-regression of $P(x = 0, \Delta t)$ on Δt.

Conditional Distributions: Returns and Levels

Motivated by the evidence on the existence of strong seasonalities in the variance of high-frequency financial data (see the references given by Goodhart and O'Hara, 1997), we examine the correlations between 30-minute returns during different periods of the day. More specifically, we concentrate on two non-overlapping GMT trading epochs: 09:00 to 16:00 (the day epoch), and 16:30 to 08:30 the following day (the night epoch), and compare the results with those obtained over the whole 24-hour day. The day trading epoch covers the period between the peaks of activity in the London and New York markets, while the night epoch covers the second half of the New York market's opening hours and the Tokyo market. It has been documented by several studies (e.g. Zhou, 1996) that volatility will be at its highest levels during what we define as the day trading epoch.

For each epoch and for the complete period, the correlation matrix of currency returns is estimated and then used to construct the 13 principal components. The marginal explanatory power of individual and combined principal components over each of the three time periods is depicted in Figures 2 and 3. We observe that over all periods the first principal

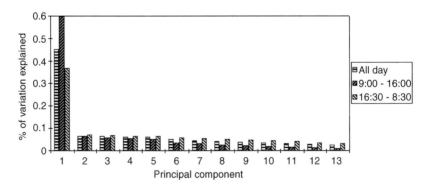

Figure 2   Percentage of variation explained by individual principal components.

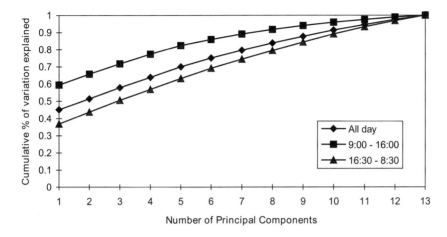

Figure 3 Cumulative percentage of variation explained by principal components.

component explains a large proportion of the variation in the data and that this explanatory power is much higher during the day epoch.

Since the inclusion of more than one component seems to add little explanatory power, only the three first components are included in further analysis, the results of which are given in Table 5 and summarized below:

- The magnitude of factor loadings appears consistent with the relative importance of the currencies in terms of trading volume. GBP is perhaps the most influential currency in our data since it enters with a high factor loading in all three (in fact all 13) of the principal components.

- Based on the sign and magnitude of factor loadings, we conclude that GBP and JPY varied somewhat independently of the other 11 European currencies considered.

- As expected, the first principal component explains the variation in the most important of the European currencies. Additional components are required to explain the behaviour of non-European (JPY) and small European currencies. This is consistent with the finding that significant diversification investments may exist for inter-continental and small-country investors.[15]

- The strength of contemporaneous information flows, as measured by the average correlation coefficients and the R^2s of the first principal component, depends significantly on the time of day: during the day

Table 5 Correlation and principal component analysis of FX returns over three trading epochs.

	All day				9:00 to 16:00 GMT				16:30 to 08:30 GMT			
	AvgCor	PC1	PC2	PC3	AvgCor	PC1	PC2	PC3	AvgCor	PC1	PC2	PC3
GBP	0.247	−0.190	−0.345	−0.306	0.327	−0.182	−0.331	−0.298	0.195	−0.193	−0.353	−0.300
DEM	0.468	0.503	0.026	0.138	0.614	0.459	−0.069	−0.104	0.375	0.118	0.192	0.090
CHF	0.406	0.768	−0.086	−0.090	0.545	0.792	0.011	0.081	0.310	0.724	0.072	0.162
FRF	0.407	−0.269	−0.096	0.003	0.581	0.282	−0.100	−0.110	0.308	−0.623	0.146	0.196
NLG	0.424	0.167	0.023	−0.005	0.596	0.212	−0.036	−0.140	0.323	0.031	0.043	0.034
BEF	0.416	−0.087	0.046	0.145	0.613	−0.041	−0.018	0.043	0.300	−0.069	0.054	0.055
ITL	0.270	−0.055	−0.048	−0.031	0.358	−0.055	0.060	0.306	0.225	0.001	−0.064	−0.253
ESP	0.326	0.087	−0.210	−0.535	0.512	0.016	0.062	0.594	0.240	−0.162	0.138	0.524
DKK	0.444	−0.036	−0.028	−0.020	0.576	0.004	0.151	−0.612	0.363	0.039	0.060	0.142
FIM	0.360	0.010	−0.066	−0.680	0.480	−0.015	−0.079	−0.125	0.291	−0.019	−0.038	−0.585
SEK	0.282	0.023	0.041	−0.107	0.389	0.008	−0.167	0.101	0.226	−0.022	−0.024	0.170
ECU	0.370	0.017	−0.149	0.084	0.547	0.005	0.598	−0.114	0.261	0.041	−0.156	0.060
JPY	0.277	0.024	−0.886	0.299	0.334	0.006	−0.672	0.014	0.243	0.028	−0.868	0.316
(Mean) R^2	(0.361)	0.451	0.064	0.063	(0.498)	0.596	0.064	0.059	(0.282)	0.368	0.070	0.070

AvgCor gives the average of the 12 correlation matrix coefficients for each currency. *PC1*, *PC2* and *PC3* give the factor loadings associated with the first three principal components, and loadings with absolute values higher than 10% are shown in bold. The percentage of variation (R^2) explained by each principal component is given in the last row of the table. For all three periods, only the first principal component has an eigenvalue that exceeds 1.

epoch, currencies are more strongly interdependent than during the night epoch. This finding is consistent with the fact that the most important news is announced in the liquid market during 09:00 to 16:00, which covers the opening periods of London and New York and the overlap between these two markets.

An effective way of interpreting and depicting the differences between correlations and information flows during the different trading epochs is to analyse the two-dimensional PCA maps of currency returns using factor loadings as co-ordinates. This analysis, given in Figure 4, confirms that correlations do depend on the trading epoch. Although GBP and CHF retain very stable co-ordinates, currencies such as FRF, ECU and JPY do change positions. The results suggest four currency groups for the

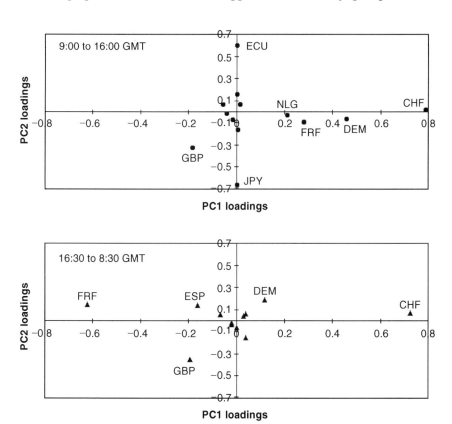

Figure 4 Two-factor PCA map of FX returns for two non-overlapping trading epochs.

day epoch: CHF-DEM-FRF-NLG, ECU, GBP and JPY. The remaining six currencies, located around the origin of the axes, cannot be explained by the first two principal components.

We proceed by analysing the conditional distributions of the exchange rate levels. First, the hypothesis of a unit root in the levels is examined by applying the Augmented Dickey-Fuller (ADF) unit root testing procedure (see Mills, 1993, chapter 3). The results, given in Table 6, indicate that for most cases the null of nonstationarity cannot be rejected at conventional significance levels. Considering the sensitivity of ADF critical values to heavy tails and infinite variance (Mittnik *et al.*, 1997), we characterise all series as $I(1)$.

We tested for cointegration between all pairs of currencies using the Johansen maximum likelihood procedure (see Mills, 1993, 176–183) and the results, given in Table 7, are summarized below:

- For 16 pairs of currencies (around 1 in 5) we find evidence at the 1 percent level of a long-run cointegrating relationship.
- Overall, JPY and GBP do not have cointegrating relationships with any of the other currencies studied. This implies that these currencies are efficiently traded relatively to the others and that they do not lead, set or follow some common trend with the other currencies.

Table 6 Augmented Dickey-Fuller unit root test results.

	Intercept and Trend		*Intercept—no Trend*	
	lag = 1	*lag = 4*	*lag = 1*	*Lag = 4*
GBP	−1.60	−1.51	0.76	0.90
DEM	−2.74	−2.70	−2.41	−2.38
CHF	−1.93	−1.89	−1.07	−1.04
FRF	−3.35	−3.16	**−3.07**	**−2.92**
NLG	−2.89	−2.77	−2.47	−2.41
BEF	−3.37	−2.98	−2.74	−2.49
ITL	***−4.76***	**−3.92**	−2.65	−2.30
ESP	**−3.69**	−3.05	−2.79	−2.38
DKK	−2.78	−2.63	−2.54	−2.44
FIM	−2.74	−2.67	−2.76	−2.69
SEK	−3.07	−2.73	−2.74	−2.40
ECU	−3.30	−2.99	**−3.23**	**−2.93**
JPY	−3.37	−3.25	−1.29	−1.23

Bold and bold italicized figures denote significance at the 5% and 1% level. For an intercept and trend (no trend) critical 1%, 5% and 10% values are: −3.96, −3.41 and −3.13 (−3.43, −2.86 and −2.57), respectively.

Table 7 Matrix of cointegration test statistics.

	GBP	DEM	CHF	FRF	NLG	BEF	ITL	ESP	DKK	FIM	SEK	ECU
GBP	—											
DEM	10.83	—										
CHF	13.13	10.65	—									
FRF	13.01	*40.43*	**16.13**	—								
NLG	10.78	*167.48*	11.50	*38.22*	—							
BEF	11.68	*363.30*	18.04	**56.21**	*629.26*	—						
ITL	9.66	14.38	8.65	**17.45**	15.21	15.18	—					
ESP	11.31	*39.46*	**16.51**	*36.22*	*53.57*	*66.25*	**15.75**	—				
DKK	10.32	*54.75*	9.22	*41.00*	*37.12*	*72.42*	13.83	*30.53*	—			
FIM	8.52	10.03	8.33	12.81	10.23	11.53	**15.71**	12.34	10.73	—		
SEK	13.97	15.05	12.57	**18.90**	**15.65**	**15.96**	11.28	14.70	14.67	13.01	—	
ECU	10.58	13.12	8.78	**16.35**	12.70	13.38	**15.78**	12.75	13.20	***23.87***	15.04	—
JPY	**19.58**	8.17	6.55	11.29	8.75	10.07	12.91	10.26	7.86	9.29	9.67	10.26

Johansen eigenvalue test statistics significant at the 5% (1%) level are emboldened (and italicized). The 5% and 1% critical values for the test statistic are 15.41 and 20.04, respectively. The test is performed with an intercept and no trend in the cointegrating VAR and 4 lags. Similar results were obtained with other test configurations and for lags ranging between 2 and 48.

- A strong common trend is found in the pairs containing BEF, NLG and DEM, and this is consistent with the strong economic ties that exist between these neighbouring countries. We would intuitively expect that DEM leads the trend in this three-currency system and that BEF and NLG revert to this trend with a delay and not instantaneously.

- Significant but less strong evidence of cointegration is found for DKK, FRF and ESP. These currencies appear to be connected both between themselves and with the DEM-BEF-NLG system identified previously.

Although the evidence concerning cointegration between spot exchange rates has been conflicting and rather weak (for example, see Baillie and Bollerslev, 1989, and Diebold *et al.*, 1994), the results shown here suggest that high-frequency data may tell a different story. Cointegration analysis of relationships between all variables, rather than between pairs, indicates the existence of around three to five common trends in the data (results varied depending on the lag structure chosen in the cointegration tests). A thorough analysis of common trends and subsequent error-correction modelling is outside the scope of this study and is left for future research.

It should be emphasized that all the evidence concerning the conditional distributions should be interpreted with much care, since the data is measured at very high frequencies and may contain significant microstructures due to, for example, non-synchronous quotes, thin trading, bid-ask bounce, fighting-screen effects, price discreteness.[16] Microstructures will bias estimates and tests of relations between returns and levels. One way of correcting for microstructures in correlation analysis involves considering cross-(auto) correlations between returns rather than correlations between returns at a single point in time.[17] To ensure that cointegration testing is not affected by short-run dynamics in the data, microstructure-related or not, we must compare the results obtained from different, sufficiently long, lag structures. Moreover, the best way of avoiding spurious cointegration is to test the validity of the results against intuition and economic theory. Finally, one must also keep in mind that data span is more important than the number of observations in terms of the power of tests for unit roots (Shiller and Perron, 1985) and cointegration (Lahiri and Mamingi, 1995).

Implications for Risk Management and Trading

Once the tails of a distribution have been characterized using the tail index ζ, the probability of extreme returns can be calculated by extrapolating the empirical distribution function outside the sample domain. This can be very useful for a number of financial applications, such as Risk-of-Ruin, Value-at-Risk, capital adequacy analysis, "safety-first" portfolio selection, etc. (see Jansen and de Vries, 1991 and de Haan *et al.*, 1994). A consistent estimate of the "excess level" $\hat{x}_p$, for which:

$$P(X_1 < \hat{x}_p, X_2 < \hat{x}_p, \ldots, X_k < \hat{x}_p) = 1 - p$$

is given by Dekkers and de Haan (1989):

$$\hat{x}_p = \frac{(0.5sk/pT)^{1/\zeta}}{1 - 2^{-1/\zeta}}(X_{(T-0.5s)} - X_{(T-s)}) + X_{(T-0.5s)} \qquad 8$$

where s is the tail truncation lag, k is the period considered and p is the probability of excess. Equation (8) can be inverted to obtain the probability $\hat{p}$ of sustaining a loss x_p. Using the left tail index estimates from Table 3, we derive two sets of results for a period (k) of one week: the first calculates the extreme negative return that is likely to occur at given probability levels (Table 8), the second reports the probability of a given extreme negative return occurring (Table 9).

We find that ESP is the riskiest currency in terms of left-tail events and that SEK and NLG follow suit, but with relatively smaller risks. It is easy to see that tail probabilities implied by a Gaussian assumption are

Table 8 Low-probability/worst-outcomes $\hat{x}_p$ implied by left tail index.

	$p = 1\%$	$p = 0.5\%$	$p = 0.1\%$	$p = 0.01\%$
GBP	−2.6%	−3.5%	−7.2%	−19.7%
DEM	−2.8%	−3.8%	−7.8%	−21.8%
CHF	−3.1%	−4.2%	−8.8%	−24.9%
FRF	−3.1%	−4.2%	−9.0%	−26.1%
NLG	−6.4%	−9.6%	−24.1%	−89.9%
BEF	−6.1%	−9.0%	−22.6%	−84.5%
ITL	−3.1%	−4.1%	−8.1%	−21.2%
ESP	−18.7%	−29.6%	−86.0%	−394.3%
DKK	−2.1%	−2.8%	−5.3%	−13.2%
FIM	−5.4%	−7.6%	−16.8%	−52.7%
SEK	−7.5%	−10.9%	−26.0%	−90.2%
ECU	−3.2%	−4.5%	−9.5%	−27.9%
JPY	−2.1%	−2.7%	−5.1%	−12.7%

Table 9 Probabilities $\hat{p}$ of various worst outcomes x implied by left tail index.

	$x = -2\%$	t (months)	$x = -5\%$	t (years)	$x = -10\%$	t (years)	$x = -20\%$	t (years)
GBP	1.804%	12.8	0.226%	8.5	0.047%	40.9	0.010%	192.3
DEM	2.077%	11.1	0.270%	7.1	0.057%	33.7	0.012%	160.3
CHF	2.638%	8.7	0.348%	5.5	0.075%	25.6	0.016%	120.2
FRF	2.519%	9.2	0.352%	5.5	0.079%	24.3	0.018%	106.8
NLG	7.731%	3.0	1.560%	1.2	0.464%	4.1	0.138%	13.9
BEF	6.910%	3.3	1.395%	1.4	0.416%	4.6	0.124%	15.5
ITL	2.777%	8.3	0.315%	6.1	0.060%	32.1	0.011%	174.8
ESP	29.080%	0.8	7.338%	0.3	2.580%	0.7	0.906%	2.1
DKK	1.133%	20.4	0.114%	16.9	0.020%	96.2	0.004%	480.8
FIM	7.247%	3.2	1.153%	1.7	0.286%	6.7	0.071%	27.1
SEK	11.578%	2.0	2.127%	0.9	0.589%	3.3	0.163%	11.8
ECU	2.755%	8.4	0.391%	4.9	0.089%	21.6	0.020%	96.2
JPY	1.086%	21.2	0.106%	18.1	0.018%	106.8	0.003%	641.0

Each specific negative excess return x is likely to occur once every t months or years. For example, the results for the GBP imply that a −10% weekly return has a probability $p = 0.047$ and will occur on average every $t = 1/(52p)$ weeks or 40.9 years.

grossly inaccurate, since the variance-derived volatilities given in Table 2 do not correspond at all with the risks of excess returns that we report here. For example, SEK and GBP, the most and least volatile currencies, respectively, are not the currencies for which we find the highest risk of a large negative return.

In addition to the fat tails, we presented evidence that most unconditional return distributions have finite variance but scaling central parts, something that is consistent with the existence of truncated Lévy flight

(TLF) processes. Under a TLF, the unconditional distribution of returns will be non-Gaussian in the short term but will eventually converge to a normal distribution. If, as suggested by the literature, we accept a point of convergence at around one month, this means that investors with horizons of one month and longer face Gaussian risks and that conventional risk management and asset pricing is applicable. On the other hand, investors at shorter horizons will face non-Gaussian fat-tailed distributions and must therefore use high-frequency data and non-Gaussian probability tools (e.g. fat-tail estimators, rare event analysis) to quantify their risks.[18] Unlike stable distributions, TLF processes do not cause significant problems for option pricing and hedging since the variance remains finite and analytical solutions are possible (Matacz, 1997).

Since in most situations we are interested in the risk associated with a basket of assets or a blend of trading positions, the relationships between currencies are also of great interest. Our empirical analysis of conditional distributions demonstrates two findings. First, contemporaneous correlations between returns have time-of-day regularities and secondly, that in some cases significant cointegration relationships between levels are present. The implication of the first finding is that *systematic* risks due to correlations vary in a regular stochastic manner with the time of the day, the "trading epoch". Other things being equal, an overnight trader does not necessarily face the same risks as a day trader and thus, should not use the same distribution of returns in evaluating positions. In general, empirical analysis should estimate the effective variances and correlations using the data that correspond to individual trading epochs and horizons. Of course, in cases where positions are carried overnight, there is no reason for estimating parameters using a selection of intra-daily data. In all cases, corrections must be made for dynamics in returns and for cointegration between levels since it is likely that these will bias correlation estimates.

Finally, with respect to trading and forecasting, we believe that cointegration analysis may have much to offer. The results we present here suggest that significant long-run relationships exist between certain exchange rates, so that error-correction modelling can be used to model deviations from these relationships. Given the nature of high-frequency data, incorporation of seasonal factors (Kunst and Frances, 1998) and nonlinearities (Markellos and Mills, 1998b) into cointegration analysis could significantly improve both inference and forecasting performance. Finally, using the notion of temporal cointegration (Siklos and Granger, 1996), it is possible that relationships hold only intra-daily and not for longer periods, e.g. two national currencies are cointegrated only temporarily during the hours that both national markets are open.

Conclusions

This paper has looked at the stochastic properties of 13 exchange rates measured at approximately 30 minute intervals. We found that most unconditional distributions of returns were substantially fat-tailed, but with finite variances and high-peaked central parts that behaved according to a stable distribution. The existence of fat tails suggests that risk management, especially of rare events, should employ non-Gaussian analytical approaches, such as tail estimators and extreme value theory. The apparently contradictory finding of distributions with tails that imply finite variances and central parts that imply infinite variance stable laws was resolved by using the recently proposed truncated Lévy flight processes. TLFs have the property of convergence to Gaussian distributions as the sampling frequency becomes lower, which is consistent with evidence from previous empirical studies on the distribution of financial returns. This implies that investors with short-term horizons face risks that are non-Gaussian/TLF but finite, while investors with longer horizons, after the point at which the TLF has dissipated, enjoy well-behaved Gaussian probabilistic environments. These conclusions agree with conventional wisdom and practice in finance and suggest that high-frequency data analysis is of little value to long-term investors.

The analysis of the conditional distributions of returns produced evidence of seasonalities in correlations and principal components of returns which imply time-of-day systematic risks. Intra-day traders with horizons of, typically, less than one day should use a selection of intra-day data in estimating the effective statistical characteristics that are relevant to their individual trading epoch. These findings are in accordance with previous research on the existence of significant intra-day seasonalities in unsystematic risks (volatility).

Preliminary results from cointegration analysis of exchange rate levels indicates that significant long-run dynamic relationships may exist between some of the currencies. These relationships are important for risk management since they may bias estimates of static association between returns, e.g., correlation coefficients and hedge ratios. Cointegration analysis may be of use to traders as a forecasting method and as a powerful and consistent way of obtaining descriptive statistics of market conditions, such as financial ratios and currency spreads.

In conclusion and in response to the question implied by the title of this chapter, *Are high-frequency financial price series random walks?*, the answer must be no. A wealth of empirical evidence from this and other studies shows that the random walk model is severely violated at very high frequencies. However, the case against random walks becomes much weaker as we move to lower sampling frequencies and eventually, at monthly or quarterly intervals, we find that financial data are well described by random walks. We also discussed a recently proposed probability model, the truncated Lévy flight, that can accommodate differences in behaviour between walks at short and long time intervals. Although the empirical findings here and elsewhere have been in favour of truncated Lévy flights, these results are preliminary; research into these new distributions is at its infancy and the robustness of the relevant testing procedures is unknown.

ACKNOWLEDGEMENT

We thank Olsen and Associates for supplying the data used in this study. Markellos acknowledges financial support from the Royal Economic Society. Corresponding author is: Professor Terence C. Mills, Dept. of Economics, Loughborough University, Leics LE11 3TU, UK.

NOTES

1. The importance and influence of Bachelier's work is described in Sullivan and Weithers (1991) and Dimand (1993), and biographical details can be found in Mandelbrot (1989). Discussions of the random walk and efficient market hypotheses in finance, along with reviews of the relevant empirical evidence, can be found in Mills (1993) and Campbell, Lo and MacKinlay (1997).
2. See "Key role for business intelligence", *Financial Times*, April 1, 1998.
3. For a comprehensive description and application of the methodology followed in the analysis of unconditional distributions see Mills (1996a).
4. Fat tails refers to the presence of more observations in the tails of empirical distributions and high peaks refers to the central part of observed distributions being more spiked.
5. For references on stable distributions in finance, see Ghose and Kroner (1995). Müller *et al.* (1990) give evidence of stable distribution scaling in high-frequency foreign exchange data. For a review of empirical evidence concerning the distribution of exchange rates, see Boothe and Glassman (1987).
6. Peters (1994, chapter 15) reviews the few theoretical asset pricing models that have been developed under stable distribution assumptions. Bouchaud *et al.* (1996) consider stable distributions with respect to option pricing.
7. For a primer on GARCH models see Mills (1993, 101–118, 137–147 and 192–196). An extensive review of empirical evidence can be found in Bollerslev, Chou and Kroner (1992).
8. A necessary though not sufficient condition for this equation to hold is that β does not exceed the value 3.56856 (see Mills, 1996a).
9. For a description, see Jackson (1991).

10. See, for example, Markellos and Siriopoulos (1997).
11. For a description of cointegration and references, see Mills (1993, chapter 6)
12. Mills (1996b) and Markellos and Mills (1998a) discuss the impact of cointegration on asset pricing with applications to the market model. Markellos and Siriopoulos (1997) study the impact of cointegration on models of international equity pricing and diversification. Markellos (1998b) is concerned with the evaluation of trading strategies using cointegration analysis.
13. For ease of exposition the following discussion will treat the case of two $I(1)$ variables; extensions to multivariate systems and fractionally integrated variables, i.e. $I(d)$ variables where d is not an integer, are possible.
14. Tail indices were estimated for truncation lags: 15, 25, 50, 75, 100, 200, 320 and 352, respectively. Results are available upon request from the authors.
15. See, for example, Markellos and Siriopoulos (1996).
16. For a review of the microstructure literature, see O'Hara (1995) and Campbell *et al.* (1997, chapter 3).
17. For example, Markellos and Mills (1998a) correct simple contemporaneous market model betas by accounting for the impact of lagged variables. Hsieh (1993) estimates capital requirements for currency futures positions under GARCH-type dynamics in the variance of returns.
18. These ideas follow Markellos (1998a) where a more extensive treatment can be found.

BIBLIOGRAPHY

Ahyankar, A., Copeland, L.S. and Wong, W. (1995), "Moment Condition Failure in High Frequency Data: Evidence from the S&P500", *Applied Economics Letters*, 2, 288–290.

Baillie, R.T. and Bollerslev, T. (1989), "Common Stochastic Trends in a System of Exchange Rates", *Journal of Finance*, 44, 167–181.

Bollerslev, T., Chou, R.Y. and Kroner, K.F. (1992), "ARCH Modelling in Finance: A Selective Review of the Theory and Empirical Evidence", *Journal of Econometrics*, 52, 5–59.

Boothe, P. and Glassman, D. (1987), "The Statistical Distribution of Exchange Rates. Empirical Evidence and Economic Implications", *Journal of International Economics*, 22, 297–319.

Bouchaud, J.-P. Iori, G. and Sornette, D. (1996), "Real-world Options" *Risk*, 9, March.

Campbell, J.Y., Lo, A. and MacKinlay, C.A. (1997), *The Econometrics of Financial Markets*, New Jersey: Princeton University Press.

Dekkers, A.L.M. and de Haan, L. (1989), "On the Estimation of the Extreme-value Index and Large Quantile Estimation", *Annals of Statistics*, 17, 1795–1832.

Diebold, F.X., Husted, S. and Rush, M. (1994), "On cointegration and exchange rate dynamics", *Journal of Finance*, 49, 727–735.

Dimand, R.W. (1993), "The Case of Brownian Motion—A Note on Bachelier's Contribution", *British Journal for the History of Science*, 26, 233–234.

Engle, R.F. and Granger, C.W.J. (1987), "Cointegration and Error Correction: Representation, Estimation and Testing", *Econometrica*, 55, 251–276.

Fama, E.F. (1965), "The Behaviour of Stock Market Prices", *Journal of Business*, 38, 34–105.

Ghose, D. and Kroner, K.F. (1995), "The Relationship between GARCH and Symmetric Stable Processes: Finding the Source of Fat Tails in Financial Data", *Journal of Empirical Finance*, 2, 225–251.

Goodhart, A.E. and O'Hara, M. (1997), "High Frequency Data in Financial Markets: Issues and Applications", *Journal of Empirical Finance*, 4, 73–114.

Granger, C.W.J. (1970), "What the Random Walk Model Does NOT Say", *Financial Analysis Journal*, May–June, reprinted in *Investment Analysis and Portfolio Management*, B. Taylor (ed.), Elek Books, London, 1970.

Granger, C.W.J. (1998), "Extracting Information from Mega-panels and High Frequency Data", *Discussion Paper*, 98–01, University of California at San Diego.

Groenendijk, P.A., Lucas, A. and de Vries, C.G. (1995), "A Note on the Relationship between GARCH and Symmetric Stable Processes", *Journal of Empirical Finance*, 2, 253–264.

Grossman, S.J. and Stiglitz, J. (1976), "Information and Competitive Price Systems", *American Economic Review*, 66, 246–253.

de Haan, L., Resnick, S.I., Rootzén, H. and de Vries, C.G. (1989), "External Behaviour of Solutions to a Stochastic Difference Equation with Applications to ARCH Processes", *Stochastic Processes and their Applications*, 32, 213–224.

Hall, P. (1982), "On some Simple Estimates of an Exponent of Regular Variation", *Journal of Royal Statistical Society, Series B*, 44, 37–42.

Hols, M.C.A.B. and de Vries, C.G. (1991), "The Limiting Distribution of Extremal Exchange Rate Returns", *Journal of Applied Econometrics*, 6, 287–302.

Hsieh, D.A. (1993), "Implications of Nonlinear Dynamics for Financial Risk Management", *Journal of Financial and Quantitative Analysis*, 28, 41–64.

Jackson, J.E. (1991), *A User's Guide to Principal Components*, New York: John Wiley and Sons.

Jansen, D.W. and de Vries, C.G. (1991), "On the Frequency of Large Stock Returns: Putting Booms and Busts into Perspective", *Review of Economics and Statistics*, 73, 18–24.

Koedijk, K.G., Schafgans, M.M.A and de Vries, C.G. (1990), "The Tail Index of Exchange Rate Returns", *Journal of International Economics*, 29, 93–108.

Koedijk, K.G., Stork, P.A. and de Vries, C.G. (1992), "Differences between Foreign Exchange Regimes: The View from the Tails", *Journal of International Money and Finance*, 11, 462–473.

Kunst, R.M. and Frances, P.H. (1998), "The Impact of Seasonal Constants on Forecasting Seasonally Cointegrated Time series", *Journal of Forecasting*, 17, 109–124.

Lahiri, K. and Mamingi, N. (1995), "Testing for Cointegration: Power versus Frequency of Observation—Another View", *Economics Letters*, 49, 121–124.

Loretan, M. and Phillips, P.C.B. (1994), "Testing the Covariance Stationarity of Heavy-Tailed Time Series. An Overview of the Theory with Applications to Several Financial Datasets", *Journal of Empirical Finance*, 1, 211–248.

Mandelbrot, B.B. (1963a), "The Variation of Certain Speculative Prices", *Journal of Business*, 36, 394–419.

Mandelbrot, B.B. (1963b), "New Methods of Statistical Economics", *Journal of Political Economy*, 71, 421–440.

Mandelbrot, B.B. (1989), "Louis Bachelier", in *The New Palgrave: Finance*, 86–88, London: Macmillan.

Mandelbrot, B.B. (1997), "Three Fractal Models in Finance: Discontinuity, Concentration, Risk", *Economic Notes*, 26, 171–211.

Mantegna, R.N. and Stanley, H.E. (1994), "Stochastic Process with Ultraslow Convergence to a Gaussian: The Truncated Lévy Flight", *Physical Review Letters*, 73, 2946–2949.

Mantegna, R.N. and Stanley, H.E. (1995), "Scaling Behaviour in the Dynamics of an Economic Index", *Nature*, 376, 46–49. Comments on this paper by A. Timmermann appear in pp. 18–19 of the same issue.

Mantegna, R.N. and Stanley, H.E. (1997), "Econophysics: Scaling and its Breakdown in Finance", *Journal of Statistical Physics*, 89, 469–479.

Markellos, R.N. (1998a), *Nonlinearities and Dynamics in Finance and Economics*, unpublished PhD thesis, Department of Economics, Loughborough University, UK (under submission).

Markellos, R.N. (1998b), "Investment Strategy Evaluation with Cointegration", *Applied Economics Letters* (forthcoming).

Markellos, R.N. and Mills, T.C. (1998a), "Asset Pricing Dynamics", *Proceedings of 5th International Conference on Forecasting Financial Markets: Advances for Exchange Rates, Interest Rates and Asset Management*, Banque Nationale de Paris/Imperial College, London.

Markellos, R.N. and Mills, T.C. (1998b), "Complexity Reduction for Co-trending Variables", *Journal of Computational Intelligence in Finance*, forthcoming.

Markellos, R.N. and Siriopoulos, C. (1997), "Diversification Benefits in the Smaller European Stock Markets", *International Advances in Economic Research*, 3, 142–153.

Matacz, A. (1997), "Financial Modelling and Option Theory with the Truncated Lévy Process", *Report*, 97–28, School of Mathematics and Statistics, University of Sydney, Australia.

Mills, T.C. (1993), *The Econometric Modelling of Financial Time Series*, Cambridge UK: Cambridge University Press.

Mills, T.C. (1996a), "Modelling Returns Distributions: A Survey of Recent Developments and some New Evidence", *Economic Research Paper*, 96/23, Loughborough University, UK.

Mills, T.C. (1996b), "The Econometrics of the 'Market Model': Cointegration, Error Correction and Exogeneity", *International Journal of Finance and Economics*, 1, 275–286.

Mittnik, S., Kim, J-R. and Rachev, S.T. (1997), "Statistical Inference in Time Series with Unit Roots in the Presence of InfiniteVariance disturbances", *Working Paper*, 105/1997, Institute of Statistics and Econometrics, Christian Albrechts University at Kiel, Germany.

Müller, U., Dacorogna, M.M., Olsen, R.B., Pictet, O.V., Schwarz, M. and Morgenegg, C. (1990), "Statistical Study of Foreign Exchange rates, Empirical

Evidence of a Price Change Scaling Law, and Intraday Analysis'', *Journal of Banking and Finance*, 14, 1189–1208.

O'Hara, M. (1995), *Market Microstructure Theory*, Cambridge MA: Blackwell.

Osborne, M.M. (1959), ''Brownian Motion in the Stock Market'', *Operations Research*, 7, 145–173.

Peters, E.E. (1994), *Fractal Market Analysis*, New York: John Wiley and Sons.

Phillips, P.C.P. McFarland, J.W. and McMahon, P.C. (1996), ''Robust Tests of Forward Exchange Market Efficiency with Empirical Evidence from the 1920s'', *Journal of Applied Econometrics*, 1–22.

Samorodnitski, G. and Taqqu, M.S. (1994), *Stable Non-Gaussian Random Processes*, New York: Chapman and Hall.

Samuelson, P.A. (1965), ''Proof that Properly Anticipated Prices Fluctuate Randomly'', *Industrial Management Review*, 6, 41–49.

Shiller, R.J. and Perron, P. (1985), ''Testing the Random Walk Hypothesis: Power versus Frequency of Observation'', *Economics Letters*, 19, 381–386.

Siklos, P.L. and Granger, C.W.J. (1996), ''Temporary Cointegration with an Application to Interest Rate Parity'', *Discussion Paper*, 96–11, University of California at San Diego.

Silverman, B.W. (1986), *Density Estimation for Statistics and Data Analysis*, London: Chapman and Hall.

Sullivan, E.J. and Weithers, T.M. (1991), ''Louis Bachelier: The Father of Modern Option Pricing Theory'', *Journal of Economic Education*, Spring, 165–171.

Zhou, B. (1996), ''High-Frequency Data and Volatility in Foreign-Exchange Rates'', *Journal of Business and Economic Statistics*, 14, 45–52.

Chapter **10**

Trading Rules Profits and the Underlying Time Series Properties

Emmanuel Acar and Pierre Lequeux

Dresdner Kleinwort Benson, Banque Nationale de Paris, London

INTRODUCTION

Investors who invest in financial markets are exposed to uncertain price changes. As a risky asset fluctuates in value, the value of the investment containing it may change. One must decide how to redefine the investment in response to such changes. Dynamic strategies are explicit rules for doing so. Dynamic strategies differ from static strategies, such as a buy-and-hold rule, in that trading in the asset occurs throughout the investment horizon, at times and in amounts that depend upon a fixed set of rules and future price changes. Dynamic strategies are developed following the expectations investors have formed about the statistical nature of the price process.

In random markets, price changes cannot be predicted. Current prices fully and correctly reflect all currently available information. Dynamic strategies are then employed to reduce the price risk exposure of an investor. The probability distribution of returns from a risky investment is tailored to suit a particular set of preferences. For instance, the most popular application of these techniques, portfolio insurance, has the objective of placing a stop-loss on the rate of return to be earned on an investment over a specified time period.

In non-random markets, price changes can be predicted. There are market imperfections, such as the existence of serial and volatility dependencies. The goal of dynamic strategies in this case is to exploit these imperfections and to outperform the market. To this end, market timing or forecasting strategies are used. On the one hand, volatility dependencies can be exploited through option strategies such as straddle. On the other hand, serial dependencies are best exploited by directional trading rules.

Financial Markets Tick by Tick
Edited by Pierre Lequeux. © 1999 John Wiley & Sons Ltd

This chapter focuses on the existence of serial dependencies in foreign exchange prices from both an academic and investor points of view by concentrating on the profitability of directional trading rules. Standard statistical tests of serial dependencies are first briefly recalled. The trading rules stochastic properties under the random walk assumption are established such that new tests of the random walk and market efficiency hypothesis can be proposed, at p 258. Previous tests are applied and compared to a set of exchange rates, at p 275. Varied time frequencies are investigated from half an hour to eight hours intervals. The last section summarizes and concludes our results.

STATISTICAL TESTS OF SERIAL DEPENDENCIES

Serial dependence refers to the notion that returns evolve nonrandomly; that is they are correlated with their prior values. One variation of serial dependence is called mean reversion. With mean reversion, returns revert to an average value or assets prices revert to an equilibrium value; the assets price will not change randomly; it will be more inclined to decrease after an increase. Conversely, if an asset is priced below its equilibrium value, it will be more likely to increase than to depreciate further. Mean reversion phenomena causes negative auto-correlations. Another variation of serial dependence is known as trending. In a trending pattern, a positive return is more likely to be followed by another positive return than a negative return, and a negative return is more likely to be succeeded by another negative return than a positive return. Trending patterns causes positive auto-correlations.

There are several ways to detect serial dependence. Historically, the two most commonly used techniques to investigate the presence of temporal dependence are the examination of a correlogram and the non-parametric runs tests. Relatively new approaches are due to Taylor (1980) and Lo and MacKinlay (1988). Both tests seem more powerful to detect dependencies in returns and will only be considered in this chapter.

Taylor Tests

In order to test the null hypothesis of a random walk against the alternative hypothesis of a trend model, Taylor (1980) considered the test statistics T and U:

$$T = \sum_{i=1}^{k} \phi^k \rho_k \Big/ \sqrt{\sum_{i=1}^{k} \phi^{2k}/n} \quad U = \sum_{i=2}^{k} \phi^k \rho_k \Big/ \sqrt{\sum_{i=2}^{k} \phi^{2k}/n} \text{ with } 0 < \phi < 1$$

If the null hypothesis is true, each ρ_k is independently normally distributed with mean zero and variance $1/n$. The T and U statistics would be asymptotically distributed with mean zero and variance unity. Under Taylor's alternative hypothesis the ρ_k are expected to be a sequence of monotonically decreasing positive values and has proposed test statistics T and U designed to be sensitive to the possibility of such an alternative hypothesis. If errors are present in a time series they will have most influence on ρ_1 and thus Taylor decides to test series with U. Experience suggests that suitable values of k and ϕ are 30 and 0.92 respectively.

Taylor points out that the high variances of conventional autocorrelation coefficients are almost certainly caused by the non-constant conditional variance of the returns. Therefore, he suggests that returns are rescaled to possess a reasonably homogeneous variance. To get reliable results, he advises to use the rescaled returns $y_t = x_t/a_t$ to calculate the coefficients T and U, now noted T^* and U^*, with $\tau = 0.1$ and a_t defined by:

$$a_t = (1 - \tau)a_{t-1} + \tau|x_{t-1}|$$

The first 20 returns are commonly used to calculate the initial value of a_t:

$$a_{20} = \frac{1}{20} \sum_{t=1}^{20} |x_t|.$$

Then for a series of n_1 returns, the coefficients are calculated from:

$$\rho_i = \sum_{t=21}^{n_1-i}(y_t - \bar{y})(y_{t+i} - \bar{y}) \bigg/ \sum_{t=21}^{n_1}(y_t - \bar{y})^2 \quad \text{where } \bar{y} = \sum_{t=21}^{n_1-i} y_t \bigg/ (n_1 - 20)$$

The term n in U^* and elsewhere now denotes the effective number of returns $n = n_1 - 20$. In this way the series y_t should have an approximately constant variance very near the expected value $1/n$. It is therefore recommended that returns are rescaled before calculating the autocorrelation coefficients.

Variance Ratio Test

The variance ratio test investigates the relation that the variance of the q-difference of uncorrelated series is q-times the variance of its first difference. Lo and MacKinlay (1988) derive an estimator for the asymptotic variance of the variance ratio, which allows for heteroskedasticity including the autoregressive conditional heteroskedastic (ARCH) process. Thus, a standard normal Z-statistic can be calculated for various q-intervals when the total number of observations is $nq + 1$. This is defined as:

$$VR(q) = \sigma_c^2(q)/\sigma_a^2(q).$$

where:

$$\sigma_c^2(q) = \frac{1}{m}\sum_{t=q}^{nq}(W_t - W_{t-q} - qu)^2 \text{ and}$$

$$\sigma_a^2(q) = \frac{1}{(nq-1)}\sum_{t=1}^{nq}(W_t - W_{t-1} - u)^2$$

and $m = q(nq - q + 1)(1 - q/nq)$; $u = (W_{nq} - W_0)/nq$ and $W_t = Ln(P_t)$ where P_t is the price at time t.

The homoskedasticity-consistent Z-statistic, $Z_1(q)$ is:

$$Z_1(q) = [VR(q) - 1](nq)^{0.5}/[2(2q - 1)(q - 1)/3q]^{0.5}$$

The heteroskedasticity-consistent Z-statistic, $Z_2(q)$, is:

$$Z_2(q) = [VR(q) - 1]/[\text{Var}(q)]^{0.5} \text{ where } \text{Var}(q) = \sum_{j=1}^{q-1}[2(q - j)/q]^2\delta(j)$$

$$\text{and } \delta(j) = \sum_{t=j+1}^{nq}(W_t - W_{t-1} - u)^2(W_{t-j} - W_{t-j-1} - u)^2 \bigg/ \left(\sum_{t=1}^{nq}(W_t - W_{t-1} - u)^2\right)^2$$

The Z-statistic can be used to test the random walk hypothesis. In both versions, homoskedastic or heteroskedastic, $Z(q)$ follows an asymptotic standard normal statistic. Therefore if the Z-statistic is greater than 1.96, it would indicate that VR is significantly different from one, suggesting that the time series is not a random walk or its increments are correlated.

TRADING RULES STOCHASTIC PROPERTIES

If investment returns are serially dependent, they are at least partly predictable. This raises the possibility that trading rules can be devised to generate abnormal profits. In the presence of negative autocorrelations, when investors observe positive returns, they revise downward their expectations and vice-versa. Thus contrarian strategies of buying the asset after a negative return and selling the asset after a positive return should earn abnormal returns. In the presence of positive autocorrelations, when investors observe positive returns, they revise upward their expectations and vice-versa. Thus, trend-following strategies of buying the asset after a positive return and selling the asset after a negative return should earn abnormal returns.

Such logic might appear counterintuitive yet it prevails in the currency markets. There is considerable evidence on the profitability of trend-following strategies in foreign exchange markets. Bilson (1990), Dacorogna *et al.* (1994), Dunis (1989), LeBaron (1991, 1992) Levich and Thomas, (1993), Schulmeister (1988), Silber (1994), Surujaras and Sweeney (1992) and Taylor (1986, 1990a, 1990b, 1992, 1994) document how past market movements can be used to presage future market movements and that this pattern is strong enough to offer profits opportunities. Lequeux and Acar (1998) have built an actively managed currency benchmark called FXDX. The market timing is based on a set of trend-following techniques whereas the currency weighting is done using Reuters volume information. The technical benchmark is not only shown to be profitable but also exhibits a high correlation with the performance of currency fund managers. This clearly demonstrates that trend-following techniques have worked over the past 10 years and have been used by currency fund managers.

What is the reason for the success of technical trading? The short answer is government intervention. Central banks spend money trying to smooth price fluctuations. They will tend to dampen short-term volatility, thereby creating an appearance of trending. Central banks' interventions are not designed to earn profits. The Bank of France, for example, bought a lot of francs in August 1993 to support their prices not to make a profit but to defend that currency from speculators. Therefore, this is an inefficiency that can be a source of profits for other investors as long as central banks' trading, on days when they are active, is a meaningful share of total currency trading. LeBaron (1994) studies to what extent foreign exchange predictability can be confined to periods of either high or low central bank activity. The results indicate that after removing periods in which the Federal Reserve is active, exchange rate predictability is dramatically reduced. More generally, Silber (1994) finds that the profitability of trend following strategies is highly correlated with the presence of price-smoothing participants in the market. His study shows that technical trading works for markets that operate under conditions similar to foreign exchange such as Treasury bills and Eurodollar time deposits, but does not work in markets without significant intervention such as gold and equities. Zask (1993) advances two other explanations specific to the profitability of trend-following strategies in the foreign exchange markets. The currency market is comprised of thousands of players in various countries of the world. Because none of these dominate the playing field the way institutional players do in other markets, there is a ripple effect in the currency market. The movement starts in one centre or location and spreads around the globe, creating trends. At last, since currency values are ultimately the market's judgement of countries and country economic policy, their movements tend to reflect macro-economic factors and thus are longer moving.

The basic assumption of technical analysis is that "everything is in the rate". Instead of analysing fundamental data in real time, this analyses the market's reaction to the participants' perception of the economic fundamentals and the supply-demand balance of the market. This reaction is seen in the price that market participants will pay for currencies. The improvement of computer speed plus the ability to feed data directly from the marketplace into trading programmes has increased the ability to measure cyclical changes. Statistical trading encompasses today a wide variety of techniques designed to identify and exploit recurrent patterns in historical prices. Even though autoregressive techniques should yield as good forecasts, the majority of futures fund managers' and spot foreign exchange traders' forecasts tend to use technical analysis. Tass management, a UK based independent consultancy that monitors the managed futures industry, report that 82 percent of its foreign exchange managers (42 out of 51) base their trading decisions on technical indicators. Unfortunately, the study of technical forecasts used for trading is relatively new. Many of the previous studies have used historical returns to exhibit the profitability of technical forecasts. Only recent work by Neftci (1991), LeBaron (1991, 1992), Brock *et al.* (1992), Levich and Thomas (1993), Taylor (1994) and Blume *et al.* (1994) have stressed the statistical properties of technical trading rules and the insight they might give us about the underlying process. Blume *et al.* (1994) have investigated how technical analysis can be valuable to traders in an economy in which the only uncertainty arises from the underlying information structure. In their model, technical analysis is valuable because current markets statistics may be sufficient to reveal some information, but not all. Although Neftci (1991) has examined the Markovian properties of trading strategies, there is only a scattered literature on their analytic properties.

Establishing trading rules stochastic properties is essential to achieving two objectives. Firstly, a proper testing of trading rules profits could be performed using expected value, variance and rules correlations under the random walk assumption. In particular it will allow the joint profitability of a set of trading rules to be tested. Brock *et al.* (1992), Surujaras and Sweeney (1992), Prado (1992) have emphasized that such a test might have power, especially against nonlinear alternatives. While much research addresses serial correlations in asset returns, researchers usually turn to mechanical trading rules to detect possible nonlinear serial dependencies. Secondly, trading rules stochastic properties might help to construct an efficient portfolio.

First our general class of forecasting strategies is defined. Some popular technical trading rules are detailed at p 263. The distributional properties of trading rule returns under the assumption of an univariate random walk without drift are given at p 264. The correlations between two technical rules applied to a same univariate random walk without drift are established at p 266. New random walk tests from the joint profitability of trading rules are proposed at p 267. Finally, expected transaction costs of trading rules when the underlying process of returns follows a Gaussian centred distribution are established at p 272.

Forecasting Strategies

Suppose that at each day (hour, minute, ...) t, a decision rule is applied with the intention of achieving profitable trades. It is the price trend which is based on market expectations that determines whether the asset is bought or sold. When the asset is bought, the position initiated in the market is said to be "long". When the asset is sold, the position initiated in the market is said to be "short". A forecasting technique is assessed as useful and will subsequently be used if it has economic value. In short, the forecast is seen as useful if in dealer terms, it can "make money". For achieving this purpose, market participants use price-based forecasts. Therefore the predictor F_t is completely characterized by a mathematical function of past prices $\{P_t, \ldots, P_{t-m}, \ldots\}$:
$F_t = f(P_t, \ldots, P_{t-m}, \ldots)$

The only crucial feature which is required from the forecasting technique is its ability to accurately predict the direction of the trend in order to generate profitable buy and sell signals. Trading signals, buy ($+1$) and sell (-1), can then be formalized by the binary stochastic process B_t:

$$\begin{cases} \text{"Sell"} & \Leftrightarrow \quad B_t = -1 \quad \Leftrightarrow \quad F_t = f(P_t, \ldots, P_{t-m}, \ldots) < 0 \\ \text{"Buy"} & \Leftrightarrow \quad B_t = +1 \quad \Leftrightarrow \quad F_t = f(P_t, \ldots, P_{t-m}, \ldots) > 0 \end{cases}$$

It must be remarked that the signal of a trading rule is completely defined by one of the inequalities giving a sell or buy order, because if the position is not short, it is long.

Only in the trivial case of a Buy and Hold (Sell and Hold) strategy, the signal B_t is deterministic and is $+1$ (-1) irrespective of the underlying process. Otherwise, trading signals B_t are stochastic variables. By nature, the signal is a highly nonlinear function of the observed price series P_t (Neftci and Policano, 1984; Neftci, 1991), and therefore it can be highly dependent through time. B_t remains constant for a certain random period, then jumps to a new level as P_t behaves in a certain way. Trading in the asset occurs throughout the investment horizon at times that depend upon a fixed set of rules and future price changes.

First we define the notations for our forecasting strategies. Let H_t and L_t be the high and low prices from day t. Let O_t and C_t be the open and close prices from day t. We shall define:

$X_t = \mathrm{Ln}(C_t/C_{t-1})$ the underlying close to close return.

$Y_t = \mathrm{Ln}(C_t/O_t)$ the underlying intra-day return.

$Z_t = \mathrm{Ln}(O_t/C_{t-1})$ the underlying overnight return.

$E_t = 0.5\{\mathrm{Ln}(H_t/O_t) + \mathrm{Ln}(L_t/O_t)\}$ the intra-day range.

Under the standard assumption in finance that the price of the asset at time t is generated by a Brownian motion, this makes X_t, Y_t, Z_t and E_t independent across days since they are functions of non-overlapping increments.

A particular class of forecasters are linear rules which can be expressed by a linear combination of logarithmic returns $X_t = \mathrm{Ln}(C_t/C_{t-1})$:

$$F_t = \sum_{j=0}^{\infty} d_j X_{t-j} \qquad\qquad 1$$

with the d_j being constants.

A more general class of forecasters are rules based on high, low, open and close rates. The usefulness of high and low data is not new and has been recognized to forecast future volatility. Because of the recognition that volatility may change over long periods of time, a highly efficient procedure should allow researchers to estimate volatility with a small number of observations. Methods based on using opening, closing, high and low prices, as published in the financial literature, have arisen in response to this need. Estimates of monthly variance that use daily data require 20 or so daily returns, whereas the high-low spread estimate requires only two prices, the high and low of the month. Readers should consult Parkinson (1980), Garman and Klass (1980), and Rogers and Satchell (1991) for details. High, low, opening and closing prices have been used as well by traders to forecast future price trends (Schwager, 1984; Kaufman, 1987). In this chapter, we will consider the family of trading rules defined by:

$$F_t = \sum_{j=0}^{\infty} a_j Y_{t-j} + \sum_{j=0}^{\infty} b_j Z_{t-j} + \sum_{j=0}^{\infty} c_j E_{t-j} \qquad 2$$

The rule is non-linear as soon as one of the coefficients c_j is different from zero. This is therefore an interesting extension of autoregressive forecasters. This has the primary advantage of including many popular technical trading rules as we will now see.

Technical Trading Rules

To be objective, buy and sell signals should be based on data available up to the current time t and should be independent of future information. Using the theory of Markov times, Neftci (1991) shows that the moving average method constitutes such a well defined methodology. The decision rule is completely defined throughout the necessary and sufficient conditions which trigger a short position on the close of the time unit (when the position is not short, it is long). This chapter will in fact consider a slightly modified version of common technical rules. More specifically, the rules instead of being based on prices are based on logarithmic prices (Table 1). The primary advantage of these logarithmic signals is that the trading rule accepts a strictly equivalent formulation in terms of logarithmic returns (Acar and Satchell, 1997). Therefore, comparisons are made possible with autoregressive models and analytic properties can be tracked further. It appears that simple, weighted moving averages and momentums are autoregressive models with constrained parameters. Consequently, they can be qualified as linear predictors. The major difference between them is that simple and weighted moving averages give decreasing weights to past underlying returns whereas the momentum gives equal weight. A separate class of rules is constituted by the typical moving averages.[2] They are non-linear predictors. Finally, all the trading rules presented above belong to the family of forecasting strategies defined by Equation 2.

Finally, it must be stressed that rules based on logarithmic prices are extremely similar to original rules based on prices when not strictly identical as in the case of the momentum method. Acar (1998) shows, using Monte-Carlo simulations, that signals are identical in at least 97 percent of the cases.

Table 1   Return/price signals equivalence.

Rule	Parameter(s)	Price Sell Signals	Equivalent Return Sell Signals
Linear rules		$Ln(C_t)$ $< \sum_{j=0}^{m-1} a_j Ln(C_{t-j})$	$\sum_{j=0}^{m-2} d_j X_{t-j} < 0$
Simple MA	$m \geq 2$	$a_j = \dfrac{1}{m}$	$d_j = (m-j-1)$
Weighted MA	$m \geq 2$	$a_j = \dfrac{m-j}{[m(m-1)]/2}$	$d_j = \dfrac{(m-j)(m-j-1)}{2}$
Momentum	$m \geq 2$	$a_j = 1$ for $j = m-1$, $a_j = 0$ for $j \neq m-1$	$d_j = 1$
Typical MA		$Ln(C_t)$ $< \dfrac{1}{m}\left\{\sum_{j=0}^{m-1} Ln(H_{t-j}L_{t-j})^{1/2}\right\}$	$\sum_{j=0}^{m-1}(m-j)Y_{t-j}$ $+ \sum_{j=0}^{m-2}(m-j-1)Z_{t-j}$ $- \sum_{j=0}^{m-1} E_{t-j} < 0$

Rule Returns Distribution Under the Random Walk Assumption

Assume a position is taken in the market for a given period $[t-1; t]$. The logarithmic return during this time is $X_t = Ln(C_t/C_{t-1})$. The nature of the position (long or short) is given by the signal triggered at time $t-1$, B_{t-1} following a given forecasting strategy, F_{t-1}. Returns at time t made by applying such a decision rule are called "rule returns" and denoted R_t. Their value can be expressed as:

$$R_t = B_{t-1}X_t \quad \Leftrightarrow \quad \left\{ \begin{array}{l} R_t = -X_t \text{ if } B_{t-1} = -1 \text{ (that is } F_{t-1} < 0) \\ R_t = +X_t \text{ if } B_{t-1} = +1 \text{ (that is } F_{t-1} > 0) \end{array} \right\} \qquad 3$$

Two important remarks should be made. Rule returns are the product of a binary stochastic signal and a continuous returns random variable. Except in the trivial case of a Buy and Hold or Sell and Hold strategy, the signal B_t is a stochastic variable and so rule returns are conditional on the position taken in the market. That is the main feature of rule returns. In addition, our rule return definition clearly corresponds to an unrealized return. By unrealized we mean that rule returns are recorded every day even if the position is neither closed nor reversed, but simply carries on.

Proposition 1[3]. If the underlying process of returns $\{X_t\}$ follows an iid centred distribution and the rule triggers long and short positions with equal probability, the process of rule returns $\{R_t\}$ follows the same iid centred distribution.

That implies in particular that if the underlying process of returns $\{X_t\}$ follows an iid normal centred distribution $N(0, \sigma^2)$, the process of rules returns $\{R_t\}$ satisfies:

$$E(R_t) = 0 \qquad\qquad 4$$

$$\text{Var}(R_t) = \sigma^2 \qquad\qquad 5$$

$$\text{Cov}(R_t, R_{t+h}) = 0 \text{ for } h > 0 \qquad\qquad 6$$

That is a very unusual case where the distribution of the rules returns is identical to the one for the underlying return and *independent of the rule itself*. These results hold for both linear and nonlinear forecasters such as the ones defined by Equation 2. The only condition which is required is that the probabilities of being long and short are of equal probability.

Under the random walk without drift assumption, not surprisingly the expected value of rule returns is zero. Indeed, using stochastic modelling, Acar (1998) shows that serial dependencies or drift are a necessary condition to the non-zero return from directional trading rules. Indeed directional trading rules cannot generate profits in the presence of volatility dependencies only. Under the random walk without drift assumption, all rules exhibit the same standard deviation which is the underlying volatility. Consequently the standard deviation seems in this case a good measure of risk, since under the random walk assumption no trading rules should be considered as riskier than others. This is the major advantage of unrealized returns over realized returns. By realized returns we mean cumulated daily returns until a position is closed and reversed from long (short) to short (long). Realized returns are known to be heteroskedastic. In fact, they exhibit for different rules very different shapes of distribution (standard deviation, skewness and kurtosis), under the random walk without drift assumption (Acar and Satchell, 1997). Subsequently, one could wrongly conclude that all rules are not equally risky under the random walk assumption, and that the higher the order of the rule, the riskier the rule is. This theoretical feature has unfortunate consequences when testing the significance of trading rules profits. Perfectly good performance records will be downgraded in comparison to others which simply possess a more nearly normal distribution (Cornew, Town and Crowson, 1984). Thus, Sharpe ratios from non-normal distributions will on average underestimate trading performance. Typically, realized returns introduce a bias in favour of models with low dealing frequency (Pictet *et al.*, 1992; Dacarogna *et al.*, 1994). The use of unrealized returns in this chapter will remove all these inconveniences and will enable us to use the Sharpe ratio or *T*-Student statistic in a meaningful way.

The distribution of the rule returns should not be surprising since past and present returns used to generate the signal and the one-ahead returns are here independent. That is, incidentally, the result provided by Broffitt (1986, example 1) who notes that although functionally dependent, rule and underlying returns are uncorrelated, the joint distribution being degenerated. This is why a study of both processes could lead to apparent differences in the results.

Non-linear Rule Returns Correlation Under the Random Walk Assumption

Proposition 2.   Assuming that the underlying asset follows a centred normal law with intra-day and overnight returns variances σ_y^2 and σ_z^2, the rates of returns $R_{1,t}$ and $R_{2,t}$ generated by forecasting strategies:

$$F_{1,t} = \sum_{j=0}^{m_1-1} a_{1,j} Y_{t-j} + \sum_{j=0}^{m_1-1} b_{1,j} Z_{t-j} + \sum_{j=0}^{m_1-1} c_{1,j} E_{t-j} \qquad 7$$

$$F_{2,t} = \sum_{j=0}^{m_2-1} a_{2,j} Y_{t-j} + \sum_{j=0}^{m_2-1} b_{2,j} Z_{t-j} + \sum_{j=0}^{m_2-1} c_{2,j} E_{t-j} \qquad 8$$

exhibit an approximated linear correlation coefficient ρ_R, given by:

$$\rho_R = \rho(R_{1,t}, R_{2,t}) = \frac{2}{\pi} \operatorname{Arc\,sin}(\rho_F) \qquad 9$$

where ρ_F is the correlation between the two nonlinear predictors. It is given by:

$$\rho_F = \frac{\left\{ \sum_{i=0}^{\text{Min}(m_1,m_2)-1} \{a_{1,i}a_{2,i} + 0.306853c_{1,i}c_{2,i} + 0.5(a_{1,i}c_{2,i} + a_{2,i}c_{1,i})\}\sigma_y^2 + \sum_{i=0}^{\text{Min}(m_1,m_2)-1} (b_{1,i}b_{2,i})\sigma_z^2 \right\}}{\sqrt{\prod_{k=1}^{2} \left\{ \sum_{i=0}^{m_k-1} (a_{k,i}^2 + b_{k,i}^2 + 0.306853c_{k,i}^2 + a_{k,i}c_{k,i})\sigma_y^2 + \sum_{i=0}^{m_k-1} b_{k,i}^2\sigma_z^2 \right\}}} \qquad 10$$

In addition, $\rho(R_{1,t}, R_{2,t+h}) = \rho(R_{1,t+h}, R_{2,t}) = 0$ for $h > 0$. $\qquad 11$

On the one hand, it must be said that when both forecasters are linear (all $c_{k,i} = 0$), formula 9 is exact and also simplifiable. An in-depth study of linear rule correlations can be found in Acar and Lequeux (1996). On the other hand, exact analytical correlations between two nonlinear rules applied to a same underlying asset seem more difficult to establish. A good proxy has been here to assume that those nonlinear rules follow, as an approximation, a normal distribution and work out what would be their correlation coefficient in this case.

Table 2 shows correlations between various systems applied to the same underlying asset. For instance $\rho[S(5), S(9)]$ means the rule returns correlation between the simple moving average of order five and the simple moving average of order nine. It is equal to 0.705. Table 2 supposes that the high and low have been calculated over the last 24 hours. This means that the opening time is equal to the previous day close and therefore $\sigma_y = \sigma_x$ and $\sigma_z = 0$. Over long periods of times, the typical moving average converges not surprisingly to the simple moving average rule. The degree of nonlinearity of the typical moving average decreases with the order of the rule. The reason is that the difference between the average of high and low data and closing price tends towards zero when averaged over long periods of times. However, over short term periods, it should be stressed that the use of high and low data can drastically reduce the correlation coefficient. For instance, the correlation coefficient between the simple moving average of order two, $S(2)$, and the typical moving average of order one, $T(1)$, using high and low data over the past twenty-four hours, is only equal to 0.757. If we now suppose that the high and low have been calculated over the last eight hours only, we have $\sigma_y / \sigma_z = \sqrt{8/16} \cong 0.707$. Then using formulae 9 and 10, the correlation coefficient between $S(2)$ and $T(1)$ drops to 0.349 which is lower than the correlation coefficient between the simple moving average of order two and ten (0.358).

Random Walk Tests from the Joint Profitability of Trading Rules

Trading rules have been widely used as a tool to detect abnormal profits and so market inefficiencies (Bird, 1985; Sweeney, 1986; Schulmeister, 1988; Dunis, 1989; Bilson, 1990; LeBaron, 1991, 1992; Brock *et al.*, 1992; Surujaras and Sweeney 1992; Levich and Thomas, 1993; Taylor 1986, 1990a, 1990b, 1992, 1994; Dacorogna *et al.*, 1994; Silber, 1994).

There are, however, pros and cons to the use of trading rule returns to test market efficiency. One of the possible benefits is that such approach might have power against non-linear alternatives (Brock *et al.*, 1992). Secondly, even if the true model is linear, standard statistical tests are often derived by minimising the mean squared error which is a sufficient but not a

Table 2 Rules returns correlations assuming high and low over the past 24 hours.

	S(2)	S(3)	S(5)	S(9)	S(17)	S(32)	S(61)	S(117)	T(1)	T(2)	T(3)	T(5)	T(9)	T(17)	T(32)	T(61)	T(117)
S(2)	1	0.705	0.521	0.378	0.272	0.196	0.142	0.102	0.757	0.631	0.549	0.45	0.349	0.26	0.192	0.14	0.102
S(3)		1	0.71	0.512	0.366	0.264	0.19	0.137	0.839	0.852	0.747	0.61	0.471	0.35	0.258	0.188	0.136
S(5)			1	0.705	0.501	0.361	0.26	0.187	0.643	0.793	0.913	0.842	0.647	0.479	0.352	0.256	0.186
S(9)				1	0.699	0.501	0.359	0.258	0.468	0.575	0.667	0.825	0.909	0.668	0.489	0.355	0.257
S(17)					1	0.707	0.504	0.361	0.336	0.411	0.475	0.585	0.763	0.951	0.69	0.498	0.359
S(32)						1	0.705	0.502	0.243	0.297	0.343	0.42	0.545	0.74	0.973	0.696	0.499
S(61)							1	0.704	0.175	0.214	0.247	0.302	0.391	0.528	0.722	0.986	0.699
S(117)								1	0.126	0.154	0.178	0.217	0.281	0.378	0.514	0.713	0.993
T(1)									1	0.809	0.696	0.564	0.435	0.323	0.238	0.173	0.126
T(2)										1	0.858	0.693	0.532	0.394	0.29	0.211	0.153
T(3)											1	0.805	0.616	0.455	0.335	0.244	0.176
T(5)												1	0.76	0.56	0.411	0.299	0.216
T(9)													1	0.73	0.533	0.386	0.279
T(17)														1	0.722	0.521	0.375
T(32)															1	0.713	0.511
T(61)																1	0.708
T(117)																	1

necessary condition to maximise profits (Acar, 1993; chapter 4). Although exhibiting some possible decisive advantages, tests based on trading rules profits have nevertheless several severe drawbacks. In particular, a trading rule can be profitable without exhibiting any market timing ability for at least two reasons. Firstly, Praetz (1976) and Acar (1998) have proved that, if the financial series follows a random walk with drift, certain trading rules can be profitable but below the unconditional mean and in consequence do not display any market timing ability. Secondly, some practitioners test for the best moving average by simulating the profitability of hundreds of alternative combinations during a particular historical period, choosing the one that has done best. Moreover, they cite the historical profitability of the winner as evidence that the system works. The problem with this approach is of course selection bias. Among one hundred rules, five can appear profitable by pure chance only, when a test is performed at a critical level of 5 percent (Taylor, 1990b). In other words, the application of filter analysis to financial markets is deficient because possible variations in models designs are infinite (Stevenson and Bear, 1976).

Previous shortcomings can be remedied by first removing the drift in the time series. Secondly, filter models require development independent on the sample upon which they are applied (Stevenson and Bear, 1976; Lukac and Brorsen, 1989). There are two ways to achieve this result. Either out-of-sample simulations are used to determine whether the trading rule works or a broad and arbitrary set of trading rules is tested instead of any single rule.

Out-of-sample simulations save recent data as "holdout period". As Markowitz and Xu (1994) underline, the problem with out-of-sample simulations is that they are routinely "data mined"; that is, if a method that did well in the in-sample period does poorly in the out-of-sample, the researcher does not abandon the project. Rather he or she tries another method that did well in the in-sample period, until one is found that also does well in the out-of-sample period. Such a procedure will eventually produce a successful method, even if all methods are equally good.

The test we describe uses instead the entire period permitted by data availability. This is based on the joint profitability of a large and arbitrary basket of trading rules. This might therefore constitute a better way to test the random walk hypothesis. Furthermore, the use of combined evidence from different trading signals best mirrors the decision process used by the human trader (Wong and Koh, 1994). The trader's decision to buy or sell is based on the combined effects of technical indicators, some of which might be conflicting. The approach is consistent with the findings of Pruitt and White (1988) and Pruitt, Tse and White (1992), who report that technical traders usually do not make decisions based on a single technical indicator. Finally, considering portfolios of technical indicators has got an additional advantage which is that portfolio rule returns exhibit a distribution more normal than single rule returns (Lukac and Brorsen, 1990). We are going to show that a variation of the usual *T*-Student test can achieve this purpose.

T-Student.   The *T*-Student is widely popular among academics and practitioners to test the hypothesis that returns to technical analysis are zero. Its attractiveness is due to its simplicity. Its use assumes that the distribution of rule returns is normal and independent. The *T*-statistic follows an asymptotic normal distribution. It can be used either as a one-tail test of the hypothesis of zero profits against positive profits or a two-tail test of the hypothesis of zero profits against non-zero profits. The *T*-statistic is formally defined as:

$$T = \sqrt{N} \frac{\overline{R}}{\hat{\sigma}_R} \qquad\qquad 12$$

with N number of observations

$\overline{R}$ the observed average returns of a portfolio of p trading rules.

$\hat{\sigma}_R$ the standard deviation of portfolio rule returns, estimated here by :

$$\hat{\sigma}_R = K\hat{\sigma} \qquad\qquad 13$$

where $\hat{\sigma}$ is the usual standard deviation estimate of the underlying returns series, and K a constant derived from the theoretical volatility and correlations between trading rules in the portfolio by:

$$K = \left\{ \begin{array}{ll} 1 & \text{for } p = 1 \\ \sqrt{p + 2\sum_{i=1}^{p}\sum_{j=i+1}^{p} \rho(R_i, R_j)} \Big/ p & \text{for } p > 1 \end{array} \right\} \qquad 14$$

and $\rho(R_i, R_j)$ is given by equation 9.

   The major advantage of such an estimate is that it only requires the estimation of underlying volatility irrespective of the portfolio of rules under consideration. It follows that comparing performances from single systems ($p = 1$) will simply be comparing mean percent returns since technical indicators display identical standard deviation, equal to the volatility of the underlying asset ($K = 1$). An important remark is that when $p = 1$, the test is valid for both linear and nonlinear forecasters. Now, portfolios of indicators can exhibit quite different standard deviations ($K < 1$) depending on the theoretical correlations between indicators and so the *T*-test applied to varied portfolios is not anymore a simple comparison of mean returns. When $p > 1$, the test is only asymptotically exact, and therefore small samples must be avoided.

The portfolio T-Statistic is a test of non-zero profit. This has power against linear and nonlinear means alternatives for which $E[X_t/X_{t-1} \ldots X_{t-k}] \# 0$ (Acar, 1993). However, the portfolio T-Statistic cannot detect or distinguish nonlinear variances models.[4] So it might be used as a tool to distinguish mean from variance non-linearity. The portfolio T-Statistic test may display a decisive advantage over T-Statistic tests derived from the use of any single trading rule. It seems to be robust for a broader range of alternatives. It appears to have the nice property of exhibiting a power almost equal to when not above the best of its components (which is unknown when the true model is unknown).

The portfolio T-test presented above proposes in fact an almost infinite number of tests, as many as there are possible different portfolios of rules. Determining what rules to incorporate into the portfolio is an extremely delicate task. There are thousands of trading systems which come in all forms. Therefore all candidates cannot be tested. The portfolio P^* including the trading rules $\{T(1), S(2), S(3), S(5), S(9), S(17), S(32), S(61), S(117)\}$ will be particularly studied because corresponding rates of returns are almost equicorrelated under the random walk assumption $\rho \cong 0.7$ (Table 2). Therefore, it can be said that portfolio P^* equally represents varied time horizons followed by investors. Larger equally weighted portfolios will be considered including rules of order 2 to 150: $S(2$ to $150)$, $W(2$ to $150)$, $M(2$ to $150)$ and $T(1$ to $149)$. However in contrast to portfolio P^*, such portfolio might slightly overweight long-term trading rules. The reason is that simple moving averages of orders 149 and 150 are correlated 0.996 when simple moving averages of orders 2 and 3 are correlated 0.705. In fact, there appears to be little need for concern about how parameters are selected in academic studies as long as they are not based on in-sample returns (Lukac and Brorsen, 1989).

It could be argued that the T-Student test is of little value because this assumes a normal, stationary and time independent rule returns distribution. There are several well known deviations from the normal distribution such as: leptokurtosis, conditional heteroskedasticity and changing conditional means. So it may be argued that the results based on single and portfolio T-Student tests may be biased. An alternative is the bootstrap approach which assumes nothing about the distribution generating function. Testing procedures based on bootstrap methodology to assess the significance of technical trading rules in financial markets are not new and have been implemented by Brock *et al.* (1992), Levich and Thomas (1993), LeBaron (1991, 1992). In fact, critical thresholds from the nonparametric bootstrap tests are extremely close to the ones issued from the parametric T-Student tests (Acar, Bertin and Lequeux, 1994). Brock *et al.* (1992) criticize parametric tests as exhibiting dubious critical thresholds. It seems that as far as rule returns are concerned, the normal assumption is more than an acceptable proxy and that T-Student based tests are as powerful and robust as bootstrap based tests. Such findings would confirm the Diebold and Nason (1990), LeBaron (1992) view that nonlinearities of financial prices can be of little economic consequence for directional predictors. This underlines that when attempting to explain directional rule returns, it is far more important to correctly model dependencies even if linear, than variance-nonlinearities. The latter haven't got, on their own, the potential to generate non-zero profits.

Transaction Costs

The profitability of dynamic strategies might be one of the most powerful statistics to detect market inefficiencies as stated by Leuthold and Garcia (1992: 53): "Relative Mean Squared Errors [however] provide only an indication of the potential for market inefficiency. A sufficient condition for market inefficiency is whether the forecasting method can generate risk-adjusted profits which are greater than the cost of usage". Therefore, market timing ability might constitute a more powerful way to detect market imperfections than standard statistical tests.

   This is why taking into account transaction costs is crucial when testing market efficiency. Jensen (1978) argues that a market should be considered efficient with respect to an information set if it is impossible to make economic profits by trading based on the information set. The random walk model requires zero risk-adjusted returns in speculative markets on the assumptions of zero transactions costs. But transaction costs in financial markets are not zero, so a market is still efficient as long as a technical trading system does not produce returns greater than transaction costs. A quantitative measure of efficiency might be derived from the bid-ask spreads of the prices in a market.

   The cost to a speculator of a currency trade depends on many variables. The total cost of taking a position is the sum of brokerage fees and liquidity costs. Liquidity costs arise because floor traders have different buying and selling prices. Trading costs can be expressed as a percentage of the goods traded (Taylor, 1986). We then assume that trading costs are equal to c, where c is a same constant for all times considered. A cost figure of $c = 0.2$ percent is suitably conservative for currencies, because such costs are still higher than most non-floor traders would pay (Taylor, 1990). Sweeney (1986), and Surujaras and Sweeney (1992) estimate transaction costs to be lower than $\frac{1}{8}$ of 1 percent ($c < 0.125$ percent). Further, large transactors or banks operating on their own account can avoid brokerage fees and only pay liquidity costs. Schulmeister (1988) reports average transaction costs based on bid-ask spreads to be at maximum 0.04 percent per trade. Satchell and Timmermann (1992) stipulate that transaction costs are very small in the foreign exchange market and less than 0.06 percent. The transaction costs used in this study will be $c = 0.2$ percent and $c = 0.05$ percent which appear upper bound for respectively private and institutional investors.

Over a period of T days, there will be a number N of round turns[5] and consequently a total trading cost equal to $TC = cN$. The number N of round turns is a stochastic variable which depends on the forecaster F_t being used. Its expected value can be established for linear rules under the Gaussian process without drift assumption.

Proposition 3

If the underlying process of returns $\{X_t\}$ follows a Gaussian centred distribution and the forecaster is unbiased, it follows that the expected number of round turns supposing that a position is opened at the beginning of the period and that the last position is closed at the end day of the period, is:

$$E(N) = 1 + (T - 2) \left[\frac{1}{2} - \frac{1}{\pi} \text{Arc} \sin(\rho) \right] \quad \text{where } \rho = \text{Corr}(F_t, F_{t-1}) \quad 15$$

Subsequently, the expected transaction cost is:

$$E(TC) = c \left\{ 1 + (T - 2) \left[\frac{1}{2} - \frac{1}{\pi} \text{Arc} \sin(\rho) \right] \right\} \quad \text{where } c \text{ is the trading cost.}$$

$$16$$

The formula is exact for linear rules and must be considered as an approximation for nonlinear predictors. Expected numbers of round turns and transaction costs over a year of 250 days are given for the simple moving average and typical rules in Table 3 under the random walk assumption. It allows one to get estimates depending only on the rule being used, not on the asset being traded. It turns out from Table 3 that transaction costs cannot be ignored if the purpose of the investor is to "make money", on a net return basis. The most active trading generated by the moving average of order 2 rule, implies for instance yearly transaction costs equal to 25 percent for small investors! It clearly appears that for equal gross returns, longer term rules must be preferred (Figure 1). This result seems to hold for nonlinear rules, such as the typical moving average or the channel rules (Taylor, 1994: Figure 1).

We now measure how transactions costs are affected by the presence of autocorrelations in the underlying time series. To do so, we assume that

Table 3   Expected yearly transaction costs under the random walk assumption.

| | | Random Walk | |
| | | E(TC)% | |
Rules/Process	E(N)	c = 0.2%	c = 0.05%
S(2)	125.00	25.00	6.25
S(3)	92.52	18.50	4.63
S(5)	67.40	13.48	3.37
S(9)	48.62	9.72	2.43
S(17)	34.92	6.98	1.75
S(32)	25.46	5.09	1.27
S(61)	18.62	3.72	0.93
S(117)	13.68	2.74	0.68
T(1)	125.00	25.00	6.25
T(2)	100.23	20.05	5.01
T(3)	82.09	16.42	4.10
T(5)	63.38	12.68	3.17
T(9)	47.14	9.43	2.36
T(17)	34.39	6.88	1.72
T(32)	25.26	5.05	1.26
T(61)	18.54	3.71	0.93
T(117)	13.65	2.73	0.68

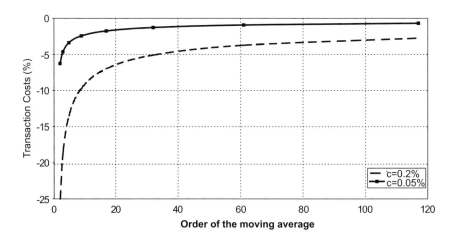

Figure 1   Expected Value of Transaction Costs under Rw.

the true process of price follows an autoregressive process of order one without drift, $AR(1)$ $X_t = \alpha X_{t-1} + \varepsilon_t$ with α being a constant and ε_t a white noise. Acar (1993) shows that in this case the strategy which maximises returns is $S(2)$ when α is positive and the reverse of $S(2)$ when α is negative.[6] The expected daily return achieved by the optimal forecaster

Table 4 Optimal $S(2)$ trading strategy.

	Random Walk	AR(1) $\alpha = 0.1$	AR(1) $\alpha = -0.1$
$E(N)$	125.00	117.09	132.91
Transaction Costs % $c = 0.05\%$	6.25	5.85	6.65

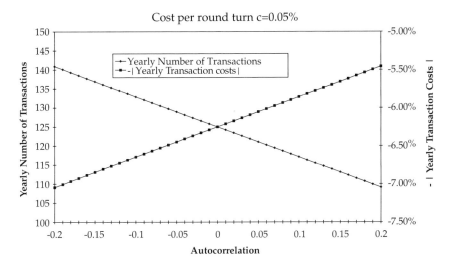

Figure 2 Optimal strategy under the $AR(1)$ assumption.

is in both cases given by $E(R) = \sqrt{2/\pi}\sigma|\alpha|$ and the transaction costs by $E(TC) = c\left\{1 + (T - 2)\left[\frac{1}{2} - \frac{1}{\pi}\text{Arc}\sin(\alpha)\right]\right\}$ since $\alpha = \text{Corr}(X_t, X_{t-1}) = \text{Corr}(-X_t, -X_{t-1})$. Numbers of round turns are higher under the random walk assumption than under positive autocorrelation alternatives but lower than under negative autocorrelations (Table 4). Indeed, the more positive autocorrelations, the more trends and the fewer transactions there are. However the number of transactions is higher when there are negative autocorrelations and therefore the expected return after transactions costs lower (Figure 2). One important implication is that negative autocorrelations will be more difficult to exploit than positive ones when transaction costs are taken into account.

RULES RETURNS AND THE PROPERTIES OF EXCHANGE RATES SERIES

Exchange rates are known in the literature to be one of the financial instruments exhibiting the strongest trends. Empirical evidence of this point is given by the profitability of path dependent strategies. Therefore, the random walk hypothesis might not be adequate for exchange rates. This paper investigates this issue by applying, in addition to standard statistical tests, the powerful and robust test based on the joint profitability of trading rules developed in this chapter.

The elementary properties of exchange rates returns are first described. The adequacy of observed volatility and correlations between trading rules with their expectations under the random walk hypothesis are checked at pp 276 and 279. The non-zero profitability of trading rule returns is tested and compared with the results with standard statistical tests of serial dependence, at p 279.

Basic Statistics

In this chapter, we have used high frequency spot prices for two currency pairs: the German Mark against the Dollar [USD/DEM] and the Japanese Yen against the Dollar [USD/YEN] for the period October 1, 1992 through September 30, 1993 inclusive. This data was provided by Olsen and Associates HFDF 93. The foreign exchange record includes the time (GMT) through a real time data feed, a bid quote $P_{\text{bid},t}$, and an ask quote $P_{\text{ask},t}$. In order to obtain high and low prices from a continuous dataset, we do not use samples with resolutions finer than 30 minutes. Then high and low data are maximum and minimum prices between two consecutive sampled prices. Other resolutions considered in this study are one, two, four and eight hours. The theoretical models of Stoll (1978), Roll (1984), Copeland and Galai (1983) and Madhavan (1992) suggest approximating transactions prices by the bid, the ask, and the average of incoming bids and offers from banks participating in the markets. We, therefore, have constructed a series of middle price using $P_t = (P_{\text{bid},t} + P_{\text{ask},t})/2$. Table 5 contains descriptive statistics on the time series of spot middle returns $X_t = \text{Ln}(P_t/P_{t-1})$.[7] Over the total period, the Usd appreciated against the Dem but decreased against the Yen (Figures 3 and 4). Both currency pairs exhibit similar magnitudes of volatility (Table 5). Excess kurtosis is evident. This sharply declines for the USD/DEM as the sampling frequency decreases. Significant autocorrelations mainly appear in the 30 minutes time series. First order autocorrelations are significantly negative for both the USD/DEM and USD/YEN.

Rule Returns Volatility

The first 150 observations have been used to trigger the signal of the longest-term trading rule used in this study. Then we have measured over

Table 5 Summary statistics for the USD/DEM and USD/YEN.

Variable:	USD/DEM			USD/YEN		
	30 MN	2 H	8 H	30 MN	2 H	8 H
Sample size	12431	3107	776	12431	3107	776
Average	1.20E-05	4.70E-05	1.88E-04	−1.00E-05	−3.90E-05	−1.59E-04
Variance	1.19E-06	4.57E-06	1.80E-05	1.12E-06	4.43E-06	1.50E-05
Standard deviation	1.09E-03	2.14E-03	4.27E-03	1.06E-03	2.10E-03	3.90E-03
Minimum	−1.30E-02	−1.30E-02	−1.55E-02	−9.35E-03	−1.49E-02	−2.35E-02
Maximum	1.44E-02	1.29E-02	2.05E-02	1.26E-02	2.79E-02	2.08E-02
Skewness	0.456	0.220	0.318	0.242	0.517	−0.334
Kurtosis	12.346	4.956	1.925	9.768	14.733	4.482
$\rho[1]$	−0.075*	0.009	0.017	−0.033*	−0.027	0.014
$\rho[2]$	0.023*	0.008	0.070	−0.020*	−0.022	0.064
$\rho[3]$	0.028*	−0.018	−0.098*	0.021*	−0.038*	−0.019
$\rho[4]$	0.011	0.021	−0.037	0.003	−0.001	−0.051
$\rho[5]$	0.006	−0.003	0.032	0.007	−0.016	0.025
$\rho[6]$	0.001	−0.011	0.012	−0.019*	0.016	−0.028
$\rho[7]$	0.003	0.007	−0.019	0.017	0.011	−0.031
$\rho[8]$	0.008	−0.022	−0.025	−0.025*	0.034	0.009
$\rho[9]$	−0.007	0.031	0.004	0.003	0.024	−0.024
$\rho[10]$	0.007	0.049*	0.023	−0.011	0.045*	−0.043

*significantly different from zero at the critical level of 5%

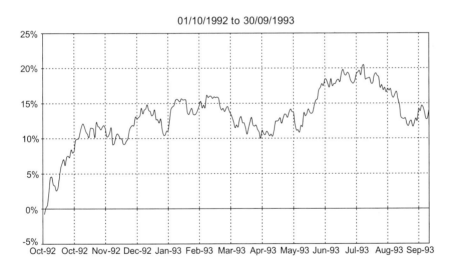

Figure 3 Cumulated log returns for USD/DEM.

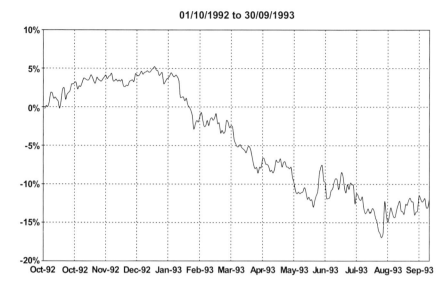

Figure 4   Cumulated log returns for USD/JPY.

the remaining sample underlying and trading rule volatility. It appears that the volatility of rule returns does not differ from the underlying market volatility (Table 6). This result is in line with what would be expected under the random walk assumption (Proposition 1). The level of risk is a direct function of the underlying volatility of the series of logarithmic returns. The relationships between rule and underlying returns do not seem to change significantly from one currency to the other.

Table 6   Yearly volatility of gross rule returns for the USD/DEM and USD/YEN.

	USD/DEM			USD/YEN		
Yearly Volatility of Rule Returns %	*30 MN*	*2 H*	*8 H*	*30 MN*	*2 H*	*8 H*
$T(1)$	11.66	11.07	10.63	11.62	11.59	11.22
$S(2)$	11.67	11.07	10.63	11.62	11.59	11.24
$S(3)$	11.67	11.07	10.62	11.62	11.59	11.24
$S(5)$	11.68	11.07	10.63	11.62	11.59	11.24
$S(9)$	11.68	11.06	10.63	11.62	11.59	11.24
$S(17)$	11.68	11.07	10.63	11.62	11.60	11.24
$S(32)$	11.68	11.06	10.63	11.62	11.60	11.23
$S(61)$	11.68	11.07	10.63	11.62	11.60	11.24
$S(117)$	11.68	11.06	10.64	11.62	11.60	11.24
Underlying	11.68	11.07	10.64	11.62	11.60	11.22

Observed big average correlations

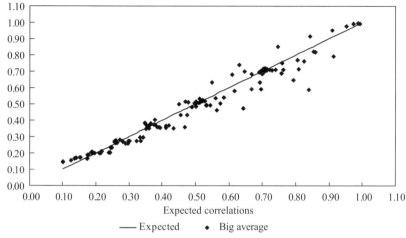

Figure 5 — Expected   ♦ Big average

Figure 5   Rule Returns Correlations.

Rule Returns Correlations

We now check the adequacy of expected rule correlations with values observed in the foreign exchange markets. It was established, at p 266, that the theoretical correlation between two technical trading rules applied to the same asset only depends on the forecasting strategies, not on the asset itself. In other words, it means that the correlation between the simple moving average of order 2 and the simple moving average of order 5 should be unique irrespective of the currency, USD/DEM, or USD/YEN and sampling frequency, from 30 minutes to eight hours. Therefore we have compared the biggest average of empirical correlations over all currencies and time frames[8] with their expected value. It appears from Figure 5 that empirical correlations are close to their expected values. The former are slightly more often above their expected value (75 cases) than below (61 cases). This result is similar to Acar and Lequeux (1996) who tested in-depth the equality of empirical correlations with their expected values for varied financial markets and linear rules.

Random Walk Tests

Random walk tests described in sections one and two are first applied. Results including annualized rule returns can be found in Table 7.

Table 7   Annualized rule returns and serial dependence statistics for the USD/DEM and USD/YEN.

Variable:	USD/DEM			USD/YEN		
	30 MN	2 H	8 H	30 MN	2 H	8 H
$T(1)$	-82.40^b	9.22	-5.59	-41.81^b	-29.48^b	-18.33
$S(2)$	-62.83^b	6.6	-4.23	-37.49^b	-24.03^b	-3.85
$S(3)$	-48.04^b	-1.86	14.37	-35.40^b	-31.15^b	-5.29
$S(5)$	-17.41	10.81	2.52	-43.47^b	-23.61^b	-2.05
$S(9)$	-15.62	11.11	0.73	-44.74^b	-28.58^b	-3.85
$S(17)$	0.42	4.21	-5.58	-32.16^b	-4.4	2.72
$S(32)$	14.13	13.96	11.75	-29.12^b	-8.28	-8.51
$S(61)$	18.76	-2.57	-3.36	-6.84	-1.43	-1.35
$S(117)$	13.48	10.55	-1.05	0.61	-3.43	-1.85
$S(2,3,5,9,17,32,61,117)$	-12.14	6.6	1.89	-28.58^b	-15.61	-3
$T(1) + S(2,3,5,9,17,32,61,117)$	-19.95^b	6.89	1.06	-30.05^b	-17.16^b	-4.71
$S(2$ to $150)$	10.52	6.98	1.31	-12.41	-5.55	-4.19
$W(2$ to $150)$	9.2	3.95	4.3	-16.83	-6.28	-6.87
$M(2$ to $150)$	4.63	6.97	3.09	-3.59	-6.25	4.1
$T(1$ to $149)$	9.88	6.82	1.41	-13.03	-5.68	-4.04
$Z_1(2)$	-8.4^b	0.4	0.4	-3.7^b	-1.5	0.4
$Z_1(3)$	-6.4^b	0.6	1.3	-4.3^b	-1.9	1.1
$Z_1(5)$	-3.4^b	0.4	0.3	-3.0^b	-2.5^b	0.9
$Z_1(9)$	-1.5	0.3	0	-2.2^b	-2.2^b	0.4
$Z_1(17)$	-0.8	0.5	0.1	-2.5^b	-0.9	-0.7
$Z_1(32)$	-0.5	0.1	0.3	-2.7^b	-0.7	-1.2
$Z_1(61)$	0.1	0.1	0.3	-1.2	-1.1	-0.5
$Z_1(117)$	-0.3	0.1	0.1	-0.9	-1.7	-0.6
$Z_2(2)$	-5.1^b	0.3	0.4	-2.1^b	-0.8	0.3
$Z_2(3)$	-3.9^b	0.4	1.3	-2.4^b	-1	1
$Z_2(5)$	-2.1^b	0.3	0.2	-1.8	-1.5	0.8
$Z_2(9)$	-1	0.2	0	-1.4	-1.4	0.4
$Z_2(17)$	-0.6	0.5	0.1	-1.6	-0.7	-0.6
$Z_2(32)$	-0.4	0.1	0.3	-1.9	-0.6	-1.1
$Z_2(61)$	0.1	0.1	0.3	-0.9	-0.9	-0.5
$Z_2(117)$	-0.2	0.1	0.1	-0.7	-1.4	-0.6
T	-0.9	0.12	0.22	-2.74^b	-1.12	-0.94
T^*	-0.9	0.78	0.16	-4.29^b	-0.87	-0.46
U	$2.62^{a,b}$	-0.09	0.04	-1.4	-0.57	-1.19
U^*	1.83^a	-0.1	-0.08	-2.12^b	-0.15	-0.38

[a] significantly above zero at the critical level of 5% (one tail test)
[b] significantly different from zero at the critical level of 5% (two tails tests)

Departures from the random walk are the strongest at the shortest time interval, 30 minutes, irrespective of the currency. Most of the trend-following rules generate significant losses for the USD/DEM and USD/YEN. Corresponding serial dependence tests also point to the presence of negative autocorrelations for the USD/DEM and USD/YEN at the 30 minutes interval. Evidence of negative autocorrelations subsists for the USD/YEN at the two hours intervals.

The problem of specifying the relationship between rule returns and standard statistical measures of serial dependency is useful because rule returns provide a measure of economic significance for serial dependencies in asset returns that otherwise might not be readily interpretable. We found here that rule returns derived from high frequency data are a positive function of serial dependence. The most striking factor is the similarity between the trading rule and variance ratio tests. Figure 6 exhibits the positive relationships between risk adjusted returns generated by simple moving averages of order q and variance ratio of length q. This may be explained by the fact that simple, weighted moving averages are autoregressive predictors with constrained parameters. Simple and weighted moving averages give decreasing weights to past underlying returns similarly to the variance ratio test which imposes declining weights on the autocorrelation estimators. These results corroborate previous academic findings. In particular, Corrado and Lee (1992) studying the time series properties of the S&P500, found a positive relationship between autocorrelations and filter rule returns. Acar (1993) similarly shows that

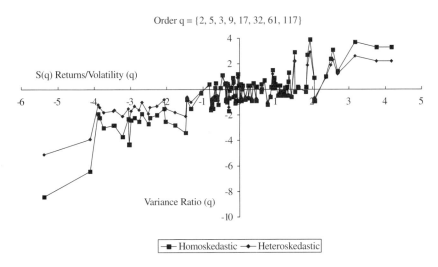

Figure 6 Variance ratio = F(risk adjusted return).

both trading rule returns and risk adjusted returns are a strong positive function of the degree of autocorrelations in daily exchange rates.

MARKET EFFICIENCY TESTS

A common problem with trading rule tests is the inability to control for institutional frictions which hinder the formation of zero net investment arbitrage portfolios. Among these are the presence of carry forward and transaction costs.

Carry Forward Cost Evaluation

The treasury cost of running the overnight positions was estimated as being the cost of carrying forward the currency positions over the period studied. In our case we look at the funding required when using trading limits, as would be the case if the activity was generated from the point of view of a dealing room. A good estimation of the funding cost as demonstrated in Sweeney (1986) would be:

$$Y = (1 - 2f)g \qquad\qquad 17$$

where g = Expected interest differential between based and quoted currencies and f = Percentage of "Long" positions

In the case of time series without drift we should expect the number of long positions to be equal to the number of short positions hence to have a near zero cost of funding. (Strictly speaking there will still be a cost due to the spread existing between the borrowing and the lending rate). In order to evaluate the cost for our sample, we first calculated in terms of base currency the frequency of long positions to short positions of our set of representative trading rules (Table 8).

Our dataset for interest rates is Olsen and Associate HFDF 93. This includes the three month maturity interbank deposit rates quotes for USD, YEN and DEM from October 1, 1992 to September 30, 1993. The summary statistics are found as in Table 9.

Then interest rate differentials between based and quoted currencies have been established as an approximation using average bid/ask interest rates (Table 10).

Therefore using Equation 17, the estimated average costs of funding are given by Table 11.

For example when we apply the simple moving average of order 117, $S(117)$, to the USD/DEM series at the eight hours sampling frequency, the

Table 8 Frequency of long positions % for the USD/DEM and USD/YEN.

	USD/DEM			USD/YEN		
	30 MN	*2 H*	*8 H*	*30 MN*	*2 H*	*8 H*
T(1)	51.74	50.91	50.24	50.83	49.63	43.22
S(2)	52.03	52.03	51.52	50.69	50.61	49.60
S(3)	50.91	51.72	51.20	49.64	49.83	47.21
S(5)	51.11	51.52	52.15	49.63	50.20	46.57
S(9)	50.95	50.98	51.67	49.43	48.65	42.58
S(17)	51.20	51.99	51.67	49.47	49.02	40.03
S(32)	51.42	53.21	49.60	49.32	46.69	37.80
S(61)	52.20	53.11	49.12	49.67	44.08	30.94
S(117)	53.68	53.68	57.42	46.73	44.76	28.71

Table 9 Interest Rates %.

	USD 3M		YEN 3M		DEM 3M	
	BID	*ASK*	*BID*	*ASK*	*BID*	*ASK*
Maximum	4	4.12	3.93	4	9.91	10.66
Minimum	2.87	3	2.38	2.5	5.94	6.06
Average	3.3024	3.4324	3.2770	3.3804	7.8052	7.9353
Sample size	3176	3176	2030	2030	2859	2859

Table 10 Interest Rates %.

	Interest Rates			Interest Rates Differentials	
	Usd	*Dem*	*Yen*	*Usd//Dem*	*Usd/Yen*
Average bid/ask	3.37	7.87	3.33	4.50	−0.04

Table 11 USD/DEM and USD/YEN Carry Forward Cost.

USD/DEM	USD/DEM			USD/YEN		
	30 MN	*2 H*	*8 H*	*30 MN*	*2 H*	*8 H*
T(1)	−0.16%	−0.08%	−0.02%	0.00%	0.00%	−0.01%
S(2)	−0.18%	−0.18%	−0.14%	0.00%	0.00%	0.00%
S(3)	−0.08%	−0.15%	−0.11%	0.00%	0.00%	0.00%
S(5)	−0.10%	−0.14%	−0.19%	0.00%	0.00%	0.00%
S(9)	−0.09%	−0.09%	−0.15%	0.00%	0.00%	−0.01%
S(17)	−0.11%	−0.18%	−0.15%	0.00%	0.00%	−0.01%
S(32)	−0.13%	−0.29%	0.04%	0.00%	0.00%	−0.01%
S(61)	−0.20%	−0.28%	0.08%	0.00%	0.00%	−0.02%
S(117)	−0.33%	−0.33%	−0.67%	0.00%	0.00%	−0.02%

cost of funding the USD position against the DEM would amount a yearly +0.67% of the position at stake since:

USD rate = 3.37%,   DEM rate = 7.87%

Frequency of long positions = 19.46%

Treasury cost = $(1 - (2^*57.42\%))^*(7.87\% - 3.37\%) = 0.67\%$

One has to note the effect of the YEN appreciation against the USD. It is worthwhile to underline the drift observed on the USD/YEN series as they impact the number of positions generated by the trading rules. The drifts in the underlying series created by this appreciation translate in a lower proportion of positions being taken by the trading rules of higher order. Indeed, higher order rules are more liable to capture the drift because of the greater information they take from the series they are applied to. As the percentage of long to short positions goes away from the 50 percent level expected from a time series without drift the inherent treasury cost/earnings ratio increases. Nevertheless, this stays low for the USD/YEN because of the small interest rate differential.

Spread Evaluation

The bid-ask spread is an important market characteristic. Various approaches have been suggested for inferring an effective bid-ask spread. Bollerslev and Domowitz (1993) examine the behaviour of quote arrivals and bid-ask spreads for a continuously recorded USD/DEM exchange rate. They find that the bid-ask spread plays an important role in determining the conditional volatility of the returns process. Another of their results is that changes in the spread are highly negatively serially correlated, with an unconditional mean of zero. The broad issue of intraday patterns in bid-ask spreads in currency markets is beyond the current study. The purpose of this section is rather to show that the knowledge of average bid-ask spreads is sufficient to accurately estimate the transaction costs generated by trading rules.

The spread between bid and ask transactions has been calculated as the logarithmic return $S_t = Ln(P_{ask,t}/P_{bid,t})$ between bid and ask prices. Summary statistics of the S_t spread are shown in Table 12. It is first interesting to note that the sampling frequency is shown to have little impact on the average spread. Given the similar volatilities of the underlying returns, one would expect, as a first guess, that currencies exhibit similar magnitude of spreads. This is not, however, the case. The USD/YEN is the more expensive currency when compared to the USD/DEM. The

Table 12 USD/DEM and USD/YEN Spread $S_t = 100^* \operatorname{Ln}(P_{ask,t}/P_{bid,t})$.

Variable:	USD/DEM			USD/YEN		
	30 MN	2 H	8 H	30 MN	2 H	8 H
Sample size	12432	3108	777	12432	3108	777
Average	0.0505	0.0507	0.0500	0.0663	0.0669	0.0668
Median	0.0586	0.0587	0.0586	0.0656	0.0662	0.0648
Standard deviation	0.0159	0.0164	0.0171	0.0248	0.0255	0.0272
Minimum	0.0115	0.0126	0.0175	0.0159	0.0170	0.0239
Maximum	0.2282	0.2282	0.1740	0.6952	0.5528	0.5145
Range	0.2167	0.2156	0.1564	0.6793	0.5358	0.4905
Lower quartile	0.0315	0.0315	0.0314	0.0453	0.0453	0.0451
Upper quartile	0.0622	0.0622	0.0622	0.0848	0.0855	0.0856
Skewness	0.5131	0.9618	1.1580	4.4452	4.6467	5.9167
Kurtosis	4.2383	7.9840	7.2566	84.1545	77.7693	93.2908
Coefficient. of variation	31.5256	32.4259	34.1947	37.3673	38.1456	40.7864
Sum	627.5929	157.4520	38.8380	824.6359	207.8867	51.8922

relative cheapness of the USD/DEM may be due to its liquidity. This is by far the most actively traded currency. This factor might explain why the USD/DEM exhibits lower and more stable spreads than currencies such as the USD/YEN which is slightly less liquid and possesses more pronounced peak trading hours.

Transaction Costs

We have first compared the actual number of round turns with what would be expected from such strategies if logarithmic returns were to follow a normal random walk. Expected values have been established using proposition 3. Table 13 tells us that for short-term trading rules $\{T(1), S(2), S(3)\}$, there are slightly more transactions for the USD/DEM and USD/YEN than expected from a random walk, especially at the 30 minutes horizon. This would tend to confirm that the USD/DEM and USD/YEN display negative autocorrelations. Long-term trading rules $\{S(32), S(61), S(117)\}$ trigger slightly fewer transactions than expected from a random walk.

Then we have worked out the transaction costs generated by such strategies (Table 14). Buy orders have been assumed to be executed at the ask and sell orders at the bid. Transaction costs are remarkably close to their expectations under the normal random walk. The expected transaction costs was obtained using Equation 16. We assumed for this the average spread $S_t = \operatorname{Ln}(P_{ask,t}/P_{bid,t})$ to be known and to constitute the only transaction cost c.

Table 13   Average number of round turns per 250 observations.

Number of Round Turns	USD/DEM				USD/YEN			
	Expected	*30 MN*	*2 H*	*8 H*	*Expected*	*30 MN*	*2 H*	*8 H*
USD/DEM *T*(1)	125.00	129.91	122.63	126.79	125.00	126.32	134.13	131.58
S(2)	125.00	131.45	127.96	133.17	125.00	131.96	135.48	134.37
S(3)	92.52	97.20	96.10	90.11	92.52	98.05	97.45	92.90
S(5)	67.40	69.80	66.35	63.00	67.40	71.59	71.59	64.99
S(9)	48.62	49.01	44.54	45.06	48.62	53.09	53.25	46.25
S(17)	34.92	34.52	29.07	39.87	34.92	36.66	33.38	27.11
S(32)	25.46	21.66	19.10	18.34	25.46	27.15	23.41	22.33
S(61)	18.62	13.72	17.24	14.35	18.62	17.87	14.45	14.35
S(117)	13.68	10.18	9.30	9.97	13.68	12.01	10.23	13.56

Table 14   Transactions costs per 250 observations.

	USD/DEM				USD/YEN			
	Expected	*30 MN*	*2 H*	*8 H*	*Expected*	*30 MN*	*2 H*	*8 H*
USD/DEM *T*(1)	6.31	6.56	6.19	6.40	8.29	8.38	8.89	8.72
S(2)	6.31	6.58	6.47	6.22	8.29	8.70	8.97	9.08
S(3)	4.67	4.89	4.78	4.32	6.13	6.49	6.51	6.25
S(5)	3.40	3.49	3.33	3.16	4.47	4.76	4.80	4.49
S(9)	2.46	2.46	2.25	2.21	3.22	3.52	3.64	3.15
S(17)	1.76	1.73	1.45	2.01	2.32	2.40	2.22	1.84
S(32)	1.29	1.10	0.97	0.95	1.69	1.79	1.59	1.56
S(61)	0.94	0.68	0.88	0.76	1.23	1.16	0.97	1.06
S(117)	0.69	0.51	0.48	0.50	0.91	0.78	0.66	0.99

Net Rule Returns

We assume here that the nature of currencies, mean-reverting or trend-following, could have been detected ex-ante. Then, we investigate the performances of the best ex-post strategies, whichever are profitable before transaction costs: contrarian or trending. When the trend following strategy is long, the contrarian strategy is short and vice-versa. Therefore the "maximum" achievable return from these trading rules is obtained by taking the absolute value of returns displayed in Table 7 and subtracting the annualized transaction costs of Table 14. Indeed, contrarian and trending strategies generate similar transaction costs because they reverse their positions at the same time. The result in Table 15 is quite disappointing since very few profits remain. Using the volatility of Table 6, there is no significant return. The USD/DEM and USD/YEN both exhibit significant negative autocorrelations. However, price reversals are always well within the bid-ask spread. Therefore, no profits remain from these

Table 15   Annualized maximum performances after transaction costs.

	USD/DEM			USD/YEN		
	30 MN	*2 H*	*8 H*	*30 MN*	*2 H*	*8 H*
USD/DEM *T*(1)	−232.48	−65.06	−13.61	−360.43	−77.2	−7.83
S(2)	−253.01	−71.04	−14.43	−380.11	−83.61	−23.39
S(3)	−186.68	−55.5	1.41	−276.12	−46.97	−13.46
S(5)	−150.11	−29.15	−6.96	−185.01	−33.99	−11.42
S(9)	−102.46	−15.89	−5.9	−124.22	−15.1	−5.6
S(17)	−82.62	−13.19	−0.45	−83.04	−22.24	−2.8
S(32)	−38.67	2.32	8.9	−56.8	−10.8	3.83
S(61)	−13.88	−7.99	1.08	−48.84	−10.21	−1.83
S(117)	−11	4.79	−0.45	−36.83	−4.49	−1.12

[a]significantly above zero at the critical level of 5% (one tail test)

contrarian strategies after transaction costs. Even traders with marginal transactions costs might expect not to earn excess returns from high-frequency trading rules.

CONCLUSIONS

Exchange rates do not follow a random walk especially at high frequency, as witnessed by both standard statistical tests and new tests based on the profitability of trading rules. The most significant autocorrelations appear at the 30 minutes interval. They are negative both for the USD/DEM and USD/YEN and statistically significant. Low frequency data have much lower significance levels. The economic significance of underlying return autocorrelations is estimated. Risk-adjusted profits from trading rules are found to be positively correlated with standard statistical tests of serial dependence. Consequently, it can be said that risk adjusted returns generated by directional trading rules are largely derived from autocorrelations. *T*-Student statistics generated by single linear trading rules might well be a reformulation of standard statistical tests of autocorrelations but with specific weights. As shown by Richardson and Smith (1994), most of the random walk tests relate statistics to linear combinations of autocorrelations. The single linear rule might not suffer this exception. This analysis helps explain why seemingly different tests may give similar conclusions. On the other hand, a portfolio of trading rules might outperform single statistics when the true model is not known or in the presence of nonstationarities.

Although exchange rates do not follow a random walk, they seem to be quite efficient at all frequencies from 30 minutes to eight hours.

No trading rule displays significant profits after transaction costs. This study is in opposition with previous researches which documented the usefulness of simple trading rules. There may be two reasons for this: the sampling frequency and the changing nature of the currency market.

Firstly, given the sampling frequency, transaction costs are of a first order significance, compared with previous researches. High frequency trading rules generate too high transaction costs to be profitable in net adjusted terms. Lower frequency trading rules should be sought because they might still exploit autocorrelations without being too sensitive to transaction costs. High-frequency data will not improve trading performances by allowing the frequency of trades to be increased. This task seems impossible given actual transaction costs. Secondly, there have been a few changes in the currency market. The two crises that rocked the European Rate Mechanism (ERM) to its foundations in 1992 and 1993, the surge of the Yen by 20 percent against the US dollar and by 30 percent against the Deutschemark after the market participants realized that any trade agreement between Japan and the US was still quite a long way off brought quite noticeable changes in the currency markets. The convergences of interest rates in Europe observed since those events are largely to blame for the decreasing currency volatilities that have been observed in the exchange rates against the dollar. The intraday ranges have been reduced by an average twofold and the dramatic decline in volatilities is providing a lot fewer profit opportunities for the market players than during the 80's. Moreover, the strong uprise of the "emerging markets" diverted a lot of funds from conventional markets, inherently unbalancing the heterogeneous structure of the currency market and possibly reducing its ability to absorb events. The time horizon of the investor seems to have been reduced leaving only the short term side of the market active. The market changed drastically from a trend-following market to a contrarian one. This brought forward new timing techniques based on non-linear mathematics like chaos, neural network, genetic algorithms, etc. It may be that as time progressed, the simple system broke down and no longer delivered good results. As time goes on and more money is driven by trading rules, one must be very conscious of the technological decay of such systems. One may need to look for ever more sophisticated and wide ranging models to manage one's money.

These factors stress the importance for the market player to establish and use reliable statistical tests in order to categorise the markets and asset classes he is trading and use the appropriate timing tools. High frequency trading rules might still be useful to currency managers in timing trades that would occur anyway. They could, for instance, postpone purchases until a trading rule triggers a "buy" signal and postpone sales until a trading rule triggers a "sell" signal. In addition, high-frequency data might be of use to construct long-term (above one day) trading rules for at least one reason. This will give the ability to vary the opening and closing times of positions which is not achievable from times series of only daily closing prices. Such a process can both enhance returns from close to close strategies (Dacorogna *et al.*, 1994) and diversify the risk (Acar and Lequeux, 1996). High frequency data should therefore enhance trading returns but it is unlikely that simple high-frequency trading rules will account for much of the profit thereby made.

APPENDIX 1: PROOFS OF PROPOSITIONS

Forecasting Strategies

We show here that the typical moving average admits a reformulation in terms of logarithmic returns.

The typical moving average triggers a sell signal if and only if:

$$\Leftrightarrow \frac{1}{m}\left\{\sum_{j=0}^{m-1} Ln(H_{t-j}L_{t-j})^{1/2}\right\} > Ln(C_t)$$

$$\Leftrightarrow \sum_{j=0}^{m-1} Ln(H_{t-j}L_{t-j}) > (2m)\,Ln(C_t)$$

$$\Leftrightarrow \sum_{j=0}^{m-1} Ln\left(\frac{H_{t-j}L_{t-j}}{O_{t-j}O_{t-j}}\right) > (2m)\,Ln(C_t) - 2\sum_{j=0}^{m-1} Ln(O_{t-j})$$

$$\Leftrightarrow 2\sum_{j=0}^{m-1}\frac{1}{2}\left[Ln\left(\frac{H_{t-j}}{O_{t-j}}\right) + Ln\left(\frac{L_{t-j}}{O_{t-j}}\right)\right] > (2m)\,Ln(C_t) - 2\sum_{j=0}^{m-1} Ln(O_{t-j})$$

$$\Leftrightarrow \sum_{j=0}^{m-1} E_{t-j} > \sum_{j=0}^{m-1} Ln(C_t) - \sum_{j=0}^{m-1} Ln(O_{t-j}) \text{ with } E_t = 0.5\{Ln(H_t/O_t) + Ln(L_t/O_t)\}$$

$$\Leftrightarrow \sum_{j=0}^{m-1} E_{t-j} > \left[\sum_{j=0}^{m-1} Ln(C_t) - \sum_{j=0}^{m-1} Ln(C_{t-j})\right] + \left[\sum_{j=0}^{m-1} Ln(C_{t-j}) - \sum_{j=0}^{m-1} Ln(O_{t-j})\right]$$

$$\Leftrightarrow \sum_{j=0}^{m-1} E_{t-j} > \left[\sum_{j=0}^{m-1} \text{Ln}(C_t) - \sum_{j=0}^{m-1} \text{Ln}(C_{t-j}) \right]$$

$$+ \left[\sum_{j=0}^{m-1} \text{Ln}(C_{t-j}) - \sum_{j=0}^{m-1} \text{Ln}(O_{t-j}) \right]$$

$$\Leftrightarrow \sum_{j=0}^{m-1} E_{t-j} > \sum_{j=1}^{m-1} \text{Ln}\left(\frac{C_t}{C_{t-j}} \right) + \sum_{j=0}^{m-1} Y_{t-j} \text{ with } Y_t = \text{Ln}(C_t/O_t)$$

$$\Leftrightarrow \sum_{j=0}^{m-1} E_{t-j} > \sum_{j=0}^{m-1} Y_{t-j} + \sum_{j=0}^{m-2} (m-j-1)X_{t-j} \text{ with } X_t = \text{Ln}(C_t/C_{t-1})$$

$$\Leftrightarrow \sum_{j=0}^{m-1} E_{t-j} > \sum_{j=0}^{m-1} Y_{t-j} + \sum_{j=0}^{m-2} (m-j-1)(Y_{t-j} + Z_{t-j})$$

$$\Leftrightarrow \sum_{j=0}^{m-1} E_{t-j} > \sum_{j=0}^{m-1} (m-j)Y_{t-j} + \sum_{j=0}^{m-2} (m-j-1)Z_{t-j} \text{ with } Z_t = \text{Ln}(O_t/C_{t-1})$$

$$\Leftrightarrow \sum_{j=0}^{m-1} (m-j)Y_{t-j} + \sum_{j=0}^{m-2} (m-j-1)Z_{t-j} - \sum_{j=0}^{m-1} E_{t-j} < 0$$

Proposition 1

We show here that the distribution of rule returns is the same as the distribution of independent underlying returns if the latter is symmetrical around zero, normal or not. If we note C_x the characteristic function of the underlying return and assume that it is symmetrical around zero, we have: $C_x(z) = E\{\exp(izX_t)\} = E\{\exp(-izX_t)\} = C_x(-z)$.

Rule returns R_t admit the characteristic function:

$$C_R(z) = E\{\exp(-izB_{t-1}X_t)\} = E(E^{\{X_{t-1}\}}[\exp(-izB_{t-1}X_t)])$$

with $E^{\{X_{t-1}\}}$ means the expected value conditional to the knowledge of past returns:

$$\{X_{t-1}\} = \{X_{t-1}, X_{t-2}, \ldots, X_{t-m}, \ldots\}.$$

By definition,

$$B_{t-1} = \begin{cases} -1 & \text{with probability} \quad \Pr(F_{t-1} < 0) \\ +1 & \text{with probability} \quad \Pr(F_{t-1} > 0) \end{cases}$$

and only depends on $\{X_{t-1}\}$. Therefore:

$$C_R(z) = E(\Pr[F_{t-1} < 0]E^{\{X_{t-1}\}}[\exp(-izX_t)]$$
$$+ \Pr[F_{t-1} > 0]E^{\{X_{t-1}\}}[\exp(+izX_t)])$$

Because X_t is independent on $\{X_{t-1}\}$, we have:

$$C_R(z) = \Pr[F_{t-1} < 0] \cdot E\{\exp(-izX_t)\} + \Pr[F_{t-1} > 0] \cdot E\{\exp(izX_t)\}$$

$\Pr[F_{t-1} < 0] = \Pr[F_{t-1} > 0] = \frac{1}{2}$ because the distribution of the linear unbiased forecaster, F_{t-1}, is symmetrical around zero, as for the underlying returns X_t. Then, it follows that:

$$C_R(z) = \tfrac{1}{2}C_x(-z) + \tfrac{1}{2}C_x(z) = C_x(z)$$

So R_t follows the same law than the underlying returns. In particular, R_t follows a centred normal law $N(0, \sigma^2)$ if X_t follows a centred normal law $N(0, \sigma^2)$. Then it implies Equations 20 and 21.

Finally, we have:

$$\text{Cov}(R_t, R_{t+h}) = E(R_t R_{t+h}) = E(B_{t-1}X_t B_{t+h-1}X_{t+h})$$
$$= E(B_{t-1}X_t B_{t+h-1})E(X_{t+h}) = E(B_{t-1}X_t B_{t+h-1})0 = 0$$

That is due to the fact that X_{t+h} is independent on X_t, B_t, B_{t+h-1}.

$$\Rightarrow \text{Cov}(R_t, R_{t+h}) = 0 \quad \text{for } h > 0. \qquad\qquad 18$$

Proposition 2

Acar and Lequeux (1996) have shown that when the underlying time series follows a centred normal law, linear rule returns, $R_{1,t}$ and $R_{2,t}$, exhibit linear correlation coefficient ρ_R, given by:

$$\rho_R = \rho(R_{1,t}, R_{2,t}) = \frac{2}{\pi} \text{Arc} \sin(\rho_F) \qquad\qquad 19$$

where ρ_F is the correlation between the two different forecasters.

We will assume here that nonlinear forecasters asymptotically follow a normal law and therefore that 19 is applicable. This is why the correlation coefficient between nonlinear rule returns must be considered as an approximation. It only remains here to establish the correlation coefficient between forecasters ρ_F.

We will consider forecasting strategies given by:

$$F_{1,t} = \sum_{j=0}^{m_1-1} a_{1,j}Y_{t-j} + \sum_{j=0}^{m_1-1} b_{1,j}Z_{t-j} + \sum_{j=0}^{m_1-1} c_{1,j}E_{t-j} \qquad\qquad 20$$

$$F_{2,t} = \sum_{j=0}^{m_2-1} a_{2,j}Y_{t-j} + \sum_{j=0}^{m_2-1} b_{2,j}Z_{t-j} + \sum_{j=0}^{m_2-1} c_{2,j}E_{t-j} \qquad 21$$

It is assumed that the underlying asset follows a centred normal law with intra-day and overnight returns variances σ_y^2 and σ_z^2. Then using the moments provided by Garman and Klass (1980) between high, low and open prices:

$$E(F_{i,t}) = 0 \text{ for } i = 1, 2$$

$$\mathrm{Var}(F_{i,t}) = \sum_{j=0}^{m_i-1} a_{i,j}^2 \sigma_y^2 + \sum_{j=0}^{m_i-1} b_{i,j}^2 \sigma_z^2 + \sum_{j=0}^{m_i-1} c_{i,j}^2 \mathrm{Var}(E_{t-j})$$

$$+ 2\sum_{j=0}^{m_i-1} a_{i,j}c_{i,j} \mathrm{Cov}(Y_{t-j}, E_{t-j}) + 2\sum_{j=0}^{m_i-1} b_{i,j}c_{i,j} \mathrm{Cov}(Z_{t-j}, E_{t-j})$$

Let us note and recall that:

$$X_t = \mathrm{Ln}(C_t/C_{t-1}), \quad Y_t = \mathrm{Ln}(C_t/O_t), \quad Z_t = \mathrm{Ln}(O_t/C_{t-1}),$$

$$U_t = \mathrm{Ln}(H_t/O_t), \quad D_t = \mathrm{Ln}(L_t/O_t),$$

and $E_t = \frac{1}{2}(U_t + D_t)$. Then Garman and Klass (1980) results stipulate that:

$$E(U_t) = 0.798 \, \sigma_y, \quad E(D_t) = -0.798 \, \sigma_y, E(U_t^2) = E(D_t^2) = \sigma_y^2,$$

$$E(U_t D_t) = -0.386294 \, \sigma_y^2, \quad E(U_t Y_t) = E(D_t Y_t) = 0.5 \, \sigma_y^2$$

Then $\mathrm{Var}(E_{t-j}) = 0.25 \, E(U_t^2 + D_t^2 + 2U_t D_t) - 0.5 \, E(U_t + D_t) = 0.306853 \, \sigma_y^2$

$\mathrm{Cov}(Y_{t-j}, E_{t-j}) = E(Y_{t-j}E_{t-j}) = 0.5 \, \sigma_y^2$ and $\mathrm{Cov}(Z_{t-j}, E_{t-j}) = 0$.

$$\mathrm{Cov}(F_{1,t}, F_{2,t}) = E(F_{1,t}F_{2,t}) = \sigma_z^2 \sum_{j=0}^{\min(m_1,m_2)-1} b_{1,j}b_{2,j}$$

$$+ \sigma_y^2 \left\{ \sum_{j=0}^{\min(m_1,m_2)-1} a_{1,j}a_{2,j} + 0.306853 \sum_{j=0}^{\min(m_1,m_2)-1} c_{1,j}c_{2,j} \right.$$

$$\left. + 0.5 \sum_{j=0}^{\min(m_1,m_2)-1} a_{1,j}c_{2,j} + 0.5 \sum_{j=0}^{\min(m_1,m_2)-1} c_{1,j}a_{2,j} \right\}$$

Therefore:

$$
\rho_F = \frac{
\begin{Bmatrix}
\displaystyle\sum_{i=0}^{\mathrm{Min}(m_1,m_2)-1} \{a_{1,i}a_{2,i} + 0.306853\, c_{1,i}c_{2,i} + 0.5(a_{1,i}c_{2,i} + a_{2,i}c_{1,i})\}\sigma_y^2 \\[1em]
+ \displaystyle\sum_{i=0}^{\mathrm{Min}(m_1,m_2)-1} (b_{1,i}b_{2,i})\sigma_z^2
\end{Bmatrix}
}{
\sqrt{\displaystyle\prod_{k=1}^{2}\left\{\sum_{i=0}^{m_k-1}(a_{k,i}^2 + b_{k,i}^2 + 0.306853\, c_{k,i}^2 + a_{k,i}c_{k,i})\sigma_y^2 + \sum_{i=0}^{m_k-1} b_{k,i}^2\sigma_z^2\right\}}
}
$$

$$22$$

Proposition 3

The expected number of round turns following a linear rule under the Gaussian process without drift assumption is now established. Again results are extend to nonlinear forecasters assuming they asymptotically follow a normal law.

The average duration of a position triggered by a technical indicator is difficult to establish because it involves truncated multivariate probabilities analytically unknown. An easier step is to determine the probability that there occurs a reversal of position on a given day, noted P[reversal].

A reversal of position on the day t means that the signal triggered by the trading rule are of opposite signs on the days $t-1$ and t. Since the underlying process is symmetrical:

$$P[\text{reversal}] = P[F_{t-1}<0, F_t>0] + P[F_{t-1}>0, F_t<0] = 2P[F_{t-1}<0, F_t>0]$$

$$P[\text{reversal}] = 2[0,0](-\rho)$$

where $\rho = \mathrm{Corr}(F_{t-1}, F_t)$, and $[0,0]$ is the bivariate truncated probability given by Johnson and Kotz (1972). As a result:

$$P[\text{reversal}] = \frac{1}{2} - \frac{1}{\pi}\,\mathrm{Arc}\sin(\rho)$$

Then the expected number of transactions over a period of T days is:

$$E(N) = T\left[\frac{1}{2} - \frac{1}{\pi}\,\mathrm{Arc}\sin(\rho)\right]$$

If we assume that a position is taken on the first day of the period and there cannot be any new position on the last day (close of position), there are in fact $T-2$ days over which a stochastic position can be triggered. Then a slight adjustment to the previous formula must be made:

$$E(N) = 1 + (T-2)\left[\frac{1}{2} - \frac{1}{\pi}\,\mathrm{Arc}\sin(\rho)\right] \quad \text{for } T \geq 2.$$

APPENDIX 2: EMPIRICAL CORRELATIONS

Table A.1 USD/DEM Rules returns correlations 30 mn (top), 2 h and 8 hours (bottom) sampling frequencies.

	S(2)	S(3)	S(5)	S(9)	S(17)	S(32)	S(61)	S(117)	T(1)	T(2)	T(3)	T(5)	T(9)	T(17)	T(32)	T(61)	T(117)
S(2)	1.000	0.708	0.556	0.424	0.299	0.257	0.235	0.158	0.613	0.710	0.634	0.531	0.410	0.317	0.253	0.234	0.159
S(3)		1.000	0.743	0.552	0.397	0.339	0.255	0.169	0.539	0.787	0.847	0.706	0.540	0.415	0.334	0.255	0.170
S(5)			1.000	0.700	0.524	0.451	0.335	0.240	0.450	0.635	0.790	0.891	0.681	0.538	0.446	0.333	0.242
S(9)				1.000	0.721	0.583	0.409	0.280	0.336	0.501	0.596	0.747	0.949	0.738	0.577	0.408	0.282
S(17)					1.000	0.750	0.540	0.351	0.242	0.359	0.446	0.558	0.746	0.960	0.752	0.537	0.352
S(32)						1.000	0.700	0.490	0.224	0.323	0.385	0.465	0.606	0.784	0.988	0.697	0.492
S(61)							1.000	0.739	0.166	0.273	0.291	0.340	0.433	0.572	0.707	0.995	0.740
S(117)								1.000	0.099	0.176	0.197	0.228	0.293	0.383	0.496	0.741	0.998
T(1)									1.000	0.687	0.567	0.452	0.343	0.262	0.221	0.165	0.101
T(2)										1.000	0.804	0.648	0.505	0.378	0.319	0.273	0.177
T(3)											1.000	0.791	0.590	0.462	0.381	0.291	0.198
T(5)												1.000	0.742	0.573	0.460	0.338	0.229
T(9)													1.000	0.764	0.601	0.432	0.294
T(17)														1.000	0.786	0.569	0.385
T(32)															1.000	0.705	0.497
T(61)																1.000	0.742
T(117)																	1.000
S(2)	1.000	0.744	0.576	0.465	0.352	0.258	0.212	0.206	0.660	0.739	0.684	0.551	0.451	0.355	0.258	0.204	0.224
S(3)		1.000	0.751	0.604	0.448	0.326	0.271	0.255	0.627	0.811	0.861	0.725	0.581	0.442	0.325	0.261	0.234
S(5)			1.000	0.793	0.562	0.393	0.298	0.299	0.524	0.690	0.812	0.950	0.767	0.567	0.392	0.290	0.278
S(9)				1.000	0.684	0.482	0.342	0.335	0.467	0.588	0.656	0.805	0.967	0.688	0.479	0.335	0.339
S(17)					1.000	0.704	0.499	0.396	0.310	0.409	0.475	0.575	0.700	0.976	0.699	0.488	0.375

	S(32)	S(61)	S(117)	T(1)	T(2)	T(3)	T(5)	T(9)	T(17)	T(32)	T(61)	T(117)
S(32)	1.000											
S(61)	0.652	1.000										
S(117)	0.485	0.708	1.000									
T(1)	0.269	0.227	0.239	1.000								
T(2)	0.290	0.261	0.268	0.765	1.000							
T(3)	0.332	0.261	0.249	0.640	0.828	1.000						
T(5)	0.398	0.287	0.285	0.537	0.677	0.811	1.000					
T(9)	0.494	0.335	0.331	0.454	0.572	0.638	0.780	1.000				
T(17)	0.727	0.505	0.412	0.328	0.415	0.479	0.579	0.705	1.000			
T(32)	0.994	0.652	0.485	0.268	0.290	0.331	0.397	0.492	0.722	1.000		
T(61)	0.642	0.985	0.717	0.214	0.251	0.251	0.279	0.328	0.495	0.644	1.000	
T(117)	0.464	0.687	0.979	0.243	0.273	0.228	0.264	0.335	0.391	0.464	0.697	1.000

	S(2)	S(3)	S(5)	S(9)	S(17)	S(32)	S(61)	S(117)	T(1)	T(2)	T(3)	T(5)	T(9)	T(17)	T(32)	T(61)	T(117)
S(2)	1.000																
S(3)	0.599	1.000															
S(5)	0.377	0.634	1.000														
S(9)	0.238	0.378	0.632	1.000													
S(17)	0.227	0.305	0.546	0.650	1.000												
S(32)	0.090	0.246	0.270	0.364	0.632	1.000											
S(61)	0.066	0.101	0.241	0.235	0.471	0.689	1.000										
S(117)	−0.003	0.033	−0.001	0.083	0.249	0.493	0.659	1.000									
T(1)	0.752	0.478	0.324	0.194	0.193	0.030	−0.021	−0.036	1.000								
T(2)	0.722	0.824	0.520	0.362	0.307	0.218	0.071	0.041	0.640	1.000							
T(3)	0.515	0.864	0.732	0.443	0.358	0.237	0.136	0.029	0.469	0.767	1.000						
T(5)	0.287	0.513	0.876	0.715	0.521	0.216	0.177	−0.014	0.248	0.434	0.623	1.000					
T(9)	0.219	0.355	0.647	0.944	0.698	0.376	0.245	0.065	0.177	0.344	0.420	0.730	1.000				
T(17)	0.210	0.288	0.529	0.663	0.981	0.617	0.456	0.233	0.176	0.291	0.342	0.504	0.711	1.000			
T(32)	0.087	0.244	0.267	0.361	0.629	0.997	0.686	0.489	0.027	0.216	0.234	0.213	0.373	0.614	1.000		
T(61)	0.066	0.101	0.240	0.234	0.471	0.689	1.000	0.660	−0.021	0.071	0.136	0.177	0.245	0.455	0.686	1.000	
T(117)	0.032	0.065	0.031	0.115	0.284	0.433	0.600	0.941	−0.004	0.072	0.061	0.018	0.098	0.269	0.430	0.601	1.000

Table A.2   USD/YEN Rules returns correlations 30 mn (top), 2 h and 8 hours (bottom) sampling frequencies.

	S(2)	S(3)	S(5)	S(9)	S(17)	S(32)	S(61)	S(117)	T(1)	T(2)	T(3)	T(5)	T(9)	T(17)	T(32)	T(61)	T(117)
S(2)	1.000	0.701	0.561	0.444	0.363	0.280	0.236	0.184	0.633	0.723	0.639	0.537	0.434	0.353	0.275	0.238	0.183
S(3)		1.000	0.742	0.593	0.460	0.362	0.300	0.222	0.603	0.807	0.851	0.714	0.576	0.451	0.365	0.301	0.222
S(5)			1.000	0.755	0.560	0.419	0.350	0.246	0.528	0.674	0.797	0.912	0.723	0.551	0.422	0.350	0.246
S(9)				1.000	0.729	0.532	0.422	0.318	0.416	0.549	0.647	0.791	0.948	0.716	0.533	0.422	0.317
S(17)					1.000	0.738	0.586	0.423	0.357	0.417	0.508	0.589	0.752	0.974	0.734	0.588	0.423
S(32)						1.000	0.754	0.549	0.281	0.330	0.405	0.447	0.555	0.750	0.976	0.755	0.550
S(61)							1.000	0.733	0.232	0.262	0.329	0.368	0.440	0.600	0.761	0.991	0.733
S(117)								1.000	0.179	0.203	0.238	0.276	0.331	0.432	0.555	0.734	0.999
T(1)									1.000	0.720	0.605	0.517	0.410	0.352	0.279	0.234	0.179
T(2)										1.000	0.815	0.663	0.538	0.408	0.337	0.266	0.202
T(3)											1.000	0.795	0.635	0.501	0.410	0.331	0.238
T(5)												1.000	0.767	0.582	0.449	0.369	0.276
T(9)													1.000	0.742	0.555	0.441	0.331
T(17)														1.000	0.747	0.601	0.432
T(32)															1.000	0.762	0.556
T(61)																1.000	0.734
T(117)																	1.000
S(2)	1.000	0.693	0.521	0.405	0.305	0.283	0.241	0.251	0.706	0.727	0.610	0.482	0.368	0.293	0.284	0.239	0.250
S(3)		1.000	0.734	0.550	0.440	0.326	0.249	0.229	0.601	0.810	0.855	0.687	0.558	0.448	0.325	0.248	0.228
S(5)			1.000	0.749	0.600	0.414	0.327	0.229	0.514	0.661	0.826	0.934	0.752	0.597	0.416	0.325	0.229
S(9)				1.000	0.732	0.554	0.430	0.315	0.396	0.489	0.637	0.796	0.944	0.728	0.556	0.428	0.315
S(17)					1.000	0.741	0.533	0.396	0.347	0.415	0.534	0.642	0.749	0.974	0.738	0.531	0.396

	S(32)	S(61)	S(117)	T(1)	T(2)	T(3)	T(5)	T(9)	T(17)	T(32)	T(61)	T(117)
S(32)	1.000	0.693	0.526	0.290	0.328	0.374	0.447	0.552	0.738	0.989	0.689	0.527
S(61)		1.000	0.757	0.238	0.273	0.303	0.327	0.417	0.546	0.696	0.997	0.758
S(117)			1.000	0.255	0.285	0.275	0.232	0.311	0.393	0.532	0.760	0.999
T(1)				1.000	0.748	0.595	0.497	0.404	0.337	0.292	0.236	0.254
T(2)					1.000	0.799	0.622	0.500	0.405	0.327	0.271	0.284
T(3)						1.000	0.794	0.639	0.542	0.373	0.301	0.274
T(5)							1.000	0.798	0.639	0.450	0.325	0.232
T(9)								1.000	0.748	0.550	0.415	0.311
T(17)									1.000	0.734	0.544	0.393
T(32)										1.000	0.693	0.533
T(61)											1.000	0.761
T(117)												1.000

	S(2)	S(3)	S(5)	S(9)	S(17)	S(32)	S(61)	S(117)	T(1)	T(2)	T(3)	T(5)	T(9)	T(17)	T(32)	T(61)	T(117)
S(2)	1.000	0.699	0.544	0.440	0.236	-0.028	0.067	0.117	0.554	0.740	0.617	0.513	0.397	0.237	-0.030	0.067	0.118
S(3)		1.000	0.685	0.522	0.317	0.035	0.150	0.185	0.612	0.851	0.812	0.658	0.500	0.318	0.037	0.150	0.186
S(5)			1.000	0.702	0.476	0.146	0.152	0.191	0.514	0.655	0.754	0.912	0.673	0.477	0.147	0.153	0.191
S(9)				1.000	0.588	0.251	0.277	0.249	0.367	0.520	0.541	0.706	0.951	0.588	0.252	0.278	0.250
S(17)					1.000	0.598	0.545	0.434	0.340	0.364	0.369	0.507	0.627	0.999	0.598	0.546	0.434
S(32)						1.000	0.787	0.452	0.102	0.111	0.085	0.194	0.286	0.598	0.998	0.787	0.452
S(61)							1.000	0.565	0.200	0.196	0.186	0.188	0.310	0.545	0.789	0.999	0.566
S(117)								1.000	0.240	0.196	0.211	0.186	0.244	0.433	0.452	0.565	0.999
T(1)									1.000	0.672	0.646	0.504	0.350	0.340	0.102	0.201	0.241
T(2)										1.000	0.843	0.680	0.542	0.365	0.112	0.197	0.196
T(3)											1.000	0.761	0.563	0.369	0.086	0.187	0.212
T(5)												1.000	0.726	0.508	0.195	0.188	0.187
T(9)													1.000	0.628	0.287	0.311	0.245
T(17)														1.000	0.598	0.545	0.434
T(32)															1.000	0.789	0.453
T(61)																1.000	0.566
T(117)																	1.000

NOTES

1. This work was carried out while Emmanuel Acar was at Banque Nationale de Paris, London Branch
2. See Appendix 1 for reformulating the typical moving average predictor in terms of logarithmic returns
3. Proofs of propositions are given in Appendix 1
4. Distinguishing nonlinear alternatives for which $E[X_t/X_{t-1}\ldots X_{t-m+1}] = 0$ is known in the literature as a difficult task. For instance it is often impossible to distinguish between Garch and stable processes (De Vries, 1991; Elie *et al.*, 1992).
5. A round turn is defined as reversing a position from one unit long to one unit short or vice-versa.
6. $S(2)$ is defined by

$$\left\{ \begin{array}{lll} Buy & when & X_t > 0 \\ Sell & when & X_t < 0 \end{array} \right\},$$

and the reverse of $S(2)$ by

$$\left\{ \begin{array}{lll} Buy & when & X_t < 0 \\ Sell & when & X_t > 0 \end{array} \right\}.$$

7. An alternative definition would have been $\tilde{X}_t = \frac{1}{2}\{\mathrm{Ln}(P_{\mathrm{ask},t}/P_{\mathrm{ask},t-1}) + \mathrm{Ln}(P_{\mathrm{bid},t}/P_{\mathrm{bid},t-1})\}$. The numerical difference between X_t and $\tilde{X}_t$ is however insignificant.
8. See for detailed results Appendix 2.

BIBLIOGRAPHY

Acar, E. (1993), "Economic Evaluation of Financial Forecasting", Ph.D thesis, City University London.

Acar, E. (1998), "Expected Returns of Directional Forecasters", in E. Acar and S. Stachell (eds) *Advanced Trading Rules*, Butterworth and Heinemann, 913–123.

Acar, E., Bertin, C. and Lequeux, P. (1994), "Tests de marche aléatoire basés sur la profitabilité des indicateurs techniques", *Analyse Financiere*, 100, 82–86.

Acar, E. and Satchell S.E. (1997), "A Theoretical Analysis of Trading Rules: An Application to the Moving Average Case with Markovian Returns", *Applied Mathematical Finance* 4(3), 165–180.

Acar, E. and Lequeux, P. (1996), "Dynamic Strategies, a Correlation Study", in C. Dunis (ed.) *Forecasting Financial Markets*, John Wiley and Sons, 113–123.

Bilson, J.F.O. (1990), "Technical Currency Trading", in L.R. Thomas (ed.), *The Currency Hedging Debate*, London: IFR Publishing Ltd., 257–275.

Bird, P.J.W.N. (1985), "The Weak Form Efficiency of the London Metal Exchange", *Applied Economics*, 17, 571–587.

Blume, L., Easley, D. and O'Hara, M. (1994), "Market Statistics and Technical Analysis: The Role of Volume", *Journal of Finance*, 49, 153–181.

Bollerserlev, T. and Domowitz, I. (1993), "Trading Patterns and Prices in the Interbank Foreign Exchange Market", *Journal of Finance*, 48, 1421–1443.

Brock, W., Lakonishok, J. and LeBaron, B. (1992), "Simple Technical Rules and the Stochastic Properties of Stock Returns", *Journal of Finance*, 47, 1731–1764.

Broffitt, J.D. (1986), "Zero Correlation, Independence and Normality", *The American Statistician*, 40(4), 276–277.

Copeland, T.E. and Galai, D. (1983), "Information Effects on the Bid-ask Spread", *Journal of Finance*, 38, 1457–1469.

Cornew, R.W., Town, D.E. and Crowson, L.D. (1984), "Stable Distributions, Futures Prices, and the Measurement of Trading Performance", *Journal of Futures Markets*, 4(4), 531–557.

Corrado, C.J. and Lee, S.H. (1992), "Filter Rule Tests of the Economic Significance of Serial Dependencies in Daily Stock Returns", *Journal of Financial Research*, 15(4), 369–387.

Dacorogna, M.M., Müller, U.A., Jost, C., Pictet, O.V., Olsen R.B. and Ward J.R. (1994), "Heterogeneous Real-Time Trading Strategies in the Foreign Exchange Market", Presentation at the *International Conference on Forecasting Financial Markets: New Advances for Exchange Rates and Stock Prices*, 2–4 February 1994, London

De Vries, C.G. (1991), "On the Relation between GARCH and Stable Processes", *Journal of Econometrics*, 48, 313–324.

Diebold, F.X. and Nason, J.A. (1990), "Non Parametric Exchange Rate Prediction?", *Journal of International Economics*, 28, 315–332.

Dunis, C. (1989), "Computerised Technical Systems and Exchange Rate Movements", in C. Dunis and M. Feeny (ed), *Exchange Rates Forecasting*, Woodhead-Faulkner, 165–205.

Elie, L., Karaoui, N.El., Jeantheau, T. and Pfertzel, A. (1992), "Les Modèles ARCH sur les Cours de Change", La Revue Banque—Supplément Banque and Marchés, No. 525 Mars, 12–16.

Garman, M.B. and Klass, M.J. (1980), "On the Estimation of Security Prices Volatilities from Historical Data", *Journal of Business*, 53, 67–78.

Jensen, M.L. (1978), "Some Anomalous Evidence Regarding Market Efficiency", *Journal of Financial Economics*, 9, 95–101.

Johnson, N.L. and Kotz, S. (1972), *"Distributions in Statistics: Continuous Multivariate Distributions"*, New York: John Wiley and Sons.

Kaufman, P.J. (1987), *The New Commodity Trading Systems and Methods*, New York: John Wiley and Sons.

LeBaron, B. (1991), *Technical Trading Rules and Regime Shifts in Foreign Exchange*, Working Paper 9118, Social Science Research, University of Wisconsin.

LeBaron, B. (1992), *Do Moving Average Trading Rule Results Imply Nonlinearities in Foreign Exchange Markets*, Working Paper 9222, Social Science Research, University of Wisconsin.

LeBaron, B. (1994), *Technical Trading Rule Profitability And Foreign Exchange Intervention*, Working Paper 9445, Social Science Research, University of Wisconsin.

Lequeux, P. and Acar, E.(1998), "A Dynamic Index for Managed Currencies Funds using CME Currencies Contracts", forthcoming in *European Journal of Finance*.

Leuthold, R.M. and Garcia, Ph. (1992), "Assessing Market Performance: An Examination of Livestock Futures Markets", in B.A. Goss (ed.), *Rational Expectations and Efficiency in Future Markets*, 52–77.

Levich, R.M. and Thomas, L.R. (1993), "The Significance of Technical Trading-rule Profits in the Foreign Exchange Market: A Bootstrap Approach", *Journal of International Money and Finance*, 12, 451–474.

Lo, A.W. and MacKinlay, A.C. (1988), "Stock Market Prices Do Not Follow Random Walks: Evidence", *Review of Financial Studies*, 1, 41–66.

Lukac, L.P. and Brorsen, B.W. (1989), "The Usefulness of Historical Data in Selecting Parameters for Technical Trading Systems", *Journal of Futures Markets*, 9(1), 55–65.

Lukac, L.P. and Brorsen, B.W. (1990), "A Comprehensive Test of Futures Market Disequilibrium", *The Financial Review*, 25(4), 593–622.

Madhavan, A.N. (1992), "Trading Mechanisms in Securities Markets", *Journal of Finance*, 47, 607–641.

Markowitz, H.M. and Xu, G.L. (1994), "Data Mining Corrections", *Journal of Portfolio Management*, Fall 60–69.

Neftci, S.N. (1991), "Naive Trading Rules in Financial Markets and Wiener-Kolmogorov Prediction Theory: A Study of Technical Analysis", *Journal of Business*, 64, 549–571.

Neftci, S.N. and Policano, A.J. (1984), "Can Chartists Outperform the Market? Market Efficiency Tests for Technical Analysis", *Journal of Futures Markets*, 4(4), 465–478.

Parkinson, M. (1980), "The Extreme Value Method for Estimating the Variance of the Rate of Return", *Journal of Business*, 53, 61–66.

Pictet, O.V., Dacorogna, M.M., Müller, U.A., Olsen, R.B. and Ward, J.R. (1992), "Real-time Trading Models for Foreign Exchange Rates", *Neural Network World*, 2(6), 713–744.

Prado, R. (1992), *Design, Testing, and Optimization of Trading Systems*, John Wiley and Sons.

Praetz, P.D. (1976), "Rates of Return on Filter Tests", *Journal of Finance*, 31, 71–75.

Pruitt, S.W. and White, R.E. (1988), "The CRISMA Trading System: Who Says Technical Analysis Can't Beat the Market", *Journal of Portfolio Management*, Spring, 55–58.

Pruitt, S.W., Tse, K.M. and White, R.E. (1992), "The CRISMA Trading System: The Next Five Years", *Journal of Portfolio Management*, Spring, 22–25.

Richardson, M. and Smith, T. (1994), "A Unified Approach to Testing for Serial Correlation in Stock Returns", *Journal of Business*, 67(3), 371–399.

Roll, R. (1984), "A Simple Implicit Measure of the Effective Bid-ask Spread in an Efficient Market", *Journal of Finance*, 39, 1127–1139.

Rogers, L.C. and Satchell, S.E. (1991), "Estimating Variance from High, Low, and Closing Prices", *Annals of Applied Probability*, 1, 504–512.

Satchell, S. and Timmermann, A. (1992), *An Assessment of the Economic Value of Nonlinear Foreign Exchange Rate Forecasts*, Discussion papers in Financial Economics, Birkbeck College, University of London, September.

Schulmeister, S. (1988), "Currency Speculations and Dollar Fluctuations", *Banco Nationale del Lavaro, Quaterly Review*, 167 December, 343–366.

Schwager, J. (1984), *A Complete Guide to the Futures Markets*, John Wiley and Sons.

Silber, W. (1994), "Technical Trading: When it Works and When it Doesn't", *The Journal of Derivatives*, Spring, 39–44.

Stevenson, R.A. and Bear, R.M. (1976), "Reply to P.D. Praëtz", *Journal of Finance*, 31, 980–983.

Surujaras, P. and Sweeney, R.J. (1992), "Profit-making Speculation in Foreign Exchange Markets", *The Political Economy of Global Interdependence*, Westview Press.

Stoll, H. (1978), "The Supply of Dealer Services in Securities Markets", *Journal of Finance*, 33, 1133–1152.

Sweeney, R.J. (1986), "Beating the Foreign Exchange Market", *Journal of Finance*, 41, 163–182.

Taylor, S.J. (1980), "Conjectured Models for Trends in Financial Prices, Tests and Forecasts", *J.R. Statist. Soc. A*, 143, 338–362.

Taylor, S.J. (1986), *Modelling Financial Time Series*, Chichester, UK: John Wiley and Sons.

Taylor, S.J. (1990a), "Reward Available to Currency Futures Speculators: Compensation for Risk or Evidence of Inefficient Pricing?", *Economic Record (supplement)*, 68, 105–116.

Taylor, S.J. (1990b), "Profitable Currency Futures Trading: A Comparison of Technical and Time-series Trading Rules", in L.R Thomas (ed.), *The Currency Hedging Debate*, IFR Publishing Ltd., London, 203–239.

Taylor, S.J. (1992), "Efficiency of the Yen Futures Market at the Chicago Mercantile Exchange", in B. A Goss (ed.), *Rational Expectations and Efficiency in Future Markets*, 109–128.

Taylor, S.J. (1994), "Trading Futures Using the Channel Rule: A Study of the Predictive Power of Technical Analysis with Currency Examples", *Journal of Futures Markets*, 14(2), 215–235.

Wong, Y.K. and Koh, A. (1994), "Technical Analysis of Nikkei 225 Stock Index Futures Using an Expert System Advisor", *Review of Futures Markets*, 1005–1025.

Zask, E. (1993), "Currency Management", in A.W. Gitlin (ed.), *Strategic Currency Investing*, London: Probus Publishing, 47–92.

Part III

High Frequency Financial Series and Market Practitioners Applications

The Sources, Preparation and Use of High Frequency Data in the Derivatives Markets

Paul MacGregor

LIFFE Market Data Services

INTRODUCTION

Much has been written in recent years about the benefits of using high frequency data to analyse financial markets, rather than the traditional daily open, high, low, close information. A lot of interest has been generated by both academics and traders alike; traders are trying to analyse intra-day movements on price historically to "back-test" theories and therefore improve trading performance; academics are generally trying to illustrate a theoretical point which they hope will be proven by increasing the data set.

The majority of the drive to make exchanges and other organisations deliver good, clean, historical tick data, has come from a particularly technically advanced section of the trading community, loosely referred to as the "alternative investments industry". It is made up of hedge funds, commodity trading advisors, corporate treasurers, mutual funds, unit trusts and pension fund managers. Depending on size, all will have positions in the major financial and commodity markets (both cash and derivative), in order to maximise returns for their investors, whilst trying to minimise the downside of investment risk. This section of the trading community, depending on their relative technical bias, will employ entire departments to purchase, clean and analyse data, spending huge budgets in the process. The driving force behind the release of LIFFE Tick Data on CD-Rom (September 1995) and the re-launch of the "LIFFE*data*" historical CD-Roms (March 1998) was demand from this section of the trading community. Indeed, some of the most technically advanced managed futures professionals will not consider trading a particular market without

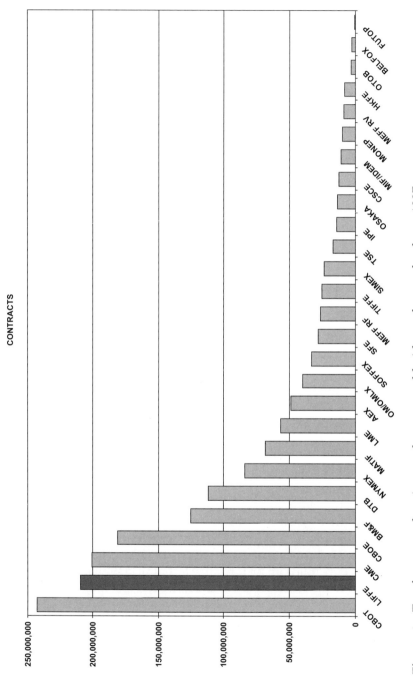

Figure 1 Top futures and options exchanges worldwide total annual volume 1997.

access to historical Tick Data. There is strong evidence that LIFFE's delivery of Tick Data on CD-Rom has been a major contributory factor to the growth in volumes over 1996 and 1997, and the subsequent movement into the number two spot in the world futures and options exchanges ranking (Figure 1).

However, little attention has been paid to the onerous task of collecting this data and preparing it in such a way that it is useful to the analyst. After all, Tick Data is no longer a product which can only be used by highly sophisticated market specialists; the growth in desktop computing power has meant that individuals can now download, access and analyse millions of records in a very short period of time.

The first section of this chapter gives an overview of how tick data is generated on different markets; the second part deals with the highly sophisticated software developed by LIFFE to deal with high frequency data.

What is Tick Data?

Even the terminology can be confusing—I have been asked in the past "What is the difference between time and sales, Tick Data and intra-day data?" The answer is—essentially nothing! But for the purist, here is a definition:

1. Tick Data—All bids, offers and trades timestamped, including flags (i.e. alpha markers indicating daily highs and lows).
2. Time and Sales—All trades with timestamps.
3. Intra-day Data—trades with timestamps which are between the open and close, but not necessarily every trade—often minute by minute.
4. Timebar Data—intra-day open, high, low and close information, usually displayed in 5, 15, 30 or 60 minute bars.

Definitions 2–4 are therefore a variation on the underlying theme, that every quote that is sent down a real-time feed, captured historically, constitutes "Tick Data".

How is Tick Data Generated?

There are three main types of market which generate Tick Data in the derivatives industry; open outcry, automated trading and over-the-counter

(OTC). As LIFFE is a hybrid exchange, having both open outcry and automated sessions, I am lucky enough to have witnessed the generation of Tick Data first hand.[1]

OPEN OUTCRY

In open outcry markets, prices are "discovered" by traders registering—often shouting—bids and offers with pit observers. At LIFFE, the pit observers have distinctive blue jackets to differentiate themselves from the other brightly coloured jackets of the traders on the LIFFE floor. The pit observers, whilst insuring that all behaviour in the pit conforms with the rules of the market, will also report prices, in real time, via microphones, to price reporters, who are located off the trading floor.

Pit Observers at LIFFE are obliged to report price, whether the price represents a bid, offer, or trade, and the delivery month to which that bid, offer or trade refers to. Delivery months are typically referred to by colours—e.g. "Blue" refers to the highest traded delivery month in the nearest year, "White" refers to the remaining delivery months in the nearest year, whilst "Red", "Green" and "Gold" refer to further delivery months, respectively. The annotation of using colours instead of actual calendar months and years whilst reporting prices improves the price reporting process.

There will be a number of Price Reporters per contract, and in contracts where a large amount of delivery months are traded, e.g. Three Month Euromark Future, there will be several Pit Observers and Price Reporters assigned to differing delivery months. Price reporters, on receiving the information direct from the trading floor, will then enter the prices, in real-time, into terminals. The average delay in prices being voice transmitted from Pit Observer to Price Reporter and being entered into a Price Reporting terminal, *is less than one second*. The data from Price Reporting terminals is then disseminated to Quote Vendors, who redistribute the data worldwide. At the end of the day price reporting files are transferred to a secure area. The data within the files at LIFFE is retrospectively enhanced, using an algorithm that matches deleted quotes with their previous erroneous entries. Via this methodology, all deleted quotes are flagged with a "D", so that a user of Tick Data can be entirely aware of deletions and exclude them from their analysis. Occasionally, users of Tick Data will want to see deletions from the feed in order to check that erroneous bids/offers or trades—perhaps noted by themselves during the trading day—have been deleted. Generally speaking, the high volumes and high frequency of quotes associated with open outcry trading, generating a high volume data set for end users, leads to useful and meaningful analysis by both traders, quantitative analysts and academics alike. This more than outweighs the occurrence of errors in price reporting, especially if exchanges are diligent in retrospectively correcting their Tick Data.

AUTOMATED TRADING

Automated trading is a completely different trading method to open outcry; there is no trading floor, and the role of the pit observer is no longer to report prices but to observe orders as they are matched and ensure an orderly marketplace.

LIFFE's Automated Pit Trading Session runs from 16:20 to 18:00 GMT, with some time variation amongst contracts, for all financial futures. The Japanese Government Bond (JGB) trades on APT all day, as does the Euroyen, Bund and BTP futures contracts.

The idea of the LIFFE APT screen (Figure 2) is to replicate the trading floor as much as possible. The system can be used as an order book (i.e. you enter your bid or offer in the hope that it will be matched at a later time) or an order matching system (i.e. you match an earlier bid/offer with your own bid/offer).

As can be seen from the above screen, two delivery months in the same contract can be displayed on one APT screen, therefore facilitating the possibility of spread trading. Best bids and offers, with volumes, are entered in the centre of each screen. The traders "in the pit" are dotted around each screen with their company and trader mnemonics. Their current bids and offers are displayed at the bottom and top of their trader "blocks" respectively.

Collection of tick data in an automated trading system is fully computerised as one would expect. There is no call for price reporters, and prices are collected from APT and appended to the Tick Data files generated from the trading floor.

In February 1998, LIFFE announced that LIFFE CONNECT^{TM}, the new electronic trading platform for individual equity options, will be launched on November 30 1998. The market will operate in an anonymous, order driven environment with orders matching according to a strict price and time priority. The new environment is expected to increase the overall

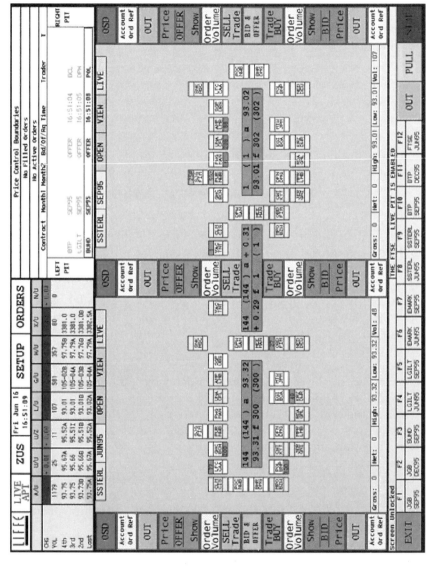

Figure 2 LIFFE APT (Automated Pit Trading) screen

quality of the market bringing significant benefits to users of individual equity options.

FOREIGN EXCHANGE

Another area where large streams of data are collected in the financial markets is foreign exchange. The foreign exchange forwards and swaps market in London alone is vast, estimated at $464 bn, nominal average daily turnover in 1996.[2] In the UK, all dealing is done on an "Over the Counter" basis—i.e. no exchange acts as an intermediary. In this marketplace, dealers at their individual desks enter bids and offers into electronic dealing systems. A proprietary network of ticker prices, therefore, is created in the process, and this can be distributed on request by information vendors. The major global distributor of proprietary currency quotes is Reuters.

There are two areas in which Reuters collect and distribute data on the OTC currency markets, *Contributed Rates* and *Dealt Rates*.

Reuters contributed rates system is a mechanism whereby major market makers will input prices for currencies in the market. Prices can be sent to individual records containing prices for one specific instrument e.g. Deutschmark, or contributors can choose to include price data with textual commentary/information on individual pages.

Reuters then consolidates the data and outputs to records with labelled fields e.g. bid/offer. These fields of data can then be used by market participants in other applications—e.g. spreadsheets. The contributed rates are indicative prices of what may be on offer in the marketplace dependent on size of trade and counterparty. The rates are updated on a real-time basis with the latest quote superceding the previous ones; prices are sourced from Banks and Brokers globally. The integrity of prices is maintained through spread and jump checks based on moving averages, e.g. a price with a spread of 10 pips or greater will be rejected from the consolidated quote. The level of checks in place will depend on the market conditions.

Dealt rates are sourced from a separate network, Reuters Dealing 2002, then displayed on information screens (Figure 3). In this case the output is from actual matched trades conducted over the Reuters D2002 system. Top of the book bid and offer are also included. Subscribers must be active participants on D2002 to have access to these rates.

As regards history, Reuters Graphics system (Figure 4) contains ten years of monthly data, five years of weekly data and two years of daily

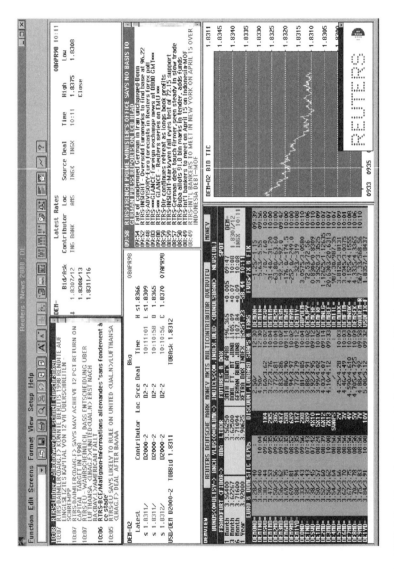

Figure 3   DEM dealt and contributed rates via Reuters 2000.

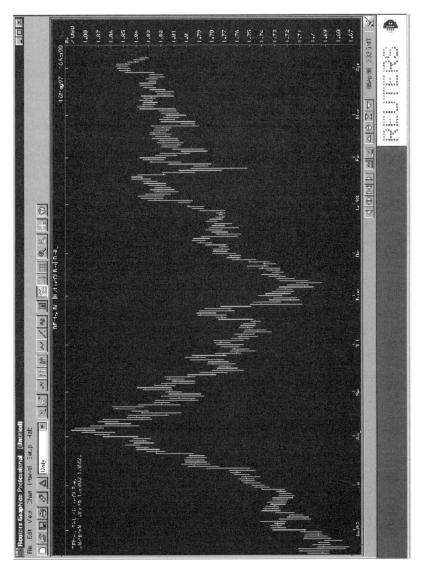

Figure 4   Typical Reuters' graphics currency screen.

data. The historical data along with real-time prices can be accessed via a number of Reuters' products such as the Reuters 3000 series.

SOURCING AND PREPARING LIFFE TICK DATA

So how does an individual deal with such enormous streams of data? Typically, there are 10 million quotes on the LIFFE market in the space of one year (or nearly 40,000 per day), equalling about 170 MB of data per contract. This is not easy to prepare or analyse, so exchanges and data vendors have begun to look at ways of viewing and extracting such large streams of data.

In this section, I will discuss the viewing and extraction software LIFFE uses for its historical data, known as "LIFFE*style*".

LIFFE*style*

LIFFE originally developed and pioneered Tick Data on CD-Rom in September 1995. Since then we have worked hard to continuously improve our historical data product range, and develop products that meet customer demands. Feedback from customers has focused on the fact that data quality was good, but the speed and "ease of use" of the viewing and extraction software was poor. As a result, LIFFE contracted Intelligent Financial Systems Ltd (see Chapter 13) to write a new viewing and extraction software, which we have called "LIFFE*style*".

As an end user, it is extremely hard to choose correctly the period of tick data to analyse. You may, for example, wish to analyse certain periods of high market volatility—but how are you to identify these periods without downloading and viewing large amounts of data initially? As mentioned above, this can be an overlong process, so LIFFE*style* delivers visualisation at the very start-up of the software. The idea is to "view" tick data immediately upon entering the software, rather than selecting your date range, exporting the data and then discovering you required a differing time period. In this case, the user has selected the year 1996 to study using the slider bars to select the required time period (Figure 5).

By clicking on the "Apply" icon, the user has selected the entire year of 1996 Gilt Futures, tick by tick, to analyse. The time delay between selecting the entire year of 1996 (nearly 2 m records) and the construction of the chart of each delivery month is approximately 3–4 minutes.

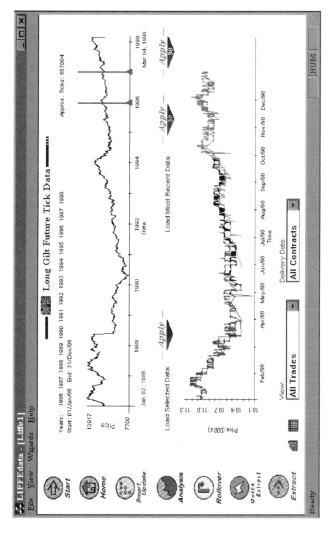

Figure 5 Viewing all delivery months for 1996.

The user actually views each of the delivery months on the same chart, but this is not the only option available. As can be seen from the dialog box below the "Applied" chart, all trades are currently being viewed, but there are many more options—1 minute, 5-minute, 15-minute, 30-minute and 60-minute samples can all be selected and viewed. In the following example, I have chosen 15-minutely samples.

We have now created a continuous time series of the Gilt Futures contract in 1996, over 15 minutely time periods (Figure 6). This entire process has taken the end user around 5–6 minutes, whereas using the normal methods of preparing tick data would have taken considerably longer. Estimates as to how much longer vary—but I have been quoted between several hours and two days!

Another lengthy process when preparing historical futures data for analysis is the creation of a "continuous contract". This is the method by which individual quarterly expiry months are "strung together" to make analysis of a long time series possible. Normally, an historical data user would download several years of data, choose his/her rollover strategy, and apply it, using some not insignificant data manipulation skills. But what is a rollover strategy? There are many differing methodologies that can be used, varying from volume crossover (i.e. the volume in the far contract overtakes that in the near contract), volume threshold (i.e. the volume in the far contract rises above a certain threshold level) to a fixed date. These features are fully complemented in the LIFFE*style* software, and save the end user precious time whilst being very flexible.

As can be seen from the screenshot (Figure 7), the default rollover strategy used by LIFFE*style* is a daily check on when the far contract volume rises above the near contract volume. When this occurs, the software will automatically rollover the prices. Pushing the "Rollover Analysis" key will deliver a text file letting us know which exact dates were employed (Table 1).

Having created our own continuous contract and evaluated the rollover points, the user may want to do some further analysis, whilst still in the LIFFE*style* package prior to exporting the data. At the time of writing, the LIFFE*style* software includes such indicators as historical volume, intra-day volume, returns history and returns distribution.

The shape of intraday volume gives the analyst a clear idea of when the most active periods take place throughout the day. As can be seen from Figure 8, trading activity is high at the open, steadily declines towards lunchtime, then picks up rapidly in the early afternoon. A factor which contributes to explaining this pattern is the opening of the US markets in the afternoon GMT.

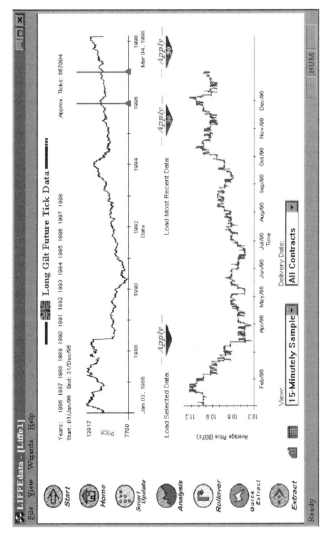

Figure 6 Viewing 1996 gilt futures tick data in 15 minute samples.

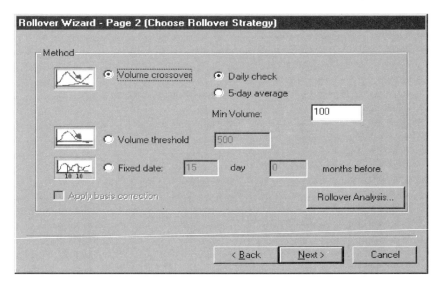

Figure 7   The LIFFE*style* rollover wizard.

Table 1   Rollover analysis of the daily volume check on the gilt futures contract in 1996.

Total Rollovers: 3
Rollover 1 occured at date Mon, Mar-04, 1996 Near Contract: Mar96 Far Contract: Jun96 Near Volume: 10364 Far Volume: 12724 Near Price: 10800.0 Far Price: 10713.0
Rollover 2 occured at date Tue, Jun-04, 1996 Near Contract: Jun96 Far Contract: Sep96 Near Volume: 13829 Far Volume: 18554 Near Price: 10606.0 Far Price: 10505.0
Rollover 3 occured at date Thu, Sep-05, 1996 Near Contract: Sep96 Far Contract: Dec96 Near Volume: 7523 Far Volume: 20863 Near Price: 10628.0 Far Price: 10604.0

The Returns distribution of the Gilt shown in (Figure 9) yields the typical "bell shaped" normal distribution—though with very long tails.

Many users, particularly of high frequency data, have their own advanced trading packages that evaluate all the technical indicators that they require, once they have exported the data. For the more advanced end users therefore, technical indicators are not required, but simply a "Quick Extract" function, which allows the data to be downloaded virtually instantly.

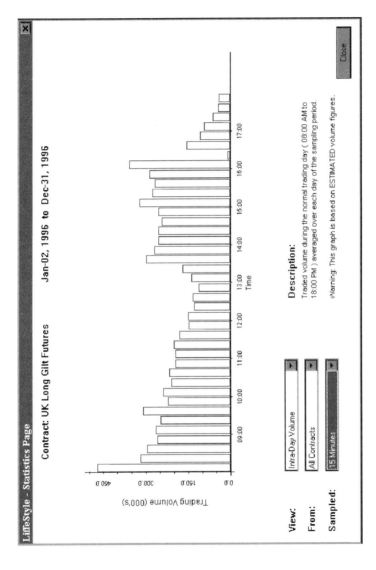

Figure 8 Intra-day volume in the gilt futures contract 1996.

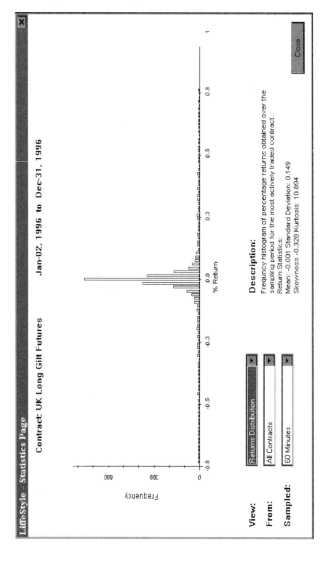

Figure 9   Returns distribution of the gilt futures contract 1996.

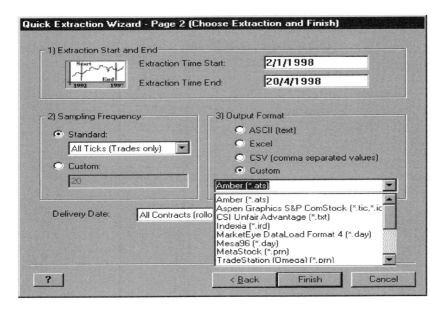

Figure 10   The LIFFE*style* Quick Extraction Wizard.

In the above example (Figure 10), the end user has chosen to extract all Gilt Futures Tick Data for 1996, in 15-minutely samples, into Amber Software. This "quick extract" facility allows advanced users of Tick Data to simply go in to the software and get out the data they require very quickly.

One of the most common questions posed by historical data users to LIFFE over the years has been "Will it work in my favourite trading software package?" Hence LIFFE have made the effort to contact and sign up the major third party application providers worldwide. At the time of writing, LIFFE*style* will export into the following custom built data formats:

Amber
Aspen Graphics S&P Comstock
CSI Unfair Advantage
Indexia
MarketEye Dataload Format 4
Mesa
Metastock
Tradestation (Omega).

There are a couple more levels of functionality at hand when using the Full Extraction Wizard (Figure 11).

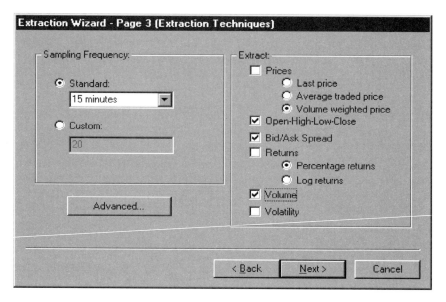

Figure 11 Defining differing outputs in the Extraction Wizard.

In Figure 11, the end user has defined again a 15-minute frequency, but has also had the opportunity to define the display to be Open, High, Low, Close, with Bid/Ask spreads and Volumes also displayed.

CONCLUSION

The use of high frequency data for trading has become increasingly popular over recent years; this has been driven by:

- The growth of technical trading within the alternative investment industry
- The recognition by exchanges of the value of "Tick Data"
- The growth in desktop computing power

LIFFE, a pioneer in the provision of Tick Data to historical data users, has seen significant benefits in terms of rising contract volumes, and the message from end users has been clear: make good, clean historical Tick Data available, and we will continue to look at your marketplace. The preparation of Tick Data into a format that becomes useful to the end user is a considerable process. Once the correct period for useful analysis has been chosen, continuous contracts need to be created and the data must be exported quickly into a useful format. LIFFE has recognized the above issues and is confronting them via a sophisticated software application called "LIFFE*style*".

NOTES

1. Information on the generation of Tick Data into OTC FX markets was supplied by Mark Beerts at Reuters.
2. Survey conducted by the Bank of England in Spring 1996.

BIBLIOGRAPHY

Bank of England (1955–6), *"Survey into the OTC Derivatives Market."*
Beerts, M. (1996) *"Product Manager Money 2000"*, London: Reuters.
Lequeux, P. (1997) "On the Impact of High Frequency Data in the Financial Markets", *Derivatives Use, Trading and Regulation*, 3(2).
Wurtz, D., Schnidrig, R. and Labermeier, H. (1995) "Archiving of High Frequency Data from Global Financial Markets", *IPS Research Report.*

Chapter **12**

The Design of a Quantitative Currency Overlay Program

Haijo H. J. Dijkstra, Marcel A. L. Vernooy and Dr Tjark Tjin

Rabobank International

INTRODUCTION

Seeking higher and more stable returns, fund managers increasingly diversify their portfolios by investing in foreign assets. Inherent in any foreign investment, however, is a foreign currency position. Of course international investors are well aware of this fact. Usually they deal with it by passively hedging their FX-positions. That is, given their foreign exchange position, they sell forward a fixed part of their exposure against the home currency. Usually this forward sale does not involve the full amount, for even though this would eliminate most of the FX-risk, it also eliminates a large part of the benefits of foreign investments. For example, consider a Dutch investor who has, in order to benefit from the high interest rates in the US, invested in an American zero-coupon bond paying 10 USD one year from now. In doing so, the Dutch investor has acquired a USD position. By selling forward 10 USD, the investor can eliminate his exposure to dollars. However, at the same time he then removes the benefits of investing abroad, because he could have received the same return by putting his money on deposit in a Dutch bank: the return is simply the risk free interest rate in the home currency. Furthermore, if during the year the dollar were to strengthen, the investor would not benefit at all. It is for these reasons that investors usually take a more moderate view and hedge only part of their FX-exposure. In the example, the Dutch investor might have sold forward only 5 USD.

In general, currency positions are perceived as unwanted by-products of international investment. Fund managers are interested in picking stocks and bonds, not in taking currency positions. Nevertheless, they inevitably and passively do. The question therefore arises, whether a more active approach to the currency position inside an internationally diversified portfolio might be fruitful in decreasing foreign exchange risk without eliminating the benefits of international investment. This chapter deals with such an approach.

The approach presented is purely quantitative. Discretionary trading is not allowed. Trading decisions are made by trading models relying on high frequency data. This paper concentrates on the theory behind a currency overlay program *based on* trading models. Furthermore, special emphasis is given to practical matters. It is possible to actually implement the overlay program described in this chapter. The most important legal and accounting constraints are addressed.

The question that is answered in this chapter is how foreign exchange trading models can be used to construct effective currency overlay strategies. It is always assumed that the underlying investment portfolio is given by the client. The overlay program then superimposes on this portfolio a set of static hedges and trading models that together dynamically hedge the currency exposures. The weights that are given to the trading models and the static hedges are calculated by the overlay program based on the principle that the risk should be minimized, for a given return. The trades initiated by the trading models are then executed in the forward market.

The currency overlay programs described in this chapter are based on the ideas developed in Müller (1994) and Lundin *et al.* (1997). The trading models that are used have been developed by Olsen and Associates.

Pages 325 to 333 of this paper introduce the necessary theoretical background behind the design of quantitative currency overlay programs. The rationale behind investments in currencies and an example of performance obtained by such a program is provided at pp 336 to 340.

TRADING MODELS

This section provides a formal setting for trading models and their risk/return characteristics. It is not meant to be a description of how to build trading models. As we want to show how trading models can be used to construct overlay strategies, we need to define first what it means to speak about the return and risk of a trading model.

Let X^α and X^β be two currencies,[1] that is a currency pair. The exchange rate related to this currency pair, denoted by $S^{\alpha\beta}$, is a process[2] such that $S^{\alpha\beta}$ is a positive real number for all $t \in [T_I, T_F]$ (where $T_I < T_F$ are positive numbers[3]). Below we always use the convention that 1 unit of currency X^α is equal in value to $S^{\alpha\beta}(t)$ units of currency X^β at time t.

Other relevant processes are the term structure of interest rates and the forward rates. Denote by $R^\alpha(t; T)$ the (annualized) interest rate on a zero coupon bond denominated in currency X^α and maturing at time T. The forward rate for a forward contract maturing at time T is then given by

$$F^{\alpha\beta}(t;T) = S^{\alpha\beta}(t)\frac{[1 + R^\beta(t;T)(T-t)]}{[1 + R^\alpha(t;T)(T-t)]}, \qquad 1$$

where the unit of time is 1 year. In this paper it is assumed that all trading is done in the forward market.

Let $Y = \{0, \pm\frac{1}{2}, \pm 1\}$. A trading model $TM^{(\alpha\beta)}$ in the currency pair (X^α, X^β) consists of a process $g^{(\alpha\beta)}$, such that $g^{(\alpha\beta)}(t) \in Y$ for all $t \in [T_I, T_F]$, together with a positive number $l^{(\alpha\beta)}$. For reasons that will become clear in a moment, the process $g^{(\alpha\beta)}$ is called the 'gearing process', while $l^{(\alpha\beta)}$ is called the 'trading limit' of the trading model. Furthermore, X^α is called the 'trading limit currency', while X^β is called the 'P&L currency' of $TM^{(\alpha\beta)}$.

The process $g^{(\alpha\beta)}(t)$ represents the gearing of the trading model at time t. The fact that the model has gearing $g^{(\alpha\beta)}(t)$ actually means that, at time t, the X^α account contains an (unrealized) amount of $l^{(\alpha\beta)}g^{(\alpha\beta)}(t)$, if the account started out with 0 at $t = T_I$. Now, suppose there are gearing changes at times $\{t^{(k)}\}_{k=0}^N$, where $T_I \leq t^{(0)} < \cdots < t^{(N)} \leq T_F$, then[4] the X^β account will contain an (unrealized) amount[5] of

$$-l^{(\alpha\beta)}\sum_{k=0}^N [g^{(\alpha\beta)}(t^{(k)}) - g^{(\alpha\beta)}(t^{(k-1)})]F^{\alpha\beta}(t^{(k)};T_F). \qquad 2$$

Here, of course, $t^{(-1)} = 0$.

Let us now consider the total value of the position the trading model is in at time $T_I \leq t \leq T_F$. Denote by $f^{\alpha\beta}(t;t',T)$ the value at time t of a foreign exchange forward contract, entered into at time t' and maturing at time T, to buy 1 unit of currency X^α in exchange for $F^{\alpha\beta}(t';T)$ units of currency X^β. It is well known to follow from no-arbitrage arguments (see Appendix A) that

$$f^{\alpha\beta}(t;t',T) = \frac{S^{\alpha\beta}(t)}{[1 + R^\alpha(t,T)(T-t)]} - \frac{F^{\alpha\beta}(t',T)}{[1 + R^\beta(t,T)(T-t)]}. \qquad 3$$

The value of the position at time t, measured in the currency X^β, is then

$$l^{(\alpha\beta)}\sum_{k=0}^N [g^{(\alpha\beta)}(t^{(k)}) - g^{(\alpha\beta)}(t^{(k-1)})]f^{\alpha\beta}(t;t^{(k)},T_F). \qquad 4$$

Often the home currency of the investor is not equal to the P&L currency of the trading model. Let X^0 be the home currency of the investor, then the unrealized profit of the trading model position at time t in the home currency is given by

$$L^{(\alpha\beta)}C^{(\alpha\beta)}(t; T_I, T_F), \qquad\qquad 5$$

where

$$C^{(\alpha\beta)}(t; T_I, T_F) = \frac{S^{\beta 0}(t)}{S^{\alpha 0}(T_I)} \sum_{k=0}^{N} [g^{(\alpha\beta)}(t^{(k)}) - g^{(\alpha\beta)}(t^{(k-1)})] f^{\alpha\beta}(t; t^{(k)}, T_F), \qquad 6$$

for $T_I \leq t \leq T_F$, and $L^{(\alpha\beta)} = l^{(\alpha\beta)}S^{\alpha 0}(T_I)$. Note that $L^{(\alpha\beta)}$ is denominated in home currency, while $l^{(\alpha\beta)}$ is denominated in X^α. So, $C^{(\alpha\beta)}(t; T_I, T_F)$ is the value at time t of the trading model position if the exposure limit that is given to the trading model at time T_I is equivalent to 1 unit of home currency at that time.

Now, let Δt be some time interval. From now on, $\Delta t = (T_F - T_I)/M$, for some (preferably large) number M. Usually Δt will be one week or one month. The change in the value of the trading model $TM^{(\alpha\beta)}$, per unit home currency, over a period of length Δt is[6]

$$D^{(\alpha\beta)}(t; T_I, T_F) = C^{(\alpha\beta)}(t; T_I, T_F) - C^{(\alpha\beta)}(t - \Delta t; T_I, T_F). \qquad 7$$

For notational convenience, $t_k = T_I + k\Delta t$, where $k = 0, 1, \ldots, N$, and $D_k^{(\alpha\beta)} \equiv D^{(\alpha\beta)}(t_k; T_I, T_F)$.

Above we expressed trading model profit in terms of forward contracts maturing at time T_F. Now, T_F might be several years in the future. In the actual execution of an overlay strategy, however, forward contracts that mature at most one year from now are used. Long forwards are approximated by successively rolling over several short forwards. In principle these procedures are not strictly equivalent, as shown in Appendix 2, due to unknown changes in the term structure. Here we assume, for simplicity, that the term structure remains approximately constant.

HEDGING CURRENCY EXPOSURES

In this section we will discuss how trading models can be used to construct overlay strategies. Essentially this boils down to superimposing on the original portfolio a set of static hedges and trading models. These together dynamically hedge the currency exposure embedded in the underlying investments.

Static Hedges

Let $P(t)$ denote the value in home currency of an internationally diversified investment portfolio. It consists of a set of foreign assets denominated in their own currency. In currency X^α there may be several distinct investments. In the USD there may, for example, be bond investments and stock investments. Let $A^{(\alpha,m)}(t)$ be the value in currency X^α of the mth asset. The total value at time t of the investment portfolio in the home currency is then

$$P(t) = \sum_\alpha \sum_m A^{(\alpha,m)}(t) S^{\alpha 0}(t).$$

8

This investment portfolio is considered to be given. Usually the stock and bond picking is done by the investor himself or by his asset manager. As one can clearly see from equation 8, there are two sources of risk: risk due to the fact that the value of an asset may fluctuate relative to the currency in which it is denominated, and risk related to foreign exchange fluctuations against the home currency. It is the latter risk factor that currency overlay tries to address.

The usual way foreign exchange risk is dealt with, is by superimposing on the primary investment a set of forward contracts to sell forward (part of) the foreign exchange exposure. In other words, one adds to the primary investment a portfolio of forward contracts. The static-hedge portfolio then becomes

$$P_s(t; \mathbf{h}) = \sum_\alpha h^{(\alpha)} H^{(\alpha)} f^{\alpha 0}(t; T_I, T_F),$$

9

where it was assumed that the time at which the hedge was initiated was T_I. Furthermore, $-1 \le h^\alpha \le 0$ and $\mathbf{h} = \{h^\alpha\}$. These are the "hedge ratios". The quantities H^α are chosen differently by different investors and for different assets. Often H^α is chosen to be the value at time $t = T_I$ of the original investment portfolio, that is

$$H^{(\alpha)} = \sum_m A^{(\alpha,m)}(T_I).$$

10

On the other hand, this choice will not lead to a so called 'future value hedge'. That is, any changes in the value of the underlying asset compared to the currency in which it is denominated will lead to additional FX-exposures. In Appendix 3 it is shown that the risk is minimized by choosing $h^\alpha = -1$ and

$$H^{(\alpha)} = \sum_m E[A^{(\alpha,m)}(T_F)],$$

11

which is the expected value at the end of the period of the investments denominated in currency X^α.

Many investors use portfolios of forward contracts in the way described above. Usually all the hedge ratios $h^{(\alpha)}$ are chosen to be equal. Often they are all chosen to be equal to, or close to, $-\frac{1}{2}$. It is fair to say, however, that this choice is based usually on not much more than the argument that $-\frac{1}{2}$ sounds like a nice compromise between 0 and -1.

Currency Overlay

The next and crucial step in a currency overlay program, is to superimpose on $P_s(t)$ a set of trading models, which form the dynamic part of the overlay strategy. Suppose that there are associated with each currency pair (X^α, X^β) a number of trading models $TM^{(\alpha\beta;p)}$, where $p = 1, \ldots, n^{(\alpha\beta)}$. Then the total unrealized profit of the trading models at time t is given by

$$P_D(t; \mathbf{L}) \equiv \sum_{\alpha > \beta} \sum_{p=1}^{n^{(\alpha\beta)}} L^{(\alpha\beta;p)} C^{(\alpha\beta;p)}(t; T_I, T_F), \qquad 12$$

where $\mathbf{L} = \{L^{(\alpha\beta;p)}\}$. Adding this portfolio of trading models to $P_s(t)$ one obtains the currency overlay portfolio

$$\Pi(t; \mathbf{h}, \mathbf{L}) = P(t) + P_S(t; \mathbf{h}) + P_D(t; \mathbf{L}). \qquad 13$$

CONSTRAINTS AND RESTRICTIONS

The objective is to optimize Π $(t; \mathbf{h}, \mathbf{L})$ in some sense. There are, however, certain constraints that need to be dealt with. These arise due to accounting rules, laws or simply investment policy. In this section, we will consider some of the most important constraints encountered in the market place.

No-Proxy Hedging

Let C be the set of all currencies. Furthermore, let C_P be the set of currencies represented in the underlying investment portfolio. That is, C_P is the set of all $\alpha \in C$ such that $A^{(\alpha,m)}(T_I) > 0$ for at least one m. No-proxy hedging means that $l^{(\alpha\beta;p)}$ is constrained to zero whenever either α or β is not an element of C_P.

Over-Hedging

According to most investors, the realized and/or unrealized position in each currency may not exceed a certain maximum, nor can it fall below some minimum (usually zero). The unrealized position in, or equivalently, the exposure to currency X^α due to the positions of the trading models, is

$$E_D^\alpha(t;1) \equiv \sum_{\beta<\alpha} \sum_m l^{(\alpha\beta;m)} g^{(\alpha\beta;m)}(t) - \sum_{\beta>\alpha} \sum_m sum_{k=0}^N l^{(\beta\alpha;m)}$$

$$\times [g^{\alpha\beta}(t^{(k)}) - g^{\alpha\beta}(t^{(k-1)})] F^{\beta\alpha}(t^{(k)};T_F) \qquad 14$$

Now, in most cases the client will restrict the currency overlay program such that, for all t,

$$0 \leq \left[\sum_p A^{(\alpha,p)}(t) + h^{(\alpha)}H^{(\alpha)} + E_D^\alpha(t;1) \right] \leq \sum_p A^{(\alpha,p)}(t). \qquad 15$$

In other words, the total exposure to currency X^α may never exceed the exposure due to the underlying investment portfolio. Furthermore, a long position may not be turned into a short position. Equation 15 is an awkward time dependent constraint. Usually the constraint imposed on an overlay program will be simplified to

$$-\sum_p A^{(\alpha,p)}(T_I \leq [h^{(\alpha)}H^{(\alpha)} + E_D^\alpha(t;1)] \leq 0. \qquad 16$$

Note that the constraints 15 and 16 both imply that proxy hedging is not allowed. For $\Sigma_p A^{(\alpha,p)}(T_I) = 0$, which means that there is no (net) exposure to currency X^α, then we *must* have $h^{(\alpha)} = 0$ and $E_D^\alpha(t) = 0$ due to the fact that $h^{(\alpha)}H^{(\alpha)}$ does not depend on t, while $E_D^\alpha(t)$ does.

Equations 15 and 16 cannot be satisfied in general. The reason for this is that $E_D^\alpha(t;1)$ is not bounded from above or below. If the model performs extremely well or badly, or if the forward rate changes dramatically, $|E_D^\alpha(t;1)|$ can become arbitrarily large. A way out of this predicament is to trade only against the home currency. That is, only consider the trading models $TM^{(\alpha0;m)}$. In that case $E_D^\alpha(t;1)$ reduces to

$$E_D^\alpha(t;1) = \sum_m l^{(\alpha0;m)} g^{(\alpha0;m)}(t), \alpha \neq 0, \qquad 17$$

which is bounded from above and below. All Profit and Losses (hence forth P&L) effects are then realized in the home currency X^0. Summarizing, the constraints that prevent overhedging are

$$l^{(\alpha\beta;p)} = 0 \qquad\qquad 18$$

when either α is not an element of C_P or $\beta \neq 0$. Furthermore, equation 16, with $E_D^{\alpha}(t; 1)$ given by (17), must be satisfied for all α. This means that

$$h^{(\alpha)} H^{(\alpha)} + \sum_m l^{(\alpha 0;m)} \leq 0 \qquad\qquad 19$$

and at the same time

$$\sum_m l^{(\alpha 0;m)} - h^{(\alpha)} H^{(\alpha)} \leq \sum_p A^{(\alpha,p)}(T_I). \qquad\qquad 20$$

Sometimes it will happen that an investor allows P&L to be realized in some currencies other than the home currency.[7] Let $I_{P\&L} = \{X^0, X^1, \ldots, X^M\}$ be the set of such currencies. Equation 16 can be satisfied by imposing the constraint $l^{(\alpha\beta;p)} = 0$ when either α is not a portfolio currency or β is not an element of $I_{P\&L}$. Again, if we impose this constraint, then for all $\alpha > M$ the exposure to currency X^α at time t is given by 17, while unknown and in principle unbounded P&L effects are generated in the currencies $X^0, X^1, \ldots, X^M$.

Constraints on the Static Hedge

These constraints arise when the investor stipulates that the static part of the hedge must be equal to, for example, his benchmark. In that case all $h^{(\alpha)}$ are fixed and the optimization is performed only over the set of trading limits $l^{(\alpha\beta;m)}$.

Rounding of Trading Limits

The trading limit $l^{(\alpha\beta;m)}$ is denominated in currency X^α. If the trading model $TM^{(\alpha\beta;m)}$ signals the trader to change his gearing for example from 0 to +1, then the trader will have to buy $l^{(\alpha\beta;m)}$ units of currency X^α. Due to market conventions, however, he will not be able to complete such a deal unless $l^{(\alpha\beta;m)}$ has a minimum size and is rounded to conform to market standards. This imposes two additional constraints on the optimization routine.

FINDING THE OPTIMAL OVERLAY STRATEGY

As was mentioned before, the objective is to optimize $\Pi(t; \mathbf{h}, \mathbf{L})$ in some sense. Precisely in what sense will be discussed now.

Once again denote $\Pi_k(\mathbf{h}, \mathbf{L}) = \Pi(t_k; \mathbf{h}, \mathbf{L})$ and let $B(t)$ be a (client specific) benchmark. The change in the value of Π from period $k-1$ to k, denoted $D_k(\mathbf{h}, \mathbf{L}) \equiv \Pi_k(\mathbf{h}, \mathbf{L}) - \Pi_{k-1}(\mathbf{h}, \mathbf{L})$, is given by

$$D_k(\mathbf{h}, \mathbf{L}) = \sum_{\alpha,m} R_k^{(\alpha,m)} + \sum_{\alpha} h^{(\alpha)} \tilde{H}^{(\alpha)} D_k^{(\alpha)} + \sum_{\alpha > \beta} \sum_p L^{(\alpha\beta;p)} D_k^{(\alpha\beta;p)}, \qquad 21$$

where

$$\tilde{H}^{(\alpha)} = H^{(\alpha)} S_0^{\alpha 0},$$

$$R_k^{(\alpha,m)} = A_k^{(\alpha,m)} S_k^{\alpha 0} - A_{k-1}^{(\alpha,m)} S_{k-1}^{\alpha 0}, \qquad 22$$

$$D_k^{(\alpha)} = \frac{f_k^{\alpha 0} - f_{k-1}^{\alpha 0}}{S_0^{\alpha 0}},$$

$$D_k^{(\alpha\beta;p)} = C_k^{(\alpha\beta;p)} - C_{k-1}^{(\alpha\beta;p)}.$$

Here we used the simplified notation $f_k^{\alpha 0} \equiv f^{\alpha 0}(t_k; T_I, T_F)$ and $C_k^{(\alpha\beta;p)} \equiv C^{(\alpha\beta;p)}(t_k; T_I, T_F)$. Note that $L^{(\alpha\beta;p)}$ and $\tilde{H}^{(\alpha)}$ are quantities denominated in home currency, in contrast to $l^{(\alpha\beta;p)}$ and $H^{(\alpha)}$, which are denominated in X^α. Similarly, we define the change in the benchmark by $D_k^B \equiv B_k - B_{k-1}$ and $\text{Out}_k(\mathbf{h}, \mathbf{L}) \equiv D_k(\mathbf{h}, \mathbf{L}) - D_k^B$. The average out-performance, tracking-error and t-value compared to the benchmark are then given by

$$\text{Out}(\mathbf{h}, \mathbf{L}) = \frac{1}{N} \sum_{k=1}^{N} \text{Out}_k(\mathbf{h}, \mathbf{L}),$$

$$\text{Track}(\mathbf{h}, \mathbf{L}) = \sqrt{\frac{1}{N-1} \sum_{k=1}^{N} [\text{Out}_k(\mathbf{h}, \mathbf{L}) - \text{Out}(\mathbf{h}, \mathbf{L})]^2},$$

$$t(\mathbf{h}, \mathbf{L}) = \sqrt{N} \frac{\text{Out}(\mathbf{h}, \mathbf{L})}{\text{Track}(\mathbf{h}, \mathbf{L})} \qquad (23)$$

Given a certain out-performance, one would like to find those $\mathbf{h}$ and $\mathbf{L}$ that minimize the tracking-error. Or conversely, given a tracking-error, one would like to optimize the out-performance. Furthermore, this optimization may be subject to some, or all, of the constraints discussed in the previous section.

In most cases, the benchmark is simply the underlying portfolio plus a certain static hedge. In other words,

$$B(t) = P(t) + P_s(t; \mathbf{h}_B),\tag{24}$$

where $\mathbf{h}_B$ are the static hedge ratios the client uses as benchmark. It is easy to show that the underlying investment portfolio drops out of the out-performance, and therefore from the entire optimization procedure, in that case. In fact, it reduces to

$$\text{Out}_k(\mathbf{h}, \mathbf{L}) = \sum_\alpha (h^{(\alpha)} - h_B^{(\alpha)}) \tilde{H}^{(\alpha)} D_k^{(\alpha)} + \sum_{\alpha > \beta} \sum_p L^{(\alpha\beta;p)} D_k^{(\alpha\beta;p)}.\tag{25}$$

This is a considerable simplification, for it means that we do not have to consider the correlation between the underlying portfolio performance and the static and dynamic parts of the overlay strategy. In other words, the performance of the underlying portfolio becomes irrelevant. It only enters the calculation through boundary conditions and constraints.

Having laid off the theoretical backgrounds necessary to understand the mechanics and constraints behind a quantitative currency overlay program we now look at the rationale for investment in currencies.

RATIONALE FOR INVESTMENTS IN CURRENCIES

Currencies are a Separate Asset Class

Currencies are weakly correlated to bond and stock markets, and are therefore treated as a separate asset class by professional investors. Currencies have their own dynamics, their own volatility patterns and their own risk and return profile. Most fund managers periodically decide how to protect the value of their investment portfolio against adverse movements in the underlying currencies. The reason is that the currency impact on the value of a bond or stock portfolio can be quite large. Taking a one month horizon, the effect of a currency movement in relation to the home currency varies between 30–90 percent of the monthly return, as illustrated by the following graph.

On a longer term horizon, the effect of currency movements on the value of investment portfolios is generally smaller, but can still be substantial. Clearly, active currency management is a necessity for professional investors, who wish to keep the risks and returns of their managed assets under control.

Currency decisions are commonly separated from investment decisions. Consequently, in the investment process, risk is not only allocated to

The Currency Factor

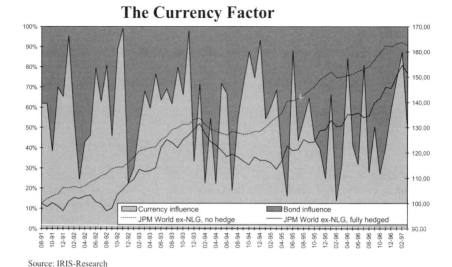

Source: IRIS-Research

Figure 1   Effect of currency movement on monthly returns.

stocks, bonds and real estate, but also to cash. In the past, currencies were seen as unwanted byproducts of international diversification of bond and stock portfolios. Nowadays, currencies are treated as a separate asset class and which active management can prove worthwhile.

Quantitative currency overlay specialists usually have a very clinical look with regard to hedging of FX-exposure or investing in specific currencies. Based on a huge database of high frequency tick-data, quantitative models are used to detect new trends in liquid currencies at a very early stage. In this way, value can be added. This approach can be used for both currency overlay as for currency investments. This quantitative approach works for the following reasons:

The Currency Market is Very Liquid, but not Efficient in the Short Term. The currency market is highly inefficient at short time intervals. This has been conclusively shown by using unprecedented databases of high frequency price data. The distribution of price changes 'looks' Gaussian only for weekly intervals. For shorter time lags the leptocurticity (fat tails) of the distribution increases, while its fourth moment starts to diverge. This is one manifestation of the more general result that FX markets are particularly less efficient when considered on time scales ranging from a few seconds to several weeks.

Long Term Memory Exists in FX Markets. The autocorrelation of absolute price changes declines hyperbolically (not exponentially) as the time lag increases, indicating long term memory. For periods of up to six weeks, auto-correlation in price returns is non-zero, even when correlation due to seasonal effects have been eliminated. Also, the Hurst coefficient is significantly larger than 0.5, effectively rejecting the efficient markets hypothesis. The properties described above are universal in the sense that they can be observed in all liquid and freely floating FX-markets.

Market Participants React Differently on New Information: Heterogeneous Markets Hypothesis. Market participants react differently on new information. According to the efficient markets hypothesis (EMH), prices only move when new information is received. When this happens, the financial markets are temporarily pushed out of equilibrium, causing the market participants to start adjusting their positions. This is done in response to the news, but also in response to each other's response, etc. In an efficient market this process converges quickly to a new equilibrium. In reality it is highly unlikely that exchange rates absorb news as quickly as implied by the EMH. One reason for this is the fact that markets are non-homogeneous. That is, not all market participants have the same objectives, time horizons and constraints. This causes them to react differently to new information, while their reaction times differ. A FX-trader will usually rebalance his position immediately, whereas pension funds usually invest strategically over longer time horizons.

They weigh and evaluate many news items and try to determine a medium-term and/or long-term strategy. As a consequence, the time lag between an individual news flash and the time at which the position is changed can be substantial for these types of investors.

Using the high frequency database, it is possible to uncover some of the mechanisms underlying the way in which information is propagated through the financial markets and the influence this has on rate movements. This makes statistical arbitrage possible, exploiting statistical market properties and inefficiencies on short time scales. This approach has its foundation in more then a decade of intensive empirical and mathematical research on the world's largest database of high frequency FX data. Using the high frequency database, it is possible to uncover some of the mechanisms underlying the way in which information is propagated through the financial markets and the influence this has on rate movements.

From these studies statistical arbitrage opportunities have emerged, that allow investors to effectively hedge their FX risks or invest in currencies on a short time scale, while enhancing the total return.

The dynamic approach:

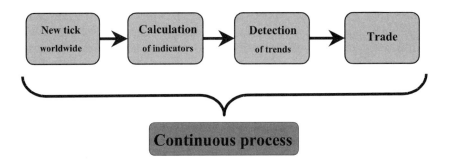

Figure 2   The dynamic approach.

Quantitative currency overlay managers also can design investment opportunities for fund managers and high net-worth individuals.

In the following Section, we show some of the possible investment alternatives. The returns shown are on top of the risk free interest rate in the home currency. As examples, we designed three types of currency baskets. Each basket is related to a specific base-currency. The currency overlay manager takes position in the major currencies in order to obtain the best possible risk-return combination and add value for the investors. The expected risk-returns are optimizations based on past performance. It is important to realize that past performance is no guarantee for future performance. The currency baskets are linked to the following base currencies: USD, DEM and JPY. The returns are expressed as percentages of the base currency. They exclude returns of the underlying investment (in cash, stocks or bonds).

Possible Investment Opportunity with a Return in USD[8].
- Un-leveraged currency basket
- Base currency = USD
- Return in USD.
- Positions are taken in USD/DEM, USD/JPY, GBP/DEM and USD/CHF
- The returns are expressed as percentages of the base currency. They exclude returns of the underlying investment (in cash, stocks or bonds) and can be considered as extra return, on top of the return on the underlying investment.

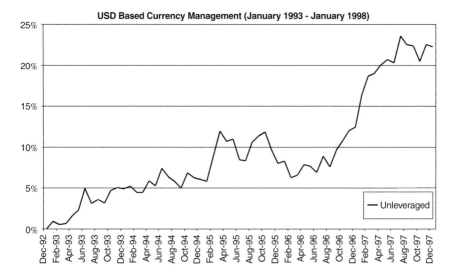

Figure 3 Cumulative return per USD-based currency basket.

USD-based currency basket	Un-leveraged
Annualized monthly return	4.37%
Annualized monthly risk	5.12%
Sharpe ratio	0.85
Total backtest return since 1993	22.30%
Average profit	0.76%
Average loss	(0.39)%
Profit/loss ratio	1.22
Maximum draw down (%)	5.66%
Maximum draw down (period)	334 days

Possible Investment Opportunity with a Return in DEM[9].

- Unleveraged currency basket
- Base currency is DEM
- Return in DEM
- Position taking in: USD/DEM, DEM/JPY, GBP/DEM and USD/CHF
- The returns are expressed as percentages of the base currency. They exclude returns on the underlying investment (in cash, stocks or bonds) and can be considered as extra return, on top of the return on the underlying investment.

DEM-based currency basket	Unleveraged
Annualized monthly return	6.75%
Annualized monthly risk	5.38%
Sharpe ratio	1.25
Total backtest return since 1993	33.10%
Average profit	0.89%
Average loss	(0.34)%
Profit/loss ratio	1.73
Maximum draw down (%)	4.33%
Maximum draw down (period)	91 days

Possible Investment Opportunities with a Return in JPY[10].

- Unleveraged currency basket

- Base currency is JPY

- Return in JPY

- Position taking in USD/FRF; USD/JPY, DEM/JPY and USD/CHF

- The returns are expressed as percentages of the base currency. They exclude returns on the underlying investment (in cash, stocks or bonds) and can be considered as extra return, on top of the return on the underlying investment.

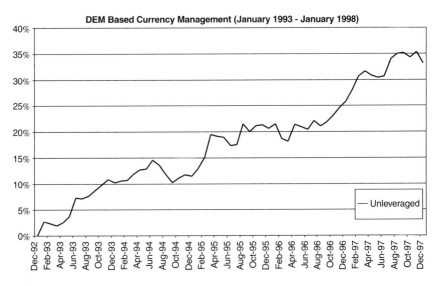

Figure 4   Cumulative return per DEM-based currency basket.

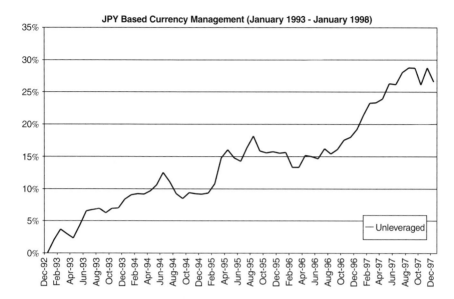

Figure 5   Cumulative return per JPY-based currency basket.

JPY-based currency basket	Unleveraged
Annualized monthly return	5.53%
Annualized monthly risk	4.81%
Sharpe ratio	1.15
Total backtest return since 1993	26.58%
Average profit	0.77%
Average loss	(0.33)%
Profit/loss ratio	1.61
Maximum draw down (%)	4.86%
Maximum draw down (period)	213 days

FINAL REMARKS

The international equity and bond markets are full of investment opportunities. It is often apparent that some markets are lagging behind and offer potential for future growth. When investing in foreign currency denominated assets, a decision has to be made about the currency exposure. The exposure simply follows from the investment decision. More and more, investors look at currencies as a separate asset class, which deserves its own trade-off in terms of risk and return. When accepting currency risks, the investor has to manage the exposure within predefined risk-limits. This takes time. If he also is interested in dynamic currency management, he should be able to work on a global basis, since fewer currencies are traded in longer time-frames. This also consumes management time. The dynamic approach allows a more frequent adjustment of the hedge-ratio around the benchmark, triggered by a trend in the foreign currencies versus the base-currency. The difficult point of course is spotting trends at an early stage. This can best be done by using a high frequency tick-by-tick database, which contains second-per-second information on the prices of liquid currencies. Studies show that statistical arbitrage opportunities exist that allow investors to effectively hedge their foreign exchange risk or invest in currencies, while enhancing the total return. Dynamic hedging and investing is a time-consuming activity and can best be done on a 24-hours basis. In this context, specialist Currency Overlay managers are always available to help you out in this respect.

APPENDIX 1: THE VALUE OF AN FX-FORWARD CONTRACT

For completeness we recall the derivation of the no-arbitrage value of a forward contract in this Appendix.

At time t, consider a forward contract to exchange 1 unit of currency X^α in return for K units of currency X^β at time T. Denote the value of this forward by f. We will determine f using the usual no-arbitrage arguments. For this we:

1. Borrow an amount

$$\frac{K}{1 + R^\beta(t; T)(T - t)} \qquad 26$$

of currency X^β;

2. Buy

$$\frac{1}{1 + R^\alpha(t; T)(T - t)} \qquad 27$$

units of currency X^α against X^β. This will cost you

$$-\frac{S^{\alpha\beta}(t)}{1 + R^\alpha(t; T)(T - t)} \qquad 28$$

units of currency X^β;

3. Sell forward one unit of currency X^α in return for K units of X^β at time T.

The cash-flow at time t is therefore

$$\frac{K}{1 + R^\beta(t;T)(T-t)} - \frac{S^{\alpha\beta}(t)}{1 + R^\alpha(t;T)(T-t)} + f.$$

29

Furthermore, you own $[1 + R^\alpha(t;T)(T-t)]^{-1}$ units of currency X^α. At time T this will have turned into precisely 1 unit of X^α due to interest. In currency X^β this is equal to $S^{\alpha\beta}(T)$. Furthermore, at that time you also have to repay the loan, which will set you back $-K$. On the other hand, the forward requires that you deliver 1 unit of X^α in exchange for K units of X^β.

Therefore, buy one unit of X^α. This will cost you $-S^{\alpha\beta}(T)$ of X^β. Then exchange it under the terms of the contract for K units of X^β. The cash-flow associated with the forwards is therefore $K - S^{\alpha\beta}(T)$. The total cash-flow at time T is $S^{\alpha\beta}(T) - K + K - S^{\alpha\beta}(T) = 0$. In other words, the cash-flow at time T is zero. Therefore, in order to have no arbitrage opportunities, it must be true that

$$f(t) = \frac{S^{\alpha\beta}(t)}{[1 + R^\alpha(t,T)(T-t)]} - \frac{K}{[1 + R^\beta(t,T)(T-t)]}.$$

30

By definition, the forward exchange rate $F^{\alpha\beta}(t;T)$ is that K for which the value of the forward becomes zero. It is clear from equation (30) that

$$F^{\alpha\beta}(t;T) = S^{\alpha\beta}(t)\frac{[1 + R^\beta(t;T)(T-t)]}{[1 + R^\alpha(t;T)(T-t)]}.$$

31

APPENDIX 2: FORWARD EXPIRATION DATES

Above we have assumed that all forward contracts expire at T_F, the end date of the analysis. Now, $T_F - T_I$ will usually be several years. This means that the forward contracts have expiration dates which are, on average, more than several months away. Trading in the market for long forward contracts can be quite expensive due to transaction costs caused by a lack of liquidity. It is therefore better in practice to consecutively roll over several short forwards. Usually one uses for this 3 month or 6 month forward contracts. In this way one can also ensure that all cash flows are generated at regular intervals. However, the question arises whether one can simulate a long forward by consecutively rolling over several short ones.

Suppose at time $T_I \leq t \leq T_F$ we sell forward an amount ϕ of currency X^α against the home currency X^0. The expiration date is $t = T_F$, as before. Now, at expiration the gain on the forward is

$$\phi[F^{\alpha 0}(t; T_F) - S^{\alpha 0}(T_F)]. \tag{32}$$

At time T_F this is the cash flow from/to the home currency account.

Let us now try to simulate such a long forward using two short forwards. Let $t < t' < T_F$. First we sell forward at time t an amount ϕ' expiring at t'. Then we roll over this deal to the period starting at t' and ending at $t = T_F$. At time t' the position is rolled over[11], which gives rise to a cash flow of

$$\phi'[F^{\alpha 0}(t; t') - S^{\alpha 0}(t')]. \tag{33}$$

This amount will then gain interest at the home currency (annualized) rate of $R^0(t', T_F)$ until T_F. At time T_F the position is closed, giving rise to a cash flow of

$$\phi[F^{\alpha 0}(t'; T_F) - S^{\alpha 0}(T_F)]. \tag{34}$$

The total gain on the two-step procedure at time T_F is therefore

$$\phi'[F^{\alpha 0}(t; t') - S^{\alpha 0}(t')]\{1 + R^0(t', T_F)(T_f - t')\} + \phi[F^{\alpha 0}(t'; T_F) - S^{\alpha 0}(T_F)]. \tag{35}$$

It is a straightforward calculation to show that (32) and (35) are equal if and only if

$$\phi' = \frac{\phi}{1 + R^\alpha(t'; T_F)(T_F - t')}, \tag{36}$$

and

$$\frac{1 + R^0(t; T_F)(T_F - t)}{1 + R^\alpha(t; T_F)(T_F - t)} = \frac{[1 + R^0(t; t')(t' - t)][1 + R^0(t'; T_F)(T_F - t')]}{[1 + R^\alpha(t; t')(t' - t)][1 + R^\alpha(t'; T_F)(T_F - t')]}. \tag{37}$$

Clearly it is not possible to satisfy these equations in general as the evolution of the term structure is unknown. In other words, there is an inherent term structure exposure associated with the two step procedure. Note that Equation 37 would be satisfied if $R^\alpha(t'; T_F)$ turns out to be equal to the forward interest rate. In general this is not true of course. A casual observer might remark that this can be solved by entering into a forward rate agreement (FRA). The problem, however, is that there is always a known notional amount associated to a FRA. However, in this case the notional is not known in advance.

APPENDIX 3: FORWARD VALUE HEDGING

Let $A^{(\alpha)}(t)$ be the value in foreign currency of a certain asset, where $T_I \leq t \leq T_F$. Suppose we want to hedge the foreign exchange exposure inherent in owning this asset.

The profit on the foreign security, measured in home currency, is

$$A^{(\alpha)}(T_F)S^{\alpha 0}(T_F) - A^{(\alpha)}(T_I)S^{\alpha 0}(T_I). \tag{38}$$

Suppose we enter into a forward contract at time T_I to sell forward, with expiration date T_F, an amount M of currency X^α against the home currency. At time T_F the payoff of this forward contract is

$$M[F^{\alpha 0}(T_I; T_F) - S^{\alpha 0}(T_F)]. \tag{39}$$

The total return of the entire position is the sum of (38) and (39), which is equal to

$$
A^\alpha(T_F)S^{\alpha 0}(T_F)\left[1 - \frac{M}{A^\alpha(T_F)}\right]
$$
$$
+ A^\alpha(T_I)S^{\alpha 0}(T_I)\left[\frac{M}{A^\alpha(T_I)}\frac{1 + R^0(T_I; T_F)(T_F - T_I)}{1 + R^\alpha(T_I; T_F)(T_F - T_I)} - 1\right]. \tag{40}
$$

Note that the first term is unknown as $A^\alpha(T_F)$ and $S^{\alpha 0}(T_F)$ are unknown at time T_I. One would like to choose M such that the risk in the total return is minimal. For this we need to calculate the variance of the total return. As the second term is deterministic, it drops out of the variance. We therefore obtain

$$\sigma^2 = E[[A^\alpha(T_F)S^{\alpha 0}(T_F) - MS^{\alpha 0}(T_F)]^2]$$
$$- E[A^\alpha(T_F)S^{\alpha 0}(T_F) - MS^{\alpha 0}(T_F)]^2, \tag{41}$$

where $E[\ldots]$ denotes the expectation value. In order to minimize σ^2 we put its derivative with respect to M to zero. What we obtain is that the standard deviation is minimized for

$$M_{\min} = \frac{E[A^{(\alpha)}(T_F)S^{\alpha 0}(T_F)^2] - E[A^{(\alpha)}(T_F)S^{\alpha 0}(T_F)]E[S^{\alpha 0}(T_F)]}{E[S^{\alpha 0}(T_F)^2] - E[S^{\alpha 0}(T_F)]^2}. \tag{42}$$

APPENDIX 4

Definitions

Average monthly loss	Average loss value of a hedging strategy over the analysis period.
Average monthly profit	Average profit value of a hedging strategy over the analysis period.
Information ratio	Average monthly return on a yearly basis divided by the standard deviation of monthly out-performance returns on a yearly basis.
Maximum drawdown	The maximum loss sustained by the relevant strategy between any two dates within the analysis period.
	The accompanying time period (in days) defines the time interval associated with this drawdown.
Profit/loss ratio	Number of profits (monthly) divided by the number of losses (monthly).
Sharpe ratio	Annualized excess return/annualized monthly risk.
	Where the "annualized excess return" is the actual return minus the risk free return.
	The risk free return is the return from a cash investment held at the risk free interest rate.
Success ratio	Total number of months with out-performance divided by the total number of months with under-performance.
Tracking error	The standard deviation of outperformance returns.
T-value	SQRT (Nob) *average out-performance return/standard deviation of performance returns
	Where: SQRT (x) = square root of x Nob = Number of observations
	Where "out-performance return" corresponds to the actual return minus the risk free return.
	The risk free return is the return from a cash investment held at the risk free interest rate.

Suppose $A^{(\alpha)}(t)$ is a zero coupon bond maturing at T_F. Then $A^{(\alpha)}(T_F) = A^{(\alpha)}(T_I)\,[1 + R^{\alpha}(T_I; T_F)(T_F - T_I)]$. Inserting this into (42) we obtain $M = A^{(\alpha)}(T_F)$ and

$$\text{Total return} = A^{(\alpha)}(T_I)S^{\alpha 0}(T_I)R^0(T_I; T_F)(T_F - T_I), \qquad 43$$

which is equal to the risk-less return on the initial investment in home currency.

More generally, if $A^{(\alpha)}(T_F)$ and $S^{\alpha 0}(T_F)$ are uncorrelated, or weakly correlated, then $M \simeq E\,[A^{(\alpha)}(T_F)]$.

NOTES

1. Here α and β are integers: $\alpha > \beta \geq 0$. X^0 is defined to be the home currency of the investor.
2. Whenever we speak of processes in this paper, we mean 'adapted processes' on some filtered probability space.
3. T_F can be, for example, the benchmark date. T_I is the time at which the analysis starts.
4. Assuming, for notational simplicity, that the trading model is neutral at T_I.
5. It will be unrealized until time $t = T_F$.
6. The usual definition of the return on, for example, a piece of stock is not appropriate in this context. A share has a certain price for which one can buy it. One physically exchanges money for the share. After a certain time one intends to sell the share in return for cash. That is, one starts out with a certain amount of cash and (hopefully) increases it. The stock itself can be bought and sold at any time. A person buying the stock at a later time, when the stock has changed in value, will nevertheless expect the same return on his invested capital. This means that even though the price has changed, the return expectation remains the same, no matter how much was invested. This is why one divides the change in the value of the stock by the amount of capital initially invested in the definition of return.
   The situation is completely different in case of a trading model as it is not a tradeable asset, or any asset, with a certain value. When one decides to use a trading model, there is no initial investment (except maybe fee payments to the vendor of the trading model). In a sense it is far more useful to think of trading model profits as dividends on an asset with value zero. Or even more appropriately, a (statistical) arbitrage opportunity.
7. This may happen, for instance, if a certain foreign currency is strongly correlated with the home currency. For example, a Dutch investor will not care whether his P&L is realized in NLG or DEM. On the other hand, the FX-markets in DEM are much deeper than the markets in NLG, which means that transaction costs will be less. For this reason, a Dutch investor may wish to trade against DEM instead of NLG. Effectively, such investors no longer consider DEM as a foreign currency.
8. Past performance is no guarantee for future performance.
9. Past performance is no guarantee for future performance.
10. Past performance is no guarantee for future performance.
11. This is done by buying spot ϕ' of X^{α} to close and selling ϕ forward.

BIBLIOGRAPHY

Lundin, M., Dacorogna, M. and Müller, U. (1997), *Currency Overlay using O&A trading models—Design document*, Rabobank/O&A Preprint MCL-1996-28-10, February.

Müller, U.A. (1994), *Hedging currency risks—Dynamic hedging strategies based on O&A trading models*, O&A preprint UAM-1994-01-31, February.

Chapter **13**

Constructing A Managed Portfolio Of High Frequency LIFFE Futures Positions

Darren Toulson, Sabine Toulson and Alison Sinclair

Intelligent Financial Systems Ltd

INTRODUCTION

In this chapter, we explore the practical elements involved in the creation of a high frequency quantitative portfolio management model. The managed portfolio consists of a set of positions in five LIFFE futures contracts. The risk of the overall futures portfolio is managed such that the expected return volatility (risk) of the positions in the five future contracts matches the expected risk of a simple buy-and-hold strategy for the FTSE-100 index. The optimal portfolio weightings (futures positions) are assessed intra-daily and the portfolio re-balanced every 240 minutes during normal LIFFE trading hours, assumed to be 8:30 AM – 4:05 PM.

The first step in the construction of the portfolio management model involves the acquisition and pre-processing of the historical price data used to produce the forecasting models. This process is described in some detail at p 348. In this study, we examine over two years of historical tick-by-tick data obtained from the five futures markets. This time period contains over 5,000,000 individual bid/ask quotes and trades. We begin by transforming the irregularly recorded tick-by-tick data into a minute-by-minute representation and describe the process by which this transformation is achieved. We conclude this Section with a simple analysis of the descriptive statistics and auto-correlation structure of the constructed 15-minutely prices in each of the five futures contracts.

We next describe the building of prediction models for each of the futures. In recent work (Toulson and Toulson, 1996a, 1996b, 1997) we have demonstrated the combined use of the Discrete Wavelet Transform (DWT) (Daubechies, 1992; Chui, 1992; Szu and Telfer, 1992) and neural networks applied to the task of financial forecasting. This has resulted in

Financial Markets Tick by Tick
Edited by Pierre Lequeux. © 1999 John Wiley & Sons Ltd

the development of the Wavelet Encoding A Priori Orthogonal Network (WEAPON) architecture. This architecture is based on the familiar Multi Layer Perceptron (MLP) (Rummelhart *et al.*, 1986) neural network architecture, but is enhanced through the use of a layer of *wavelet* processing nodes. The *complexity* of the network is controlled through the use of Bayesian regularisation techniques (MacKay, 1992a,b; Williams, 1993). At p 354, we give a brief description of the key features of the WEAPON architecture and describe its use in the prediction of the conditional mean of the expected returns of the five futures contracts.

At p 365, we proceed to examine prediction models composed of committees of WEAPON networks for each of the five futures used to estimate both the expected future return and expected future volatility (risk) of each future. For comparison purposes, we also estimate the future volatility of the markets using a more standard GARCH technique (Bollerslev, 1986). The prediction models are built using historical data covering the period January 1995 to March 1996. The prediction models are then used to manage a portfolio consisting of positions in the five futures over the period April 1996–April 1997. How the portfolio management is performed using a standard Markowitz Mean-Variance approach (Markowitz, 1959) is described at p 370. The WEAPON predictors provide the required estimates for the conditional mean of the five futures in the managed portfolio. The conditional variance is determined by a GARCH model for each of the five futures. The correlations of the returns between the five futures are estimated using a simple exponentially weighted moving average.

Finally, simulation results for managing the futures portfolio over 6 months of unseen test data are examined in considerable detail, at p 372. In particular we give details of the overall return performance, Sharpe Ratio, maximum draw-down and volatility of the managed portfolio.

THE HISTORICAL DATA

Partitioning the Price Data

The first step in any quantitative analysis or trading model simulation involving financial time series is to obtain a suitable set of historical price data and to then define precisely how that data is to be used. In this study the historical price data is firstly used to develop and parameterize the forecasting models for the estimation of future returns and risks in our chosen markets. Secondly, the historical price data is used to obtain simulated results for the overall performance of the portfolio management model based on these forecasting models. To obtain genuine *ex ante* simulated trading performance, we define four clear partitions of the historical price data:

1. *Training data*—This portion of the historical price data is used to formulate forecasting strategies, and to parameterise or *train* the forecasting models.

2. *Validation data*—This data is used to validate (i.e. predict the out-of-sample generalisation ability of) the forecasting models. It may be used more than once in an iterative forecasting model development cycle.

3. *Optimisation data*—This portion of the data is used to test different portfolio management strategies and optimise any parameters that may be associated with the portfolio management model. It usually does not contain training data (as this would produce biased forecasting accuracies) but may contain validation data.

4. *Test data*—This is the data that the final optimised portfolio management model is applied to, *only once*, to obtain the simulated real trading performance.

The historical price data used in this work consists of tick-by-tick records from five LIFFE futures contracts (shown in Figure 1 below), namely BTP

Figure 1   Price histories of the five futures contracts used in the portfolio.

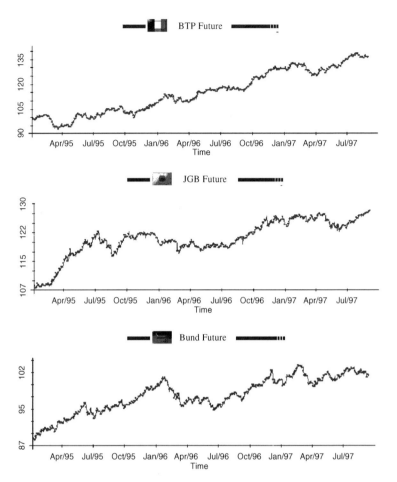

Figure 1   *(continued).*

(Italian Government Bond), Bund (German Government Bond), FTSE-100 index, JGB (Japanese Government Bond) and Long Gilt.

Table 1   The four data periods used in developing and testing a portfolio management model.

Period	Start	End
Training	July 1, 1995	Dec 31, 1995
Validation	January 1, 1995	June 30, 1995
Optimisation	January 1, 1996	June 30, 1996
Test	July 1, 1996	September 1, 1997.

The historical data cover the period January 1, 1995–September 1, 1997. The four data periods defined above, were partitioned as shown in Table 1.

Pre-processing the Data

The historical price data used in this study consists of over $2\frac{1}{2}$ years of tick-by-tick records from five LIFFE futures contracts. We refer to the tick data using the following notation. Each tick, i, on a particular market is denoted by four values, a time stamp $T(i)$ expressed in seconds, a price $P(i)$, a volume $V(i)$ and a type $H(i)$ where $H(i) \in Q$, $Q = \{bid, ask, trade\}$. The ticks do not have any particular spacing between their time-stamps, and may contain quite large discontinuities, for instance at the beginning and end of each trading day.

To build the forecasting and portfolio management models we convert the raw tick-by-tick data into a set of evenly spaced 15-minute price samples. We do this by forming volume weighted traded price averages within these 15-minute time bars. To illustrate this, we define the 15-minute volume weighted traded price average at time t to be

$$\tilde{p}_t = \frac{\displaystyle\sum_{\substack{i, t < T(i) < t+300, \\ H(i)=\text{trade}}} P(i)v(i)}{\displaystyle\sum_{\substack{i, t < T(i) < t+300, \\ H(i)=\text{trade}}} v(i)} \qquad 1$$

From the unevenly spaced tick data, we can obtain a set of evenly spaced fifteen-minute volume weighted price averages for the duration of each trading day. There still exist, however, obvious discontinuities (in time) at the beginning and end of each trading day.

Difficulties occur in intervals in which the overall traded volume is zero. We use the following strategies to cater for different possible situations in which no tradable price ticks were recorded in a particular 15-minute interval.

Strategy 1 – Bids and Asks Exist. In some intervals in which there is no actual traded volume, there may, however, exist a number of bid and ask ticks. In such cases we define the price for that interval to be the simple average of the mean bid, $\tilde{b}_t$, and mean ask prices, $\tilde{a}_t$, i.e.

$$\tilde{b}_t = \frac{\displaystyle\sum_{\substack{i, t < T(i) < t+300, \\ H(i)=\text{bid}}} P(i)}{\displaystyle\sum_{\substack{i, t < T(i) < t+300, \\ H(i)=\text{bid}}} 1}, \quad \tilde{a}_t = \frac{\displaystyle\sum_{\substack{i, t < T(i) < t+300, \\ H(i)=\text{ask}}} P(i)}{\displaystyle\sum_{\substack{i, t < T(i) < t+300, \\ H(i)=\text{ask}}} 1}, \quad \tilde{p}_t = \frac{\tilde{a}_t + \tilde{b}_t}{2} \qquad 2$$

Strategy 2–Either Bids or Asks Exist. In other cases, it may be that either
only bids or only asks exist in the 15-minute interval, i.e. perhaps three
bids but no corresponding asks. In this case we take the values we have
(for example the three bids) and either add or subtract half of the mean
bid-ask spread measured from the previous 20 intervals. So in the case of
bids but no asks,

$$\tilde{p}_t = \tilde{b}_t + \frac{\tilde{s}_t}{2},$$ 3

where $\tilde{s}_t$ is the mean bid-ask spread at time t. In the case of asks only,

$$\tilde{p}_t = \tilde{a}_t - \frac{\tilde{s}_t}{2}$$ 4

Strategy 3–No Ticks At All. In the case in which there are no recorded
ticks at all in the 15-minute period, we simply carry forward the price of
the previous 15-minute interval, i.e.

$$\tilde{p}_t = \tilde{p}_{t-1}$$ 5

NB: Tradability of prices

The 15-minute weighted average prices described above are used for
information and model building purposes only. That is, once actual trading
model simulations are performed, the system does **not** trade the averaged
15-minute prices. What occurs instead is that if, for instance, a long
position is recommended by the system at a particular time then the
"price" actually traded is the price of *the next recorded ask.* Similarly, if a
short position is required, then the price used is that for the next available
bid. The time lag between the system recommending a position and the
system actually taking that position may thus be anything between a
couple of seconds in active trading and up to several minutes in sparse
trading. Also, the system does not "know" in advance the price it will
receive for a particular desired trade.

Basic Statistics

For each of the five contracts, the summary statistics for 15-minute returns
were estimated. Table 2 shows the mean, standard deviation, skewness
and kurtosis for each of the contracts. All 15-minute returns distributions
are slightly positively skewed. The kurtosis values show that, as expected,
all distributions exhibit fat tails.

Figure 2 depicts the autocorrelation structure of the returns for the
first 15 lags for each of the contracts. Considering only the first ten

Table 2   The descriptive statistics for the 15-minutely returns for each of the five futures markets.

Future	Mean	SD	Skewness	Kurtosis
BTP	0.0012	0.1016	0.3745	28.09
Bund	0.0015	0.0537	0.5996	39.24
FTSE 100 Index	0.0025	0.1198	0.7543	13.82
JGB	0.0013	0.0718	0.4533	93.82
Long Gilt	0.0013	0.1213	0.1298	19.33

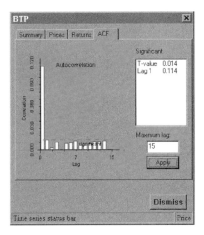

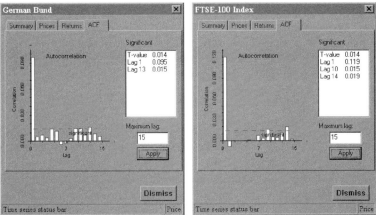

Figure 2   The autocorrelation structure of the five futures markets showing the significant lags (based on a 95% confidence band) in the right-hand box of each screenshot.

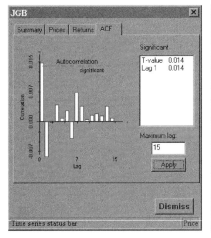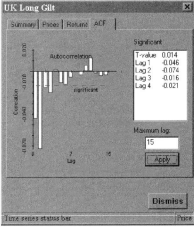

Figure 2   (*continued*).

lags, it can be seen that for all but one market only the first lag exhibits significant autocorrelation. The exception is the Long Gilt, for which the first four lags are significant. However, the first two lags are much more significant then the last two. The autocorrelation structure is considered in more detail at p 370 where we develop combined $AR(p) - GARCH(1, 1)$ models to estimate the conditional variance of the 15-minute returns.

FORECASTING CONDITIONAL RETURNS

Background

Our aim is to develop a portfolio management model that attempts to maximize the return whilst managing the risk of a portfolio of positions taken in five futures contracts. The risk management is performed using a fairly standard Mean-Variance (Markowitz) model adjusted for transaction charges (for more detail see p 370). A key requirement for the success of the Mean-Variance model is the accurate and robust estimation of the future conditional returns, risks and correlations for each of the assets in the portfolio (in this case, the five futures contracts). In much of the financial literature, these estimates tend to be based on simple historical moving averages. Such estimates are suitable when managing a portfolio over long time periods, in which case short term market trends may be effectively ignored. However, in this chapter we are looking at a portfolio management model that re-balances a portfolio of futures positions every 240-minutes and hence shorter term, possibly non-linear forecasting techniques may be more suitable.

There has recently been much interest in attempting to improve the accuracy of future conditional return and risk estimates using non-linear neural networks (primarily for conditional return estimation), and (G)ARCH and stochastic volatility methods for volatility (risk) estimates. In this section we describe the combined use of wavelets and neural networks to build 4-hour ahead prediction models for future *returns* for each of the five contracts.

Forecasting Returns Using Neural Networks

In this section we examine the use of *committees* of neural network models to predict future 4-hourly returns. We use as input to each of the neural networks the previous 96 lagged 15-minute returns for each of the five markets (corresponding to three full 480-minute trading days). The required output of the neural network models is the predicted future conditional return for a particular market four hours into the future. This process is illustrated in Figure 3.

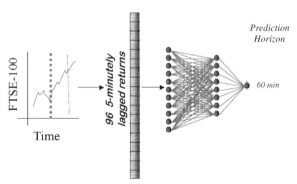

For instance, 96 15-minutely-lagged returns are input to the neural network for the FTSE-100 Index future. The network then outputs a prediction for the future conditional 4-hour return.

Figure 3 Predicting future returns for each of the five LIFFE future markets.

A key consideration in this type of prediction strategy is the encoding of the 96 lagged 15-minute returns as a neural network input vector. One possibility is to simply use all 96 *raw* inputs. The problem with this approach is the relatively high dimensionality of the input vectors. This requires the use of an extremely large set of training examples to ensure that the parameters of the model (the weights of the neural network) may be properly determined. Due to computational complexities and the non-stationarity of financial time series the use of extremely large training sets is seldom practical. A preferable strategy is to reduce the dimension of the input information to the neural network.

A popular approach to reduce the dimension of inputs for neural networks is Principal Components Analysis (PCA). PCA is used to reduce redundancy in the input vectors due to inter-component correlations. However, as we are working with lagged returns from a single high frequency financial time series we know, in advance, that there is little (auto) correlation in the lagged returns. In other work (Toulson and Toulson, 1996a,b), the problem of dimension reduction was addressed by the use of Canonical Discriminant Analysis (CDA) techniques. These techniques were shown to lead to significantly improved performance in terms of prediction ability of the trained neural networks. However, such techniques do not, in general, take any advantage of our knowledge of the temporal structure of the input components, which are sequential lagged returns. Such techniques are also implicitly linear in their assumptions of separability, which may not be generally appropriate when considering inputs to (non-linear) neural network prediction models. We consider, as an alternative means of reducing the dimension of the input vectors, the use of the discrete wavelet transform (DWT).

The Discrete Wavelet Transform (DWT)

Background. The Discrete Wavelet Transform (Telfer *et al.*, 1995; Meyer, 1995) has recently received much attention as a powerful technique for the pre-processing of data in applications involving both the compact representation of the original data (i.e. data compression or factor analysis) or as a discriminatory basis for pattern recognition and regression problems (Casasent and Smokelin, 1994; Szu and Telfer, 1992). The transform operates by projecting the original signal onto a sub-space spanned by a set of *child wavelets* derived from a particular Mother wavelet (see Figure 4). The projection of the original signal into the lower dimensional sub-space

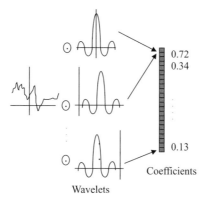

Wavelets

The time series is convolved with a number of child wavelets characterised by different dilations and translations of a particular mother wavelet.

Figure 4 The discrete wavelet transform.

can then be used, for instance, as a compressed input representation for a neural network.

Definition. Let us select the Mother wavelet to be the Mexican Hat function:

$$y(t) = \frac{2}{\sqrt{3}}\pi^{1/4}(1 - t^2)e^{-(t^2/2)}.$$ 6

The wavelet *children* of the Mexican Hat Mother are the dilated and translated forms of 6, i.e.

$$\phi^{\tau,\zeta}(t) = \frac{1}{\sqrt{\zeta}}\phi\left(\frac{t - \tau}{\zeta}\right)$$ 7

Now, let us select a finite subset C from the infinite set of possible child wavelets. Let the members of the subset be identified by the discrete values of position τ_i and scale ζ_i, $i = 1, \ldots, K$,

$$C = \{\tau_i, \zeta_i \quad i = 1, \ldots, K\}$$ 8

where K is the number of children.

Suppose we have an N dimensional discrete signal $\vec{x}$. The jth component of the projection of the original signal $\vec{x}$ onto the K dimensional space spanned by the child wavelets is then

$$y_j = \sum_{i=1}^{N} x_i \phi^{\tau_j, \zeta_j}(i) \qquad\qquad 9$$

The reduced dimension vector $\vec{y} = (y_1, y_2, \ldots, y_k)$ is then the wavelet transform of the original signal, $\vec{x}$.

Choice of Child Wavelets. The significant questions to be answered with respect to the practical use of the DWT to reduce the dimension of input vectors to a neural network are:

1. How many child wavelets should be used?
2. What values of τ_i and ζ_i should be chosen given the number of child wavelets?

For "representational" problems, the child wavelets are generally chosen such that together they constitute a *wavelet frame*. There are a number of known Mother functions and choice of children that satisfy this condition (Debauchies, 1988). With such a choice of mother and children, the projected signal will retain all of its original information (in the Shannon sense, see Shannon, 1948), and reconstruction of the original signal from the projection will be possible. There are a variety of conditions that must be fulfilled for a discrete set of child wavelets to constitute a frame, the most intuitive being that the number of child wavelets must be at least as great as the dimension of the original discrete signal. However, the choice of the optimal set of child wavelets becomes more complex in discrimination or regression problems. In such cases, reconstruction of the original signal is not relevant and the information we wish to preserve in the transformed space is the information that *distinguishes* different classes of input signal (i.e. positive and negative future returns).

   In the following Section, we present a method of choosing a suitable set of child wavelets such that the transformation of the original data (the 96 lagged 15-minute returns of the five future markets) enhances the non-linear separability of different classes of signal whilst significantly reducing the dimension of the data. We show how this may be achieved naturally by implementing the wavelet transform as a set of *wavelet neurons* contained in the first layer of a multi-layer perceptron (Rummelhart *et al.*, 1986—*henceforth R86*). The shifts and dilations of the wavelet nodes are found along with the other neural network parameters through the minimisation of a penalised least squares objective function. We extend this concept to include automatic determination of a suitable number of

wavelet nodes by applying Bayesian priors on the child wavelet parameters during training of the neural network and enforcing orthogonality
between the wavelet nodes using soft constraints.

The Wavelet Encoding A Priori Orthogonal Network (WEAPON)

We now derive a neural network architecture that includes wavelet
neurons in its first hidden layer (WEAPON). We begin by defining
the wavelet neuron and its use within the first layer of the WEAPON
architecture. We then derive a learning rule whereby the parameters of
each wavelet neuron (dilation and position) may be optimized with respect
to the accuracy of the network's predictions. Finally, we consider issues
such as wavelet node orthogonality and choice of the optimal number of
wavelet nodes to use in the architecture (skeletonisation).

The Wavelet Neuron. The most common activation function for neurons
in the Multi-Layer Perceptron architecture is the sigmoidal activation
function, see Equation 10.

$$\varphi(x) = \frac{1}{1 + e^{-(x/x_0)}} \qquad 10$$

The output of a neuron y_i is dependent on the activations of the nodes
in the previous layer x_k, and on the weighted connections between the
neuron and the previous layer $\omega_{k,i}$, as shown in Equation 11.

$$y_i = \varphi \left(\sum_{j=1}^{I} x_j \omega_{j,i} \right) \qquad 11$$

Due to the similarity between Equations 9 and 11, we can implement
the Discrete Wavelet Transform as the first layer of hidden nodes of a
multi layer perceptron (MLP). The weights connecting each wavelet node
to the input layer $\omega_{j,i}$ must be constrained to be discrete samples of a
particular wavelet child $\phi^{\tau_j, \zeta_j}(i)$ and the activation function of the wavelet
nodes should be the identity transformation $\varphi(x) = x$. In fact, we ignore
the weights connecting the wavelet node to the previous layer and instead
characterise the wavelet node purely in terms of values of translation and
scale, τ and ζ. The WEAPON architecture is shown below in Figure 5.

The WEAPON architecture is a standard four-layer MLP with a linear
set of nodes in the first hidden layer and in which the weights connecting
the input layer to the first hidden layer are constrained to be wavelets.
This constraint on the first layer of weights acts to enforce our *a priori*

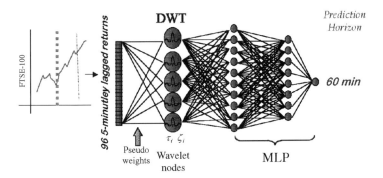

Figure 5 The WEAPON architecture.

knowledge that the input components are not presented in an arbitrary fashion, but have a defined temporal ordering, i.e. they are, in fact, 96 sequential values of 15-minute lagged returns.

Training the Wavelet Neurons. The standard MLP is usually trained using error backpropagation (backprop) (R86) on a set of training examples. The most commonly used error function is simply the sum of squared error over all training samples E_D

$$E_D = \sum_{i=1}^{N} |\vec{y}_i - \vec{t}_i|^2 \qquad 12$$

Backprop requires the calculation of the partial derivatives of the data error E_D with respect to each of the free parameters of the network (usually the weights and biases of the neurons). For the case of the wavelet neurons suggested above, the weights between the wavelet neurons and the input pattern are not free but are constrained to assume discrete values of a particular child wavelet. The free parameters for the wavelet nodes are therefore not the weights, but the values of translation and dilation τ and ζ. To optimise these parameters during training, we must obtain expressions for the partial derivatives of the error function E_D with respect to these two wavelet parameters. The usual form of the backprop algorithm is shown in Equation 13.

$$\frac{\partial E}{\partial \omega_{i,j}} = \frac{\partial E}{\partial y} \frac{\partial y}{\partial \omega_{i,j}} \qquad 13$$

The term $\partial E/\partial y$, often referred to as δ_j, is the standard backpropagation of error term, which may be found in the usual way for the case of the wavelet nodes. The partial derivative $\partial y/\partial \omega_{i,j}$ must be substituted with the partial derivatives of the node output y with respect to the wavelet parameters. For a given Mother wavelet $\phi(x)$, consider the output of the wavelet node, given in Equation 11. Taking partial derivatives with respect to the translation and dilation yields Equations 14.

$$\frac{\partial y_j}{\partial \tau_j} = \frac{\partial}{\partial \tau_j} \left(\sum_{i=1}^{N} x_i \frac{1}{\sqrt{\zeta_j}} \phi \left(\frac{i - \tau_j}{\zeta_j} \right) \right)$$

$$= -\sum_{i=1}^{N} x_i \frac{1}{\zeta_j^{3/2}} \phi' \left(\frac{i - \tau_j}{\zeta_j} \right)$$

$$\frac{\partial y_j}{\partial \zeta_j} = \frac{\partial}{\partial \zeta_j} \left(\sum_{i=1}^{N} x_i \frac{1}{\sqrt{\zeta_j}} \phi \left(\frac{i - \tau_j}{\zeta_j} \right) \right)$$

$$= -\frac{1}{2} \sum_{i=1}^{N} x_i \frac{1}{\zeta_j^{3/2}} \phi \left(\frac{i - \tau_j}{\zeta_j} \right) - \sum_{i=1}^{N} x_i \frac{(i - \tau_j)}{\zeta_j^{5/2}} \phi' \left(\frac{i - \tau_j}{\zeta_j} \right)$$

14

Using the above equations, it is possible to optimize the wavelet dilations and translations. For the case of the Mexican Hat wavelet we note that:

$$\phi'(t) = -\frac{2}{\sqrt{3}} \pi^{-1/2} 2t(2 - t^2) e^{-(t^2/2)}$$

15

Once suitable expressions for the above have been derived, the wavelet parameters can be optimized in conjunction with the other parameters of the neural network by using any of the standard gradient based optimization techniques.

Orthogonalisation of the Wavelet Nodes. A potential problem that might arise during the optimisation of parameters associated with the wavelet neurons is the duplication of parameters of some of the wavelet nodes. This leads to redundant correlations in the outputs of the wavelet nodes and hence to an overly complex final neural network model (in terms of number of parameters). One way of avoiding this type of parameter duplication is to apply a soft constraint of orthogonality on the wavelets of the hidden layer. This is done through the use of an additional error term in the standard data misfit function, as shown in Equations 16, 17 and 18.

$$E_W^\phi = \sum_{i=1, j \geq i}^{N} \langle \phi^{\tau_i \zeta_i}, \phi^{\tau_{ji} \zeta_{ji}} \rangle$$

16

where $\langle\ \rangle$ denotes the projection

$$\langle f, g \rangle = \sum_{i=-\infty}^{\infty} f(i)g(i) \qquad 17$$

In the previous section, backprop error gradients were derived in terms of the unregularized sum of squares data error term, E_D. We now include an additional term for the orthogonality constraint to yield a combined error function $M(W)$, given by:

$$M(W) = \alpha E_D + \gamma E_W^{\phi} \qquad 18$$

To implement this new error term within the backprop training rule, we must derive the two partial derivatives of E_W^{ϕ} with respect to the dilation and translation wavelet parameters ζ_i and τ_i. Expressions for the partial derivatives above are obtained from 16 and are given by:

$$\frac{\partial E_W^{\Phi}}{\partial \tau_i} = \sum_{j=1}^{K} \sum_{t=1}^{N} \phi^{\tau_j,\xi_j}(t) \frac{\partial}{\partial \tau_i} \phi^{\tau_i,\phi_i}(t)$$

$$\qquad\qquad\qquad\qquad\qquad 19$$

$$\frac{\partial E_W^{\Phi}}{\partial \xi_i} = \sum_{j=1}^{K} \sum_{t=1}^{N} \phi^{\tau_j,\xi_j}(t) \frac{\partial}{\partial \xi_i} \phi^{\tau_i,\phi_i}(t)$$

These terms may then be included within the standard backprop learning algorithm. The ratio α/γ determines the balance made between obtaining optimal training data errors against the penalty incurred by the network

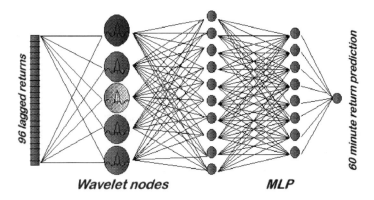

Figure 6   Marginalization of wavelet nodes. In this case wavelet nodes 1 and 3 are marginalized.

containing overlapping or non-orthogonal nodes. The value of this ratio may either be estimated or optimized using the method of cross validation.

During training the orthogonalisation terms make the wavelet nodes *compete* with each other to occupy the most *relevant* areas of the input space with respect to the mapping being performed by the network. In the case of an excessive number of wavelet nodes in the hidden layer this process generally leads to the *marginalization* of a number of wavelet nodes. The marginalized nodes are driven to areas of the input space in which little useful information with respect to the discriminatory task performed by the network is present (see Figure 6).

Weight and Node Elimination. The *a priori* orthogonal constraints introduced in the previous section help to prevent significant overlap in the wavelets by encouraging orthogonality. However, *redundant* wavelet neurons remain in the hidden layer though they will have been marginalized to irrelevant (in terms of discrimination) areas of the time/frequency space. At best, these nodes play no significant role in modelling the data. At worst, they are used to model noise in the output targets and lead to poor generalization performance. It is, therefore, preferable to eliminate these redundant nodes.

A number of techniques have been suggested in the literature for node and/or weight elimination in neural networks. We adopt the technique proposed by Williams (1993) and MacKay (1992a,b) and use a Bayesian training technique, combined with a Laplacian prior on the network weights as a natural method of eliminating redundant nodes from the WEAPON architecture. The Laplacian prior on the network weights implies an additional term in the previously defined error function (18), i.e.

$$M(W) = \alpha E_D + \gamma E_W^\phi + \beta E_W \qquad\qquad 20$$

where E_W is defined as

$$E_W = \sum_{i,j} |\omega_{i,j}| \qquad\qquad 21$$

A consequence of this prior is that during training, weights are forced to adopt one of two positions. A weight can either (1) adopt equal data error sensitivity as all the other weights, or (2) be forced to zero.

This leads to *skeletonization* of the network. During this process, weights, hidden nodes or input components may be removed from the architecture. The combined effects of the soft orthogonality constraint on the wavelet nodes and the use of the Laplacian weight prior leads to what we term

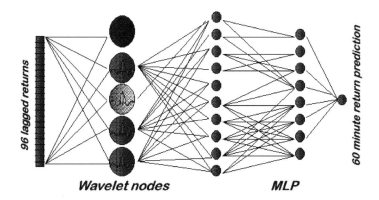

Wavelet node 1 is now completely disconnected and can be removed. Wavelet node 3 has only one connection left.

Figure 7   The WEAPON neural network after applying the Marginalize & Murder training algorithm.

Marginalize & Murder (M&M) training. At the beginning of the training process, the orthogonality constraint forces certain wavelet nodes to *insignificant* areas of the input space with regards to the discrimination task being performed by the network. The weights emerging from these redundant wavelet nodes will then have little data error sensitivity and are forced to zero and deleted due to the effect of the Laplacian weight prior (see Figure 7).

WEAPON Summary

In this section, we have developed a neural network prediction model in order to forecast future 4-hourly returns for the five LIFFE futures contracts on the basis of 96 lagged 15-minute returns. The neural network model used (WEAPON) operates by encoding the 96 lagged input returns using a Discrete Wavelet Transform. The model allows the shifts and dilations of the Wavelet Transform to be determined as part of the standard back-propagation of error training algorithm. A term is included in the learning rule to attempt to maintain a degree of orthogonality in the wavelet neurons during training. Also included in the training regime of the WEAPON model is a set of regularisation constraints on the weights of the network that prevent *over-training* which results in a model with better generalization capability. These constraints are expressed as a Bayesian prior on the weights of the network. During training this prior (modelled as a Laplacian) tends to both limit the magnitude of the weights (associated with model complexity) and also to identify *redundant* weights that are eliminated from the model during training.

In the next section we report the practical results of training WEAPON networks to forecast 240-minute ahead returns for the five LIFFE future contracts.

FORECASTING RESULTS

To test the effectiveness of the WEAPON forecasting model, committee network prediction models are built for each of the 5 LIFFE futures. Each committee is composed of five WEAPON networks. To train each of the WEAPON networks, example input and output vectors are generated using 6 months of historical data. This yields approximately 5,000 training examples. Each training example consists of a 96-dimensional input vector of lagged 15-minute returns and a 1-dimensional target or output vector which contains the actual return 240 minutes ahead (see Figure 8). Each of the five WEAPON networks is initialized with a 96-20-20-1 architecture and then trained using the Marginalize & Murder training scheme described in the previous section. Training is continued

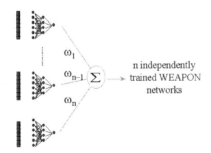

Each WEAPON network is trained to predict the four-hourly return for the asociated futures market. The five resulting predictions are then combined using a simple arithmetic average to obtain a single four hour return prediction for the futures market.

Figure 8   A committe of independently trained WEAPON networks.

until the combined data-misfit/orthogonality/weight magnitude error function is minimized. Optimal values for the hyper-parameters, α, β, and γ are obtained by cross validation.

Once the five trained WEAPON architectures have been obtained for each futures market, the overall prediction model for that market is then defined to be a simple average of the predicted future conditional returns generated by each of the five independent WEAPON architectures. The forecasting abilities of the final trained committees are shown in Tables 3 to 6. As a comparison, the accuracies of a simple, single MLP trained with cross validation and a weighted average forecasting model are also shown. The WEAPON networks quite clearly offer the best forecasting ability.

Table 3   Results for FTSE 100 index future.

Architecture	% Accuracy	Large % Accuracy	RMSE
WEAPON committee	53.54%	54.24%	0.23432
Single MLP	51.26%	55.26%	0.24879
EWMA	52.13%	56.71%	0.24127

Figures are shown for predicting the four-hour return in terms of percentage turning point accuracy, large percentage turning point accuracy and root mean square prediction error.

Table 4   Results for the Bund future.

Architecture	% Accuracy	Large % Accuracy	RMSE
WEAPON committee	53.37%	53.51%	0.0972
Single MLP	52.91%	51.73%	0.1062
EWMA	52.55%	53.29%	0.1045

Figures are shown for predicting the four-hour return in terms of percentage turning point accuracy, large percentage turning point accuracy and root mean square prediction error.

Table 5   Results for BTP future.

Architecture	% Accuracy	Large % Accuracy	RMSE
WEAPON committee	53.85%	56.63%	0.1804
Single MLP	52.60%	53.08%	0.1922
EWMA	51.87%	51.98%	0.1901

Figures are shown for predicting the four-hour return in terms of percentage turning point accuracy, large percentage turning point accuracy and root mean square prediction error.

Table 6 Results for JGB future.

Architecture	% Accuracy	Large % Accuracy	RMSE
WEAPON committee	50.34%	48.43%	0.0633
Single MLP	50.42%	49.65%	0.0659
EWMA	49.72%	49.30%	0.0642

Figures are shown for predicting the four-hour return in terms of percentage turning point accuracy, large percentage turning point accuracy and root mean square prediction error.

Table 7 Results for Long Gilt future.

Architecture	% Accuracy	Large % Accuracy	RMSE
WEAPON committee	52.51%	56.04%	0.1843
Single MLP	49.98%	52.74%	0.1982
EWMA	51.59%	53.04%	0.1972

Figures are shown for predicting the four-hour return in terms of percentage turning point accuracy, large percentage turning point accuracy and root mean square prediction error.

VOLATILITY ESTIMATION

To manage a risk-controlled portfolio of positions we need estimates for the associated *risks* (predicted future volatilities or forecasting errors) of each contract traded. It is possible to extend the neural network model described in the previous sections to forecast future volatility as well as future conditional return. However, we have found the performance of non-linear neural networks in forecasting volatility to be rather unstable particularly in markets containing strong heteroskedasticity. Instead, in this section we examine the use of a combined $AR(p) - GARCH(1, 1)$ model for volatility forecasting.

Volatility Forecasting using AR(P)−GARCH(1,1)

Consider the basic linear AR(P) time series model

$$y_t = \alpha_0 + \alpha_1 y_{t-1} + \alpha_2 y_{t-2} + \cdots + \alpha_p y_{t-p} + \varepsilon_t \qquad 22$$

The conditions on the noise process, ε_t for this model are that the noise should be independent identically distributed and have constant unconditional variance, σ^2, i.e.

$$E[\varepsilon_t] = 0$$

$$E[\varepsilon_t \varepsilon_{t-\tau}] = \begin{cases} \sigma^2 & \text{if } \tau = 0 \\ 0 & \text{otherwise} \end{cases} \qquad 23$$

Now, although the *unconditional* variance of ε_t is constant, it is possible to specify the *conditional* variance of ε_t to be non-constant. One possible way in which this non-constant conditional variance may be modeled is to use one of the families of Auto-Regressive Conditionally Heteroskedastic (ARCH) models. We consider the GARCH(1,1) model in which the noise process ε_t is modeled using

$$\varepsilon_t = \sqrt{h_t w_t} \qquad 24$$

where w_t is a zero mean unit variance white noise process and h_t is

$$h_t = \beta_0 + \beta_1 \varepsilon_t^2 + \gamma_1 h_{t-1} \qquad 25$$

It should be stressed that the GARCH(1,1) models the magnitude of the conditional variances of the forecast residuals of the forecasting model (i.e. the AR(p) model in this case). The parameters of the GARCH(1,1) model must therefore be estimated in conjunction with the forecasting model (if any is used). However, in cases where the "forecastability" of the time series is low (as is certainly the case with financial time series analysis) the prediction errors of a simple linear AR(P) model approximates the overall volatility of the time series. We thus can use the value of h_t as a proxy for the volatility of the time series.

Estimating the AR(P)−GARCH(1,1) Models

To obtain estimates for the parameters of AR(P) − GARCH(1, 1) models we use the following 2-stage procedure.

- First, given the partial autocorrelation functions for the five markets, suitable values for the *order* of the AR(p) models were selected.
- Second, parameters for the combined AR(p) − GARCH(1, 1) models are estimated for each of the five contracts using Maximum Likelihood and the method of Berndt *et al.* (1974).

Table 8 below shows the final parameter values with significance levels for each of the five markets obtained from examining price data for the combined training and validation periods.

Forecasting Volatility

After parameterising the $AR(P) - GARCH(1, 1)$ models, a one-step ahead forecast of the value of conditional forecast error variance is simply

$$\hat{h}_t = \beta_0 + \beta_1 u_{t-1}^2 + \gamma_1 h_{t-1} \qquad 26$$

where u_{t-1} is the prediction error for the previous time step, i.e.

$$u_{t-1} = y_{t-1} - \alpha_0 - \alpha_1 y_{t-2} - \alpha_2 t_{t-3} - \cdots - \alpha_p y_{t-p} \qquad 27$$

Table 8 $AR(p) + GARCH(1, 1)$ results for the five futures.

Future	Parameter	Value	SE
BTP	α_0	0.0053	0.00057
	α_1	0.1719	0.00945
	β_0	0.0041	0.00007
	β_1	0.6762	0.01347
	γ_1	0.2290	0.01095
Bund	α_0	0.0017	0.00031
	α_1	0.1140	0.01296
	β_0	0.0005	0.00001
	β_1	0.4594	0.00980
	γ_1	0.5543	0.00445
FTSE 100 Index	α_0	0.0014	0.00099
	α_1	0.1545	0.01272
	β_0	0.0034	0.00013
	β_1	0.2983	0.00843
	γ_1	0.5407	0.01097
JGB	α_0	0.0014	0.00083
	α_1	0.0426	0.01246
	β_0	0.0004	0.00002
	β_1	−0.0026	0.00013
	γ_1	0.9171	0.00441
Long Gilt	α_0	0.0012	0.00036
	α_1	0.0746	0.01198
	α_2	−0.0419	0.00843
	α_3	−0.0221	0.00543
	α_4	0.0379	0.00396
	β_0	0.0048	0.00004
	β_1	1.994	0.04434
	γ_1	0.187	0.00455

PORTFOLIO MANAGEMENT MODEL

In previous sections we developed methods of estimating future conditional risks and returns for five LIFFE futures contracts. This section describes a portfolio management model that manages a set of varying positions on each of these markets so as to attempt to maximize the return for a pre-defined level of risk. We begin with a brief description of the mean-variance model used to manage the portfolio.

The Mean Variance Model

Assume that we hold a portfolio of N assets. Let the size of our holding in each asset be determined by a set of weightings, ω_i. In the context of a portfolio of futures positions these weightings represent the number (and sign) of contracts held in each futures market. It is convenient to scale the weightings such that a 1 percent positive change in the price of the futures market would lead to a 1 percent return in the nominal portfolio value. This means that the value of ω_i depends on the number of contracts held, the monetary value of the contract, and the nominal total value of assets held in the portfolio.

The expected return of the portfolio is then given by

$$E(r) = \sum_{i=1}^{N} \omega_i \tilde{r}_i \qquad\qquad 28$$

where $\tilde{r}_i$ is the expected return of asset i. These return estimates are provided by the WEAPON committee networks described at pp 354 and 365. The expected risk (future conditional variance) of the portfolio is given by Equation 29.

$$E(V) = \sum_{i=1}^{N} \sum_{j=1}^{N} \omega_i \omega_j \tilde{\sigma}_{i,j} \qquad\qquad 29$$

where $\sigma_{i,j}$ is the covariance between the returns of assets i and j as defined in Equation 30

$$\tilde{\sigma}_{i,j} = \tilde{\sigma}_i \tilde{\sigma}_j \tilde{\rho}_{i,j} \qquad\qquad 30$$

In order to estimate the portfolio risks we need estimates of the univariate risks of each asset, σ_i along with the inter-asset correlations, $\rho_{i,j}$. We have shown, at p 370, how the individual market risks may be estimated using a GARCH model. We therefore only require estimates for the inter-asset correlations, $\rho_{i,j}$. We estimate these using a simple Exponentially Weighted Moving Average Model (EWMA) given in Equation 31.

$$\rho_{i,j}(t) = \sum_{\tau=1}^{T} \frac{(r_i(t-\tau) - \mu_i)(r_j(t-\tau) - \mu_j)e^{-\lambda\tau}}{e^{-\lambda\tau}} \qquad 31$$

where $r_i(t)$ is the historical return of asset i at time t and μ_i is the mean return of asset i between times and $t - \tau$ and t. The parameter λ is set to be 0.99 and the time period T is set to be 5 days. Historical returns are calculated at 15-minute intervals. Because we are considering a portfolio of futures positions there are none of the usual constraints placed on the weights of the portfolio (such as positivity of individual asset weightings or the asset weightings summing to unity).

Managing the Portfolio

The equations for portfolio risk and return introduced in the previous Section allow us to monitor the expected risk and return of a given portfolio. To manage the portfolio, however, we need to define the desired properties of the portfolio risk and return over time. These constraints are:

- The portfolio will at all times be balanced such that the expected return of the portfolio is maximized, *subject to the constraint* that the portfolio risk should not exceed the implicit estimated risk in adopting a buy and hold position of the FTSE 100 index cash market.

- The risk of the spot FTSE 100 index is calculated using an Exponentially Weighted Moving Average measure.

The portfolio is *re-balanced* at 240-minute intervals, that is every 240 minutes the optimal set of asset weightings, ω_i, is determined and trades performed such that these asset weightings are realized. The calculation of the optimal portfolio weightings is carried out using a quadratic programming technique. It is assumed that the total value of the managed portfolio is sufficiently large such that the discrete nature of contracts in the futures market can be ignored.

PORTFOLIO MANAGEMENT RESULTS

The portfolio of futures positions is simulated over a 6-month test period. During this period, every 240 minutes during each trading day, the portfolio weightings are re-balanced in the following manner,

- Estimates of future four-hourly returns for the five futures contracts were made using the committees of trained WEAPON networks described at pp 354 and 365.
- Estimates of the future four-hourly variances (risks) of the five futures contracts were made using the GARCH model described at p 370.
- Estimates of the inter-market correlations are made using an Exponentially Weighted Moving Average model.
- The risk of the spot FTSE 100 index is estimated using an Exponentially Weighted Moving Average model.
- The asset weightings that optimize the return of the portfolio subject to the risk being less than or equal to the risk of the FTSE 100 index are determined.
- Contracts are traded (if necessary) in the five futures markets to achieve these optimal weightings.

During simulation, the total asset value of the portfolio is monitored at all times net of any transaction costs. The trading conditions assumed during the simulation are as follows:

- We do not know the exact price we will obtain in any market. That is, for instance, if we wish to re-balance a position in one of the contracts at 9:00 am then the price at which the re-balancing takes place is the first relevant ask or bid tick *after* 9:00 am. This strategy means we do not need to take into account any bid-ask spread.
- We assume a round trip transaction cost of four ticks per trade for all markets.

The results of managing the portfolio are shown in Figure 9. The overall profitability, estimated annualized volatility and estimated annualized Sharpe Ratio are presented in Table 9.

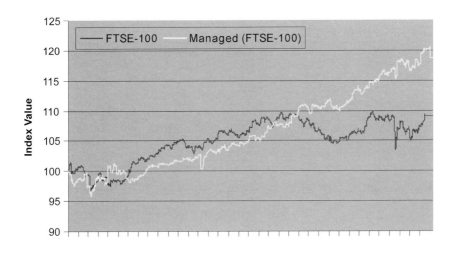

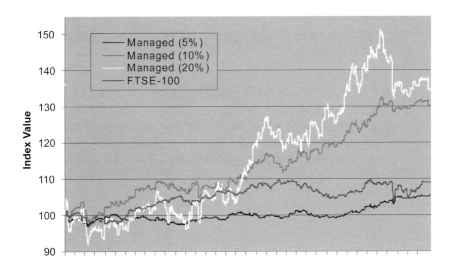

As a comparison the FTSE 100 index value is also shown

Figure 9   The total asset value of the managed portfolio over the previously unseen test period.

Table 9 Table of results comparing the FTSE 100 Index with a number of different managed portfolios.

Series	Return (6 months)	Sharpe Ratio (annualized)	Volatility (annualized)
FTSE 100 Index	9.12%	1.19	10.04%
Managed (5%)	5.32%	1.47	07.21%
Managed (10%)	30.43%	3.43	15.84%
Managed (20%)	34.46%	1.99	32.34%
Managed (FTSE-100 Index)	18.66%	3.08	11.33%

CONCLUSIONS

In this chapter, we have presented a set of methodologies to quantitatively manage a high-frequency portfolio of positions on five LIFFE futures contracts. In order to do this we have:

- Made forecasts of future returns for each market using the Wavelet Encoding A Priori Orthogonal Network.

- Made forecasts of risk for each market using a combined $AR(p)$ – $GARCH(1, 1)$ method.

- Made forecasts of inter-market correlation using a simple Exponentially Weighted Moving Average (EWMA) technique.

- Combined these estimates to allocate positions in the futures markets using a risk management methodology that attempted to balance the portfolio of positions such that the risk of the futures positions did not exceed the corresponding risk of a buy and hold strategy in the FTSE-100 index.

The resulting portfolio management model appears to function correctly in terms of its realized risk (volatility), with the returns modestly in excess of buy and hold strategies on any of the underlying markets.

BIBLIOGRAPHY

Berndt, E.K., Hall, B.H., Hall, R.E. and Hausman, J.A. (1974), "Estimation and Inference in Nonlinear Structural Models", *Annals of Economic and Social Measurement*, Vol. 3, 653–665.

Bollerslev, T., "Generalized Autoregressive Conditional Heteroskedasticity", (1986), *Journal of Econometrics*, 31, 307–327.

Casasent, D.P. and Smokelin, J.S. (1994), "Neural Net Design of Macro Gabor Wavelet Filters for Distortion-Invariant Object Detection In Clutter", *Optical Engineering*, 33(7), 2264–2270.

Chui, C. (1992), *An Introduction To Wavelets*, New York: Academic Press.

Daubechies, I. (1992), "The Wavelet Transform, Time Frequency Localisation and Signal Analysis", *IEEE Transactions on Information Theory*.

MacKay, D.J. (1992a), "A Practical Bayesian Framework For Backprop Nets", *Neural Computation*, 4(3) 448–472.

MacKay, D.J. (1992b), "Bayesian Interpolation", *Neural Computation*, 4(3), 415–447.

Markowitz, H.M. (1959), *Portfolio Selection: Efficient Diversification of Investments* New York: John Wiley and Sons.

Meyer, Y. (1995), *Wavelets and Operators* Cambridge UK: Cambridge University Press.

Rummelhart, D.E., Hinton, G.E. and Williams, R.J. (1986), "Learning Internal Representations by Error Propagation", in *Parallel Distributed Processing* 1, ch 8, Cambridge MA: MIT Press.

Shannon, C.E. (1998), "A Mathematical Theory of Communication", *The Bell System Technical Journal*, 27(3), 379–423 and 623–656.

Szu, H. and Telfer, B. (1992), "Neural Network Adaptive Filters For Signal Representation", (1992), *Optical Engineering*, 31, 1907–1916.

Telfer, B.A., Szu, H. and Dobeck, G.J. (1995), *Time-Frequency, Multiple Aspect Acoustic Classification*, World Congress on Neural Networks, 2, II-134–II-139, July.

Toulson, D.L. and Toulson, S.P. (1996a), *Use of Neural Network Ensembles for Portfolio Selection and Risk Management*, Proceedings of Third International Chemical Bank/Imperial College Conference on Forecasting Financial Markets, London.

Toulson, D.L. and Toulson, S.P. (1996b), *Use of Neural Network Mixture Models for Forecasting and Application to Portfolio Management* Proceedings of Sixth International Symposium on Forecasting, Istanbul.

Toulson, D.L. and Toulson, S.P. (1997), *Intra-Day Trading of the FTSE-100 Futures contract using Neural Networks with Wavelet Encodings* Proceedings of Fourth International Banque Nationale de Paris/Imperial College Conference on Forecasting Financial Markets, London.

Williams, P.M. (1993), "Bayesian Regularisation and Pruning Using A Laplace Prior", *Neural Computation* 5(3).

Chapter **14**

Is Short Term Better? An Insight Through Managed Futures Performances

Pierre Lequeux and Philippe Michelotti

Banque Nationale de Paris, London, Bank Austria Creditanstalt Futures Ltd, London

INTRODUCTION

Wider availability of high frequency data and consequent research on market micro-inefficiencies lead by market practitioners and academics have been the catalysts behind the growth of a new breed of traders (short term also called "noise traders"). These traders concentrate on short time frames as they try to capture micro-trends/counter-trends in the financial markets. They tend to ignore fundamentals and to use complex trading techniques to exploit the non-linearity of financial markets at high frequency. The research of "tick data" can reveal very profitable trading opportunities for traders that can access low transactions costs (Coy, 1997) since there is some evidence on the short term predictability of the markets (Pitt, 1995). Short term traders have been in high demand over recent years due to their generally low correlation with other type of trading and the consequent diversification they can bring in a multi-advisor portfolio (Peltz, 1998). But high frequency trading does not come cheap; the highly quantitative nature of the trading methodology usually requires big investments in computing technology and know-how to guarantee a high probability of success (Alley, 1996). The short term trader needs to access large amount of data to back test his/her strategies (Meaden and Fox-Andrews, 1991); this has been a particularly costly issue in the past. This might have been one of the main factors that slowed the growth of high frequency traders. In the following, we quantify the economic value of short term trading and consequently the use of high frequency data. For that purpose, we analyse the performance of a universe of managed

Financial Markets Tick by Tick
Edited by Pierre Lequeux. © 1999 John Wiley & Sons Ltd

futures trading advisors operating over three distinct time horizons: Long term, Medium Term and Short term.

Managed Futures are investments in the derivatives markets, either on commodities, interest rates, stock indices or currencies. These highly regulated investments are monitored in the States by the National Futures Authority (NFA), and in the United Kingdom by the Securities and Futures Authorities (SFA). Tight control of the back office procedures by the regulators ensures a reliable and steady level of reporting; the performance statistics released by the fund manager are usually audited and standardized. Consequently, there is a wealth of detailed information about the various fund managers' trading programs, also known as Commodities Trading Advisors (CTA) in this industry. The readily available information on past performance, evolution of the assets under management as well as a detailed description of the trading programs and methodologies gives a good insight on how CTAs run their operation. This permits accurate analysis of the managed futures industry performance as well as a better understanding of trading advisor's results when compared to other types of investments. Investors can make a more precise decision with respect to investing or not in a program. The main feature of these investments is their low correlation to traditional assets whilst having similar risk/reward profiles. Consequently, they bring a higher level of diversification to portfolios made of traditional assets. The benefit of managed futures in the institutional portfolio has been extensively reported upon (Schneeweiss and Spurgin, 1997). This might partly explain the strong growth of assets managed by this sector (Figure 1).

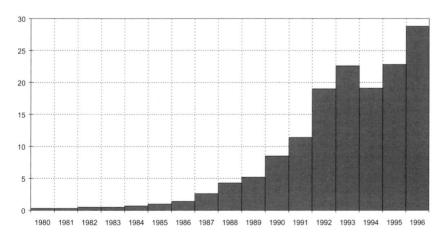

Figure 1 (Source: MAR). Evolution of the assets under management (1980–1996) in US$ billions.

DATA AND DESCRIPTIVE STATISTICS

The data used in this research comes from a database compiled by Refco Capital Advisor Inc. This database reports the information listed in Table 1 as well as the monthly returns and assets under management for each of the trading programs it tracks. It covers the period from July 1992 through June 1997 (60 months).

Out of the 536 CTAs listed in the database we found that 54 have been operating for at least 60 months, managing a minimum of US$ 2 m and belonging to a specific trading time horizon: short, medium or long term. We ignored the numerous CTAs that position themselves on two or more trading time frames, to simplify our analysis. Our sample comprises US$ 4.8 bn out of the US$ 23 bn of assets managed by the 536 programs listed in the database. Table 2 shows what was the average number of transactions and assets under management for each time horizon.

On average, the higher the frequency of trading the higher the number of transactions and the smaller the amount of assets under management.

Table 1   Information on CTA.

Program Name	Program name
Assets In Program	140,000,000.00
Minimum Account Size	5,000,000.00
Management Fee	3%
Incentive Fee	20%
Trading Methodology	Highly sophisticated statistical techniques are used to search historical data for trading rules. Very short-term oriented, the system is designed to control risk through greater diversification of trades as well as through low correlation of trades across various markets.
Markets Traded	Financial, Currency
Round turns/Million $/Year	3000
Market Codes	Short-term

Table 2   Average number of transactions and assets managed per time horizon.

	Round turns/Million $/Year	Average money under management	Number of managers
Short Term	3141	39,630,067	13
Medium Term	2002	77,243,694	17
Long Term	1893	125,503,282	24

The smaller size of assets under management could be due to various reasons. First, it is possible that short term traders, due to their more recent nature and higher technicality, are not yet fully recognized by investors who still need to gain a better understanding of their trading approach. Secondly, the time horizon on which they operate does not allow large transactions to be executed without being noticed by other market participants. Managing large amounts would imply incurring slippage offsetting the potential profits they target. Consequently, the growth in the assets they have under management might be restrained by the market inefficiencies they try to exploit.

We deducted the T-Bill return that would have been earned in each of the 54 CTAs track records to obtain the excess return net of fees that an investor would have earned. We split each track record in five non-overlapping 12 months sub-periods starting from July 1993. We calculate yearly return,[1] volatility,[2] maximum drawdown,[3] Sharpe ratio for each sub-periods and time horizon. Tables 3 to 5 shows the descriptive statistics per time horizon over the whole period.

Table 3 Descriptive statistics for the short term traders.

	Return	*Volatility*	*Sharpe*	*Max. Drawdown*
Mean	12.45	14.97	0.84	−8.88
Median	9.48	13.04	0.87	−5.85
Standard Deviation	20.93	8.74	1.34	8.70
Kurtosis	0.85	0.60	−0.07	11.66
Skewness	0.65	0.97	0.23	−2.75
Range	110.64	37.58	5.99	55.18
Minimum	−35.62	2.81	−2.30	−55.18
Maximum	75.02	40.39	3.69	0.00
Count	65	65	65	65

Table 4 Descriptive statistics for the medium term traders.

	Return	*Volatility*	*Sharpe*	*Max. Drawdown*
Mean	9.58	19.09	0.46	−12.67
Median	8.26	17.11	0.55	−11.75
Standard Deviation	18.85	10.20	0.98	8.40
Kurtosis	1.71	0.06	0.19	0.80
Skewness	0.75	0.82	0.14	−1.07
Range	107.41	42.73	4.74	36.71
Minimum	−25.68	2.98	−1.43	−38.20
Maximum	81.73	45.70	3.31	−1.49
Count	85	85	85	85

Table 5   Descriptive statistics for the long term traders.

	Return	Volatility	Sharpe	Max. Drawdown
Mean	15.63	23.94	0.63	−14.56
Median	14.60	22.02	0.74	−10.95
Standard Deviation	23.04	11.75	0.96	10.06
Kurtosis	2.43	0.49	1.08	2.14
Skewness	0.37	0.82	−0.31	−1.46
Range	165.39	53.83	5.69	51.63
Minimum	−53.64	4.65	−2.26	−52.17
Maximum	111.75	58.47	3.43	−0.54
Count	120	120	120	120

The average performance of CTAs has a volatility, return and Sharpe ratio comparable to stocks. This agrees with previous research underlining that CTAs have the same type of risk return profile as the S&P500 (Schneeweis and Spurgin, 1997). The short term trader tends to have the best Sharpe ratio and the smallest maximum drawdown out of the three groups observed, probably due to the lower volatility of their returns. The kurtosis of the returns points towards the non normality of CTAs performance. This is more marked for the long term traders indicating that the shorter the time horizon, the less extreme observations. This might be due to the more active management of the trading positions by the short term managers and to the fact that they are more often "out of the market" than long term traders.

Selecting and monitoring trading programs is paramount to the success of a well structured multi-advisor portfolio. When investors consider allocating to a program they select amongst numerous possible traders. Their choice is made by following a strict methodology of performance evaluation, primarily centred on criteria of risk analysis. The use of risk analysis is threefold. First, to forecast risks relevant to their current exposure, secondly, to measure investment past performance and, thirdly, to design new optimal portfolios (Kahn, 1995). In what follows we look at how the performance of the three groups has fared over the years in absolute and risk adjusted terms. We also look at the higher diversification value that the short term trader may provide.

PROGRAM PERFORMANCE PER TIME HORIZON

Quite often, when selecting a CTA, the investor looks at the past history of performance and tries to make a projection of future returns. A lot of

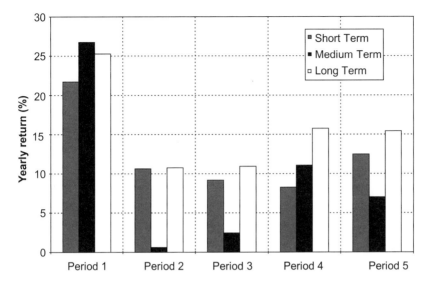

Figure 2   Average yearly return per period and group.

studies have been recently conducted on the significance of trading advisor past performance and also on the predictive nature of returns (Schwager, 1996; Irwin *et al.*, 1994; Edwards and Park, 1996). Overall, the results of these studies have been quite inconclusive with respect to the significance of the historical returns generated by such investments and they found that there is little evidence of predictability in the managed futures returns (Irwin *et al.*, 1994). The findings on the significance of the returns is often attributed to the fact that most of these studies have been conducted on public futures funds which compare unfavourably due to their high fee structure (Edwards and Parks, 1996).

We found that the average level of return between short and long term was quite similar and relatively stable over the years. Medium term traders were found to under-perform the two other groups in three out of five periods.

VOLATILITY AND LOSS

Over recent years, emphasis has been placed on a better understanding and control of market risk. Being able to monitor the level of risk taken by

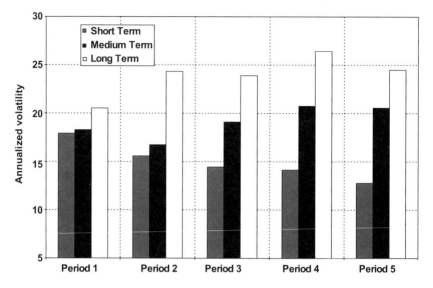

Figure 3   Average yearly volatility per period and group.

a trading advisor is of prime importance for an investor as the maximum loss he might potentially suffer will be a function of this level of risk. The probability of loss, defined as the probability of showing a loss at the end of an investment period T is given by: $P_L = \Pr(R_T < 0)$ where R_T is the return generated by the investment. If we assume that an investment manager's returns follows a normal distribution: $P_L = \Pr(R_T < 0) = \Phi(-\mu/\sigma)$ with μ being the expected return of his performance and σ the standard deviation of his returns (Φ is the cumulative function of a $N(0,1)$), minimizing the probability of loss will be obtained through the maximization of the ratio μ/σ. This is easier to achieve through a minimization of the volatility since the predictability of returns has been proven to be very difficult. Overall this implies a maximization of the Sharpe ratio.

We found that the volatility of the performance was pretty much a function of the time horizon adopted by the investment manager. Maybe more interesting was the decrease in volatility of the short term traders, whereas long term traders did seem to keep their high level of volatility through time (Figure 3).

We also noted in accordance with their respective level of volatility that short term traders had a lower maximum drawdown than their medium and long term peers (Figure 4). This agrees with the remarks of some long-term traders on the subject of time horizon and risk (Basso, 1997).

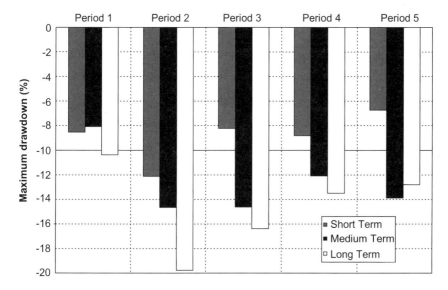

Figure 4   Average maximum drawdown per period and group.

RISK ADJUSTED RETURN RELATIONSHIP

The ratio of reward per unit of risk taken was presented by Sharpe in 1966 as a good measure of risk adjusted performance. The ratio is now widely used by the investment community where it is now a general practice to report performance in absolute terms as well as in a risk adjusted form (De Rosa, 1996).

One of the drawbacks of the Sharpe ratio is that it is not weighted by the number of observations and, consequently, does not reflect the impact of time nor does it reward long-term performance. The Sharpe ratio will mechanically decrease over time and cannot distinguish between intermittent and consecutive losses because the measure of risk (standard deviation) it uses is independent of the order of the data. Attempts have been made to design a modified measure to overcome this drawback, but, to date, none of the proposed ratios have been able to retain the simplicity of the Sharpe ratio.

We find that short term traders were an optimal choice in terms of Sharpe ratio in four out of the five periods. This was most certainly due to their more controlled level of volatility.

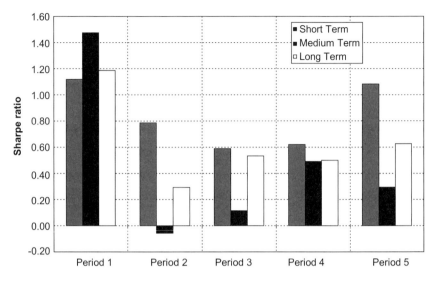

Figure 5   Average Sharpe ratio per sub-period and group.

CORRELATION

Differently to other assets, futures need to be associated with some sort of active management to yield significant returns. Consequently, trading managers use a wide spectrum of trading strategies to base their decision as to when to buy or sell into a financial market. The correlation of a CTA's performance to another program or asset will depend more on the trading approach used than on the underlying traded asset. This is of great importance when the initial decision of investing is made within a portfolio context, as the investor will have to make sure that the trading style of the CTAs keeps the same level of correlation and risk characteristics as other assets in his portfolio. In the following, we try to evaluate the level of correlation between each program within each class. For doing so, we calculate a correlation matrix for the programs within each time horizon.

Short term traders are usually more de-correlated between themselves than the other two groups (Figure 6). This is, without any doubt, due to the more active management of their trading positions when compared to longer term approaches. One of the reasons might be the higher diversity of trading methods available to short term traders. Consequently, it should be easier to achieve a higher level of diversification when using a portfolio of short term traders than long term traders. However, the analysis and selection of short term traders will be more demanding for an investor due to the variety of trading styles within the same class.

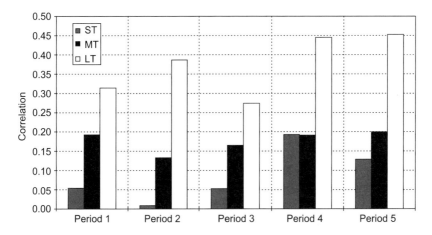

Figure 6 Average correlation within each group.

WEIGHTING THE TIME HORIZON IN A PORTFOLIO

Here we evaluate the need for short term traders versus long term traders within a context of portfolio allocation. We make the hypothesis that our typical investor is rational and that, therefore, he will try to obtain the maximum return for the minimum level of risk. To simulate this we use our 54 track records and optimize a weighting system to obtain the specific mix that would have maximized the Sharpe ratio for each sub-period. The results are shown in Table 6.

We note that, for each period, there is a need to allocate to short term traders in order to maximize the Sharpe ratio of our hypothetical portfolio, in contrast to medium and long term traders. This is due to the lower level of volatility and correlation found amongst short term traders than within the two other groups.

Table 6 Allocation between time horizons to maximize the Sharpe ratio.

	Short Term	Medium Term	Long Term
Period 1	50.73%	35.48%	13.79%
Period 2	73.08%	26.92%	0.00%
Period 3	28.28%	57.28%	14.44%
Period 4	22.04%	56.85%	21.11%
Period 5	95.08%	0.00%	4.92%
Average	53.84%	35.31%	10.85%

CONCLUSION

The advent of more readily available high frequency data has, without any doubt, contributed to the increase in number of short term traders over recent years. We have shown that the features of a short term trader are quite different to those of a long term trader. Generally speaking, the short term trader is less volatile than his medium and long term peers and has, consequently, a more controlled maximum drawdown. On a risk adjusted basis, the average short term trader has been the best alternative over the period studied. The level of diversification available from short term traders is higher than for the medium and long term traders. Overall, these features justify the use of a high proportion of short term traders within a multi-advisor fund. The better performance of traders positioned on a short term horizon justify their use of high frequency data. But high frequency data is not restricted to short term traders only. It is also justified for longer term traders that try to have a better understanding of the heteroscedacity of the financial markets and a better control of their liquidity and transaction cost. It contributes to the growth of trading strategies that are more apt to answer the investor requirement in terms of risk and diversification.

NOTES

1. Sum of the 12 monthly returns for each non overlapping year (five observations per CTA).
2. Standard deviation of returns for each of the non overlapping year of track record, multiplied by square root of 12.
3. Maximum adverse excursion in performance for each year of track record.

BIBLIOGRAPHY

Alley, J. (1996), "Wall Sheet's King Quant", *Fortune* magazine, February .
Basso, T. (1997), "Technical Analysis" in *FX: Managing Global Currency Risk* G. Klopfenstein, (ed.), Glenlake Publishing.
Coy, P. (1997), "Mining Profits from Microdata", *Business Week*, December.
DeRosa, D. (1996), *Managing Foreign Exchange Risk*, Homewood, IL: Irwin.
Edwards, F. and Park, J. (1996), "Do Managed Futures Make a Good Investment?", *Journal of Futures Markets*, 16(5), 475–517.

Irwin, S.H., Zulauf, C.R. and Ward, B.W. (1994), "The Predictability of Managed Futures Returns", *Journal of Derivatives*, Winter, 20–27.

Kahn, R. (1995), *Quantitative Measures of Mutual Fund Risk: An Overview*, BARRA, Research Paper.

Meaden, M. and Fox-Andrews, M. (1991), *Futures Fund Management*, Woodhead-Faulkner Publishing.

Peltz, L. (1998), "Short-term traders continue to attract assets", Managed Account Report, February.

Pitt, J. (1995), "When your investment horizon is minutes", *Global Finance*, June.

Schneeweis, T. and Spurgin, R. (1997), "The Benefits of Managed Futures", in Peters, C. and Warwick, B. (eds), *The Handbook of Managed Futures*, Homewood, IL: Irwin.

Schwager, J. (1996), *Managed Trading: Myths and Truths*, New York, John Wiley and Sons.

Index

LIFFE*data*

Deutschmark Products

Lira Products

Euro/Swiss/Yen Products

Sterling Products

See overleaf for details . .

Purchasing this publication has entitled you to an automatic 10% discount on all LIFFE Tick Data titles. Save £30 per CD-Rom title when you order using this promotional card only.

Tick Data CD-Rom Title	Normal Subscription Price	Special Discounted Price	*Quantity*	*Total*
Deutschmark Products Tick Data	£300	£270		
Lira Products Tick Data	£300	£270		
Sterling Products Tick Data	£300	£270		
Euro/Swiss/Yen Products Tick Data	£300	£270		
All 4 Tick Data Titles (save £200)	£1,000	£880		
Postage and Packaging for each CD-Rom Title per annum		£10		

Please note:

1. VAT: UK = 17.5%, EU = zero (if a VAT number is stated otherwise 17.5%), Outside EU = zero. EU members please supply a VAT number:

Sub total £	
VAT £	
Total + VAT £	

Payment

Please tick ☐ I have read the terms and conditions at http:www.liffedata.com/ and agree to subscribe to the LIFFE*data* service under them

Payment must be made by Sterling cheque/draft (payable to **LIFFE Data Services**) or by credit card.

Please charge my credit card £ _____

Please tick credit card type: ☐ Access/Mastercard   ☐ Visa/Barclaycard   ☐ Amex

Credit card number: | | | | | | | | | | | | | | | | | | Expiry date | | |

Cardholder's name   Signature

Delivery Address

Name
Address

Postcode/Zip   Country
Telephone   Fax
E-mail

Please return the completed form, together with requisite fee to: LIFFE Data Services, Concept House, Bell Road, Basingstoke, Hampshire RG24 8FB. Tel: +44 171 379 2900 Fax: +44 171 379 2901